INSTRUCTOR'S NOTES

The St. Martin's
Handbook

INSTRUCTOR'S NOTES

The St. Martin's
Handbook
Fifth Edition

Andrea A. Lunsford
STANFORD UNIVERSITY

Cheryl Glenn
PENNSYLVANIA STATE UNIVERSITY

Alyssa O'Brien
STANFORD UNIVERSITY

BEDFORD / ST. MARTIN'S
BOSTON ◆ NEW YORK

Manufactured in the United States of America.

7 6 5
f e d c b

For information, write: Bedford/St. Martin's, 75 Arlington Street, Boston, MA 02116
(617-399-4000)

ISBN: 0-312-39831-X

Acknowledgments

"1993 Doublespeak Quiz" and "1993 Doublespeak Awards" from *Quarterly Review of Doublespeak XX* (January 1994). Copyright © 1994 by the National Council of Teachers of English. Reprinted by permission.

Jeff Jarvis. "Frasier" review. From *TV Guide,* November 26-December 2, 1994. Copyright © News America Publications. Reprinted with permission from TV Guide.

James Kirkpatrick. Column on "style." From "A Conservative's View" column by James J. Kilpatrick. © Dist. By Universal Press Syndicate. Reprinted with permission. All rights reserved.

Queen Latifah. "Ladies First." Excerpt of 7 lines. From *Ladies First.* © 1992 T-Boy Music LLCo./b/o itself & Queen Latifah Music. Forty-Five King Music. Forked Tongue Music/ Warner Chappell Music, Inc. (ASCAP). All rights reserved. Used by Kind Permission.

"Sentence." *Redefinition from A Dictionary of Modern English Usage,* Second Edition by H.W. Fowler and Sir Ernest Gowers. Copyright © 1965 by Oxford University press. Reprinted by permission of Oxford Univeristy press.

"Unique." Entry as defined in *Webster's New World™ Dictionary, Third World Dictionary, Third Edition.* Updated. Copyright © 1997, 1996, 1991, and 1988 by Simon & Schuster, Inc. Reprinted with permission of Macmillan USA, A Simon Macmillan Company, Inc.

Marilyn vos Savant. "Ask Marilyn" column. From *Parade* Magazine, © 1996 and reprinted with the permission of Parade Publications and the author.

"War of 1912." Entry from *World Book, Inc.* Copyright © 1988 by World Book, Inc. Reprinted with permission.

▼ Preface

The *Instructor's Notes* grew out of the extensive marginal notes orginally created for the *The St. Martin's Handbook* by Cheryl Glenn, Roger Graves, R. Gerald Nelms, Dennis Quon, and Andrea Lunsford. In subsequent editions, the *Notes* were revised and expanded by other important contributors, including Melissa Goldthwaite, Jennifer Cognard-Black, and Jeff Loew. The Fifth Edition of the *Instructor's Notes* builds on this pedagogical foundation and works to improve and extend the usefulness of the *Notes* for teachers of writing today.

The present book signifies a major revision, corresponding to the revamped Fifth Edition of the *Handbook*: not only have we updated resources, added a significant number of practical strategies, and responded to current trends in the field of teaching writing, but we have also developed two additional notes— "Attending to Disabilities" and "Teaching with Technology" —and produced over fifteen new chapters to match the new organization of *The St. Martin's Handbook*.

In order to explore these aspects of writing and teaching, we have tested the materials for the new edition in the crucible of our classrooms, thereby making the necessary, if not always successful, connection between theory and practice. In this way, the current edition continues a tradition developed with each incarnation of this project. Once again we found ourselves collaborating in the same ways we ask our students to do, and, like our students, we struggled with the concept of audience, attempting to address both beginning and experienced instructors of composition. At the end of the day, creating the revised *Instructor's Notes* offered us a rich opportunity to practice what we so often preach and to provide a set of notes for use by teachers in the writing classroom.

In approaching the question of audience for this edition, our first thought was again of everyday classroom needs—teaching suggestions, additional activities for student writers, answers to exercises, and so on. As we began work, however, we came upon materials and ideas for teaching that expanded our original horizons, providing not only the *what* to teach but, more important, the *how* and the *why*. Our experience mirrors the recent history of composition scholarship. In the past thirty years, the *what* has changed from a product-oriented approach to a process approach, and now this in turn has become what some refer to as a "post-process" approach. Our teaching today focuses on the material conditions for student writing (and our teaching of it); on the social nature of writing and reading; on an enriched sense of rhetorical situations and the key writing occasions they entail; on changes in the nature, status, and scope of writing; on recently emerging genres of writing; and on the impact of technologies and visual culture on writing. Accompanying this shift in *what* we focus on has been increasingly sophisticated pedagogy and research—the *how*— and greater justification—the *why*. In our experience, the *what* cannot be separated from the *how* and the *why*.

This book, therefore, contains various materials that respond not only to everyday classroom needs but also to broad pedagogical concerns. In this significant revision, we have kept the best of the earlier notes, now linking each heading to the language of the *Handbook* rubrics for greater ease in cross-referencing. We have greatly expanded the presence of notes on multilingual writers, and we've developed two new sets of notes to help teachers make the most of new technologies in the composition classroom and to attend to all students' needs:

Background notes, prefaced with **"On,"** present useful historical, theoretical, and contextual information.

For Teaching notes offer practical classroom strategies, exercises, and assignments.

For Collaborative Work notes provide suggestions for group work and exercises that students can do in peer-review pairs and small groups.

For Multilingual Writers notes, now substantially expanded for this edition, offer suggestions for teaching writers whose home language is not English.

Teaching with Technology notes offer classroom-tested strategies for using new technologies effectively to teach writing.

Attending to Disabilities notes provide theoretically informed and classroom-tested advice on how to teach *all* our students as well as concrete strategies for transforming classroom culture to rethink the ways in which we conceptualize the writers in our communities.

Useful Readings provide an annotated reference list of books, articles, and Web sites that explore issues addressed in the chapter.

Quotes about writing suggest a starting point for class discussion; they can also illuminate the subject at hand or simply entertain.

We're also pleased to be able to offer a revision of Michael Hennessy's guide to "Using *The St. Martin's Handbook* with Sample Syllabi." In this opening chapter to the *Instructor's Notes,* Michael offers wonderfully clear and cogent suggestions for teaching students how to use a handbook, for using a handbook as a classroom tool, and for developing your course through his sample syllabi by pairing *The St. Martin's Handbook* together with a thematic reader, a literature anthology, or an argument/rhetoric.

Our collaboration on this most recent revision includes a number of friends and colleagues to whom we are indebted. At Bedford/St. Martin's, we wish to thank our development editor extraordinaire, Joanna Imm, as well as our managing editor, Erica T. Appel, and our project editor, Sarah Ludwig. The editorial and production team for *The St. Martin's Handbook,* Fifth Edition, Stephanie Carpenter, Nick Wolven, and Kristin Bowen, provided excellent assistance for our questions about these notes. We are especially grateful to our colleagues at Stanford University, including Marvin Diogenes, Christine Alfano, and Stacey Stanfield Anderson, whose timely advice and innovative classroom practices helped provide material for these new and expanded *Instructor's Notes*.

In an important sense, however, this group extends to include all the instructors to whom this book is addressed. Everything in this book is written for you—but in fact much, perhaps most, of it has been inspired by you.

Andrea A. Lunsford
Alyssa J. O'Brien

Contents

x   Contents

Contents   **xi**

INSTRUCTOR'S NOTES

The St. Martin's
Handbook

Using *The St. Martin's Handbook*

WITH SAMPLE SYLLABI

BY MICHAEL HENNESSY, Southwest Texas State University

Some books are to be tasted, others to be swallowed, and some few to be chewed and digested; that is, some books are to be read only in parts; others to be read, but not curiously; and some few to be read wholly and with diligence and attention.

– FRANCIS BACON, "Of Studies"

A comprehensive handbook for college writers — and *The St. Martin's Handbook* is a classic example of the genre — slips somewhat uneasily between Bacon's categories. Most of us would agree that such a book is primarily "to be tasted," to be read "in parts," rather than "swallowed" or "chewed and digested." Handbooks are essentially reference works, books we more often "consult" than read in long stretches. But this statement belies the fact that many of us own an old handbook, perhaps from our college days or earlier, that looks very much "chewed and digested" from repeated use. Over the years, we may have read the book "wholly and with diligence and attention": we know it inside out. And while we may ask our students to read parts of their handbooks "not curiously" — that is, quickly rather than carefully — there are other parts we want them to read and read again with great "diligence and attention."

This discussion suggests, perhaps, that a contemporary writing handbook is actually several books in one — a text we use in different ways at different times, a book whose function varies from teacher to teacher, course to course, and student to student. Any book in a composition class, of course, can vary in function depending on the pedagogical preferences of the instructor or the focus of the class. But handbooks are especially adaptable because of their encyclopedic qualities: they bring together large amounts of material, ranging — in the case of *The St. Martin's Handbook* — from information about the recursive nature of the writing process and the qualities of memorable prose to minutiae about the placement of footnote numbers and the use of emoticons. Handbooks include an ambitious and — for some students — baffling array of grammatical rules, sample papers, charts, lists, checklists, style sheets, glossaries, and exercises — a compendium of information not designed for start-to-finish reading.

Because handbooks are by nature highly adaptable, instructors employ them in myriad ways. Some use a handbook as the backbone of a composition course, taking students systematically through large parts of the text; the work of the term is tied closely to the structure of the book itself. With *The St. Martin's Handbook,* for example, an instructor might begin at the beginning, moving from the larger elements of invention and arrangement toward smaller matters of style and convention. Another instructor, working from a different set of assumptions, might start with detailed in-class coverage of Chapters 31 through 36, the material on sentence grammar. At the other end of the spectrum are instructors whose classroom use of the *Handbook* may consist of little more than holding the book up for students to see on the first day of the term. Such instructors may assign students to read some sections, perhaps the advice in Chapters 1 through 6 about the writing process. Beyond that, students are on their own with the book, using it as a reference tool, a guide for revising and editing their work. Between these extremes, of course, are many other points of balance.

I work in an English department whose faculty members generally see a handbook more as a reference work than as a teaching text. The composition program I direct at Southwest Texas State University employs about eighty faculty members (thirty of them graduate assistants) who teach approximately 120 sections of first-year composition each semester. Several years ago, we decided to adopt a single handbook — currently *The St. Martin's Handbook* — as a common text for all sections of our required two-semester composition sequence. In addition to the *Handbook,* faculty members use a reader, which they select individually from a list of approved titles: a collection of expository essays for the first course and a thematic literature anthology for the second.

Because our program is large and because our faculty members range from longtime full professors to first-time graduate assistants, there are naturally wide variations in the way *The St. Martin's Handbook* is used in combination with the various readers. Nevertheless, we see the book as a way to help bring focus and coherence to our program. Every student we teach carries the book from the fall to the spring term; thus, the *Handbook* helps define a common set of expectations and standards for good writing in the department. And when students move beyond first-year composition, we urge them to take the book with them as a guide in any course that requires writing papers and essay tests.

In the next few pages — from my perspective as a composition director, a supervisor of graduate assistants, and a teacher of writing — I offer a number of suggestions for using *The St. Martin's Handbook* in a first-year composition course. I regularly conduct my classes as writing workshops in which students review one another's drafts and revise their work under my supervision. I therefore assign the *Handbook* mainly as a reference tool that students use on their own. I do make assignments from the book, but I rarely have time to "teach" them in class. And so, rather than attempting to offer a broad survey of the various ways the book might be used, I focus here on a few specific ways that instructors can help their students make the best use of the book as a writing guide and reference tool. My advice is aimed chiefly at new teachers of composition and at experienced teachers using the *Handbook* for the first time.

Each year, in training and advising graduate assistants, I get dozens of questions about the *Handbook:* "How should I use it in class?" "How can I integrate it with selections from the reader?" "Is there a way I can use the book during writing workshops and peer-editing sessions?" "How can I encourage students to use the book as they revise their own papers outside of class?" "Should I use the symbols on p. I-43 when I grade papers?" "How can I get students to read the sections that I advise them to read when I comment on their drafts?" I have tried to keep these and other questions about the *Handbook* in mind in offering the advice that follows.

Orienting Students to the *Handbook*

Whether you assign *The St. Martin's Handbook* as your primary classroom text or mainly as a guide for students to use on their own as they draft, revise, and edit their work, you will want to provide a thorough orientation to the book at the beginning of the term. Neglecting to do so can leave students frustrated in their efforts to understand the book's advice and to master its reference system. The *Handbook* is a rich source of information, and a powerful tool, but like any tool, its effectiveness depends on the skill of the person using it. A personal computer is worthless unless you know how to operate it. So, too, a writing handbook.

I am reminded of a junior transfer student who visited my office to discuss a paper she had written during her first term on campus. The paper had earned a low grade partly because of numerous surface errors. I asked the student if she owned a handbook in which she might review the problems identified in her paper. Her response was, "Yes, I still have the one I used in my freshman year, but I never have been able to figure out how to use it to fix problems in my writing." This anecdote goes to the heart of the matter: that many students find handbooks baffling, even mysterious texts, something altogether unfamiliar. Such students need *to be taught about the way a handbook works:* its organization, its language, its conventions. A text that seems perfectly transparent, logical, and "natural" to a writing teacher — a member of the discipline — may look strange, new, and "unnatural" to an uninitiated student.

One of the most essential things an instructor can do, then, is to demystify the *Handbook* for students, to make them feel comfortable working with it, flipping through its pages, reading it, consulting it. Taking class time to describe, demonstrate, and practice the use of the book is always time well spent.

Even after students have grown relatively comfortable finding their way around in the book, they still may harbor misconceptions that you will want to address. A superficial familiarity with the text may lead them to conclude, for example, that good writing is essentially a matter of managing details — constructing error-free sentences, avoiding misspelled words, and putting commas where they belong. That students might develop such an impression is not altogether surprising: like most handbooks, *The St. Martin's Handbook* has roughly as many pages about spelling (Chapter 30) or about commas (Chapter 48) as it does about planning and drafting an essay (Chapter 3). And the book as a whole devotes more pages to the third rhetorical canon — style — than it does to the first two — invention and arrangement.

Students need to be told why this is so. They need to know that the author of the *Handbook,* and the teacher using the book, do not necessarily endorse the idea that grammatical correctness and spelling take precedence over the work of developing substantial, convincing ideas. It will be useful, then, to explain at the beginning of the term that the truly "basic" information in the book is located in Part 1, Chapters 1 through 6, on the writing process. You will want to tell students that the book emphasizes rhetorical choices rather than hard-and-fast rules. Like any comprehensive handbook, *The St. Martin's Handbook* covers hundreds of details of style, but these details matter most during the revising and editing stages of the writing process, *after* the writer has dealt with larger issues of content, organization, and presentation. Students will be pleased to hear that they already follow, without thinking much about it, most of the "rules" and mechanical conventions that occupy a good portion of the book — and that those rules are there for reference, to be "read only in parts" rather than "wholly."

Here are four strategies that you might use at the beginning of the term to help orient yourself and your students to the book, to help students learn its conventions, and to undercut any faulty perceptions they may have about handbooks in general.

1. **If you are a new teacher, or if you are using the *Handbook* for the first time, take time to familiarize yourself with the book.** Learn how it differs from other handbooks you have used. The Preface describes the book's distinguishing features, explains how the book was developed, and spells out the author's assumptions about rhetoric, writing, reading, and the role of "correctness" in academic English. While the preface may not be of particular interest to students, it provides essential information for instructors planning to use the book. The more you know about the *Handbook,* the better equipped you will be to show students how it works.

2. **Give students a guided tour of the *Handbook*.** Your doing so sends a clear message: that the book plays an essential role in the course you are teaching and that you expect students to consult it regularly. The tour need not take more than half a class period. Show students the book's endpapers and explain how the information found there can be useful in tracking down important advice about writing. Review the table of contents to give students an overall sense of what the book includes. Finally, lead students through two chapters — one that gives advice about composing and one that deals with a particular grammatical or mechanical concern — highlighting various types of information and identifying useful features of the text. You will especially want to point out the editing tips on the second page of most chapters; these help students edit independently by showing them how to apply the "rules" to their own work.

3. **Give students practice in using the *Handbook*.** In "A Note to Students" near the front of the book, a tutorial on using the *Handbook* is provided to help students become familiar

with the types of information contained in the text. Students can do the tutorial on their own, but taking time in class to work through parts of it will go a long way toward reinforcing the book's usefulness. Because the tutorial gives ample attention to the *Handbook*'s coverage of the larger elements of composition, assigning it is one way to undermine any misperceptions that the book — or that good writing in general — is mainly about learning rules and avoiding errors. Students need to know from the outset that, above all, the book is about making informed rhetorical choices, even in matters of "correctness."

4. **Make assignments from the *Handbook* early in the term.** Even if you expect students to use the book mainly on their own as a reference guide, give at least one substantial reading assignment to the whole class during the first week of the course. A good choice is the Introduction, "Learning from Your Errors." Take time to talk about this section, asking students to discuss what they learned and, in particular, to consider how the book's advice may help them as they draft and revise their papers later in the term. This sort of discussion can help establish a connection between the *Handbook* and the rest of what students will do in the course.

After using an earlier edition of *The St. Martin's Handbook* for a semester, one of my colleagues observed that she was starting to know the book well and was becoming increasingly "comfortable" with it. If we can likewise bring students to feel a certain level of "comfort" with *The St. Martin's Handbook,* we will do them an important service. Taking time at the beginning of the course to show them how the book works will pay off later on.

Teaching Students to Use the *Handbook* as a Writing Guide

Much of the advice given in the preceding section anticipates what I want to say here. Demystifying the *Handbook,* teaching students how it works, is the necessary condition for using it effectively as a writing guide. Simply telling your students that they *should* consult the book is not likely to get results. And even after you have given them a thorough introductory tour of the text, students are apt to leave the book on the shelf unless you make an ongoing effort to see that they don't.

To assign the book as a writing guide means, in effect, to give it a prominent place in your course, even though you might not teach from it regularly. Other texts, perhaps a collection of readings or your students' own writing, may occupy most of the available class time. Students may spend a typical class period discussing a reading from an anthology, analyzing a sample paper, or working in groups on their drafts. While you may assign readings from the *Handbook* to the entire class, you will not generally spend time going over the readings. The book thus becomes a resource that students use, mainly outside of class, to locate advice about writing, revising, and editing their work. Especially in classes organized as workshops, with the emphasis on practice and peer review, taking time to teach directly from the book, to use it as a classroom text, can disrupt the core activities of the course. Still, most instructors who conduct their classes in this fashion feel the need for an anchor text, a book that students can study and consult as needed for authoritative advice about writing. The *Handbook* can fill this need. But without "teaching" the book, how can you ensure that your students will actually benefit from its advice?

Following are some suggestions for integrating *The St. Martin's Handbook* into a course without making it the primary teaching text. These strategies require little class time, and should promote students' active use of the book as a writing guide and reference tool.

1. **Make the *Handbook* a presence in the classroom.** Bring the book to class, even when you don't plan to teach from it, and encourage students to do likewise. By keeping the book in a handy spot on your desk—perhaps alongside a dictionary—you can easily consult it when needed during class discussions, demonstrating in a tangible way its value as a writing guide and *showing* students how to use the book to answer questions. If, for example, a student asks you during an editing session, "Should I use a semicolon or a colon here?" turn to the book with the student and look up the answer. Doing so will take a bit more time, of course, than simply saying which mark is appropriate, but looking up the information will *show* the student how to use the book for reference. And the next time an editing question comes up, the student may turn to the *Handbook* before asking you.

   You can also spend a few minutes with the book at the beginning of each class as a way to start the conversation. For example, you might ask a student to read aloud one of the vignettes about language in everyday use that open most chapters. Discussing a vignette can help link the *Handbook*'s advice to the world outside the classroom. Alternatively, you can draw attention to some other spot in the book—one of the many shaded guidelines boxes or a fine point of usage that you want students to review. Any of these activities

should take no more than five minutes, but if one of them leads to a longer discussion about writing, so much the better.

2. **Ensure that reading assignments from the *Handbook* reinforce other activities in the course.** Even if you don't "teach" the *Handbook*, you can ask your students to read particular sections that directly support the work they are doing at the time. This may seem like an obvious point, yet I have seen many syllabi over the years that take precisely the opposite tack, having students read about sentence grammar while writing first drafts. Though there may be a certain logic in reviewing "basics" in the early part of a course, it is nearly always preferable, I think, to make as close a match as possible between *Handbook* readings and the actual writing tasks that students are working on at the time. If, for example, you plan to have students bring draft thesis statements and outlines to class for discussion, you might ask them to read Chapter 3 of the *Handbook* in advance. You may not discuss the chapter explicitly, but the students' reading will be directly relevant to the planned activity.

   The goal is to make as close a match as possible between the book's advice and what you want your students to accomplish. The first time students revise a paper, they should be reading Chapter 4, on reviewing, revising, and editing. Later, when they are revising, say, the third paper of the term, you might want them to pay close attention to sentence style. During that week of revision, you could assign one or more of the chapters in Part 8, "Sentences: Making Stylistic Choices." For instance, you might ask students to study Chapter 47, "Creating Memorable Prose," and apply one or two of its lessons in reshaping their drafts. Or, if you want students to pay special attention to the use of commas during the final edit of a paper, you could assign

Chapter 48, "Using Commas," just prior to the edit. At that juncture, students will have a more pressing need for advice about commas (your pointed insistence that they get them right) than they will later. Again, the closer link you can make between the *Handbook* and the students' writing projects, the more likely they are to use the book and to become comfortable with it as a guide to writing.

Other sorts of links are possible, too. If you plan to use a reader with the *Handbook,* you may spend a good deal of class time discussing selections from the reader. *The St. Martin's Handbook* can be a useful adjunct: section 1c, "Considering the processes of reading," includes a detailed set of guidelines for critical reading, and these might serve over the term as a way to help students approach all their assignments from the reader. Likewise, if you plan to teach students to read argumentative essays or newspaper editorials, you might ask them to review Chapter 11, "Analyzing Arguments." Or, if you are using the book in a literature-based course, section 64c, on writing about literature, will help students make reading-writing connections. Finally, at various points in the term, you may want to link the *Handbook*'s advice on using computers (Chapter 7) or creating Web texts (Chapter 9) with work your students are doing online.

3. **Teach students to use the Introduction as a mini-*Handbook*.** In addition to using the Introduction, "Learning from Your Errors," as a way of orienting students to the book, this section has another potential use: it can serve throughout the term as a "mini-*Handbook*," a freestanding section that students can use as a point of first reference to answer many of their most pressing questions. You may find it worthwhile, then, to spend time during the first week of class discussing the principles set forth in the Introduction and teaching students how to use these pages for reference.

You can begin by explaining that the Introduction is research-based, that its discussion of what constitutes good writing is grounded in the actual responses of college teachers to thousands of student papers. You should explain, in particular, that the material about broad content issues, organization, and presentation gives a decidedly realistic picture of what readers expect. Students should study this material early in the course and, if necessary, review it each time they begin a new paper.

What makes this material especially helpful is its emphasis on making students *independent,* its insistence that they take responsibility for their own writing. Students are advised to step back and look critically at their work — at details of expression as well as at larger issues of purpose, organization, and supporting evidence. The *Handbook* shows them that good writing is always based on rhetorical choices made by responsible, well-informed writers.

The book's emphasis on responsibility is nowhere more apparent than in the discussion of surface errors. Here the author urges students to take charge of their writing by charting their errors and learning to edit independently. As with the advice about content and organization, the treatment of surface errors is research-based, identifying the twenty most common errors actually marked in student papers and showing several examples of each error. Examples are shown hand-edited, so that students can see the error and its correction at a glance.

If the book as a whole can overwhelm some students with its comprehensive coverage of grammar, punctuation, and mechanics, the Introduction should help sort things out. The information found in this part of the book is focused and to the point. Students can use it quickly at the beginning of the course to identify the errors most apt to appear in their work. Later, when they get back their marked drafts and finished papers, they can turn to the Introduction for quick reference. What they find there may be all they need. But if they want more advice, cross-references will send them to the relevant parts of the book. In marking papers, you might even want to do what one of my colleagues does: note errors in the margins with numbers (1 through 20), referring students directly to the condensed information in the Introduction. If students learn to use that information intelligently, they are well on their way to becoming competent editors and proofreaders of their own work.

4. **Encourage students to use the *Handbook* during peer-review sessions.** Most of the faculty members in the program I direct make collaboration a regular part of their courses. For each paper, students spend time in small groups, responding to classmates' drafts and revising their work in light of the commentary they receive. These peer-review sessions provide good opportunities for students to use the *Handbook* as a reference guide. You can even require that they do so.

Tell students in advance the specific issues you will ask them to consider when reading drafts, and ask them to study—before coming to class—the sections of the book relevant to those issues. With the first paper of the term, for example, a peer-review session might focus on issues of thesis and organization, which are covered in sections 3b–3e and 4d–4e. Having reviewed these sections of the book beforehand, students will be prepared to use a shared vocabulary and set of assumptions in discussing one another's work. The *Handbook* thus becomes a point of reference as well as a tool they can use to teach one another. Instead of saying (or writing on a peer-review sheet), "Your thesis is kind of vague," a stu-

dent might say, "Your thesis states a topic, but it doesn't make a comment on the topic," or "Your thesis contains a workable comment, but is the idea really manageable for a four-page paper?" Students can refer to the text to make their points, showing one another where to find additional advice. Thus, the book can give students the terms—and the terminology—they need to become effective peer reviewers. With practice, even inexperienced writers can develop considerable facility in helping their peers, and themselves, to use the book skillfully.

The same principles apply, of course, to students working independently outside of class: the more skillful they become at using the *Handbook,* the more likely they are to keep it open on their desks as they revise. To encourage them, you might even ask that they turn in a brief response with a draft, or with the final copy of a paper, telling you two or three specific questions that they were able to resolve with help from the book.

5. **Use the *Handbook* when marking drafts and grading finished papers.** Graduate assistants often ask me whether they should use revision symbols, such as those found at the back of the *Handbook,* when marking papers. I usually equivocate. On the one hand, the symbols are a convenient form of shorthand that can save a good deal of "grading time." On the other hand, if overused, the symbols can overwhelm students, who are more apt in theory than in practice to look up the indicated pages and read the information they find there. My advice usually comes down to this: use a few key symbols to identify common surface errors, but concentrate on larger issues (thesis, development, structure) and on persistent *patterns* of error that need attention. How is the *Handbook* best used for this sort of marking?

Perhaps the best strategy is to mark selectively and to tie marginal and terminal comments as closely as possible to advice in the book. If, for example, a central weakness of a draft happens to be paragraph coherence, you might describe the problem in a sentence or two. Your comment, like a revision symbol, can send the student to the *Handbook,* but whereas the symbol *(coh)* gives the student an entire section to read, your advice can be more specific: "Revise this paragraph by adding transitions between the sentences I've marked. See p. 124 in the *Handbook.*" Supplying this degree of specificity takes time, but if marking is selective, if you focus on one or two major issues per paper, students are more likely to revise — and to use the book as a reference tool — than they are if you mark every error. Your terminal comment can help focus a student's attention, highlighting strengths to exploit and problems to avoid in the next draft.

The *Handbook* can also be used in a like manner to mark surface errors. If you notice a persistent error in a student's writing — say, sentence fragments — you can repair two or three examples of the error (rather than marking all of them), and write a marginal comment to give advice: "There are several fragments here besides the ones I noted. Review Chapter 40 in the *Handbook,* especially the box on p. 679, and try to locate and repair as many additional fragments as you can." Again, this is the sort of advice that students can apply during revision, using your comments in tandem with a specific section of the book. The more selective and pointed you can make your comments, even if this means making fewer of them, the more your students will be inclined to act on the advice you give them — and to develop the habit of using the *Handbook* for reference when working on their own.

Encouraging Students to Use the *Handbook* beyond First-Year Composition

Just as you may have started your first-year composition course by orienting students to the book, you may want to end it by explaining how the text can serve them in their other college courses. You might even choose to devote part of a class period to another "guided tour" of the book, highlighting sections that students will find most helpful in subsequent courses.

You can begin the tour by letting students know that the kind of writing they have been doing in your class has much in common with the writing they will be asked to do later. For that reason, the Introduction is a piece they may want to revisit often; its research-based overview of the qualities of good academic writing, its emphasis on rhetorical effectiveness, and its attention to reader expectations apply to written communication in all disciplines. It is also worth reminding students of the enormous amount of all-purpose information in the *Handbook* — advice about the writing process, chapters on surface errors and punctuation, two helpful glossaries, chapters on word choice, and much more.

Many parts of the book offer advice and information particularly suited to the academic world beyond first-year composition. For example, Part 4 on research includes a fund of information about gathering and using source material as well as about the various documentation styles students might use in later courses. In addition, Part 12 covers academic and professional writing; Part 2 introduces students to the use of various media, including oral presentations; and Part 11 includes five reference chapters for multilingual writers.

Reminding your students of the various ways they might use the *Handbook* beyond first-year composition helps place the courses you teach in a larger academic context. Students at the outset of their college years rarely see the "big picture"; they often have little sense of the interconnectedness of the curriculum they are beginning to pursue. You should do what you can to show them the connections — especially the way in which writing, as a way of learning and as a means of communication, cuts across disciplinary boundaries. In a small but significant way, teaching students to make the *Handbook* a trusted guide and reference companion contributes to that effort.

Three Sample Syllabi

The syllabi included here suggest how *The St. Martin's Handbook* might be used as a writing guide in three first-year composition courses. Each course has a distinct set of objectives, and each combines the *Handbook* with a different type of reader. But all share one key assumption: that student writing is an important "text" in any composition course. A significant amount of class time is thus reserved for discussions of student papers and for workshops in which students review one another's plans and drafts.

A sample syllabus is necessarily generic; while it can suggest an overall pattern for a course, it cannot account for the many variations in departmental policy, student ability, teacher preference, and academic scheduling that inevitably shape an actual syllabus. But if you are new to teaching composition, or if you are using the *Handbook* for the first time, the following sample syllabi may give you a broad idea of how to integrate *The St. Martin's Handbook* into your course. The syllabi have been written for a fourteen-week term, but you can adapt them for a shorter schedule by modifying the reading selections and reducing the number of papers.

Syllabus 1: The *Handbook* with a Collection of Essays

This syllabus outlines an introductory course in expository writing. Students learn to draft, revise, and edit short papers in which they state and develop a thesis. The reader in the course, *The Presence of Others,* is a collection of seventy readings and forty visual texts designed to provoke thinking about a range of contemporary concerns. Students thus practice critical reading in close conjunction with writing, using selections from the reader — along with their own ideas and experiences — to generate material for papers.

Students write a total of six short papers: an in-class diagnostic sample at the beginning of the term, four out-of-class essays, and a final exam. Instructors may also want to include informal writing activities, such as exercises and responses to readings.

Books: Andrea A. Lunsford, *The St. Martin's Handbook,* 5th ed. (Bedford/St. Martin's, 2003) = *SMH*

Andrea A. Lunsford and John J. Ruszkiewicz, *The Presence of Others: Voices and Images That Call for*

Response, 3rd ed. (Bedford/St. Martin's, 2000) = *PO*

Schedule: Early in the term, students read the *Handbook* chapters about the larger elements of composition—invention and arrangement. As the term progresses, they study increasingly smaller matters of style, first the paragraph, then the sentence, and finally diction. On days when papers are collected and returned, the syllabus allows time for covering the "tools" of writing—grammar, punctuation, mechanics. Any *Handbook* assignments for these class meetings should be geared to the needs of students at that point in the course.

■ WEEK 1

1. **Paper 1 written in class** (diagnostic writing sample)
2. Introduction to the course; *SMH* Introduction (learning from errors); *PO* Chapter 1 (reading and thinking critically)
3. Paper 1 returned and discussed; selection(s) from *PO*

■ WEEK 2

1. Paper 2 assigned; selection(s) from *PO; SMH* Chapter 1 (reading and writing)
2. Selection(s) from *PO; SMH* Chapter 2 (rhetorical situations)
3. Selection(s) from *PO; SMH* Chapter 3 (planning and drafting)

■ WEEK 3

1. Working thesis and plan for Paper 2 due; workshop to review theses/plans
2. Workshop continued
3. Draft of Paper 2 due (two copies); peer-review workshop, with emphasis on thesis, organization, and development; *SMH* Chapter 4 (reviewing, revising, and editing)

■ WEEK 4

1. **Paper 2 due;** workshop—papers annotated, proofread, and discussed; bring *SMH* to class for review
2. Selection(s) from *PO*
3. Paper 3 assigned; selection(s) from *PO*

■ WEEK 5

1. Paper 2 returned and discussed; bring *SMH* to class for review
2. Selection(s) from *PO*
3. Selection(s) from *PO; SMH* 5a–5e (constructing paragraphs)

■ WEEK 6

1. Working thesis and plan for Paper 3 due; workshop to review theses/plans
2. Workshop continued; *SMH* 5f (introductory and concluding paragraphs)
3. Draft of Paper 3 due; peer-review workshop, with special attention to introductions, conclusions, and body paragraphs

■ WEEK 7

1. **Paper 3 due;** workshop—papers annotated, proofread, and discussed; bring *SMH* to class for review
2. Selection(s) from *PO*
3. Paper 4 assigned; selection(s) from *PO*

■ **WEEK 8**

1. Paper 3 returned and discussed; bring *SMH* to class for review
2. Selection(s) from *PO*
3. Selection(s) from *PO*; *SMH* Chapter 43 (effective sentences)

■ **WEEK 9**

1. Working thesis and plan for Paper 4 due; workshop to review theses/plans
2. *SMH* Chapter 46 (varied sentences)
3. Draft of Paper 4 due; peer-review workshop, with special attention to revising for effective and varied sentences

■ **WEEK 10**

1. **Paper 4 due;** workshop — papers annotated, proofread, and discussed; bring *SMH* to class for review
2. Selection(s) from *PO*
3. Paper 5 assigned; selection(s) from *PO*

■ **WEEK 11**

1. Paper 4 returned and discussed; bring *SMH* to class for review
2. Selection(s) from *PO*
3. Selection(s) from *PO*; *SMH* Chapter 47 (memorable prose)

■ **WEEK 12**

1. Selection(s) from *PO*
2. Selection(s) from *PO*; *SMH* Chapter 27 (diction)

3. Working thesis and plan for Paper 5 due; workshop to review theses/plans

■ **WEEK 13**

1. Draft of Paper 5 due; peer-review workshop, with special attention to revising for memorable prose
2. Peer-review workshop continued, with special attention to revising for effective diction
3. **Paper 5 due;** workshop — papers annotated, proofread, and discussed; bring *SMH* to class for review

■ **WEEK 14**

1. Preparation for final exam (Paper 6) — an essay in which students assess their strengths and weaknesses as writers; review Introduction to *SMH* (learning from errors)
2. Workshop — review of students' writing portfolios (all drafts and graded papers) in preparation for final exam
3. Paper 5 returned and discussed; review of portfolios continued

Syllabus 2: The *Handbook* with a Literature Anthology

This syllabus outlines a course in writing about literature. Such courses are typically offered as the second half of a two-part composition sequence, taken after students have completed an earlier course in expository writing. In the version that follows, students develop critical reading skills, write literary analyses, and use secondary sources to support their ideas. They learn to quote, summarize, and paraphrase, demonstrating these skills in short essays and in a longer documented paper. The reader in the course—*Literature: The Human Experience*—is organized thematically and includes work in four genres (fiction, poetry, drama, and the essay).

Students write three short papers, a longer research paper, and, near the end of the term, an in-class essay. This last piece helps prepare them for the final exam, an additional in-class essay. Instructors may also want to add informal writing assignments, such as entries in a reading journal.

Books: Andrea A. Lunsford, *The St. Martin's Handbook*, 5th ed. (Bedford/St. Martin's, 2003) = *SMH*

Richard Abcarian and Marvin Klotz, *Literature: The Human Experience*, 8th ed. (Bedford/St. Martin's, 2002) = *L*

Schedule: In the early part of the course, *Handbook* assignments provide an overview of the writing process and teach students about literary analysis. Later, students make extensive use of Part 14 on doing research and using sources. They also bring the *Handbook* to class for review on days when papers are collected and returned. And throughout the term, they consult the book on their own as a tool for drafting and revising their papers.

■ **WEEK 1**

1. Introduction to the course: analytical reading and writing
2. *L* 3–6, and *SMH* 64c (reading and writing about literature); story selected from *L*

3. *L* 35–46; poem selected from *L*

■ **WEEK 2**

1. Paper 1 assigned (500-word literary analysis with citations from text); *SMH* Chapter 3 (review of the writing process: exploring, planning, and drafting); *L* 71–74 (preliminary information about quoting and documenting)
2. Selection(s) from *L*
3. Selection(s) from *L*

■ **WEEK 3**

1. Working thesis and plan for Paper 1 due; workshop to review theses/plans; *SMH* Chapter 4 (review of the writing process: reviewing, revising, and editing)
2. Draft of Paper 1 due; peer-review workshop
3. **Paper 1 due;** workshop—papers proofread and discussed; bring *SMH* to class; selection(s) from *L*

■ **WEEK 4**

1. Selection(s) from *L*
2. Paper 2 assigned (750-word literary analysis with citations from primary text and one secondary source); selection(s) from *L*
3. Paper 1 returned and discussed; bring *SMH* to class; selection from *L*

■ **WEEK 5**

1. Selection(s) from *L; SMH* 17b, 17c, and 17d (using sources: quotation, paraphrase, summary)

2. Working thesis and plan for Paper 2 due; workshop to review theses/plans; using sources continued

3. Draft of Paper 2 due; peer-review workshop

■ WEEK 6

1. **Paper 2 due;** workshop — papers proofread and discussed; bring *SMH* to class; Paper 3 assigned (750-word literary analysis with citations from primary text and minimum of two secondary sources)

2. Selection(s) from *L*

3. Selection(s) from *L*

■ WEEK 7

1. Paper 2 returned and discussed; bring *SMH* to class; thesis and plan for Paper 3 due; workshop to review theses/plans

2. *SMH* Chapters 16–18 (using sources) and Chapter 20 (MLA style)

3. Draft of Paper 3 due; peer-review workshop

■ WEEK 8

1. Paper 4 assigned (1,500-word literary analysis with citations of primary text[s] and minimum of five secondary sources); writing from sources continued

2. **Paper 3 due;** workshop — papers proofread and discussed; bring *SMH* to class

3. *SMH* Chapter 19 (writing for a research project)

■ WEEK 9

1. Working thesis and plan for Paper 4 due; workshop to review theses/plans

2. Paper 3 returned and discussed; bring *SMH* to class; selection(s) from *L*

3. Selection(s) from *L*

■ WEEK 10

1. Review material from *SMH* Chapters 15–20

2. Draft of Paper 4 due; peer-review workshop

3. Peer-review workshop continued

■ WEEK 11

1. Peer-review workshop continued

2. **Paper 4 due;** workshop — papers proofread and discussed; bring *SMH* to class

3. Selection(s) from *L*

■ WEEK 12

1. Selection(s) from *L*

2. Selection(s) from *L*

3. Preparation for Paper 5 (500-word in-class literary analysis)

■ WEEK 13

1. Paper 4 returned and discussed; bring *SMH* to class; preparation for Paper 5 continued

2. **Paper 5 drafted in class**

3. Paper 5 revised and edited in class

■ WEEK 14

1. Selection(s) from *L* for use in final exam — a 500-word in-class essay

2. Selection(s) from *L*; preparation for final exam continued

3. Paper 5 returned and discussed; bring *SMH* to class

Syllabus 3: The *Handbook* with an Argument Reader

This syllabus outlines another course typically taught as part of a year-long sequence. After learning to write short expository papers in a first-year composition course, students concentrate in a second (or later) course on argumentation and the research paper. In the version that follows, students read and analyze argumentative essays, construct their own arguments, and write a research paper in which they quote, summarize, and paraphrase secondary sources to support their ideas. The reader in the course, *Everything's an Argument, with Readings,* contains argumentative essays along with advice about analyzing and writing arguments.

Students write three short papers, a longer research paper, and, near the end of the term, an in-class essay. This last piece helps prepare them for the final exam, an additional in-class essay. Instructors may also want to add informal writing assignments, such as exercises or impromptu responses to the readings.

Books: Andrea A. Lunsford, *The St. Martin's Handbook,* 5th ed. (Bedford/St. Martin's, 2003) = *SMH*

Andrea A. Lunsford, et al., *Everything's an Argument, with Readings,* 2nd ed. (Bedford/St. Martin's, 2001) = *EA*

Schedule: In the first few weeks of the course, *Handbook* assignments provide an overview of the writing process and teach students about analyzing and constructing arguments (Chapters 11–13). Later, students make extensive use of Part 4 (doing research and using sources). They also bring the *Handbook* to class for review on days when papers are collected and returned. And throughout the term, they consult the book on their own as a tool for drafting and revising their papers.

■ WEEK 1

1. Introduction to the course: analyzing and writing arguments
2. *EA* Chapter 1 (introduction to argument)
3. *EA* Chapters 2–3 (reading arguments); sample argument(s) selected from *EA*

■ WEEK 2

1. Paper 1 assigned (500-word analysis of an argument with citations from text); *SMH* Chapter 11 (analyzing arguments); *EA* Chapter 22 (preliminary information about using sources)
2. Selection(s) from *EA; SMH* Chapter 3 (review of the writing process: exploring, planning, and drafting)
3. Selection(s) from *EA*

■ WEEK 3

1. Working thesis and plan for Paper 1 due; workshop to review theses/plans; *SMH* Chapter 4 (review of the writing process: reviewing, revising, and editing)
2. Draft of Paper 1 due; peer-review workshop
3. **Paper 1 due;** workshop—papers proofread and discussed; bring *SMH* to class; selection(s) from *EA*

■ **WEEK 4**

1. Selection(s) from *EA*
2. Paper 2 assigned (750-word comparative analysis of two newspaper editorials with citations from both); selection(s) from *EA*
3. Paper 1 returned and discussed; bring *SMH* to class; selection(s) from *EA*

■ **WEEK 5**

1. Selection(s) from *EA*; *SMH* 17b, 17c, and 17d (using quotation, paraphrase, summary)
2. Working thesis and plan for Paper 2 due; workshop to review theses/plans
3. Draft of Paper 2 due; peer-review workshop

■ **WEEK 6**

1. **Paper 2 due;** workshop — papers proofread and discussed; bring *SMH* to class; Paper 3 assigned (750-word argumentative essay with citations from a minimum of two sources)
2. *SMH* Chapter 13 (writing an argument); selection(s) from *EA*
3. Selection(s) from *EA*

■ **WEEK 7**

1. Paper 2 returned and discussed; bring *SMH* to class; thesis and plan for Paper 3 due; workshop to review theses/plans
2. *SMH* Chapters 16–18 (using sources) and Chapter 20 (MLA style)
3. Draft of Paper 3 due; peer-review workshop

■ **WEEK 8**

1. Paper 4 assigned (1,500-word argument with citations from minimum of five sources); writing from sources continued

2. **Paper 3 due;** workshop — papers proofread and discussed; bring *SMH* to class
3. *SMH* Chapter 19 and *EA* Chapter 18 (writing for a research project)

■ **WEEK 9**

1. Working thesis and plan for Paper 4 due; workshop to review theses/plans
2. Paper 3 returned and discussed; bring *SMH* to class; selection(s) from *EA*
3. Selection(s) from *EA*

■ **WEEK 10**

1. Review material from *SMH* Chapters 15–20
2. Draft of Paper 4 due; peer-review workshop
3. Peer-review workshop continued

■ **WEEK 11**

1. Peer-review workshop continued
2. **Paper 4 due;** workshop — papers proofread and discussed; bring *SMH* to class
3. Selection(s) from *EA*

■ **WEEK 12**

1. Selection(s) from *EA*
2. Selection(s) from *EA*
3. Preparation for Paper 5 (500-word in-class analysis of an argument)

■ **WEEK 13**

1. Paper 4 returned and discussed; bring *SMH* to class; preparation for Paper 5 continued
2. **Paper 5 drafted in class**
3. Paper 5 revised and edited in class

■ **WEEK 14**

1. Selection(s) from *EA* for use in final exam — a 500-word in-class essay
2. Selection(s) from *EA;* preparation for final exam continued
3. Paper 5 returned and discussed; bring *SMH* to class

▼ INTRODUCTION: Learning from Your Errors

Recent research on students' approaches to college-level writing indicates that students are deeply invested in improving their rhetorical and argumentative skills in a way that confirms our scholarly insistence on "process" methodologies. As Richard Light discovered through his interviews with Harvard undergraduates, students not only are open to working through the acts of invention, organization, revision, and editing but in fact desire the opportunity to do so. In his study entitled *Making the Most of College: Students Speak Their Minds*, Light reflects:

> The findings from our survey dramatize the extraordinary importance that students put on good writing. . . . I was surprised by students' strong attitude toward writing. I would have guessed that they value good writing, but I didn't realize how deeply many of them care about it, or how strongly they hunger for specific suggestions about how to improve it.

Similarly, students at Stanford University told a group of writing teachers that they desired the freedom to make mistakes in their writing and rhetoric classes. They also voiced a hunger to take risks, receive suggestions, and analyze texts that they might use as models.

Our challenge as teachers is to provide the space for such risk-taking to occur. We might reconceptualize writing as an inevitable process of working through errors. In the words of Malcolm Gladwell, journalist for the *New Yorker* and author of *The Tipping Point*, the writer's inclination is to err. "Journalists write a lot," Gladwell told an audience at Stanford University in January 2002, "so sometimes you are just wrong."

Allowing — even encouraging — our students to embrace experimentation and error as integral parts of the writing process empowers them as practitioners and rhetoricians; it also provides us as teachers the opportunity to take risks in our facilitation of writing exercises and assignments. Above all, our task is to foster *critical thinking* about the errors — and the exceptional rhetorical strategies — in all writing. In this way, we can invite students to develop the ability to analyze the rhetorical situations in the textual, visual, and multimedia world around them and to transform their engagement into effective writing that contributes to the public sphere.

The Introduction to *The St. Martin's Handbook* serves as a guide to facilitating such critical thinking. It also encourages students to begin taking risks — not to fear failure, but to seize the opportunity to shape language into elegant, persuasive texts of rhetorical power and significance.

(pp. 2–3)

FOR TEACHING: TAKING A WRITING INVENTORY

One way to encourage students to begin actively learning from their errors is through the use of writing inventories. If you want students to take a full inventory of their writing, you might consider working through the beginning of a hypothetical inventory with them. To do so, distribute copies of a student essay (from your files or from another class) and ask the students to work with you to identify the three categories of features dealt with in this section: broad content issues, organization and presentation, and surface errors.

To give students practice in taking a writing inventory on a more detailed level, ask them to examine a piece of writing for some specific feature — looking for every organizational "cue," for instance, or every transitional word or phrase. They can do this part of the assignment particularly well in groups. Then ask them to reflect on their findings and to draw one or more conclusions on whatever feature they have looked for. Such an exercise asks students to move from observation to generalization, to "metadiscourse" about their own writing, or to what Shirley Brice Heath calls building theories about their own language use. The more students are able to make such mental moves, the better they will be at monitoring their own learning and learning from their errors.

(p. 4)

On Looking for Strengths in Student Writing

Peter Elbow reminds us that it is characteristic of good teachers to *like* student writing, even though they see its weaknesses or failures. Elbow urges teachers to cultivate their enjoyment of student writing by: (1) looking for "strengths, both real and potential"; (2) practicing "conscious, disciplined, positive reinforcement"; and (3) getting to know students through conferences, journals, and free topic choices. Elbow concludes:

It's not improving our writing that leads us to like it, but rather our liking it that leads us to improving it. Liking writing makes it easier to criticize it — and makes criticism easier to take and to learn from.

(Lecture delivered at Bread Loaf School of English, July 17, 1991.)

On Assessing Broad Content Issues   **(p. 4)**

It is important for students to recognize the larger questions informing the writing process: What is the purpose of this writing project? Who is the audience? What is the main argument? Is there sufficient evidence?

When you present a writing assignment to your students, provide them with a detailed list of questions or criteria to follow in composing their work. Recall that research shows students need to continue to work on broad content issues, including the categories on p. 4 of the *Handbook*. Provide a rationale for understanding each of these broad content issues as part of your assignment sheet in order to facilitate students' own critical thinking about broad content issues in their writing.

FOR TEACHING: USE OF SUPPORTING EVIDENCE   **(p. 5)**

Ask students to look at essays or assignments written recently for instructors' comments on the logic or use of evidence and support. Ask them to bring examples of such comments to class for discussion.

TEACHING WITH TECHNOLOGY: USE OF SOURCES   **(p. 5)**

Using a computer projector, display sample writing passages from student papers in order to demonstrate the effective use of sources. A large computer screen or shared plasma screen works particularly well so that all students can see the text on the screen.

Once you display a sample text, ask students to participate in analyzing the use of the source as evidence: Is there an effective lead into the citation? Does the passage identify the source of the citation? Is there an effective comment on the citation to propel the argument forward? Solicit suggestions for revision from the students and make changes with the keyboard, demonstrating the correction to the class.

Try to offer different kinds of examples when teaching proper use of sources. For instance, demonstrate a paraphrase, summary, and direct quotation. Show students how to integrate visual sources into their writing. Provide a Web source, an e-text of a published article, and a book entry. Use this opportunity to begin a conversation about the evaluation of sources and the importance of consulting a range of sources.

(p. 6) **FOR TEACHING: ACHIEVEMENT OF PURPOSE**

When designing your writing assignments, list "Purpose" as a separate category in order to develop students' critical thinking about the importance of purpose in the writing process. Ask students to compare the purposes of writing done for different classes and different audiences. Have students bring in the prompts for writing assignments distributed in other classes and participate in a group analysis of the language of these documents. A class dialogue on purpose, using concrete examples from students' courses of study and extracurricular activities, will help illuminate this concept.

(p. 7) **FOR MULTILINGUAL WRITERS: ATTENTION TO AUDIENCE**

An exercise on audience can help multilingual writers begin to distinguish between different kinds of writing in English. On the first day of class, ask students to write a brief paragraph addressed to you explaining what they hope to gain from your course. Then have students rewrite the paragraph with two different audiences in mind — their parents, their best friend from home, their summer employer, their coach, and so on. When the students finish writing, take some time to discuss the changes in diction, tone, and appeals that accompany each rhetorical situation.

(p. 7) **FOR TEACHING: OVERALL IMPRESSION**

Surprisingly few studies have been done on the nature of teachers' written comments on student writing, and no studies have looked at large numbers of essays commented on by large numbers of teachers. For the second edition of *The St. Martin's Handbook,* Lunsford and Connors analyzed teachers' global comments on three thousand student essays, a stratified sample of twenty-one thousand marked student essays gathered from teachers throughout the United States. Of the three thousand essays, 77 percent carried global comments — those that address issues of rhetoric, organizational structure, longitudinal writing development, mastery of content, and so on. This finding suggests that teachers care a great deal about such matters and that, contrary to popular opinion, they comment on them rather than only pouncing on every surface error. The most commonly used form of global comment is one that begins positively, with praise for some element in the essay, and then details the negative points.

On Assessing Organization and Presentation   (p. 8)

Often students overlook the importance of organization and presentation in their focus on content and purpose. Ask them to consider the impression that one makes going to a job interview with the appropriate clothes and demeanor. Would someone wear crumpled, dirty, or inappropriate clothing? It's just as crucial for writers to attend to formal qualities of their writing, including overall organization, sentence structure and style, paragraph structure, format, and documentation.

FOR TEACHING: OVERALL ORGANIZATION   (p. 9)

Ask each student to check an essay or assignment written recently for the instructor's comments on organizational issues and to bring the example to class for discussion. Ask students to write a short letter to that teacher. Their letters should do three things:

1. Respond to the teacher's comments, telling the teacher what they think he or she is asking them to do.
2. Explain why they organized their writing that way in the first place.
3. Explain how they would reorganize the writing according to the teacher's comments and their own improved understanding.

FOR COLLABORATIVE WORK: SENTENCE STRUCTURE AND STYLE   (p. 9)

Have students exchange papers in peer-review groups and use a pen to circle repetitive phrases in their sentence patterns. Often a particular tendency will emerge in student writing, and each student can develop an awareness of his or her own individual preferences by having peers help identify these patterns. Students can use a highlighter to emphasize particularly compelling phrases in the work of their writing groups. Ask students to share their findings with each other and to discuss the benefits of different sentence lengths, sentence sequences, and ordering strategies.

(p. 10)

FOR TEACHING: PARAGRAPH STRUCTURE

An excellent way to emphasize the importance of logical paragraph structure in the writing process is through the use of post-draft outlines. Ask students to make an outline of the points covered in their drafts, and then have them assess the effectiveness of the paragraph order and structure. You might give students a list of questions to answer, including the following:

Do the paragraphs help readers follow the thread of thought?

Is there a tendency for underdeveloped paragraphs (one or two sentences in length)?

Does each paragraph deal with one significant idea — or too many?

Is there a cumulative development of ideas from beginning to end?

Does the argument build or do the paragraphs need to be rearranged/restructured to provide a more forceful progression?

Are there strong transitions between paragraphs?

(p. 11)

FOR TEACHING: FORMAT

Sylvan Barnet and Hugo Bedau describe the necessity of assessing format and presentation in terms of visual persuasion. Their rationale may be helpful to share with students in your classes: "Every paper uses some degree of visual persuasion, merely in its appearance: perhaps a title page, certainly margins (ample — but not so wide that they tell the reader that the writer is unable to write a paper of the assigned length), double-spacing for the convenience of the reader, paragraphing (again for the convenience of the reader), and so on" (96). Ask students to complete a format checklist in peer-review groups or on their own before handing in the revised versions of their drafts.

FOR COLLABORATIVE WORK: DOCUMENTATION   (p. 11)

Students respond well to checklists that help them assess proper documentation. You can provide the following questions to help them work on their drafts in peer-review groups before turning in a final revision.

Are there specific primary sources cited throughout the essay?

Are there secondary sources integrated as frame and support for the argument?

Is all the material in the quotes necessary and appropriate?

Are quotes integrated well (with proper signal phrases), so that the context or source is understood?

Is there sufficient analysis/explanation after each quotation to propel the argument forward?

For MLA Citation:

Is there a source reference for every quotation?

Are page numbers or paragraph numbers cited parenthetically after each quotation?

Does the citation list the author's last name (or, if no author, the title's key words)?

Are quotes of four lines or more introduced with a colon and indented five spaces?

Are quotes of less than four lines set off with quotation marks?

Does the format follow MLA style with punctuation after the parenthesis?

Is the works-cited list in correct MLA format?

In addition to distributing checklists to students, it is worth spending time in class discussing the importance of proper documentation. Analogies to scientific notation (for science majors), correct "code" (for computer science majors), or proper form and training (for athletes) often work to open students' minds to considering the value of proper format.

On Learning from Your Surface Errors   (p. 12)

The greater the writer's fixation on error, the greater the difficulty that writer will have writing. The more the instructor focuses on error, the more the student will worry about error. In *The Concept of the Mind* (New

Give me a fruitful error any time, full of seeds, bursting with its own corrections.
        – VILFREDO PARETO

Any fool can make a rule and every fool will mind it.
        – HENRY DAVID THOREAU

But enough of these errors. The good writer masters grammar in order to control his words, and meaning is his target.
        – KEN MACRORIE

York: Barnes and Noble, 1949) British philosopher Gilbert Ryle wrote that "errors are exercises in competence." And this new concept of error as "portals to discovery" became the mainstay of Mina Shaughnessy's study of basic writing. By 1981, Isabella Halsted was writing that errors are *"not* Sin, not Crime punishable by F." Errors are simply mistakes that we are all capable of, given the wrong circumstances: lack of sleep, deadline pressure, unfamiliarity with formal English. Halsted describes her own attitude toward error:

> Like soot on the pane, Error is something that gets in the way of the clear vision. . . . Error on all levels is distracting, annoying, obstructive. Error is inexcusable ultimately, yes, [but] not because it is Wrong per se. . . . In plain pragmatic terms, the absence of Error is useful; but when our students take pains to avoid it — by writing short sentences, by sticking to one tense, by writing as little as possible — I doubt very much that they do so in order to better communicate with a reader, but rather to play safe, to avoid the red marks.

At the same time, however, research by Larry Beason, in "Ethos and Errors," suggests that errors impede more than communication; they also endanger a writer's credibility and character. Through quantitative research on fourteen businesspeople, Beason offers a rhetorical analysis of errors in terms of how textual transgressions lead readers to produce judgments of character and consequently construct "a negative ethos of the writer."

Beason's study provides compelling reasons for teachers to spend time helping students identify common errors in their writing: "Whether we believe it to be the optimum situation or not, errors have an impact on the writer's image and communicability. Error avoidance, I submit, should have a presence in the composition curriculum — but without overpowering it" (60). Focusing students' attention on the "Twenty Most Common Errors" listed in the *Handbook* (p. 14) can go a long way toward remedying such ethos-damaging errors.

(p. 12)

ATTENDING TO DISABILITIES: LEARNING FROM SURFACE ERRORS

"[M]any of our students would gladly avoid composition classes because they fear any difficulties they have with writing will (once again) be interpreted as intellectual or moral flaws," writes Brenda Jo Brueggemann in "Becoming Visible." This is especially true for students with disabilities who may already be at a disadvantage if the institution does not have the resources to facilitate their learning. Be sure to identify and meet with students at the beginning of the course in order to assess their writing fears and capabilities. A student information sheet can provide a quick way to ascertain students' perspectives, but be sure to follow up with individual conferences as soon as the course is under way. The reason for such early dialogue is clear. As Brueggemann asserts:

> For decades we have spoken about "writing" as learning. We know that writing is about complex intellectual processes. We know that writing is intimately connected with issues of authority, identity, power, and confidence, and that if students are to become more sophisticated thinkers and writers, they should be both challenged and taken seriously. The rhetoric of the learning disability backlash interferes with this critical dynamic between writer and reader, between student and teacher, by introducing stereotype into the equation. (379)

FOR TEACHING: THE TWENTY MOST COMMON ERRORS

(p. 14)

Here are twenty passages taken from the group of student essays on which Lunsford and Connors's research is based. Each passage contains one of the twenty most common student writing errors, and these passages are numbered to correspond with the "top twenty" list on p. 14. These passages may be used in at least three different ways: (1) You might reproduce this list and use it as a diagnostic test early in the semester to see how practiced your students are at recognizing these errors; (2) you might use them as a review test at the end of the semester or after concluding your class's study of this introduction; (3) you may simply want to use them as examples of the top twenty errors, supplementing those given in the text.

1. The Beast which is one of the biggest roller coasters, has a thunderous ride of steep hills and turns. As you race down the first and biggest hill your coaster is engulfed by a tunnel at the end of the hill.

2. Once you find where other surfers are, you can set up your camp. This entails claiming your own territory. You do this by laying out your oversized beach towel and by turning your radio on loud enough to mark your domain without disturbing anyone else. This should help you blend in with the locals.

3. I was gaining speed and feeling really good but when I looked back he wasn't there. I panicked. I saw him and my parents down at the other end of the street and forgot to look forward. When I finally did turn forward, I saw that I was rapidly closing in on my neighbor's car. How ironic; I was about to hit the car of the man who was trying to teach me how to ride a bike.

You can be a little ungrammatical if you come from the right part of the country.
– ROBERT FROST

4. Assateague is perfect for those who want to simply lay out in the sun, go swimming, and walk along the coast. But for those who crave a little more excitement, Ocean City is just a few minutes away by car. Ocean City hosts all the hotels, restaurants, and gift shops one could desire.

5. The knights with armor and horses beautifully decorated participate in battles of jousting, target shooting with spears, archery, and duels of strategy and strength using swords and shields. During the evening, there is a break from the fighting, and a beautiful ceremony of marriage is acted out.

6. I decided to begin searching for an outfit while the rollers in my hair cooled. I began throwing everything out of my closet. Nothing fits my mood, and not one thing caught my eyes as they fell on the bed. I had no idea what I was even looking for since I didn't know where I was going.

7. You should also think about how far you want to walk to class from your apartment. You may want to live in an apartment that is a shorter walking distance to campus, especially if it is important for you to be independent from public transportation.

8. Chips and sauces are not the only thing that you get free refills on, you also get free refills on all non-alcoholic beverages, such as soda and tea. The servers are very good about getting you more of both things when you need refills, usually you do not even have to ask.

9. What I'm trying to get at is that because of this persons immaturity, many people have suffered. This persons lack of responsibility has turned peoples lives upside down.

10. The good thing about its location is that it is right off the main highway, very easy to spot. There are also plenty of road signs pointing you in the direction of the park. And if you got extremely lost, pulling off and asking would be the easiest way to get on track.

11. After deciding to begin your college career, many students are then faced with the predicament of where to live. This is not such a problem for students from out of town, but it is if you live in the same city or area in which you chose a school.

12. When I got to half court, the guy that was playing center on my team stood between the defensive player and me. As I dribbled around the center, he stopped the defensive player. Not by using his hands but by his big body. This is a strategy used to get a player open for a shot.

13. I thought about all of the work we had done this quarter in English. I had not done well on my spelling tests even when I had cheated on them. I did my reading assignments with other people so I never answered the question by myself completely.

14. Their hands are folded and it seems as though they are mumbling to themselves. They try to get the person's attention but never does what they planned to do.

15. I was driving along behind an older Volkswagen Jetta, following closely, but not close enough that I couldn't see everything that was going on around me. My eyes were watching the brake lights the curbs the side walks, and the car in front of me.

16. On the other hand, what if you don't care for your partner — or even worse — they don't care for you? You know now that it is still okay to separate without the problem of obtaining a divorce. Many divorces that take place within the first years of marriage might have been avoided if the couple had lived together before marrying.

17. There is also a stand up roller coaster called, the King Kobra, which goes up-side down in the first loop, with plenty of tossing and turning. Like I said previously, King's Island also keeps the people with weaker stomachs in mind; there are rides all throughout the park which are a little slower paced.

18. I felt someone's hand shaking my shoulder. I lifted my head up to see my best friend Stephanie looking down at me. "That must have been some dream. Come on the bell rang class is over."

19. Trying to keep parents happy is a constant effort made by kids to keep in good standing with mom and dad. After all, it is they who will support us until we are capable of living on our own with things like money, food, and clothes.

20. You cannot just decide to have a party and have it the same day. You have to prepare for it. All the things that you do before, during, and after the party determines it's success. The better you prepare for it, the better time everyone will have.

FOR COLLABORATIVE WORK: THE TWENTY MOST COMMON ERRORS   **(p. 14)** ·······································

Ask students to work in groups of three to compare findings and plans for improvement after working through the twenty passages. Their first plan should be to categorize the errors they make according to the catalog of errors in this chapter. Then, they may want to determine the frequency of errors they make in each category. This simple exercise will establish their ability to evaluate their own work, an important skill each writer needs to develop.

■ **USEFUL READINGS**

Bartholomae, David. "The Study of Error." *CCC* 31 (Oct. 1980): 253–69.

Beason, Larry. "Ethos and Error: How Business People React to Errors." *CCC* 53.1 (Sept. 2001): 33–64.

Bérubé, Michael. *Life as We Know It: A Father, a Family, and an Exceptional Child.* New York: Vintage-Random, 1998. In this important text about breaking stereotypes and not viewing your students through the lens of disabilities, Bérubé describes his own child with Down syndrome.

Booth, Wayne C. "The Rhetorical Stance." *Now Don't Try to Reason with Me: Essays and Ironies for a Credulous Age.* Chicago: U of Chicago P, 1970. Booth posits a carefully balanced tripartite division of rhetorical appeals, including "the available arguments about the subject itself, the interests and peculiarities of the audience, and the voice, the implied character, of the speaker" (27).

Brueggemann, Brenda Jo. *Enabling the Humanities: A Sourcebook for Disability Studies in Language and Literature.* New York: MLA, 2002.

———. *Lend Me Your Ear: Rhetorical Constructions of Deafness.* Washington, DC: Gallaudet UP, 1999. Writing out of both professional and personal experience with deafness, Brueggemann provides an astute analysis of rhetorical constructions and institutional traditions that limit deaf people; interviews and poetry make this a compelling text for the classroom.

Brueggemann, Brenda Jo, Linda Feldmeier White, Patricia A. Dunn, Barbara A. Heifferon, and Johnson Cheu. "Becoming Visible: Lessons in Disability." CCC 52.3 (Feb. 2001): 368–98. The authors scrutinize constructions of normalcy, writing, and composition in this groundbreaking article in disability studies.

Connors, Robert J., and Andrea Lunsford. "Teachers' Rhetorical Comments on Student Papers." CCC 44 (May 1993): 200–24. This article represents part of the research described in the Introduction to the *Handbook*.

Corbett, Edward P., Nancy Myers, and Gary Tate. *The Writing Teacher's Sourcebook.* 4th ed. New York: Oxford UP, 2000.

Daiker, Donald A. "Learning to Praise." *Writing Response: Theory, Practice and Research.* Ed. Chris Anson. Urbana: NCTE, 1989. 103–13.

Epes, Mary. "Tracing Errors to Their Sources: A Study of the Encoding Processes of Adult Basic Writers." *Journal of Basic Writing* 4 (Spring 1985): 4–33. Epes makes a cogent argument for grammatical instruction that reflects standard academic English.

Halasek, Kay, Tara Pauliny, Edgar Singleton, Rebecca Greenberg Taylor, Kathleen R. Wallace, and Matt Wanat. *The Writer's Companion: A Guide to First-year Writing.* Needham Heights: Pearson, 1999.

Halsted, Isabella. "Putting Error in Its Place." *Journal of Basic Writing* 1 (Spring 1975): 72–86.

Hartwell, Patrick. "Grammar, Grammars, and the Teaching of Grammar." CE 47 (1985): 105–27. Rpt. in *The St. Martin's Guide to Teaching Writing.* Ed. Cheryl Glenn, Robert Connors, and Melissa A. Goldthwaite. Boston: Bedford, 2003. 000–00. Hartwell defines and explains the purposes of the various grammars.

Holberg, Jennifer, and Mary Tyler, eds. *Pedagogy: Critical Approaches to Teaching Literature, Language, Composition, and Culture.* Durham: Duke UP, 2000.

Jarratt, Susan C., and Lynn Worsham, eds. *Feminism and Composition Studies: In Other Words.* New York: MLA, 1998. An excellent collection of scholarship on feminist approaches to teaching.

Kolln, Martha. "Closing the Books on Alchemy." *CCC* 32 (May 1981): 139–51. While no direct relation exists between grammar instruction and writing improvement, there are other important reasons for studying grammar—to analyze and to build shared vocabulary and conceptual frameworks.

Krishna, Valerie. "The Syntax of Error." *Journal of Basic Writing* 1 (Spring 1975): 43–49. Unlike the "classical" errors—verb agreement, punctuation, pronoun case—that are easily categorized, students' structural errors are unique. Krishna directs us in understanding that students' structural errors are the direct outgrowth of "a weak structural core" that is disjoined from the idea that a writer is trying to express.

Lanham, Richard A. *Analyzing Prose.* 2nd ed. New York: Continuum, 2002. Lanham applies Aristotelian classifications of style (such as noun and verb styles, parataxis and hypotaxis, periodic and running styles) in order to provide both a descriptive and an evaluative approach to analyzing modern prose style.

Light, Richard J. *Making the Most of College: Students Speak Their Minds.* Cambridge: Harvard UP, 2001.

Lindemann, Erika. *A Rhetoric for Writing Teachers.* 4th ed. New York: Oxford UP, 2001. Lindemann provides background material for the teaching of writing, including a history of rhetoric, a survey of linguistics, and a useful bibliography.

Lunsford, Andrea A., and Lisa S. Ede. "Audience Addressed/Audience Invoked: The Role of Audience in Composition Theory and Pedagogy." *The Writing Teacher's Sourcebook.* 4th ed. Ed. Nancy Myerson, Gary Tate, and Edward P. J. Corbett. New York: Oxford UP, 1999. Lunsford and Ede point out the limitations of two prominent concepts of audience, that of "audience addressed," which emphasizes the concrete reality of the writer's audience, and that of "audience invoked," which focuses on the writer's construction of an audience. They argue that a writer's audience may be both addressed and invoked.

Miller, Susan. "How Writers Evaluate Their Own Writing." *CCC* 33 (May 1982): 176–83. Miller argues that all writers should always end their writing process by evaluating the written product according to two criteria: How well did the audience respond to the piece of writing? How well did the writers meet their original intentions? But finally, writers should measure their growth as writers, what Miller calls "author growth."

Pemberton, Michael A. *The Ethics of Writing Instruction: Issues in Theory and Practice.* Stamford: Ablex, 2000.

Pytlik, Betty P., and Sarah Liggett. *Preparing College Teachers of Writing: Histories, Theories, Programs, Practices*. New York: Oxford UP, 2002.

Schwegler, Robert. "The Politics of Reading Student Papers." *The Politics of Writing Instruction*. Ed. Richard Bullock, Charles Schuster, and John Trimbur. Portsmouth: Boynton, 1991. 203–26.

Shaughnessy, Mina. *Errors & Expectations: A Guide for the Teacher of Basic Writing*. New York: Oxford UP, 1977. Since the publication of this book, every scholarly work on error has referred to it.

Tate, Gary, Amy Rupiper, and Kurt Schick. *A Guide to Composition Pedagogies*. New York: Oxford UP, 2001.

Williams, Joseph M. "The Phenomenology of Error." *CCC* 32 (1981): 152–68. Williams argues that we need to view errors as simply socially inappropriate, easily remedied behavior.

——. *Style: Ten Lessons in Clarity and Grace*. 7th ed. New York: Longman, 2003. Intended as a how-to manual for writers, this book outlines four principles of effective style: clarity, cohesion, emphasis, and concision. Williams also discusses punctuation and usage as matters of style.

Wolfram, Walt. "Teaching the Grammar of Vernacular English." *Language Variation in North American English: Research and Teaching*. Ed. A. Wayne Glowka and Donald M. Lance. New York: MLA, 1993. 16–27. This is a good basic guide (with bibliography) for working with speakers and writers of other Englishes.

■ USEFUL WEB SITES

The Bedford Bibliography for Teachers of Writing

    http://www.bedfordbooks.com/bb/

    A searchable database of the The Bedford Bibliography for Teachers of Writing *by Patricia Bizzell, Bruce Herzberg, and Nedra Reynolds.*

Centre for Disability Studies, University of Leeds, England

    http://www.leeds.ac.uk/disability-studies/publish.htm

    Hosts an extensive list of recent publications in disability studies in England.

Disability Studies in the Humanities

    http://www.georgetown.edu/crossroads/interests/ds-hum/index.html

    The Disability Studies in the Humanities (DS-HUM) Web site, listserv, and syllabus bank provide samples of college course syllabi that either incorporate disability as an issue or even center on that subject in the humanities classroom (especially in language, literature, and composition).

Kairos Special Issue: "Disability—Demonstrated by and Mediated through Technology"

http://english.ttu.edu/kairos/7.1

The Spring 2002 issue offers a range of articles and assignment ideas for composition.

LD Resources

http://www.ldresources.com

The online resource for Learning Disabilities: read online columns and essays, subscribe to the LD newsletter, read archived issues, keep informed on current happenings and conferences, contact people, find out about educational developments, access both high- and low-tech tools, and link to electronic books and videos.

Program in Writing and Rhetoric

http://pwr.stanford.edu

Stanford University's Program in Writing and Rhetoric site hosts a wealth of resources for students and teachers of writing.

Tools for Teaching

http://teaching.berkeley.edu/bgd/teaching.html

A compendium of resources from Barbara Gross Davis's Tools for Teaching, *(San Francisco: Jossey-Bass, 1993).*

PART 1

THE ART AND CRAFT OF WRITING

1

▼ Reading, Writing, and Research

The peace I am thinking of is the dance of an open mind when it engages another equally open one — an activity that occurs most naturally, most often in the reading/writing world we live in.

–Toni Morrison, "The Dancing Mind"

Today, the job of teaching writing is a complex blending of at least two purposes: first, to help students see that they have a voice and to help them become comfortable with developing a writing process that can express it; second, to introduce them to the conventions of academic discourse, with its genres, levels of expertise, different tones, and sense of audience.

In your class are many students who know exactly what you expect of them: flawlessly executed, fully developed essays. They are sure that you write without anxiety, false starts, or dictionaries, for you are an English instructor. Therefore, you might start by asking students how they think experienced writers work. Then discuss your writing process as well as theirs.

Your students will benefit from comparing their writing habits: how (and if) they gather their thoughts first, whether they add new information as they move through the writing assignment, if they prefer quiet or background noise, what time of day they do their best writing, how soon before the deadline they begin their assignments, and, most important, what kind of writing they do.

I believe in miracles in every area of life except *writing. Experience has shown me that there are no miracles in writing. The only thing that produces good writing is hard work.*
– Isaac Bashevis Singer

By discussing your students' writing processes, you will help them accomplish three goals: (1) They will listen and talk to one another, not just to you, thereby fostering a classroom atmosphere that lends itself to collaborative writing practices. (2) They will realize that you, too, have a unique writing process. (3) They will see that because writing is a recursive process consisting of planning, drafting, and revising, they can concentrate on one step at a time.

On Discovering New Opportunities for Writing

(1a)

The field of writing has been marked of late by new attention to teaching students with disabilities as well as by continued interest in attending to multicultural writers. Advances in teaching with technology enable us to provide our students with new opportunities both in the classroom space and beyond its four walls.

ATTENDING TO DISABILITIES: DISCOVERING NEW OPPORTUNITIES FOR WRITING

(1a)

The Americans with Disabilities Act (ADA) became law in 1990, but universities and classrooms have been slow to adapt. The goal of the ADA is to extend to Americans with disabilities the civil rights and equal access afforded to all other citizens: "Its purpose is to end discrimination, reduce barriers to employment, and ensure access to education for people with disabilities. . . . It also has led to the reshaping of the physical environment and improved communications access" (Disability Rights Movement Web site). As Ed Roberts, founder and president of the World Institute on Disability, tells us, Americans with disabilities have become an increasingly significant community:

> When people with disabilities come to the conclusion that they have the right to be in the community, to have a say in how that community treats them, they are beginning to develop a consciousness about taking control of their lives and resisting all attempts to give others that control.

Nothing about us without us.
– LEADERS OF DISABLED PEOPLE OF SOUTH AFRICA

Consequently, the changes to composition practices and to the institutional framework in which such practices take place have been sweeping. Scholars and teachers attending to disabilities have begun to recognize how doing so provides new opportunities for previously marginalized writers, and they are challenging the very definitions we use to discuss writing, texts, collaboration, and all other facets of the composition process.

FOR COLLABORATIVE WORK: NEW OPPORTUNITIES FOR WRITING

(1a)

Divide the class into groups of three and ask the members of each group to discuss their writing processes and practices. Then have them work together to write a one- or two-page description of the findings of their group, first describing, then comparing and contrasting the writing strategies of group members.

(1b)

On Considering the Process of Writing

In "Pre-Writing: The Stage of Discovery in the Writing Process," D. Gordon Rohman challenged the field of composition studies by arguing that writing is a learnable process. He begins his essay, published in *CCC* in 1965, by positing the following:

> Writing is usefully described as a process, something which shows continuous change in time like growth in organic nature. Different things happen at different stages in the process of putting thoughts into words and words onto paper. In our Project English experiment, we divided the process at the point where the "writing idea" is ready for the words and the page: everything before that we called "Pre-Writing," everything after "Writing" and "Re-Writing."

(1b)

ATTENDING TO DISABILITIES: CONSIDERING THE PROCESSES OF WRITING

Patricia Dunn suggests that we reconceptualize our notions of "writing" in order to incorporate a theorized and timely attention to students with disabilities:

> If a course requires reading logs or dialogue journals, every student might be asked to produce both oral and written ones — perhaps alternating the format throughout the semester. Good writers who might have difficulty organizing their thoughts orally, without first writing them down, would be challenged to do so. Those dynamic students who contribute much to the quality of class discussions — but who sometimes are not the best writers — would be recognized for their verbal contributions. If written proposals, outlines, or early drafts are required for inquiry-based papers, students might also experiment with drawing, sculpting, or dramatizing the plan. Being asked to conceptualize a project from a different perspective can trigger new insights for all writers, helping us generate connections we might not have made in word-locked prose. (Brueggemann et al. 381)

　　The act of rethinking writing assignments to provide new opportunities for *all* students will have far-reaching consequences: we challenge our conventional ways of thinking about what is "normal," we expand the meaning of "writing," and we reconceptualize what we signify by "disability." As Dunn argues, discovering new opportunities is a hallmark of our profession: "In a field that rightly prides itself on its self-reflective praxis, we in composition should become especially aware of cultural biases supporting limited definitions of writing in composition" (381).

FOR TEACHING: WRITING LOGS ON THE PROCESSES OF WRITING

(1b) ....

Grading students' writing logs may discourage them from analyzing their writing processes. The logs, however, can tell you what help your students need.

    An ungraded essay is a good way for you and your students to assess their current approach to composition. Assign the students to write a brief description of someone they knew well during childhood. Their essays should enable the reader to picture the person clearly and to understand how the writer felt about the subject. You may want to use this diagnostic essay as the basis for future assignments.

    After they have completed their essays, ask the students to answer the questions in the text. Then consider the following questions as you read their writing logs to determine how they might improve their writing.

1. Could the student spend more time in preparation?
2. Is the essay aimed at a particular audience?
3. Is the purpose for writing evident?
4. Did the student do any revising at all? What kind(s)?
5. Do you and the student agree on the strengths of the essay?

    Now is a good time to assure your students that you will help them improve their writing in specific ways, building on their strengths and concentrating on one problem at a time.

Writing and rewriting are a constant search for what it is one is saying.
—JOHN UPDIKE

I have never thought of myself as a good writer. Anyone who wants reassurance of that should read one of my first drafts. But I'm one of the world's great rewriters.
—JAMES A. MICHENER

Word-work is sublime . . . because it is generative; it makes meaning that secures our difference, our human difference—the way in which we are like no other life.
—TONI MORRISON

On Considering the Processes of Reading

(1b) ....

One of the primary benefits of teaching students the conventions of academic discourse is that it demonstrates to them the mutual reciprocity between the reading and writing processes. The interconnection between reading and writing has received a great deal of attention during the last decade. It has become clear that writing teachers are doing far more than teaching sentence structure—we are helping introduce students to a discourse that many of them are unfamiliar with. Standard academic discourse is more than just correctness; it is a style of presentation that involves awareness of audience, grasp of subject, and confidence in the writer's own ethos and abilities. As David Bartholomae says in "Inventing the University,"

> Every time a student sits down to write for us, he has to invent the university for the occasion — invent the university, that is, or a branch of it, like history or anthropology or economics or English. The student has to learn to speak our language, to speak as we do, to try on the peculiar ways of knowing, selecting, evaluating, reporting, concluding and arguing that define the discourse of our community. . . . The student has to appropriate (or be appropriated by) a specialized discourse, and he has to do this as though he were easily and comfortably one with his audience, as though he were a member of the academy or an historian or an anthropologist or an economist; he has to invent the university by assembling and mimicking its language while finding some compromise between idiosyncracy, a personal history, on the one hand, and the requirements of convention, the history of a discipline, on the other. He must learn to speak our language. (134–35)

In order to become part of the conversation of academic discourse, students must be exposed to it. Readings in a writing course assist this process in several ways: they provide models of good writing (as well as models of writing to be avoided); they provide content issues that can be discussed; they provide analyses of the decisions that writers have made; and they can illuminate the composing process. We will be using all of these elements in the reading exercises and the examples from works by various writers throughout the *Handbook*.

(1c)   **TEACHING WITH TECHNOLOGY: CONSIDERING THE PROCESSES OF READING**

More than ever, students are becoming online readers of Web and digital media texts. Have students review the "Guidelines for Critical Reading" exercises in the *Handbook*. They should follow the same steps for reading digital texts, including previewing, reading and annotating, summarizing, analyzing, talking with others, rereading, and responding.

(1d)   **On Doing Research**

In contrast to the narrow view of "student research," which confines it to a few weeks of hurried library activity at the end of a semester, this book sees the concept of research in a hermeneutic way: research is the process of understanding, interpreting, and applying new information *of all kinds*. We are all always engaged in research, some of which results in writing and much of which does not. Every essay a student writes is a research paper, and though some may require more library reading and correlation of information than others, it is impossible to write without having done research — even if that research is just into the shifting world of personal memories.

■ USEFUL READINGS

Bartholomae, David. "Inventing the University." *When a Writer Can't Write: Studies in Writer's Block and Other Composing Process Problems.* Ed. Mike Rose. New York: Guilford, 1985: 134–65. Bartholomae argues that in order to succeed in college, students need to learn to speak the language of the university, "to try on the peculiar ways of knowing, selecting, evaluating, reporting, concluding, and arguing" that are valued by various academic discourse communities.

Brueggemann, Brenda Jo, et al. "Becoming Visible: Lessons in Disability." *CCC* 52.3 (Feb. 2001): 368–398.

Charlton, James I. *Nothing about Us without Us: Disability Oppression and Empowerment.* Berkeley: U of California P, 1998. Examining the emergence of disability rights activists in the United States and across the globe, Charlton traces the "the political-economic and cultural dimensions" of what he calls "the dominant culture's oppression of people with disabilities" and offers pedagogues crucial reading (interviews, international research, and local practices).

Cope, Bill, and Mary Kalantzis, eds. *Multiliteracies: Literacy Learning and the Design of Social Futures.* London: Routledge, 2000. A collection of essays from the New London Group (NLG), including the famous 1996 *Harvard Educational Review* manifesto "Pedagogy of Multiliteracies: Designing Social Futures," chapters by ten founders, and South African contributions on the new multiliteracy curriculum, this volume analyzes and responds to the globalized, "fast capitalism" economy that both fragments cultures and produces new forms of writing in terms of multimedia and information technology.

Dunn, Patricia. *Learning Re-Abled: The Learning Disability Controversy and Composition Studies.* Portsmouth: Heinemann-Boynton/Cook, 1995.

Emig, Janet. *The Web of Meaning: Essays on Writing, Teaching, Learning, and Thinking.* Ed. Dixie Goswami and Maureen Butler. Upper Montclair: Boynton, 1983. Emig argues, among other things, that there is no one formula for teaching writing, that writing processes are recursive, and that writing "is as often a preconscious or unconscious roaming as it is a planned and conscious rendering of information and events" (141).

——. "Writing as a Mode of Learning." *CCC* 28 (1977): 122–28. Emig argues that writing represents a unique mode of learning, noting that it is inherently reinforcing, uses both hemispheres of the brain, and provides immediate feedback.

Henry, Jim. "Writing Workplace Cultures." *CCC* 53.2 (Dec. 2001): Online at <http://www.ncte.org/ccc/2/53.2/henry/article.html>. Henry examines the dramatic changes wrought by globalization (or "fast capitalism") on both the workplace and the writing produced in it.

Iezzoni, Lisa I. "Disability: The Reluctant Identity." *Journal of Health Politics, Policy and Law* 25.6 (2000): 1157–67. In this review of recent publications in disability studies, Iezzoni examines "the relative newcomer to identity politics, the 'disability identity'" from a cultural, historical, legal, and social point of view and concludes that "a sea change in attitudes and practices" is forthcoming.

Kelman, Mark, and Gillian Lester. *Jumping the Queue: An Inquiry into the Legal Treatment of Students with Learning Disabilities.* Cambridge: Harvard UP, 1998. While the controlling metaphor of this book suggests a "special treatment" epistemology, the authors constructively promote inclusive learning communities. A valuable source for reconsidering reading and writing processes in your classroom.

Kleege, Georgina. "Voices in My Head." *Yale Review* 85 (1997): 1–18. In this beautifully crafted essay, Kleege explores books-on-tape as a (major) way of reading, focusing on the ways that people with disabilities use this and other techniques of reading.

Lay, Nancy Duke. "Response Journals in the ESL Classroom: Windows to the World." *TETYC* (Feb. 1995): 38–44. Lay's article describes ways to use journals to help students with reading and with getting to know one another.

Leverenz, Carrie Shively. "Peer Response in the Multicultural Classroom: Dissensus—A Dream (Deferred)." *Journal of Advanced Composition* 14.1 (Winter 1994): 167–86. Consensus may not always be the best result of peer response; group questioning and dissensus may be more valuable to the students—and to the instructor.

Linton, Simi. *Claiming Disability: Knowledge and Identity.* New York: New York UP, 1998. Written by the self-proclaimed "disability ambassador," this text sounds a call to transform the curriculum of postsecondary education to include a "disability studies perspective."

Lunsford, Andrea, and Lisa Ede. *Singular Texts/Plural Authors: Perspectives on Collaborative Writing.* Carbondale: Southern Illinois UP, 1990. Lunsford and Ede trace the development of the idea of "the author" and demonstrate through extensive research that collaborative writing is quite common in business, government, and other major institutions, including the academy. They describe two modes of collaborative writing, hierarchical and dialogic, and offer guidelines and specific suggestions for incorporating collaboration in classrooms.

Murray, Donald M. "Teaching the Other Self: The Writer's First Reader." *CCC* 33 (1982): 140–47. According to Murray, all writers have an "other self" that is capable of reading a piece of writing in progress and giving advice to the writer about how the writing should proceed. Murray argues that the instructor should teach a student's "other self" by giving the writer's "other self" the chance to speak in teacher-student conferences and in small and large workshops with other writers.

Perl, Sondra. "Understanding Composing." *CCC* 31 (1980): 363–69. Rpt. in *Rhetoric and Composition: A Sourcebook for Teachers and Writers.* 2nd ed. Ed. Richard L. Graves. Portsmouth: Heinemann, 1984. Arguing that "throughout the process of writing, writers return to substrands of the overall process, or subroutines," Perl attempts to identify the features of this recursiveness.

Rohman, D. Gordon. "Pre-Writing: The Stage of Discovery in the Writing Process." *CCC* 16 (1965): 106–12.

The St. Martin's Guide to Teaching Writing, 5th ed., Chapter 7, provides more on "Teaching Composing Processes."

Williams, Wendy M., and Stephen J. Ceci. "Accommodating Learning Disabilities Can Bestow Unfair Advantages." *Chronicle of Higher Education* 6 (Aug. 1999): B4–5. The article that started an online firestorm of debate over the proper curri-cular, pedagogical, and institutional approach to students with learning disabilities.

Wilson, James C., and Cynthia Lewiecki-Wilson, eds. *Embodied Rhetorics: Disability in Language and Culture.* Carbondale: Southern Illinois UP, 2001. The editors unite rhetoric and disability studies to rethink educational practices.

■ **USEFUL WEB SITES:**

Disability Rights Movement

http://americanhistory.si.edu/disabilityrights

The Smithsonian National Museum of American History hosts a Web exhibit commemorating the tenth anniversary of the Americans with Disabilities Act (ADA).

Disability Studies Quarterly

http://www.cds.hawaii.edu/DSQ

The online site for the Center on Disability Studies at the College of Education, University of Hawaii at Manoa, Honolulu.

Disability Studies in the Humanities

http://www.georgetown.edu/crossroads/interests/ds-hum/index.html

The Disability Studies in the Humanities (DS-HUM) Web site, listserv, and syllabus bank provide samples of college course syllabi that either incorporate disability as an issue or even center on that subject in the humanities classroom (especially in language, literature, and composition).

▼ Considering Rhetorical Situations

2

It is well to understand as early as possible in one's writing life that there is just one contribution which every one of us can make; we can give unto the common pool of experience some comprehension of the world as it looks to each of us.

— DOROTHEA BRANDE

No writing takes place in isolation. As Wayne C. Booth wrote in his classic essay "The Rhetorical Stance," all good writing establishes a relationship among content, reader, and writer. In texts from emails to research papers, there is a dynamic interplay among audience, persona, and message that signifies the "rhetorical stance." Deciding to write entails engagement with this dynamic.

Within the discipline of rhetoric, the rhetorical situation has long been of paramount concern. Whether thought of in terms of Aristotle's categories of appeals a writer should consider when addressing any audience (ethos, logos, pathos), Kenneth Burke's scheme of dramatism (a pentadic method of analysis based on the categories of act, agent, agency, scene, and purpose), James Kinneavy's exploration of what he calls "the rhetorical triangle" (writer or speaker, audience or reader, and text), or Sandra Harding's examination of feminist standpoint theory, rhetoric has called for a careful investigation of the context in which any discourse appears. New historicist and other recent feminist theorists have also stressed the need to situate any act of writing within the fullest possible context or situation. In *A Pedagogy of Possibility: Bakhtinian Perspectives on Composition Studies,* Kay Halasek rereads the discipline of composition with special attention to rethinking the concept of rhetorical situation. Especially important are her applications of dialogism, heteroglossia, and other Bakhtinian concepts to composition in ways that reimagine familiar terms of the rhetorical situation — the student writer, audience, genre,

A rhetorician, I take it, is like one voice in a dialogue. Put several such voices together, with each voicing its own special assertion, let them act upon one another in cooperative competition, and you get a dialectic that, properly developed, can lead to the views transcending the limitations of each.

— KENNETH BURKE

and authority—and her description of a "pedagogy of possibility" that is based on dialogue, collaboration, and answerability.

(2a) **On Deciding to Write**

Whether the stimulus for writing comes from outside the writer (as in a class assignment) or grows from the writer's own desire to put thoughts into words, the decision to write is a deliberate act of commitment.

When we commit ourselves to writing, we *prewrite* by assessing our writing (i.e., rhetorical) situation, asking ourselves questions such as the following: Who is my audience? What does the audience expect of me? What do I already know about this subject? What must I find out? How can I best arrange my information and ideas? How much time do I have? How long should the composition be?

As soon as you make a writing assignment, encourage your students to respond to these questions by "thinking with a pencil in hand," jotting down ideas in their writing logs. Unlike experienced writers, students tend to spend little time prewriting. You might want to remind your students that almost all writers, even experienced ones, dread the blank page. Many authors say that the quickest way to face that challenge is to cover the blank page with writing, allowing anything to find its way onto the page.

(2b) **FOR COLLABORATIVE WORK: BRAINSTORMING TO IDENTIFY A PROBLEM**

Use small groups to generate ten to twenty possible topics or questions for several subject areas, such as interesting people, current controversies, cultural trends, problems on campus, scientific discoveries we'd like to know more about, possibilities for progress or decay, and so on. Students can use these topics or questions as starters for prewriting activities (see 3a), which may lead directly to an essay draft.

(2b) **FOR TEACHING: WRITING LOGS FOR IDENTIFYING A PROBLEM**

Ask your students to keep a section in their writing logs dedicated to compiling essay topics on subjects that interest them. The log can also be a place to store ideas, intriguing facts, observations, and provocative quotations from public figures or from students' reading (academic or otherwise). Organizing these entries under general subject headings (of the teacher's suggestion or the writer's invention) can provide some initial development of the topics.

FOR TEACHING: UNDERSTANDING WRITING ASSIGNMENTS   **(2c)**

Some instructors — and writing programs — believe that three to five pages is an appropriate page length for most composition-course essays. Three- to five-page papers demand development of a topic beyond simple description of a problem or narration of an event, yet they are short enough to require significant narrowing of the topic. In contrast, other instructors require progressively longer and more challenging assignments, culminating in a fifteen- to twenty-page research paper. Whatever the length of the assignment, take the time to create *detailed* and *directive* assignment sheets that explain the purpose, goals, length, format, content, and grading criteria for the assignment. It is often helpful to break down these items into categories and to offer models to help students begin the writing project.

Consider assigning due dates for drafts. A day or two after introducing invention strategies, assign an exploratory draft. A couple of days later, schedule conferences with your students to discuss their work. Within the next few days, have them bring their revisions — along with all their planning notes and earlier drafts — to class. Setting deadlines for drafts reinforces the importance of starting early.

After designing and distributing your assignment, make time in class to read through the detailed handout and answer any questions. Too often we leave this step up to the students and, consequently, problems arise concerning expectations, which could have been avoided with a general class discussion. Stress the importance of comprehending and addressing the rhetorical situation before beginning to write.

**TEACHING WITH TECHNOLOGY: ON UNDERSTANDING
WRITING ASSIGNMENTS ONLINE**   **(2c)**

One of the greatest advantages of using the Internet is the ability to post or email assignments online through a course Web site or class email distribution list. Students who miss class on a day you hand out an assignment can check online for the materials distributed in their absence. Students can also download PDFs or cut and paste Word or HTML documents — and, of course, they can print out a copy for their reference.

(2c)

ATTENDING TO DISABILITIES: UNDERSTANDING WRITING ASSIGNMENTS ONLINE

If you post materials online through a course Web site, make sure your materials can be read by a Braille screen reader for students with visual impairments. In addition, offer to provide recorded texts of your assignment sheets for those who need an aural document. For more information on complying with ADA regulations, contact your campus Web specialist or visit the Web sites listed at the end of this chapter.

(2d)

FOR TEACHING: DECIDING ON YOUR PURPOSES

Students may have trouble coming up with a succinct statement of purpose for a piece of writing they are currently working on. Often their purpose will be little more than a simple statement like "My purpose is to tell the story of how I felt after I wrecked my dad's Buick" or "My purpose is to describe how stupid it is to shoplift." Try pushing students beyond these simple statements into purpose statements that include some effect on the audience, since audience and purpose are always linked. The intended audience for most first drafts is usually either "people in the class," or "you, the instructor." Again, asking students to go beyond audiences that are immediately available will increase their repertoire of abilities. In talking with or writing to the student, keep asking how the writing would change if written for some other audience.

(2e)

On Considering Genre and Academic Discourse

You can provide students with experience writing in a variety of academic genres by offering them freedom to choose the rhetorical stance for a particular assignment. Have them select the disciplinary parameters for their essays by modeling their work on published academic writing in the fields of literary analysis, film review, scientific writing, social science research, and computer science. A good way to develop students' critical reading and writing skills in terms of genre and academic discourse is to ask them to find a contemporary article on a subject of their choice from a recent periodical or academic journal. Conduct a rhetorical analysis of the article, examining the genre for its specific writing conventions. Then have students model their own writing after the article's discipline-specific attributes.

On Considering Language   **(2f)** ················

In an interview, Maya Angelou was asked if city schools should teach the languages of their neighborhoods, or if they should teach the English language. Her strong response follows:

> I think they should teach the English language primarily. Fundamental Standard English language in every environment — because the language is so flexible, there are particularities and peculiarities which will be absorbed into the language. [The neighborhood language] becomes what the West Africans call the *sweet language*. That then makes a person bilingual. He or she speaks Standard English, which he needs in the marketplace. He or she also speaks the *sweet language,* which is used to make contact with a beloved, a family member, a lover. I think what should be taught is the Standard English language. The other languages of the neighborhood are so in flux that you can't really teach them. You can learn them, but you can't really teach them.
>
> The Council Chronicle (Feb. 1994, 8 ff.)

We may not be able to teach our students the *"sweet languages,"* but we can use examples such as the one Maya Angelou discusses to teach students about the importance of *discourse communities.* Have students develop an awareness of how different language conventions are used for different audiences across the country — whether by region, race, profession, or class. What kind of discourse communities exist in the student's hometown, on campus, in the dorms, or between different majors? When students begin writing, they should consider such differences and select the most appropriate language to match the expectations of their audience.

On Considering Your Rhetorical Stance   **(2g)** ················

The idea of the rhetorical stance was first put forward by Wayne Booth in a *CCC* article of the same name. A good rhetorical stance, said Booth, was the result of an effective balance between the three Aristotelian forms of proof: ethos, pathos, and logos. Too much emphasis on ethos, the wonderfulness of the writer, would result in an imbalance Booth called the entertainer's stance. Too much emphasis on pathos, playing to the desires of the audience, would result in the advertiser's stance. And too much emphasis on logos, the message in itself, would result in the imbalance Booth called the pedant's stance. Keeping these three elements at work but not allowing any one to predominate is the work of the successful writer.

Only presidents, editors, and people with tapeworm have the right to use the editorial "we."
– MARK TWAIN

(2h)

On Focusing on Your Audience

In *A Pedagogy of Possibility,* Kay Halasek discusses audience in ways that are helpful to teachers and students alike. Halasek briefly describes the uses of six kinds of audience that writers have available to them: projected audience (those imagined or invoked by the writer), previous audience (those the writer is responding to or is in conversation with), immediate audience (such as peer group members), textual audience (what some call the "implied" reader or the audience in the text), public audience (those to whom the text will be sent), and evaluative audience (the teacher, employer, or group that will assess the text).

(2h)

FOR TEACHING: AUDIENCE

Dealing with questions of audience is one of the most complex problems facing any writer, and face-to-face oral communication doesn't completely prepare students for the intracacies of attending to audience in written texts. Discuss the six types of audience presented above with your students and ask them to brainstorm examples of each type from their daily lives. Try the exercises that follow to continue educating students about the crucial importance of audience in the writing process. You can use the questions listed in 2h of the *Handbook* for oral or written practice in getting students more comfortable with writing for a more distant or diverse audience than they may be used to.

Ask students to prepare to write an essay describing the college health service's policies on distribution of birth control information. They should answer the questions on the list for two audiences: a women's student group at another college and a religiously based scholarship committee. This exercise can be done either individually or in groups, and in either case the writing is followed by class discussion on the kinds of problems each audience presents to a writer.

A student's first response to the question of audience is usually to assume that the instructor is the audience as well as the evaluator of the essay. Help your students distinguish between the two by asking them to write a *general audience profile*. If, for example, their general topic is "part-time worker, full-time student," their audience profile might read something like this:

> My audience is seventeen- and eighteen-year-olds who are either attending or planning to attend college and who have experienced the dual obligations of work and school.

By writing an audience profile for each paper, your students will begin to see that they are constructing an audience that goes beyond you. As they begin to visualize their audience, they can write directly to it instead of directly for you. It will also be easier for you to evaluate their work when they have defined their audience.

FOR COLLABORATIVE WORK: PEER RESPONSE ON FOCUSING YOUR AUDIENCE   (2h) ....

If your students are working on an essay, have them exchange their drafts and write audience profiles based on one another's topics. After they have returned the profiles and drafts, the students may need to rethink their original audience. Often such collaborative work helps students grasp the significance of addressing an audience and the way in which they need to revise their stance, strategic use of appeals, and language to match readers' expectations.

FOR TEACHING: ADDRESSING SPECIFIC AUDIENCES   (2h1) ....

Ask each student to bring in an article, editorial, or column from the newspaper and to circle elements in the writing that deliberately include or exclude certain kinds of audiences. Ask students to read the circled excerpts and talk about whether the writer seemed to be aware of or in control of his or her effects, and how and why the writer made the choices he or she made concerning the inclusion or exclusion of audiences. Ask students to bring in local newspapers and magazines that target speakers of languages other than English. Discuss the audiences for each periodical.

(2i)   **FOR TEACHING: ONLINE RHETORICAL SITUATIONS**

After reading and talking about this section of Chapter 2, ask students to work in groups to compile three lists: (1) of the *differences* in rhetorical situations they encountered (or expected to encounter) online; (2) of what they liked *most* and *least* about online rhetorical situations; and (3) of what they would propose as a set of guidelines for good online citizenship. Use the lists for a whole-class discussion of the ways in which working online is changing writing, reading, and research in college. For additional help regarding online rhetorical situations, consult Chapters 7 and 9.

■ **USEFUL READINGS**

Booth, Wayne C. "The Rhetorical Stance." *CCC* 14 (Oct. 1963): 139–45.

Britton, James. *The Development of Writing Abilities.* London: Macmillan, 1975.

Doheny-Farina, Stephen. *The Wired Neighborhood.* New Haven: Yale UP, 1996. This book examines how writing allows for engagement with the global village and considers the ethical implications involved in online rhetorical contexts.

Ede, Lisa, and Andrea Lunsford. "Audience Addressed/Audience Invoked: The Role of Audience in Composition Theory and Pedagogy." *CCC* 35 (1984): 155–71. Rpt. in *The Writing Teacher's Sourcebook.* Ed. Gary Tate and Edward P. J. Corbett. New York: Oxford UP, 4th ed., 2000. Ede and Lunsford point out the limitations of two prominent concepts of audience, that of "audience addressed," which emphasizes the concrete reality of the writer's audience, and that of "audience invoked," which focuses on the writer's construction of an audience.

Eldred, Janet Carey. "The Technology of Voice." *CCC* 48 (1997): 334–47. The writer explores the possibilities for online voices in rendering a series of conversations with her mother.

Faigley, Lester. "Literacy after the Revolution." *CCC* 48 (1997): 30–44. In his 4Cs Chair's Address, Faigley puts the electronic "revolution" in global perspective and reminds instructors of the economic and political concerns raised by the increasing importance of online rhetorical situations.

Farr, Marcia. "Essayist Literacy and Other Verbal Performances." *Written Communication* 10 (Jan. 1993): 4–38. Farr argues that the essayist style of discourse used in most academic writing differs from the natural discourse of students from nonmainstream groups and that "many such students face difficulties in writing instruction that mainstream students do not face" (4). It is therefore important to teach essayist discourse explicitly and to learn about other discourse styles used by students.

Halasek, Kay. *A Pedagogy of Possibility: Bakhtinian Perspectives on Composition Studies.* Carbondale: Southern Illinois UP, 1999.

Hampton, Sally. "The Education of At-Risk Students." *Practice in the Teaching of Writing: Rethinking the Discipline.* Ed. Lee Odell. Carbondale: Southern Illinois UP, 1993. 186–212. Hampton writes that "we are not likely to improve the chances of at-risk students to succeed academically until we examine the assumptions we currently hold about their needs and abilities, consider how those assumptions led to flawed educational practices, and enact new practices and assessment procedures based on what we know about what works and what does not work" (187).

Kinneavy, James. "The Basic Aims of Discourse." *CCC* 20 (1969): 297–304. This is a distilled version of Kinneavy's *Theory of Discourse,* in which he divides discourse into referential, persuasive, literary, and expressive, each emphasizing a particular element in the exchange between writer and audience about the subject of the discourse.

Kroll, Barry M. "Writing for Readers: Three Perspectives on Audience." *CCC* 35 (1984): 172–85. Kroll examines three prominent views of audience—the "rhetorical," the "informational," and the "social." For each view he offers an analysis of its theoretical assumptions, its pedagogical implications, and its limitations.

Moss, Beverly J., and Keith Walters. "Rethinking Diversity: Axes of Difference in the Writing Classroom." Rpt. in *The St. Martin's Guide to Teaching Writing,* 5th ed. Ed. Cheryl Glenn, Melissa A. Goldthwaite, and Robert Connors. Boston: Bedford/St. Martin's 2003. The authors make clear how "our" language informs the norms of the institution and how our students use language as their medium of resistance. They write that "acknowledging difference, examining it, and finding creative ways to build upon it—to make it the cornerstone of individual and corporate philosophies of educational theory and classroom practice—require that we see ourselves, our beliefs, and even our actions, from a new perspective, one that forces us, as Clifford Geertz has put it, to see ourselves among others."

The St. Martin's Guide to Teaching Writing, 5th ed., Chapter 4, provides more on "Successful Writing Assignments."

Spack, Ruth. "Initiating ESL Students into the Academic Discourse Community: How Far Should We Go?" *TESOL Quarterly* 22 (1988): 29–47. Spack argues that teachers must help students enter the academic discourse community by setting up a process-centered writing course that clearly articulates academic expectations, demands, and standards.

White, Edward. *Assigning, Responding, Evaluating: A Writing Guide.* 3rd ed. New York: Bedford/St. Martin's, 1999. Practical advice on approaching writing assessment, using evaluations, and creating assigments and tests.

■ **USEFUL WEB SITES**

American with Disabilities Act (ADA)

> http://americanhistory.si.edu/disabilityrights/exhibit_ada.html
>
> *A Web exhibit by the Smithsonian Museum.*

Disability Studies in the Humanities

> http://www.georgetown.edu/crossroads/interests/ds-hum/index.html
>
> *This Disability Studies in the Humanities (DS-HUM) Web site, listserv, and syllabus bank provide samples of college course syllabi that either incorporate disability as an issue or even center on that subject in the humanities classroom (especially in language, literature, and composition).*

Writing across the Curriculum: General Articles

> http://www.indiana.edu/~wts/cwp/lib/wacgen.html

Exploring, Planning, and Drafting

3

In any work that is truly creative, the writer cannot be omniscient in advance about the effects that he or she proposes to produce. The suspense . . . is not just in the reader, but in the writer, who is intensely curious about what will happen.

– MARY McCARTHY

Classical rhetoric consisted of five canons: *inventio* (invention), *dispositio* (arrangement), *elocutio* (style), *memoria* (memory), and *pronunciatio* (delivery). The process of discovery implied by the Latin *inventio* and the Greek *heuresis* (eureka!) parallels our modern concept of "prewriting," which is also called rhetorical "invention." Since "prewriting" is often used to refer both to "invention" and to "planning," your students might want to think of "invention" as a process of exploring what to say about a topic; of "planning" as the choices of what, when, and how to say it; and of "prewriting" as the first stage in the writing process, when "invention" and "planning" most often occur. While drafting can and should occur throughout exploring and planning, at some point you will want to help students compile all their drafting into an official "first draft." Encourage your students to be creative in their approach to a topic, their prewriting process, and planning of organizational strategies.

On Brainstorming

(3a1)

Brainstorming works particularly well with groups of three to five students, but it generates even more energy when conducted with the entire class. Whether you or your students suggest the topic is not as important as getting started. Appoint two students to record ideas as they are suggested by the rest of the class. After about ten minutes, break the class into groups of four and ask each group to choose an idea and develop a thesis from it. Share with your students the following ways to facilitate brain-storming:

- Write down as many ideas you can think of without stopping. Go back and edit your list later, selecting the most promising topics.
- Speak into a tape recorder as you walk through campus, commenting on what you notice as interesting.
- Keep a "reaction journal" in which you jot down your responses to course lectures, reading materials, news items, and public conversations in dorms or dining halls.
- Find the most provocative article you can on a topic that matters to you and forge a constructive response to it.
- Interview five people in your community on a matter of historical, intellectual, or personal interest. Transcribe their responses into a dialogue and insert your own voice in order to discover your own stance.

(3a1)

ATTENDING TO DISABILITIES: BRAINSTORMING

Barbara A. Heifferon teaches Nancy Mairs's intimate account of writing and disability, *Carnal Acts,* as a means to enable students to risk exploring the link among writing, identity, emotion, and meaning-making in the world. For one of her male students, "the disability text opened up an opportunity for him to express his own grief and loss. The introduction of her honest text and the chance to write in response to that honesty reinforce our notions that writing is closely linked to how we form our identities" (Brueggemann et al., 386–87). Heifferon's reflection on her pedagogy offers writing teachers an important lesson:

> Texts on disability, honest, real, open texts such as Mairs's essay, have a valuable place in the writing classroom, particularly in a culture that continually blasts the able-bodied, idealized, and commodified body into our eyes and ears, and in a culture that often denies men the right to express their innermost feelings. I doubt a tamer text or a text that did not confront such stereotypes could have moved students so far from the previously unquestioned assumptions they carried with them, invisible and silent assumptions that render those with disabilities invisible and silent. Thus we moved from dismay to discussion past dissonance to the discovery of a place where disability texts in the classroom help students confront issues of authority and power. Students' ability to grapple with such texts that challenge the views they take for granted increases their confidence and enables identification with persons different from themselves. (Brueggemann et al., 386–87).

Have your students respond to a powerful textual account of living with disabilities as a way to break through conventional categories of meaning-making.

On Freewriting   (3a2)

James Moffett, in *Teaching the Universe of Discourse,* and Janet Emig, in *The Composing Processes of Twelfth Graders,* posit that freewriting not only increases verbal fluency but also provides a means for discovering ideas. In *Writing without Teachers,* Peter Elbow writes:

> The habit of compulsive, premature editing doesn't just make writing hard. It makes writing dead. Your voice is damped out by all the interruptions, changes, and hesitations between the consciousness and the page. (6)

Freewriting eliminates the beginning writer's most frustrating habit: focusing on correctness rather than content. During final drafting, your students will need to focus on correctness — but not until then.

FOR TEACHING: WRITING LOGS FOR FREEWRITING   (3a2)

Elbow suggests in *Writing without Teachers* that students who sincerely want to improve their writing keep a freewriting diary:

> Just ten minutes a day. Not a complete account of your day; just a brief mind sample for each day. You don't have to think hard or prepare or be in the mood: without stopping, just write whatever words come out — whether or not you are thinking or in the mood. (9)

You might suggest that students keep a section of their logs dedicated to such a diary.

TEACHING WITH TECHNOLOGY: LOOPING   (3a3)

Looping is a way to activate students' critical thinking. If you are teaching with a course email distribution list or a bulletin board, have each student post an initial one to two sentences describing an idea that might provide the beginning of a paper. Then ask students to respond to one or two posts and identify what is most interesting about the topics. Have the first student, in turn, respond to the reactions of the class by developing and amplifying the focus of the topic. This form of collaborative looping, facilitated by technology, can offer a fast and meaningful way to encourage your students' exploration of writing topics.

(3a4)   TEACHING WITH TECHNOLOGY: CLUSTERING

The software program Inspiration enables students to follow the flow of their ideas through diagrams that resemble clouds, circles, or squares. Arrows can begin to show relations between items and, with the click of a drop-down menu, students can convert their clusters of ideas into an outline.

(3a5)   ## On Questioning

The questions in this section are meant to stimulate the writer's thinking and are based on various *heuristics* (prompts for thinking that involve questioning and other guides for investigation). Ultimately, all such heuristics derive from the *topoi,* the "topics" or "commonplaces" of classical rhetoric.

In *Classical Rhetoric for the Modern Student,* Edward P. J. Corbett explains that the topics helped writers find appropriate ways to develop any subject. Special topics are those classes of argument appropriate to particular kinds of discourse: judicial, ceremonial, or political. Aristotle names the common topics, those that could be used for any occasion, as "definition," "comparison," "relationship," "testimony," and "circumstance."

Just get it down on paper, then we'll see what to do with it.
– MAXWELL PERKINS

Like the questioning strategies in this section, the *topoi* were a way to find something to say about a subject.

(3a5)   FOR MULTILINGUAL WRITERS: QUESTIONING

Another questioning technique that works well with students comes from the yoga technique of empathetic listening. This strategy can be particularly successful with multilingual students who may be shy about voicing questions during class.

Have students sit in pairs and ask each other the questions that follow. Tell them not to respond to the answers, but to facilitate continued talk through asking a subsequent question. These prompts are particularly effective in helping students develop argumentative research papers or position papers.

> What really matters to you and why?
> Go on, can you tell me more about it?
> What do you want me to do about it?

At the end of ten minutes, have students write down what focused thoughts emerged as a consequence of this questioning/empathetic listening technique. You can modify the questions to match the purpose of your own class's particular writing assignment.

ATTENDING TO DISABILITIES: QUESTIONING   **(3a5)**

For deaf students, you can conduct the preceding questioning exercise through an email discussion group, instant messenger, or a networked classroom bulletin board. The advantage of using a word processor is that students will have a textual copy of all their work in progress, including brainstorming questions, answers, and reflections.

For students who may be visually impaired, provide a tape recorder at the time of the brainstorming/questioning session so that the conversation can be preserved for future use.

FOR COLLABORATIVE WORK: TRYING OTHER GENRES   **(3a6)**

Alternative ways of exploring an idea include using everyday communication strategies to isolate and develop an idea. Have students test one of the following strategies:

- Phone a friend from another university or college and explain the assignment and your idea in the simplest possible terms.
- Email a colloquial version of your assignment and your potential topic to a friend or a family member. Sometimes communicating with a close companion can help you develop your ideas.

FOR COLLABORATIVE WORK: DEVELOPING A WORKING THESIS   **(3b)**

Exercise 3.3 can be extended to include peer responses. After your students have critiqued their own work, ask them to exchange their preliminary working theses and then evaluate them, using questions such as the following:

1. Does the thesis arouse your interest? How can it be made more engaging?
2. Is the thesis clear and specific? How can you make it more so?
3. What is the "so what?" of the thesis? How might the writer push the argument further?
4. Does the thesis seem manageable within the limits of time and length? Does the writer promise to do too much? How can the writer narrow the thesis?

The value of this peer-review exercise is greater perspective. What is patently obvious to the writer may not be so discernible to a reader whose information is limited to the text.

(3c)   ## On Gathering Information

There are a variety of ways to orient students to the wealth of materials available to them in the form of verbal and visual information for writing projects. Your own field research into the ever-increasing information available to students will help make their research projects more exciting.

- Explore the online resources of your institution's library and research facilities in order to point students to helpful resources.
- Look into archives and special collections that host specialized information in terms of documents, visual material, digitized collections, sound collections, and more.
- Investigate your institution's office of undergraduate research to find out if there are Web sites listing faculty mentors (for possible interviews), scholarships and research grant opportunities for students (for continuation of their projects), and workshops in research skills on campus.

(3c)   **FOR TEACHING: GATHERING INFORMATION**

Many students — including juniors and seniors — have little experience with research projects or familiarity with a campus library. You might consider holding a class in the library and asking a reference librarian to describe the general resources of the library (including electronic resources) and to explain their location and usefulness.

For more about teaching library, online, and field research, see Chapter 15.

FOR COLLABORATIVE WORK: ORGANIZING VERBAL AND VISUAL INFORMATION **(3d)**

Ask your students to read and comment on one another's drafts, looking first at organizational patterns in individual paragraphs and then throughout the entire paper. Ask them to write in the margin the type of paragraph organization. Toward the end of class, call on several students to read paragraphs that illustrate different forms of organization. Some paragraphs may defy classification because of the ingenuity of the writer or the rough condition of the draft.

Another effective teaching strategy entails asking students to produce an outline *after* completing their draft essays. Use these outlines to double-check the organization and flow of the essay as well as the strategic use of both visual and verbal information.

FOR TEACHING: WRITING OUT A PLAN **(3e)**

Even the most proficient pre-draft outliners need to know that outlines are not unalterable or absolute; they are merely guides. The outline must conform to the paper — not the paper to the outline. Outlines, like the papers they help organize, must be revisable.

If you require an unchangeable, formal outline, your students may not be able to adhere to it. Instead, ask them to prepare a "writing plan," a backbone for the body of the paper. Then allow them to develop their papers as much by their drafting processes, which reveal form, as by their plan. Another possibility is to suggest that they write each idea on a notecard. They can then easily rearrange their ideas and experiment with various orders. They will also learn that some ideas are expendable.

> *. . . content determines form, yet content is discovered only in form.*
> – Denise Levertov

On Producing a Draft **(3f)**

Remind your class that first drafts are never perfect. Among many other scholars and researchers who believe that first drafts are rarely directed toward an audience, Linda Flower has listed the features of what she calls "writer-based prose." According to Flower, this stage of writing is:

1. Typically narrative or chronological in structure
2. Usually filled with private terms that may not be meaningful to another reader
3. Sometimes elliptical
4. Filled with unclear referents and causal relations
5. Frequently loaded with self-referents such as "I believe," "I feel," "in my opinion"

Flower views writer-based prose as a natural stage in the composing process, one that allows for discovery and growth and that should not be criticized because it is not yet "reader-based."

Often, proficient writers can skip the stage of writer-based prose and move directly to reader-based prose. These writers seem to internalize their writer-based drafts, unlike many beginning writers.

(3f1)

FOR TEACHING: REMAINING FLEXIBLE

Anne Lamott's famous advice to writers on "shitty first drafts" in *Bird by Bird: Some Instructions on Writing and Life* merits repeating to students embarking on producing a draft: "Now, practically even better news than that of short assignments is the idea of shitty first drafts. All good writers write them. This is how they end up with good second drafts and terrific third drafts" (21).

Help students overcome their own fears about first drafts by giving them permission to make errors, to explore intellectual content, to try strategies of argument, and to play with variations in their writing style and persona. Allow them to experiment with voice in a first draft, to be comfortable with not having all the answers, and to write for the sake of discovering meaning. The open, encouraging attitude of a teacher can go a long way toward getting that first draft down on paper.

(3f2)

FOR TEACHING: KNOWING YOUR BEST WRITING SITUATION

As students prepare to develop drafts of their papers, give them an in-class writing prompt and ask them to reflect on their own best writing situations. When and where do they write best? What time of day do the ideas flow most freely? Do they prefer to write at night, in solitude, or in the middle of a computer lab during the day? Do they listen to music to write or like to have snacks nearby? Can they write for long chunks of time or do they work best in smaller time blocks?

When they are done writing, have them exchange their responses with a partner. Then take a few moments to solicit some specific observations from the class as a whole. Tell students to honor their own writing situations. At the same time, encourage them to experiment with new methods and new approaches to writing. We are always learning, and writing situations do change over time and in different contexts.

FOR MULTILINGUAL WRITERS

Diane Belcher, director of Ohio State University's English as a second language programs, advises multilingual writers to "slow down the writing process as much as possible — to allow as much time as possible to concentrate on content and form first, grammar and style later."

While using the first or most comfortable language can be very useful during invention, Belcher warns that "thinking in a first language" at later stages of the writing process is far less likely to be beneficial and can lead to negative transfer as a result of translating rather than composing in English.

Mary Shapiro also warns that many ESL students have had little or no experience writing in English for *any* purpose, have never written a research paper, and have had no access to sources — let alone the opportunity to make proper use of them. She goes on to say that many ESL students come from backgrounds in which linear argumentation is not the norm. Many have never written an outline, do not know how to write introductions and conclusions (or seem aware that this is necessary), and have no experience writing footnotes or bibliographies.

Therefore, each ESL student must be made aware that every essay, regardless of purpose, method of organization, or intended audience, requires a title, an introduction of topic and thesis, adequate development of ideas with appropriate transitions, a conclusion, proper documentation, an appropriate style, and most often linear progression.

Here it is, My Theory about Writing: It's hard. No good writing is easy.
– Dave Barry

FOR TEACHING: FACILITATING EFFECTIVE REFLECTIONS

(3g)

The self-assessment part of the writing process is as crucial to the development of critical thinking as are the exploring, planning, and drafting stages. One way to accomplish such self-reflection is to ask students to compose a brief, two- to three-page typed letter to both the class and the instructor addressing the following aspects:

- Specific ways in which your writing has changed, developed, or improved
- Understanding of rhetorical strategies and writing strategies
- Ways in which you plan to apply insights and practices learned here to other contexts
- Closing reflections on your participation in the community of the class this term
- Anything else you want to articulate concerning your work over the term

You might also ask students to refer specifically to at least three pieces of writing (or drafts, outlines, or stages) that they have completed or to quote from their work to illustrate their points.

■ USEFUL READINGS

Ballenger, Bruce. "Methods of Memory: On Native American Storytelling." *College English* 59 (1997): 789–800. This fine example of an essay uses association as a mode of organization.

Brueggemann, Brenda Jo, Linda Feldmeier White, Patricia A. Dunn, Barbara A. Heifferon, and Johnson Cheu. "Becoming Visible: Lessons in Disability," *CCC* 52.3 (Feb. 2001): 381.

Corbett, Edward P. J., with Robert Connors. *Classical Rhetoric for the Modern Student.* 4th ed. New York: Oxford UP, 1999. Newly revised, this text still provides a thorough, cogent, and readable exposition of Aristotelian rhetoric and a brief history of the Western rhetorical tradition.

Crowe, Chris, and Keith Peterson. "Classroom Research: Helping Asian Students Succeed in Writing Courses." *TETYC* (Feb. 1995): 30–37. The authors offer concrete suggestions for helping with organization, transitions, and use of sources.

Elbow, Peter. "The Loop Writing Process." *Writing with Power.* New York: Oxford UP, 1981. 59–77. Elbow offers a refinement of freewriting that he calls loop writing — "a way to get the best of both worlds: both control and creativity" (59).

——. *Writing without Teachers.* 2nd ed. New York: Oxford UP, 1998.

Emig, Janet. *The Composing Processes of Twelfth Graders.* Urbana: NCTE, 1971.

Flower, Linda. "Writer-Based Prose: A Cognitive Basis for Problems in Writing." *CE* 41 (1979): 19.

Kaplan, Robert B. "Cultural Thought Patterns in Intercultural Education." *Composing in a Second Language*. Ed. Sandra McKay. Cambridge: Newbury House, 1984. 43–62. Different cultures produce different rhetorical patterns of discourse that ESL teachers should be aware of. Kaplan discusses Semitic, Oriental, Romance, and Russian writing and rhetorical patterns. He recommends that ESL instructors teach "contrastive rhetoric" and provides pedagogic exercises for doing just that. Though Kaplan's work is very controversial, the patterns he describes offer a starting point for thinking about rhetorical and cultural differences.

Lauer, Janice M. "Issues in Rhetorical Invention." *Essays on Classical Rhetoric and Modern Discourse*. Ed. Robert J. Connors, Lisa S. Ede, and Andrea A. Lunsford. Carbondale: Southern Illinois UP, 1984. 127–39. Various prewriting techniques imply various assumptions about the composing process. Lauer distinguishes prewriting methods according to such factors as "the genesis of writing, exploratory acts and their relationship to judgment, and the province of invention."

Moffett, James. *Teaching the Universe of Discourse*. Portsmouth: Boynton/Cook: 1987.

Reid, Joy. "The Radical Outliner and the Radical Brainstormer: A Perspective on Composing Processes." *TESOL Quarterly* 18 (1984): 529–33.

Smitherman, Geneva. "'The Blacker the Berry, the Sweeter the Juice': African American Student Writers." *The Need for Story*. Ed. Anne Haas Dyson and Celia Genishi. Urbana: NCTE, 1994. 80–101. Smitherman suggests four general ways of drawing on African American rhetorical traditions. First, capitalize on the strengths of African American cultural discourse; it is a rich reservoir that students can and should tap. Second, encourage students toward the field dependency style, which enables them to produce more powerful, meaningful, and highly rated essays. Third, design strategies for incorporating the African American imaginative, storytelling style into student production of other essay modalities. Further, de-emphasize your and your students' concerns about African American English Vernacular grammar; overconcentration on these forms frequently suppresses the production of African American discourse and its rich, expressive style.

■ **USEFUL WEB SITES**

Ohio State University's Strategies for Cubing

http://www.cohums.ohio-state.edu/cstw/tutor/invent6.htm

Paradigm Online Writing Assistant: Organizing Your Writing

http://www.powa.org/orgnfrms.htm

Purdue University's Online Writing Lab: Guides to Planning (Invention)
http://owl.english.purdue.edu/handouts/general/gl_plan1.html

Step-by-Step Guide to Brainstorming
http://www.jpb.com/creative/brainstorming.html

▼ Reviewing, Revising, and Editing

4

"I never have time to rewrite; I always wait until the night before."
"How can I improve my first draft when I don't know whether it's good?"
"I don't care about what I'm writing. I just want to get it over with."
"I'm such a bad writer that I hate to read my own writing."
"If I can't get it right the first time, I must be stupid."

Such typical attitudes toward revision support Erika Lindemann's claim that "for most students, *rewriting* is a dirty word." Students tend to view rewriting as an indication of failure, as punishment, or as simply a "filler" for classroom time. Because students have often been trained to outline carefully or to follow the format of a five-paragraph essay, revising means nothing more than making their words "prettier" or moving from handwriting to type or fixing misspelled words and mispunctuated sentences. In fact, many student writers are under the misapprehension that "real" writing is perfectly formed and flows onto the page at the touch of the Muse's hand. It is important for them to realize that almost all experienced writers revise their work repeatedly.

I have made this [letter] longer, because I have not had the time to make it shorter.
– Blaise Pascal

Marcel Proust wrote that "the real voyage of discovery consists not in seeking new landscapes, but in having new eyes." Revision *is* a process of "*re*-vision" or looking at an essay with new eyes. You can help students grasp the benefits of rigorous review and in-depth revision by sharing with them Proust's insight and teaching them to look at rewriting as a journey of discovery.

FOR TEACHING: GETTING DISTANCE FROM YOUR WRITING   (4a)

Try to structure your assignment schedules with ample time for students to be able to look at a piece of writing with fresh eyes. In particular, check to see that there is sufficient space between the due dates for the rough draft, the peer review, and the final version.

(4b)

FOR TEACHING: REREADING YOUR DRAFT

When instructing students to reread their drafts, be sure to distinguish between revising and editing. Students often confuse revising (making changes in content) with editing (correcting mechanical errors). To reinforce this important distinction:

1. Try to observe the distinction yourself.
2. Discuss revising and editing on separate days, as separate class topics.
3. Plan separate practice exercises for revising and editing.

(4b)

TEACHING WITH TECHNOLOGY: MEANING, PURPOSE, RHETORICAL STANCE, AND AUDIENCE

Have students exchange copies of their papers online or post them on a course Web site or electronic discussion board. Provide students with an online peer-review sheet, asking them questions about meaning, purpose, rhetorical stance, and audience derived from section 4b of the *Handbook*. Ask each student to assess another writer's draft and compose a short peer-review letter online.

You can vary this exercise by establishing four teams of reviewers: meaning, purpose, rhetorical stance, and audience. Ask each team to judge a group of essays and describe the qualities of each text. This assessment will prove invaluable to student writers during the revision process, for they can think critically about how to resolve problems involving intention and effect.

(4c)

On Collaborating with Others

Having students respond to each other's work is probably the most common type of collaboration in composition classes. Peer responding helps students (1) move beyond an exclusive focus on the instructor as audience; (2) learn to accept and use constructive criticism; (3) practice analyzing written texts, including their own; and (4) acquire the vocabulary of composition.

Nevertheless, many students are reluctant to share their writing with one another. They may regard the instructor as the only one qualified to give advice or criticism; hence, time spent with peers is time wasted. Some students are embarrassed to show what they fear is poor writing to peers who will judge them personally. Moreover, they lack experience in offering constructive criticism. Your students may need help in learning how to respond to another's work — how to temper excessive criticism with tact, how to balance *what* has been said with *how* it has been said, both in terms of the writer's text and the reader's comments. In this way they will learn how to respond to drafts and how to trust and help one another, both vital aspects of a productive composition course.

FOR COLLABORATIVE WORK: RESPONDING TO DRAFTS   (4c)

1. At the beginning of the term, have groups of students read and comment on one another's writing. You may wish to suggest a number of your own questions as well as those in the text to help them respond to what they read: What is most memorable or stands out most in what they are reading? What is the writer's main point — and what makes that point clear or not clear? How does the essay in question respond to the assignment?

2. Using an anonymous, imperfect model draft, provide at least one or two practice sessions before the class undertakes its first peer-responding session. During these preliminary discussions, check their responses and help students who have trouble offering comments.

3. To encourage group discussion, you may wish to share one of your own preliminary drafts or an example of a work in progress and have students comment on it.

4. Ask your students to keep a record of peer responses to their work. Do certain problems recur? As they become increasingly aware of their writing profiles, your students will develop self-critical faculties that they can apply to their own writing. What they can do today in group discussion with peers, they will be able to do individually and by themselves in the future.

ATTENDING TO DISABILITIES: COLLABORATING WITH OTHERS   (4c)

Some students may have particular learning disabilities (such as dyslexia) that merit careful and sensitive responses in peer-review situations. Identify such students at the beginning of your course and make sure they have ample support from your institution's disability resource center

Nothing about us without us.
– DISABILITY ADVOCATES

and/or writing center. In addition, reiterate to all students that their job in peer review is not to edit corrections in a negative way but to make students aware of frequent patterns of errors in their writing.

(4c1)

FOR MULTILINGUAL WRITERS: GETTING THE MOST FROM REVIEWERS' COMMENTS

Realize that students from diverse cultures have different comfort levels with giving and receiving peer feedback. Some students may feel shy about making comments, afraid of offending the writer or being rude; their reviews may be excessively formal in tone, exceedingly positive in nature, and polite to the point of being unhelpful. Gently encourage these students to develop the skill of providing *constructive criticism* and to see themselves as important readers of the texts under review. Often, these students doubt their own authority to suggest changes and they need to be coached into becoming confident, collaborative peer reviewers.

Finally, multilingual students are often able to point out the excessive use of clichés, cultural shortcuts, and other common patterns of tired writing. From their vantage point of what Karl Manheim would call "intellectuals" on the cusp between cultures, multilingual writers are invaluable members of any writing class community.

(4c2)

FOR TEACHING: REVIEWING ANOTHER WRITER'S DRAFT

To make sure your students are offering more than yes/no comments when reviewing other writers' drafts, consider collecting and evaluating their responses. Reinforce specific responses that quote a word or phrase or that refer to a specific paragraph or line. Your interest will underscore the value of peer response.

Having worked in groups, your students could have as many as four or five sets of responses to their writing. Lest they be overwhelmed by so many suggestions and questions, assure them that they need not heed all the advice, just weigh it. However, if several comments point in the same direction, the writer should take them seriously.

When students are faced with conflicting advice, they will naturally turn to you for the "right" answer. Because this is an impossible request, you will have to encourage them to reach their own decisions. Have them ask other students to respond to their particular problems. Ask about their original writing choices and about the potential effect of suggested changes. Using others' comments to make independent decisions should be a goal of every writer.

Ideally, peer-responding sessions will be so effective, profitable, and stimulating that your students will initiate sessions outside the classroom. Realistically, however, they will probably hesitate to ask others who have no peer-responding experience or training. Therefore, you may want to provide them with several questions or statements for introducing a session:

1. "Would you mind telling me what you think of this?"
2. "The point I want to make in this paper is _____."
3. "How well did I succeed?"
4. "What do you think of my support?"
5. "I had trouble with this part. Does it make sense to you? What can I do to improve it?"

At least once during the term, have your students initiate a responding session with someone other than a classmate. Ask them to report on their success.

I have not failed. I've just found 10,000 ways that won't work.
– Thomas Edison

TEACHING WITH TECHNOLOGY: REVIEWING A DRAFT ONLINE (4c3)

Have students compose online entries or threaded email responses on their perceptions of the advantages and disadvantages of peer response. Have them respond to each other's entries or put together a class Web page on the possibilities and potential problems. Knowing their concerns will allow you to explain the nature of peer response more fully and thus alleviate many of their initial concerns. Having them communicate their concerns will help build class community and alleviate individual fears. Then you can more easily model/introduce collaborative writing activities such as the ones listed in the preceding sections.

FOR TEACHING: STYLES OF REVISION (4d)

Revising styles vary considerably, depending on the purpose of the writing or on the field the writing is in. Ask students to choose a favorite or

Sometimes the delete key is your best friend.
– Steve Martin

respected faculty member on campus and set up an interview to discuss that person's specific writing process. Using the revising and editing guidelines in this chapter, ask them to draw up a list of questions they'd like to ask the interviewee about revising and editing in his or her field. (See 15f2 for tips on how to conduct interviews.) Finally, based on the notes students take during the interview, ask them to compare the resource person's revising style to their own. Remind students that all writing is recursive such that any change to one part of the text necessarily affects the whole.

(4e)

FOR TEACHING: ORGANIZATION AND VISUALS

Ask your students to locate a story, an article, or a book they especially enjoyed. Either in class or as homework, have them analyze the piece by outlining its organization. Then ask them to answer the following questions and cite examples from the text:

1. Why do you suppose the author started this way? Is there a flashback? a provocative question? a description?
2. Does the author "hook" you? If so, how?
3. At what point in the piece did you become interested and decide to go on?
4. How is the piece held together? Find appropriate transitional devices, repetition of key words, or repetitive sentence structures.
5. How does the author prepare you for the information in the middle and the end of the piece?
6. How does the author end the piece? Was it satisfying to you? predictable? surprising?
7. Look at the title. Does it seem appropriate to you now that you've finished the piece? Did it when you started? Can you improve on it or provide an alternative?
8. Are visual elements introduced properly (using the notation "Figure 1," etc.)? Are they placed next to the corresponding text?
9. Do the visual and verbal elements work in conjunction to develop the thesis? Are the visuals explained adequately in the essay?
10. Is there a source notation for the visual either beneath it or in the works-cited list?

TEACHING WITH TECHNOLOGY: TITLES

(4f1)

A great way to get students to understand the importance of titles is through an assessment of their function. Begin by discussing the crucial aspects of titles—what function they serve and what makes them effective. Students might suggest the following attributes that you can write on the board or project on a computer screen:

- Informative (or clear)
- Interesting (or captivating)
- Funny (or engaging in some way—perhaps moving or shocking)
- Relevant

Once you have established a working rubric, ask students to evaluate each other's titles. This works well in a computer-networked classroom, for you can cut and paste the titles of all the students' drafts into a Power-Point presentation while they are in peer-review groups. Then lead them through a slide show in which you show increasing levels of complexity, from simple one-word titles to more engaging, funny, and elaborate titles. Make the presentation interactive by asking students for on-the-spot revisions as you go. At the end of class, ask them to read out loud their revised titles and save them for future use.

(Note: If you can't create a PowerPoint presentation ahead of time, ask students to post or email their papers to you so you can develop the presentation before class begins.)

> *A good title should be like a good metaphor: it should intrigue without being too baffling or too obvious.*
> – E. B. White

FOR TEACHING: INTRODUCTIONS

(4f2)

"First impressions count," Emily Post wrote, speaking about one's manners and personal appearance. Similarly, the writer's introductory paragraph gives the reader a first impression of the writer. Have students work in small groups and answer the following questions about the effectiveness of their introductory paragraphs:

1. What tentative conclusions can you draw about the writer's style and tone from the introduction? Is the writer intelligent, well-informed, confident? Is the writer ill at ease or uncommitted to the topic?

2. Can you determine the intended audience from the first paragraph? Or does the introduction seem to be directed at no one in particular? Describe the intended audience.

(4f3) **FOR TEACHING: CONCLUSIONS**

Padded endings are common in student writing. Inexperienced writers may sense that the paper is finished, but lacking confidence in their own writing, may feel compelled to restate the thesis or summarize the entire essay. Have students find and copy into their logs the endings (final paragraph or sentence) of three to five essays or articles they particularly like. Have them each select an ending to share in class and discuss the features that make it effective. Then have them read the endings of their own essays aloud in small groups and see if they can identify any possibilities for making them more effective (concise, clear, powerful, and so on).

(4g) ## On Revising Paragraphs, Sentences, Words, and Tone

Students often think that becoming a better writer means that one does not have to attend to the smaller units of composition — paragraphs, sentences, words, and tone. But even the most prolific and accomplished writers struggle with revision of these small parcels of meaning. The popular humor writer Dave Barry offers the following reflection on revision, which you might want to share with your students:

> Writing humor takes discipline and hard work. I have this theory. Here it is, My Theory about Writing: It's hard. The humor doesn't just flow as easily as people think. A funny idea has to be tooled and shaped so that it's funny to others when it's read. People think that because humor is light and easy to read that it's just as simple to write. Nothing could be more untrue. You have to work at it. Writer's block, for example. Here's My Theory about Writer's Block: People simply give up and don't want to put forth the effort to work through the barriers. No good writing is easy. It has to do with overcoming the obstacles we find in the way of our creativity. You have to have the determination to do it.
> — Dave Barry, *How to Write Funny*

(4g1) **FOR COLLABORATIVE WORK: EXAMINING PARAGRAPHS**

Assign a draft due at the start of class. Ask the students to identify the best three- to five-sentence paragraph. After dividing the class into small groups, ask each student to read his or her paragraph to the rest of the group. The rest of the group then decides which passage is most effective and analyzes it for sentence length, sentence variety, word choice, and tone. Accentuate the positive and encourage possible revisions.

FOR TEACHING: SENTENCES OPENING WITH *IT* AND *THERE*   **(4g2)**

After your students have written two versions of each of the *there are* and *it is* sentences in the collaboration exercise in 4g2, ask them to see how many variations they can achieve as a class. Have your class examine these sentences according to the questions on diction in 4g3.

FOR TEACHING: EXAMINING WORDS   **(4g3)**

Joseph Williams, in *Style: Ten Lessons in Clarity and Grace,* points out that avoiding passives and agentless constructions will usually make one's choice of words more vigorous and direct. He gives these examples for comparison:

> The money was found by me.

> I found the money. (80)

However, as Williams points out, "often we don't say who is responsible for an action, because we don't know or don't care, or because we'd just rather not say." Consider the following examples.

> The president *was rumored* to have considered resigning.

> Those who *are* guilty of negligence *can be fined.*

> Valuable records *should always be kept* in a fire-proof safe. (82)

After giving students these examples, have them select one page of a current draft and highlight every passive construction they can locate. They can work individually, in pairs, or in small groups to determine if each instance of the passive voice is justified or not.

On Examining Tone   **(4g4)**

Word choice produces tone, and tone carries implications for a writer's voice. The work of theorist Mikhail Bakhtin has been particularly useful in helping to examine traditional notions of "voice" as something unique and authentic to any individual. This view, much elaborated and advo-cated by Peter Elbow, Donald Murray, and many others in composition studies, fails to recognize the constructed nature of all voices. More im-portant, it fails to recognize the multiplicity (what Bakhtin calls "hetero-geneity") of voice. Like all writers, students have many "voices" they can deploy in various ways, and these voices are always, according to Bakhtin, in dialogue with others. Teachers can help students locate differing voices in their texts, some their "own" and others that belong to institutional discourse — such as the voice of big business, or of higher education. Moreover, instructors can teach students how to study and learn from the tensions among these voices. By emphasizing that students examine care-fully their use of words or diction, teachers can begin to raise student awareness about the presence and importance of voice in writing.

(4h)   ## On Reconsidering Format

It's crucial that students become aware of the entire package and presen-tation of their work, from the opening words to the overall format of their essays. You can help facilitate such attention by providing students with a "Final Checklist" to use in assessing their last revisions. Give students a handout or post questions on your course Web site. Delineate your precise format expectations. It is also helpful to have a class dialogue about the dif-ferent format expectations across disciplines and classes.

(4i)   ### FOR TEACHING: PROOFREADING THE FINAL DRAFT

Many students cut out this final stage of the editing process because they are eager to finish, stay up too late, or lose interest in the writing. You may want to provide them a last-minute opportunity to proofread: before they hand in their papers, give them ten minutes of class time to proofread their final drafts; or ask them to trade papers and proofread one another's final drafts.

(4j)   ### FOR COLLABORATIVE WORK: IMPROVING FINAL DRAFTS

Even writing that has reached "final draft" stage can be revised, and often very effectively. Have students choose two paragraphs from Emily Lesk's final draft on pp. 106–11 and, working with two or three other students, plan and carry out a further revision. They should begin by reading the paragraphs aloud once or twice and jotting down items in three columns: a "plus" column for words, phrases, or ideas they especially like; a "minus" column for words, phrases, or ideas they *don't* like; and a "question" column for words, phrases, or ideas that seem unclear or somehow questionable. Then they can compare notes all around and, together, draft a revision. Finally, have them compare their revisions with the original paragraphs and report to the class, explaining the changes and describing what they have done to improve the paragraphs.

> *But many writers who have earned their reputations through hard work agree that one writes at first just to have something to rewrite.*
> – DAVID MADDEN

■ USEFUL READINGS

Bishop, Wendy. *Released into Language: Options for Teaching Creative Writing.* Urbana: NCTE, 1991. Bishop offers us two chapters on responding to student writing: "Responding and Revising" and "Evaluating and Responding" (131–76). Besides her fine explanations of the politics of responding to student writing, Bishop provides clearly articulated response questions that are accessible to students at any level. See also her "Helping Peer Writing Groups Succeed," in *Teaching English in the Two-Year College* 15 (1988): 120–25.

> *I have rewritten — often several times — every word I have ever published. My pencils outlast their erasers.*
> – VLADIMIR NABOKOV

Brannon, Lil, Melinda Knight, and Vera Neverow-Turk. *Writers Writing.* Upper Montclair: Boynton, 1983. Arguing that writing and revising should not be considered two separate stages in the writing process, the authors provide examples of successive drafts by both student writers and professional writers.

Cook, Devan. "Revising Editing." *TETYC* 29.2 (Dec. 2001): 154–61. Cook challenges the common distinction between revising and editing by showing how an attention to the rhetorical effects of punctuation as purposeful and meaning-making helps students discover new ideas as part of the revision process.

Faigley, Lester, and Stephen Witte. "Analyzing Revision." *CE* 32 (1981): 400–14. The authors distinguish between surface revision (usually at the phrase or word level) and text-based revision (at the structural level).

Flower, Linda. "Writer-Based Prose: A Cognitive Basis for Problems in Writing." *CE* 41 (1979): 19–37. Flower suggests that early drafts are frequently directed not to readers, but to the writer. A significant part of revision is the movement from writer-based to reader-based prose.

Flower, Linda S., John R. Hayes, Linda Carey, Karen Schriver, and James Stratman. "Detection, Diagnosis, and the Strategies of Revision." *CCC* 37 (Feb. 1986): 16–55. This award-winning essay discusses three revision methods employed by successful writers in order to move from intention to goal: detecting problems in the text, diagnosing the problems, and selecting a strategy. A focus on purpose and audience shifts attention from proofreading to more elaborate revision.

Horvath, Brooke K. "The Components of Written Response: A Practical Synthesis of Current Views." *Rhetoric Review* 2 (1984): 136–56. Horvath identifies seven types of "formative" responses to student writing that treat the text as part of an ongoing process rather than as a finished product, including responses that correct, emote, suggest, question, remind, and assign. Horvath also provides an eighty-one-item annotated bibliography.

Lindeman, Erika. *A Rhetoric for Writing Teachers.* 4th ed. New York: Oxford UP, 2001.

Rubin, Lois. "'I Just Think Maybe You Could . . .': Peer Critiquing through Online Conversations." *TETYC* 29.4 (May 2002): 382–392. Rubin's study refutes the myth that politeness in peer review signifies low power status and instead analyzes it as a strategy of negotiation that in fact increases power and effectiveness in communication.

Sommers, Nancy. "Revision Strategies of Student Writers and Experienced Adult Writers." *CCC* 31 (Dec. 1980): 378–88. Rpt. in *Landmark Essays on Writing Process.* Ed. Sondra Perl. Davis: Hermagoras, 1994. Sommers analyzes the differences between revision strategies of students and older writers, examining the range from choosing words to rearranging form in order to meet the needs of an audience. She argues that revision is a recursive process essential to developing ideas, rather than a surface cleaning of diction or the final step in a writing progression.

Tomlinson, Barbara. "Tuning, Tying, and Training Texts: Metaphors for Revision." *Written Communication* 5 (1988): 58–81.

Welch, Nancy. *Getting Restless: Rethinking Revision in Writing Instruction.* Portsmouth: Boynton/Cook, 1997. Drawing from feminist and psychoanalytic theories and utilizing ethnographic, case-study, and autobiographical research, Welch seeks to demonstrate ways composition teachers can support "revision as restlessness," a process that leads to re-visioning and making real-life changes.

Williams, Joseph M. *Style: Ten Lessons in Clarity and Grace.* 5th ed. New York: Addison, 1997. This practical guide for revising gives special attention to the sentence. Individual chapters deal with such problems as overuse of nominalization and passive voice, prose sprawl, and lack of coherence and emphasis.

5

Developing Paragraphs

Learning is fundamentally about relationships.
– RICHARD RODRIGUEZ

Earlymanuscriptsranwordstogetherlikethis

Words were not considered individual entities; rather they formed the continuum of oral language. Later manuscripts, however, began to sacrifice precious paper by leaving space between the words and putting special marks in the margin as an aid to the reader. In fact, the paragraph as we know it today — with its qualities of consecutiveness and loose order of propositions — did not begin to emerge until the late seventeenth century and did not attain full codification until the eighteenth. Not until the mid-nineteenth century did the first systematic formulation of paragraph theory appear, in Alexander Bain's *English Composition and Rhetoric* (1866).

On Paragraphing for Readers (5a)

Alexander Bain's theories on essay structure generated categories we still use today, including narration, description, exposition, and argumentation. Suddenly the text — and the units of paragraphs within it — were characterized as fundamentally relational and affective. Not only does a text attempt to influence its readers, but readers come to a text with particular expectations based on their social and cultural contexts, their purpose in reading the material, and their knowledge of the field.

FOR TEACHING: PARAGRAPHING FOR READERS

Encourage your students to browse through their favorite nonacademic reading materials — newspapers, magazines, novels, nonfiction — looking for effective long and short paragraphs. They should bring their samples to class, either copies to be distributed or one copy to read aloud, and be prepared to explain the paragraphing conventions of this particular publication and of this particular author.

As a class, they'll want to answer the following questions:

1. What idea or topic does each paragraph develop?
2. What special effect(s) do the paragraphs create, if any?
3. How do these effects move forward the main idea?

All writers tend to imitate the styles of their favorite authors, consciously and unconsciously. This exercise will heighten the students' awareness of paragraphing techniques — their own as well as their favorite authors'.

(5b)   ## On Constructing Conventional Paragraphs

In his essay "Structure and Form in Non-Narrative Prose," Richard Larson explains what he sees as the three categories of paragraph theory: paragraphs (1) as expanded sentences, governed by comparable syntactical forces; (2) as self-contained units of writing with their own unique principles; and (3) as parts of the overall discourse, informed by the strategies a writer chooses for the overall piece.

Today, partially as a result of the poststructuralist and feminist critique, scholars are challenging conventional paragraph norms. In *Marxism and the Philosophy of Language,* V. N. Volosinov notes that "to say that a paragraph is supposed to consist of a complete thought amounts to absolutely nothing." Beginning with this provocative insight, Kay Halasek's book *A Pedagogy of Possibility* shows the ways in which composition textbooks have traditionally taught the paragraph in strictly traditional ways, as unified, coherent, and tightly linear. But Halasek works to redefine the paragraph as dialogic, as a negotiation among writer, audience, subject, and other textual elements that surround it. Most important, Halasek insists, is for instructors of writing to understand that the process of producing "unified," "cohesive" paragraphs calls for ignoring, erasing, or otherwise smoothing out a diversity of discourses and voices. Thus teaching students to be aware of this process can not only illuminate a great deal about how "good" paragraphs get constructed but also introduce them to a philosophy of language that is not based on current traditional positivism or objectivism.

FOR TEACHING: CONSTRUCTING CONVENTIONAL PARAGRAPHS **(5b)**

For many of the reasons Halasek identifies, students often have problems with conventional academic paragraphing — with development and cohesion. And their problems are often diagnosed in various ways. For instance, George Goodin and Kyle Perkins argue that because students fail to subordinate effectively, their writing is replete with digressions and afterthoughts. Betty Bamberg argues that cohesion comes with the successful movement from "writer-based" to "reader-based" prose. "Writer-based" prose often consists of elliptical expressions, sentences that have meaning for the writer but that omit information necessary for the reader's understanding.

Successful prewriting — and the kind of analysis Halasek calls on both students and instructors to do — may be the best cure for both of these paragraphing "problems." By planning ahead what to say and how to say it, writers can better stay on course. Therefore, reaffirm the need for prewriting as you introduce paragraphing. Adequate prewriting will result in the more orderly text characteristic of academic paragraphs.

On Focusing on a Main Idea **(5c)**

The notion that one sentence in every paragraph should announce the main idea of that paragraph was derived from the fourth law of Alexander Bain's "seven laws" for creating paragraphs: "Indication of theme: The opening sentence, unless obviously preparatory, is expected to indicate the scope of the paragraph."

Although most compositionists agree with Bain that every paragraph should have a unifying theme or purpose, not all agree that it should be announced by a topic sentence. In his study of professional writers, Richard Braddock found that topic sentences are used far less than we have traditionally believed; his research calls into question the teaching of topic sentences. On the other hand, Frank D'Angelo argues that despite

Braddock's findings, the use of topic sentences improves the readability of a paragraph.

(5c1)

FOR TEACHING: POSITIONING A TOPIC SENTENCE

If your class uses a reader, have students turn to *any* essay in it and see whether they can find a topic sentence in each paragraph. (1) What is the placement of the topic sentence? (2) What are the key terms in that topic sentence? (3) How does the information in that paragraph relate to those key words?

(5c1)

TEACHING WITH TECHNOLOGY: POSITIONING A TOPIC SENTENCE

Ask students to complete the same analytical exercise described above on their own drafts. With students working in small groups of two or three, project each student's essay on a shared plasma screen. Change the font color of the topic sentence of each paragraph. At the end of the allotted time, ask students to select three paragraphs from their papers that show different strategies for positioning a topic sentence. Display the models for the entire class, and discuss the pros and cons of each approach. Allow students to speak about their selections and to describe how the placement functions as a persuasive act.

(5c2)

FOR COLLABORATIVE WORK: RELATING EACH SENTENCE TO THE MAIN IDEA

One practical way to have students check whether each sentence relates to the main idea of the paragraph is through a collaborative highlighting exercise. Ask students to exchange papers in writing groups. Have each student go through one essay, highlighting the main idea of each paragraph and noting the relevance of each sentence in a given paragraph to the highlighted one. Then ask the groups to discuss their reviews together. Provide them with the following questions to help their analysis:

Does each paragraph stand on its own as a unified whole?

Are there too many new ideas in a given paragraph?

Do the details of each paragraph fit together to support the topic sentence?

Encourage the peer-review groups to revise one paragraph from each essay collaboratively by relying on the strengths of each group member.

On Making Paragraphs Coherent **(5d)**

The notion of relational unity within discrete units received an added boost when Alexander Bain helped transform the field of rhetoric by emphasizing contiguity and similarity as the key processes of association implicit in rhetorical acts. You can encourage your students to think through these terms in order to produce associational paragraphs in which the details fit together in contiguous or similar ways. By allowing students to experiment with different types of organization — spatial, chronological, logical, and associational — you can teach them to see the pattern of relationality in all writing.

FOR TEACHING: ORGANIZING IDEAS **(5d1)**

To give students practice using *spatial order,* suggest that they write about their bedrooms, dorm rooms, sleeping rooms — their view upon waking. After they record the information, ask them to read their essays to see if they started out or ended up with a controlling idea. Ask them to identify the topic sentence.

To give students practice using *chronological order,* suggest that they write a paragraph about their morning routines. After they've written it, ask them to mark the controlling idea. Do they have a topic sentence? Or did they come to one after they wrote the paragraph?

Have students practice using *logical order* by writing a paragraph describing their possessions — academic/personal; from home/from school; old/new; personal/public. They may want to look around their rooms as they write. Did they start out or end up with a controlling idea? What is it? Do they have a topic sentence?

Ask students to attempt a chain of *associations* in order to experiment with this type of organization. Have them study an advertisement from a popular magazine and freewrite a series of sentence fragments in response. Then have them revise the freewrite into a short opinion essay to be submitted to the magazine. When they are done, encourage them to reflect on the process: Did they begin with a strong response and move toward a conclusion? Did they discover unexpected ideas as they wrote?

How is the presentation of controlling ideas different in this short opinion piece than in a full-length essay?

(5d2)

FOR TEACHING: REPEATING KEY WORDS AND PHRASES

Repetition of key words and phrases is an age-old technique for pulling together thematically related units; moreover, the rhythm of such verbal/visual echoing effectively holds the audience's attention. We are all familiar with various repetitive devices.

Single word

Vanity of vanities, saith the preacher, vanity of vanities; all is vanity.
— ECCLESIASTICUS 1:1

Syntactic structure

The thoughts are but overflowings of the mind, and the tongue is but a servant of the thought. — PHILIP SIDNEY

Anaphora (initial repetition)

Say that I was a drum major for justice. Say that I was a drum major for peace. That I was a drum major for righteousness. And all of the other shallow things will not matter. — MARTIN LUTHER KING JR.

Why am I compelled to write? Because the writing saves me from this complacency I fear. Because I have no choice. Because I must keep the spirit of my revolt and myself alive. Because the world I create in the writing compensates for what the real world does not give me. By writing I put order in the world, give it a handle so I can grasp it. — GLORIA ANZALDÚA

(5d2)

FOR MULTILINGUAL WRITERS: REPEATING KEY WORDS AND PHRASES

Students from non-English-speaking cultures will often mention the rich variations in language that exist in their home countries, particularly with regard to patterns of repetition and common phrases. You can encourage all students to develop an awareness of culturally based patterns of repetition by sharing with them translated texts from other languages. Alternatively, ask students to bring in materials from language and literature courses for collective study, or assign readings of your own. Gloria Anzaldúa, for instance, uses a unique blend of eight languages — two variations of English and six of Spanish—in *Borderlands/La Frontera: The New Mestiza.*

FOR TEACHING: USING PARALLEL STRUCTURES AND REPETITION   **(5d2–3)**

Ask students to read the following paragraph from a famous essay by a woman who wants a "wife," and to identify every use of repetition and parallel structure. In addition, ask them to explain, in a brief paragraph, how the writer uses these structures to build coherence in the paragraph.

> I would like to go back to school so that I can become economically independent, support myself, and, if need be, support those dependent upon me. I want a wife who will work and send me to school. And while I am going to school I want a wife to take care of my children. I want a wife to keep track of the children's doctor and dentist appointments. And to keep track of mine, too. I want a wife to make sure my children eat properly and are kept clean. I want a wife who will wash the children's clothes and keep them mended. I want a wife who is a good nurturant attendant to my children, who arranges for their schooling, makes sure that they have an adequate social life with their peers, takes them to the park, the zoo, etc. I want a wife who takes care of the children when they are sick, a wife who arranges to be around when the children need special care, because, of course, I cannot miss classes at school. My wife must arrange to lose time at work and not lose the job. It may mean a small cut in my wife's income from time to time, but I guess I can tolerate that. Needless to say, my wife will arrange and pay for the care of the children while my wife is working.   —JUDY BRADY, "I Want a Wife"

FOR TEACHING: USING TRANSITIONAL DEVICES   **(5d4)**

Read aloud to the class the following selection from *Jane Eyre.* As you read, your students should jot down the transitional devices they hear.

> My first aim will be to *clean down* . . . Moor House from chamber to cellar; my next to rub it up with beeswax, oil, and an indefinite number of cloths, till it glitters again; my third, to arrange every chair, table, bed, carpet, with mathematical precision; afterwards I shall go near to ruin you in coals and peat to keep up good fires in every room; and lastly, the two days preceding that on which your sisters are expected will be devoted by Hannah and me to such a beating of eggs, sorting of currants, grating of spices, compounding of Christmas cakes, chopping up of materials for mince-pies, and solemnising of other culinary rites, as words can convey but an inadequate notion of to the

uninitiated like you. My purpose, in short, is to have all things in an absolutely perfect state of readiness for Diana and Mary before next Thursday; and my ambition is to give them a beau-ideal of a welcome when they come. (Chapter XXXIV)

Diane Belcher, director of the ESL program at Ohio State University, notes that overuse of taxonomies of transitions are of very limited help to multilingual writers, noting that such lists may lead students to conclude an essay with "at last" rather than "in conclusion" — *without* humorous or ironic intent (personal correspondence).

(5d4)

FOR COLLABORATIVE WORK: COMMONLY USED TRANSITIONS

Ask students to review the list of commonly used transitions in section 5d4. Then have them break into groups and trade drafts of current essays. As they read one another's papers, have them draw arrows between or circles around key terms, ideas, and pronouns, and mark transitional phrases with heavy underlining and parallelism with //*sm*. By stopping to analyze patterns in their writing, students can come to a better understanding of the elements of unity and coherence necessary for constructing effective paragraphs.

(5e1)

On Patterns of Development

No such thing as a pure definition or division/classification or comparison/contrast essay exists outside of the classroom, and to teach or assign these techniques as discourse structures is to confuse means with ends. Discourses are, perhaps without exception, motivated by multiple aims. However, we can identify primary aims and primary organizing principles in order to construct essays using dynamic and reciprocal notions of function and form.

(5e1)

TEACHING WITH TECHNOLOGY: DIVIDING AND CLASSIFYING

As a way of introducing the idea of classifying, consider asking the class to answer the following series of questions on their computers or through a threaded email discussion:

1. What are your strengths and weaknesses as a writer?

2. Is your writing process linear or recursive?
3. How do you learn in this class: from writing? from taking notes? from reading and responding to your friends' work?
4. What are your reasons for taking this course?

Then, with students working in groups of three, have them use their answers to these questions to classify each other into different groups. Ask students to draft a chart presenting the results of their classifications and to discuss different strategies for dividing and classifying. Project the results on a shared overhead screen to enable further class discussion.

FOR COLLABORATIVE WORK: COMPARING AND CONTRASTING   **(5e1)**

Ask students to break into groups to discuss the contrasts between high school and college or between life with and life without children. Students should keep notes, then write a short essay on one of the topics.

FOR TEACHING: DETERMINING PARAGRAPH LENGTH   **(5e2)**

Modern stylist William Zinsser advises nonfiction writers to keep their paragraphs short. Visually, such paragraphs are more inviting because they have more white space around them. But he does not mean that all paragraphs should be the same length.

Paragraph length should vary with purpose: long paragraphs often introduce a character, a setting, a situation, while short paragraphs add emphasis or move the reader through the text.

Ask your students to find a magazine article and a newspaper article that cover the same story. Which medium has more consistent paragraph length? Is one story more in-depth? Does one have longer, more developed paragraphs that continue to introduce new information? Can your students account for the different styles and lengths of paragraphs?

FOR TEACHING: COMPOSING SPECIAL-PURPOSE PARAGRAPHS   **(5f)**

Ask students to bring in magazine articles in which you will highlight the various purposes served by particular paragraphs, especially the introductory and concluding paragraphs. Alert students to the presence and function of transitional paragraphs in especially long prose texts.

It is important to stress that of all the paragraphs in a piece of writing, none is more important than the first. In fact, outside of classroom assignments — in job applications, newspaper articles, and fund-raising appeals, for example — the quality of the opening paragraph often determines whether readers bother to read further. One high school student, Ted Frantz, found himself concentrating hard on his opening paragraph as he worked on an essay describing his "major academic interest" to accompany his college application. Following is the paragraph he came up with to get his readers' attention and introduce his subject.

> Picture a five-year-old boy with a stack of cards in his hands, not baseball cards but presidential flash cards. He would run around asking anybody to question him about presidents; this kid knew incredible facts and could name every president in the correct order from Washington to Bush. I was this little boy, and ever since I was five, I have had a passion for studying history.

Consider asking students to take some time to look at the opening paragraphs in the reading they normally do: newspapers or magazines, textbooks, junk mail. How well do such paragraphs get and hold their attention? Ask students to bring the paragraphs to class for discussion.

(5f2) FOR COLLABORATIVE WORK: CONCLUDING PARAGRAPHS

Ask students to draft three different attempts at concluding their essays. Have them share these samples in writing groups and talk about what works and what doesn't in each draft. If the essay is only two or three pages in length, you can ask students to read through to the penultimate paragraph and then jot down their thoughts on how best to conclude the essay *before* turning to the three conclusion attempts.

(5g) On Composing Paragraphs Online

The very process of writing online, or through technologically mediated methods, has raised new challenges complicating our attempts to conform to Alexander Bain's prescription for unified and coherent discourse broken into succinct paragraphs. But we can look at such new writing sites as opportunities for creativity rather than as cause for complaint. As Cynthia Selfe and Susan Hilligoss argue in *Literacy and Computers,* "Technology, along with the issues that surround its use in reading- and writing-intensive classrooms, both physically and intellectually disrupts the ways in which we make meaning—the ways in which we communicate. Computers change the ways in which we read, construct, and interpret texts. In doing so, technology forces us to rethink what it means to be human. We need more problems like this."

TEACHING WITH TECHNOLOGY: PARAGRAPHING IN MESSAGES AND POSTINGS   **(5g)**

Ask students to respond to the course texts through online message boards or postings, and direct them to experiment with different paragraph structures: short, long, informative, bulleted, associative, logical, chronological. You can have students create two different online texts in response to the same prompt and then analyze the different meanings produced by variations in paragraph unity, length, and composition.

On Linking Paragraphs   **(5h)**

You might ask students to think of linking paragraphs in terms of the game of dominos. Each paragraph needs to share a similarity with the previous one: just as in dominos, you can only connect two game pieces that have the same number of points on them. Drawing a spatial model of the dominos game on the board for students often opens their eyes to the way in which writing also works as a series of relationships within and between paragraphs.

■ USEFUL READINGS

Bain, Alexander. *English Composition and Rhetoric.* 1866.

Ball, Arnetha F. "Cultural Preference and the Expository Writing of African-American Adolescents." *Written Communication* (Oct. 1992): 501–32. Researcher Arnetha Ball identifies embedded narrative and two other patterns of development that are characteristic of spoken discourse.

Bamberg, Betty. "What Makes a Text Coherent?" *CCC* 34 (1983): 417–29.

Braddock, Richard. "The Frequency and Placement of Topic Sentences in Expository Prose." *Research in the Teaching of English* 8 (Winter 1974): 287–302. After analyzing the use of topic sentences by professional writers, Braddock concludes that topic sentences are used far less than textbooks claim. We should not deceive our students on the subject.

Christensen, Francis. "A Generative Rhetoric of the Paragraph." *CCC* 16 (1965): 144–56. Christensen exemplifies the view that paragraphs are determined by forces similar to those that determine sentences and explains the three principal kinds of paragraphs: coordinate, subordinate, and a mixture.

D'Angelo, Frank. "The Topic Sentence Revisited." *CE* 37 (1986): 431–41. Citing work in psycholinguistics, D'Angelo argues that the use of topic sentences improves readability, which justifies teaching them.

Fleckenstein, Kristie. "An Appetite for Coherence: Arousing and Fulfilling Desires." *CCC* 43 (1992): 81–87. The author urges instructors to help students practice looking at parts of their texts from the reader's point of view, as a means of understanding what devices can be used to make the text "cohere" for the reader.

Goodin, George, and Kyle Perkins. "Discourse Analysis and the Art of Coherence." *CE* 44 (1982): 57–63.

Halasek, Kay. *A Pedagogy of Possibility: Bakhtinian Perspectives on Composition.* Urbana: Southern Illinois UP, 1999. Halasek devotes a significant part of one chapter to a rereading of paragraph pedagogy from a Bakhtinian perspective, suggesting that we have lost quite a bit in a narrow drive for "unity" and "coherence" at all costs.

Halliday, M. A. K., and Rugaiya Hasan. *Cohesion in English.* London: Longman, 1976. The authors provide a classification of cohesive ties in paragraphs and essays: reference, substitution, ellipsis, conjunction, and lexical ties.

Larson, Richard. "Structure and Form in Non-Narrative Prose." Rpt. in *Ten Bibliographic Essays.* Ed. Gary Tate. Fort Worth: Texas Christian UP, 1987. 39–82. Larson provides an exposition of his own paragraph theory as well as an overview of contemporary theory.

Markels, Robin Bell. *A New Perspective on Cohesion in Expository Paragraphs.* Carbondale: Southern Illinois UP, 1984. Investigating paragraph cohesion from a perspective that focuses both on semantics and structural (syntactic) cohesiveness, Markels offers useful alternative backgrounding to the grammatical concept of unity.

Root, Robert L., Jr. "Beyond Linearity: Writing the Segmented Essay." *Writing on the Edge* 9.2 (Spring 1998): 27–34. Root argues that we should teach "segmented" essays, which are not traditional, beginning with a thesis and presenting a linearly linked set of supports. In contrast, the segmented essay organizes by juxtaposition, parallelism, accumulation, or patterning. He offers examples of a number of assignments.

Selfe, Cynthia, and Susan Hilligoss. *Literacy and Computers: The Complications of Teaching and Learning with Technology.* New York: MLA, 1994.

The Sentence and the Paragraph. Urbana: NCTE, 1963. This important collection includes essays by Francis Christensen on the generative rhetoric of the sentence and the paragraph, Alton L. Becker's "A Tagmemic Approach to Paragraph Analysis," and a symposium on the paragraph by Francis Christensen, A. L. Becker, Paul C. Rodgers, Jr., Josephine Miles, and David H. Karrfalt.

Witte, Stephen P., and Lester Faigley. "Coherence, Cohesion, and Writing Quality." CCC 32 (1981): 189–204. Using an adjusted version of Halliday and Hasan's classifications, the authors conclude that cohesion is connected to our perceptions of how well the text fits to its context.

6

▼ Collaborating—
Online and Off

*Technology in the classroom clearly warrants new ways of teaching
. . . those new ways of teaching should steer clear of traditional lecture-based instruction, and focus on doing.*
                                                    – Scott Kirsner

Recent works in philosophy and literary theory have undercut the concept of the "solitary creator and interpreter," who strives alone to read and write and to make sense of the world. One of the most important facts to have come out of recent research into writing is that most real-world writing is done collaboratively. Lisa Ede and Andrea Lunsford explain that people in a range of professions regularly write as parts of teams or groups, and their ability to participate successfully in such collaborative writing efforts is essential both to their productivity and job satisfaction. In an effort to determine just how many people in the "real world" write collaboratively, they surveyed 1,400 randomly selected members of seven professional associations. Of the members surveyed, nearly 50 percent completed the questionnaire, 87 percent of whom reported that they have written as part of a team or group.

Although it is often extremely difficult to set up, collaborative work in composition classes provides important preparation for the writing tasks that students will find when they leave the classroom. The emphasis this book puts on collaboration will help use class time more efficiently, and it will get students used to learning together in ways that reflect how reading, writing, and research work together.

On Collaborating Online

In the past ten years, technology in higher education has transformed our classroom practices and the pedagogical opportunities available to us.

Such changes come in a variety of forms, but no innovation has been more fundamental for the composition classroom than the advent of computers for collaboration and peer review.

Identifying class discussion as "perhaps our most prominent and widely used pedagogical tool," Patrick Sullivan argues that conversing with computers enhances such collaboration—both online and off:

> With the presence of the Internet in a majority of our schools, with access to an increasing number of computer labs for teaching purposes, and with Internet-related technology and software becoming an increasingly significant part of our students' lives, it is time to think creatively about how we might use this new technology in our classrooms to enhance class discussion. . . . [A] networked classroom environment—either to supplement or to replace traditional face-to-face class discussion—offers English teachers opportunities that can help make class discussion more engaging, more worthwhile, and significantly more effective as a teaching tool. ("Reimagining" 393)

Indeed, working together in technologically mediated environments offers unprecedented opportunities for teachers and students to learn from each other through collaboration in ways that transform the very nature of education. Describing this shift, Sheila Offman Gersh reflects:

> Today, we are finding that the learning environment encourages many to work together, to learn from each other, and to allow learning to happen in a variety of ways. No longer is the textbook and the teacher the sole provider of information. Students can learn from others via the Internet; they can learn with their teachers; they can teach their teachers; and they can learn at a distance with hundreds of other students. (par. 25)

On Collaborating in College

(6a) ....

Rose Pringle, writing about Web-mediated discourse learning communities, describes the way in which teaching can respond to new opportunities for collaboration through computers:

> Today, asynchronous learning tools on the Web have opened up possibilities and potential for a new environment for teaching and learning. The central pedagogical idea in an asynchronous learning network is collaborative learning at the time and place of the individual learner's convenience which allows for multiple discussions to occur simultaneously, while slowing down the dynamic face-to-face interactions characteristic of the traditional classrooms. (par 4)

Teachers — we are empowered by our collective strengths. We have the ability to change children's lives and collectively, we bring skills that allow for the education of kids in our classrooms.
– RICK FEUTZ, founder of the Learning Space

(6b)

FOR TEACHING: IMPROVING INDIVIDUAL WRITING THROUGH COLLABORATION

As teachers using technology, we need to change our approaches to writing when leading a computer-facilitated writing class. As David McConnell reminds us:

> [P]eople learn best when they have the opportunity to work with other people, through processes of cooperation and collaboration. . . . [W]ithout an underlying educational philosophy which emphasizes the importance of cooperation, no Computer Supported Cooperative Learning system will in itself be effective. (158)

Becoming a part of an online community has put me in touch with colleagues who have similar beliefs about teaching and technology. . . . It is the connection with these teachers that has helped me to use technology to change the way I teach and my students learn.
— CAROLYN HINSHAW, commenting on the Learning Space

More and more, teachers are sharing suggested methods of collaboration at conferences, in electronic journals, through listservs, and on Web sites such as the Learning Space (<www.learningspace.org>). The collaboration between professionals translates into better classroom practices to improve student writing. Explore some of the resources available online for your own pedagogical and professional development. Bookmark the Web sites listed at the end of this chapter. Exchange your ideas with colleagues through email and electronic discussion lists in order to help improve your students' writing.

(6b)

ATTENDING TO DISABILITIES: COLLABORATING ON GROUP PROJECTS

John Slatin recommends a number of group activities for raising student awareness about attending to disabilities. These work particularly well for collaborating both online and off. One exercise entails making an auditory file accessible to hearing-impaired students. Slatin suggests the following:

> Starting from a substantive block of text (for example, an historical narrative, an explanation of economic data, a news item, or an exposition of a complex concept), ask students to locate or create alternative visual or auditory representations to help people with learning disabilities or other cognitive impairments understand what's being said. Alternatively, start with a piece of audio — a recorded interview, for example — and have students create a verbatim transcript; or, if the audio material is part of a video soundtrack, have students write captions and synchronize them with the soundtrack using the National Center for Accessible Media's free software, MAGpie (available at http://ncam.wgbh.org/webaccess/magpie/). (Persons with certain types of cognitive disabilities may be helped by visual symbols like those afforded by the Bliss symbol language; see http://www.handicom.nl/english/Bliss/BfW_Edt

.html. See also "LDD Symbols" at http://www.learningdifficulty.org/develop /symbols.html.) (par. 32)

By asking students to collaborate on projects that take all modes of learning into account, you help them realize the rhetorical purpose of each aspect of the project: what audience it addresses and what role it serves as part of the whole. Moreover, challenging students to work with technology to include all readers and participants helps expand their imaginative range and fulfill a legal and ethical call to greater inclusivities.

FOR MULTILINGUAL WRITERS: USING EMAIL AND WEB SITES FOR COLLABORATION   **(6c)**

Exchanging messages with peers can be an excellent way to develop language and writing skills for multilingual writers. Encourage this development by pairing students at the beginning of the term and asking them to exchange informal feedback about their writing throughout the term. You might suggest that they email each other with research tips, exciting source finds, and problems encountered during the research process. Also, keep in mind that students from other countries may often keep in touch with you over the years; help facilitate their continued writing development by corresponding with them by email and continuing the collaborative learning process.

In addition, multilingual writers often benefit from online collaboration in the classroom itself. As Patrick Sullivan points out, collaborating online presents unique opportunities to engage multilingual students who might be reserved about conventional participation methods:

> In an online environment, the teacher doesn't have to call on quiet students, draw them out, and encourage them to share their ideas and feelings. Students typically must participate if they want to pass the course. Since the time restraints of the traditional classroom setting are not a factor, all students can contribute, usually in as much depth and detail as they wish. The online format often leads to more class participation than in traditional classrooms and the opportunity to encounter a variety of voices and perspectives. ("Gender," 363)

FOR COLLABORATIVE WORK: WORKING WITH WEB DESIGN

Billie J. Jones offers an excellent idea for collaborative work in which students construct a Web page that explores the role of technology in our society. "Great ideas generate in groups," is the philosophy behind the assignment. Jones arranges the groups "on the basis of Web writing experience, giving each group both experienced and inexperienced Web writers." Jones explains that collaborating online and off helps students learn to work together and develop their collective abilities: "I believe Web design is an excellent project for collaborative work because, used at its best, collaboration allows students to pool their individual experiences and skills to complete a project. Groups can even be structured with varying levels of prior Web expertise to maximize the possibility of learning-through-sharing."

For students who voice what Barbara Duffelmeyer, in a recent article in *Computers and Composition*, describes as "oppositional" and "negotiated" stances toward technology in composition classes, such collaborative projects take the pressure off students to perform individually. At the same time, presenting a group project with technology trains students to become engaged public citizens, proficient in production, and computer literate.

■ USEFUL READINGS

Barber, Margaret M., Laura L. Sullivan, and Janice R. Walker. "Letter from the Guest Editors." *Body, Identity, and Access: Diversity and Networked Environments.* Spec. issue of *Computers and Composition* 14 (1997): 163–67. Warning against viewing computers as the sole means of developing a progressive pedagogy, the authors remind us of the dangers of erasing difference in the name of multiculturalism.

Duffelmeyer, Barbara Blakely. "Critical Computer Literacy: Computers in First-Year Composition as Topic and Environment." *Computers and Composition* 17.3 (2000), 289–308. Online at <http://corax.cwrl.utexas.edu/cac/Current_Issue/dufflemeyer.html>.

Ebest, Sally Barr, Thomas Fox, and David Bleich, eds. *Writing with New Directions in Collaborative Teaching, Learning and Research.* Albany: SUNY P, 1994.

Forman, Janis, ed. *New Visions of Collaborative Writing.* Portsmouth: Boynton/Cook, 1992. This collection of essays offers teachers many ways to consider and use collaboration in their classrooms. Establishing authorship, working face-to-face, writing electronically, and exploring the ethics of collaboration are issues covered well.

Gersh, Sheila Offman. "Technology's Role in Creating the Shared-Learning Environment." *Tech Learning: The Resources for Education Technology Leaders* 1 Nov. 2001. Online at <http://www.techlearning.com/db_area/archives/WCE/archives/sheilag.htm>. Gersh details the new collaboration opportunities afforded to teachers, teacher-librarians, and students with the increased turn to electronic spaces for pedagogical work.

Gimbert, Belinda, and Carla Zembal-Saul. "Learning to Teach with Technology: From Integration to Actualization." *Contemporary Issues in Technology and Teacher Education* 2.2 (2002). Online at <http://www.citejournal.org/vol2/iss2/current practice /article1.cfm>. Citing the national need to integrate training in technology into teacher preparation, the authors offer concrete models for implementation from a program at Penn State.

Goodburn, Amy, and Beth Ina. "Collaboration, Critical Pedagogy, and Struggles over Difference." *Journal of Advanced Composition* 14.1 (Winter 1994): 131–47. Goodburn and Ina explore the intersection of critical pedagogy and collaborative processes and encourage teachers to question their own assumptions and expectations about collaboration.

Jones, Billie J. "Great Ideas: Collaborative Web Assignment." *Kairos* 7.2 (Summer 2002). Online at <http://english.ttu.edu/kairos/7.2/binder.html?sectiontwo /jones/ TechPopJones.html>.

McConnell, David. *Implementing Computer Supported Cooperative Learning*. London: Kogan, 1994. McConnell argues for an emphasis on collaboration through technology rather than a reliance on computers alone.

McNenny, Geraldine, and Duane H. Roen. "Collaboration or Plagiarism—Cheating Is in the Eye of the Beholder." *Dialogue: A Journal for Writing Specialists* 1 (Fall 1993): 6–27. Besides providing a tantilizing and often wry overview of the issues central to collaboration, McNenny and Roen include a splendid bibliography of relevant works.

Meloni, Christine. "The Internet in the Classroom." *ESL Magazine* 1.1 (1998): 10-16. A discussion of how email and Internet technology can help facilitate the writing development skills of non-English speakers.

Pringle, Rose. "Developing a Community of Learners: Potentials and Possibilities in Web Mediated Discourse." *Contemporary Issues in Technology and Teacher Education* 2.2 (2002). Online at <http://www.citejournal.org/vol2/iss2/current practice/article2.cfm>. Pringle discusses how asynchronous learning reduces competition and encourages a sense of community.

Selfe, Cynthia. "Technology and Literacy: A Story about the Perils of Not Paying Attention." *CCC* 50.3 (Feb. 1999): 411–36. The 1997 CCCC Chair's Address in which Selfe cautions teachers to attend to the structural dynamics of computer usage that can perpetuate gender and racial inequities.

Selfe, Cynthia L., and S. Hilligoss, eds. *Literacy and Computers: The Complications of Teaching and Learning with Technology*. New York: MLA, 1994.

Selfe, Cynthia L., and Richard J. Selfe. "The Politics of the Interface: Power and Its Exercise in Electronic Contact Zones." *CCC* 45 (1994): 480–504. An important warning against a utopian view of computer-aided teaching.

Slatin, John. "The Imagination Gap: Making Web-based Instructional Resources Accessible to Students and Colleagues with Disabilities." *Currents in Electronic Literacy* 6 (Spring 2002). Online at <http://www.cwrl.utexas.edu/currents /spring02/slatin.html>.

Sullivan, Patrick. "Gender and the Online Classroom." *TETYC* 26.4 (1999): 361–71. Arguing that "a carefully designed and skillfully moderated asynchronous Internet classroom environment can help minimize problems related to gender in traditional classrooms," Sullivan proposes ways for collaborating online in order to reduce gender disparity in writing classes.

——. "Reimagining Class Discussion in the Age of the Internet." *TETYC* 29.4 (2002): 393–410. In this comprehensive assessment of approaches to class discussion and the difficulties presented by conventional classrooms, Sullivan looks to networked environments as reconfiguring class discussion to produce a collaborative learning environment.

■ USEFUL WEB SITES

Collaborate!

http://www.stanford.edu/group/collaborate/index.htm

Devoted to collaborative writing and research in higher education, this Web site was established in conjunction with MLA President Linda Hutcheon's call for "alternatives to the adversarial academy" (MLA Convention, Dec. 2000). The site provides information about ongoing collaborative efforts and invites the participation of all who wish to move beyond the academy's traditional agonistic individualism.

Computers and Composition Online

http://www.cwrl.utexas.edu/~ccjrnl

The Web site for Computers and Composition: An International Journal for Teachers of Writing.

Currents in Electronic Literacy

http://www.cwrl.utexas.edu/currents

Special issue on "Computers, Writing, Research, and Learning in the Lab."

Kairos: A Journal of Rhetoric, Technology, and Pedagogy

http://english.ttu.edu/kairos

The summer 2002 issue has a special focus on technology, popular culture, and the art of teaching that is particularly enlightening to teachers interested in designing syllabi and assignments for collaborating online and off.

The Learning Space: Evolving Tools for Evolving Minds

http://www.learningspace.org

Funded by the US West Foundation, this nonprofit, teacher-based organization aims to break down professional isolation by providing an ongoing support network for teachers to teach each other through Internet communications and Web sites.

PART 2

CONSIDERING MEDIA

7

▼ Writing with Computers: The Basics

With the development of the Internet, and . . . networked computers, we are in the middle of the most transforming technological event since the capture of fire.

—JOHN PERRY BARLOW

Now that students are raised in a computer-mediated environment, most of them see writing with computers as natural, even as easier than writing with pen and paper. One student at Stanford University's 2002 summer session lecture on "Writing Your Life" admitted to learning to write on a keyboard, not by hand. This revolution is widespread across the United States, as most students have grown up with a relationship with computers that Cynthia Selfe calls indicative of "critical technological literacy" (432). While discrepancies remain in underprivileged schools, neighborhoods, and families, and while some students take "oppositional" or "negotiated" stances toward technology, the majority of today's college students report what Barbara Duffelmeyer calls "comfortable oneness with technology." Knowing this can transform the way you implement writing with computers in your curriculum and syllabus.

At many colleges and universities, however, the implementation of technology in our teaching has not yet been optimized. As Chris M. Anson, a specialist in computers and composition, argues in a recent article: "Online communication with students is an idea that seems stale by now but is by no means fully exploited; only some teachers eagerly invite email from students, and only some students end up using it when invited" (270).

At the same time, working with computers means making sure that you have access to proper and timely training in new technologies and support for your pedagogical innovations. Anson argues as much in his assessment of national and institutional trends: "The quality of faculty interaction with students is a product of our *work* — our training, the material conditions at our institutions, how much support we get for developing our teaching and keeping up on research" (273). Check with your institution's technology center or ask your chairperson for training workshops as part of your professional development.

On Writing with Computers

While the research study cited in *The St. Martin's Handbook* solicited information from nearly twenty-five hundred students from a variety of colleges and universities across the country, we know from looking closely at the responses from each school that access to technology and experience with online writing vary widely from one campus to another. As a result, the information on these pages may be interesting and provocative to you — but it may not match the experiences of your students.

You might do a brief survey of students in your class (or in your larger writing program) to find out how many of them have access to computers and the Internet from their dorm rooms; how many use the Web frequently — and for what purposes; and so on.

ATTENDING TO DISABILITIES: WRITING WITH COMPUTERS

When working with online writing, be sure to comply with the Americans with Disabilities Act (ADA). A screen reader for visually impaired students can help facilitate complete participation in online analysis and writing activities. Software that translates spoken words into computer text is readily available and can ensure that all students contribute to in-class writing exercises. When posting material on a course Web site, ask your academic technology staff about design considerations that help meet ADA requirements and provide alternative pages for specially adapted Web browsers that might not be able to read fancy graphics or frames. Look to your institution's disability resource center for training sessions and a plethora of information to help you make writing projects accessible to all members of your class community. For more information, see the Learning Disabilities Resources Web page at < www.ldresources .com >.

To introduce the issue of accessibility with your students, John Slatin suggests the following exercises that you can conduct with the entire class:

> The Virtual Keyboard activity gives you a very slight hint of what using the Web and other software is like for people who cannot use their hands or voices to control the computer. It works like this: Download and install a virtual keyboard (for example, the Click-N-Type from Lake Software available at < www.ac.net/~lakerat/cnt >). A virtual keyboard is an on-screen keyboard designed for people with limited or no use of their hands. People in that situation might use a puff-stick to aim a stream of breath at the screen, or a head-mounted pointer to select each key. For this exercise, you can use your mouse to select the keys you need. Use the virtual keyboard for a week; again, you'll want to keep your journal handy to record your experiences and observations and to keep track of the problems you encounter — including the ones you solve and those you don't. (par. 21)

Slatin also recommends experimenting with the talking computer by installing a screen reader and putting away the mouse. This exercise enables students to "gain an understanding of what the Web and other applications are like as *auditory* experiences for people who are blind" (par. 22). Screen readers are available at no charge at < www.gwmicro.com > and < www.freedomscientific.com >.

(7a)   **FOR TEACHING: EMAIL ETIQUETTE**

In order to establish the ground rules for online communication in your class, review the guidelines in *Handbook* Chapter 7 as a group. You might also include a list of specific policies in your syllabus. Patrick Sullivan provides an excellent example of such a list of email etiquette in "Reimagining Class Discussion in the Age of the Internet" and urges teachers to "establish a strong online netiquette policy":

> Establishing such a policy is essential for creating a learning environment where students feel safe and comfortable enough to share their ideas and feelings. . . . It is important to establish ground rules about class discussion to ensure that conversations will not be confrontational, competitive, or unnecessarily argumentative. Some level of conflict is, of course, usually desirable in a class discussion, but teachers who hope to create a positive class environment online need to make it very clear that class discussions will also be collaborative in nature and collegial in tone. (401–02)

In addition, you can model appropriate email style, tone, content, and use in your own correspondence with students.

FOR COLLABORATIVE WORK: EMAIL ETIQUETTE

(7a)

Ask students to work in small groups to draw up a description of the ways in which email and listserv postings seem to differ from postal letters and from the academic writing they do for most of their classes. You can use their small group reports to generate a discussion about netiquette and about issues of style in different genres of writing.

FOR MULTILINGUAL WRITERS: EMAIL

(7a)

Spend some time in class discussing the new digital dialogue found in Internet chat rooms, which may be hard for multilingual writers to follow. "To save time typing, chat room visitors and instant messaging users scrimp on the keystrokes to produce abbreviations for a variety of phrases and actions," explains *Telegraph Herald* writer Erik Hogstrom. This shorthand manifests itself in acronyms such as IDG (I don't get it), BBL (be back later), CMIIW (correct me if I'm wrong), and *VEG* (very evil grin).

Semicolons also have come to figure prominently in the newest of writing genres, e-mail correspondence. A semicolon is an essential component in the wink or smirk: ;-).
—Julia Keller

FOR TEACHING: WORD PROCESSING

(7b)

Ask students to respond briefly to the following questions:

1. When you are writing on a computer, how often do you "save"?
2. Do you print out copies of each draft of an assignment? Why, or why not?
3. Do you keep an extra copy of your assignments on a floppy disc?
4. When you save documents, do you use a folder system to keep related pieces of writing separate from others? For example, do you have folders for English assignments, history assignments, family correspondence, or other such categories?
5. Do you use your spell-checker consistently? If possible, have you personalized it to include words you use frequently?

You can use student responses to these questions to lead a discussion on how to use the computer most efficiently — and to save a lot of headaches.

TEACHING WITH TECHNOLOGY: WORD PROCESSING

(7b)

Roger Ebert, discussing the differences between writing on a typewriter and writing using a word processor, describes how using technology has become an inherent part of his composition process:

The old L.C. Smith sat ignored, except for addressing envelopes. Since then, on a series of computers, I have written so many words that the act of writing and the act of word processing have become the same thing. I realized that the computer keyboard is now an extension of my mind.

Begin a dialogue in class with your students about the way they write: Do they compose primarily on a computer? Do they write rough drafts with a word processor? How many still write down ideas and first attempts with pen and paper?

I have keyboarded in so many e-mails, so many forum messages, so many arguments and replies, that I instinctively think of this activity as a conversation.
— ROGER EBERT

If you are in a technology classroom, you might also experiment with in-class writing prompts. Have students first respond to a prompt through a class discussion list at the start of class and then take a moment to comment on another person's response. You'll find that writing with word processors can get the thinking-through-writing process started for most students, since their primary mode of composition is now through technology. Consult Sarah R. Wakefield's comparative study of mediated and traditional discussions for more evidence that word processing can work as a communication tool in the writing classroom.

(7b)   FOR MULTILINGUAL WRITERS: WORD PROCESSING

Students familiar with many languages may have various defaults built into their keyboard preferences. They may also be particularly concerned by the auto-grammar function of popular programs such as Microsoft Word. You can encourage students to disable these functions so that they focus on the writing process and save the editing for later. Have them work with the computer staff in their dorms or residence halls to set up the preferences on their computers to work best for their own approach to writing.

In addition, alert students to technologies that enable them to write electronically in their own language. Apostolos Syropoulos describes a modern typesetting tool called Omega that enables Cherokee, Inuktitut, and Cree students to compose texts on computers. Omega is freely available from the Comprehensive TeX Archive Network (CTAN), and other technology syllabaries are worth investigating for use in your classes.

(7b)   FOR TEACHING: WORD PROCESSING

Remind your students to save their work often and in various forms. This includes backing up files on a remote server and printing out hard copies of drafts to keep in course folders. Another way to prevent loss of word-processed work is to have students email or send files to each other. They can collaborate in a shared file system. You can integrate this safety measure as part of your peer-review guidelines. Students can open a peer's document and use the "Comment" feature of Microsoft Word to provide feedback.

"Computer Haiku"
What if, instead of
cryptic, geeky text, your
computer gave error
messages in haiku . . .

Having been erased,
The document you're
seeking
Must now be retyped.

Rather than a beep
Or a rude error
message,
These words: "File not
found."

Windows NT has
crashed.
I am the Blue Screen of
Death.
No one hears your
screams.

■ **USEFUL READINGS**

Anson, Chris M. "Distant Voices: Teaching Writing in a Culture of Technology." *CE* 61.3 (1999): 261–80. An overview of how teaching writing has changed with the emergence of technology-enhanced classrooms.

Belcher, Diane D. "Authentic Interaction in a Virtual Classroom: Leveling the Playing Field in a Graduate Seminar." *Computers and Composition* 16 (1999): 253–67. Belcher presents her experimentation with an ESL composition teaching methods class in which multilingual students in an electronic discussion list participated with entries of greater length and reflection than they would have in conventional oral communication in class.

Duffelmeyer, Barbara Blakely. "Critical Computer Literacy: Computers in First-Year Composition as Topic and Environment." *Computers and Composition* 18 (Summer 2002). Online at < http://corax.cwrl.utexas.edu/cac/Current_Issue /dufflemeyer.html >. Duffelmeyer offers a perspective on first-year students' computer literacy by examining their attitudes toward technology as well as the influence of cultural assumptions about technology.

Ebert, Roger. "In Cyberspace, Writing Is a Performance." *Yahoo Internet Life Magazine* Mar. 2002. Online at < http://www.yil.com/columns/column.asp?columnist =ebert&date=020301&page=01 >. Ebert uses this regular column to describe his writing process.

Hogstrom, Erik. "Bite-size Jargon: Internet Conversations Chock Full of Acronyms." *Telegraph Herald* 10 Mar. 2002: D10.

Irvin, L. Lennie. "The Shared Discourse of the Networked Computer Classroom." *TETYC* 26.4 (1999): 372–79. Irvin argues that networked classrooms offer a number of opportunities for more effective writing instruction.

Selfe, Cynthia. "Technology and Literacy: A Story about the Perils of Not Paying Attention." *CCC* 50 (1999): 411–36. In the 1997 *CCCC* Chair's Address, Selfe cautions teachers to attend to the structural dynamics of computer usage that can perpetuate gender and racial inequities.

Slatin, John. "The Imagination Gap: Making Web-based Instructional Resources Accessible to Students and Colleagues with Disabilities." *Currents in Electronic Literacy* 6 (Spring 2002). Online at < http://www.cwrl.utexas.edu/currents /spring02/slatin.html >. Slatin reminds teachers of their legal and ethical obligations to make their Web materials accessible to students with disabilities; he also suggests excellent group activities for raising student awareness of universal design.

Sullivan, Patrick. "Reimagining Class Discussion in the Age of the Internet." *TETYC* 29.4 (2002): 393–410. In this comprehensive assessment of approaches to class discussion and the difficulties presented by conventional classrooms, Sullivan looks to networked environments as reconfiguring class discussion to produce a collaborative learning environment.

Syropoulos, Apostolos. "Typesetting Native American Languages." *Journal of Electronic Publishing* 8.1 (2002). Online at < http://www.press.umich.edu/jep/08 -01/syropoulos.html >. Syropoulos has created software that can typeset the syllabaries used in the Cherokee, Inuktitut, and Cree languages and thereby facilitate students' writing in their own languages.

Wakefield, Sarah R. "Comparing Traditional and Computer-assisted Composition Classrooms." *Currents in Electronic Literacy* 6 (Spring 2002). Online at <http:// www.cwrl.utexas.edu/currents/spring02/wakefield.html>. A revealing examination of two composition courses, one taught in a traditional classroom and the other in a computer classroom.

■ **USEFUL WEB SITES**

Alliance for Computers and Writing

http://english.ttu.edu/acw

The Alliance for Computers and Writing is a national, nonprofit organization committed to supporting teachers at all levels of instruction in their intelligent, theory-based use of computers in writing instruction. Its operating principle is that writing teachers will provide the shared knowledge necessary for doing their job well if someone gives them the means to share that knowledge.

Interpersonal Computing and Technology Journal

http://jan.ucc.nau.edu/~ipct-j

Focusing on computer-mediated communication, this journal provides articles on the use of computers and technology in educational settings.

Journal of Electronic Publishing

http://www.press.umich.edu/jep

A host of articles on how writing has changed, on multimedia as informative medium, and on various forms of electronic communication.

▼ Considering Document Design

8

Good visual design complements good writing; it does not replace it. Together writing and design are part of finding the best available means to communicate with readers.

– SUSAN HILLIGOSS

When addressing an audience, a speaker is judged visually and aurally. The speaker's appearance, tone of voice, the degree to which he or she meets the audience's eyes, all create an impression. Our rhetorical sense tells us that we ought to dress appropriately when we go before a committee to be interviewed for a scholarship. Classical rhetoricians viewed this aspect of our behavior as one aspect of rhetoric's five arts or canons, *actio* (or *pronunciatio*), which we translate today as "delivery."

In classical rhetoric, *actio* referred exclusively to the delivery of a speech to an audience. In our literate culture, however, rhetoric must also include written communication, where the audience is removed from the writer's immediate proximity. The writer has a different set of cues than the speaker on which to rely to get his or her image across to the reader. Some primary cues, of course, must come from the writing itself: what it says, how it presents the writer's ideas and feelings, how it reflects him or her. But increasingly in this digital age, the visual rhetoric of documents is taking center stage. Thus, today, students *and* instructors need to pay special attention to the elements of design that add so much to the effectiveness of print documents.

For many instructors of writing, it has been all too easy to neglect *delivery*, which has long been cut out of the rhetorical tradition. Yet *actio* is of great importance to students' writing and may well become more so in the future. You should consider the importance of such issues to your own writing and share your thoughts with students. Also, you need to make very clear your requirements concerning visual rhetoric — perhaps even spelling them out in your syllabus.

FOR TEACHING: DOCUMENT DESIGN

In a recent issue of *College English*, Craig Stroupe argues that English studies "needs to decide not only whether to embrace the teaching of visual and information design in addition to verbal production, which some of the more marginalized elements of English Studies have already done, but, more fundamentally, whether to confront its customary cultural attitudes toward visual discourses and their insinuation into verbal texts" (608). Similarly, teachers in writing classes need to confront the idea that visual images are subordinate to the verbal, and that they serve as decoration to the true heart of the text that lies in its prose.

You can alert students to these preconceptions by asking them to take short articles from magazines and campus newspapers and analyze how the texts function when paired with visual images. How do placement, color, size, and relationality affect the power of persuasion inherent in visual-verbal combinations? Have students draw up a brief list of "visual rhetoric" criteria on which to evaluate the design of texts containing images. Then ask them to experiment with manipulating the images: What happens when a different image is used in conjunction with a text? How does changing the visual structure produce a change in rhetorical meaning?

(8a)

FOR TEACHING: CREATING A VISUAL STRUCTURE

Ask students to discuss their options for document design. How many students have their own computer and printer? How many share with a roommate? Does the university library have a computing center, available to all enrolled students? Does your school have a writing center that is networked? Does the university community offer a variety of computing and printing services where students can bring their computer discs? The students will be a rich source of information and advice for one another — as well as for the instructor.

(8a)

ATTENDING TO DISABILITIES: CREATING A VISUAL STRUCTURE

When considering document design — especially with the use of technology — it is important to keep all members of an audience in mind. Invite students to break from their standardized way of conceptualizing particular audience or class members. Often this means reconsidering peers with disabilities as group members with individual strengths, not weaknesses. John Slatin describes this paradigm shift in terms of an act of imagination:

> I become more convinced each day that practicing accessibility means closing the imagination gap that separates most people from people with disabilities. It means *imagining disability*, and working at it long enough to get over the first shock of being *un*able to do what you're accustomed to doing in the way you're accustomed to doing it — long enough so that you begin to find solutions and workarounds, long enough so that you can begin to tell the difference between good design and bad design, between things that you can't do because you haven't learned how to do them yet and things that you can't do because there's no way for a person in your (imagined) circumstances to do them. (par. 16)

When teaching students to create a visual structure, encourage them to use their imaginations and find solutions to include all audience members, no matter what their functional limitations (sight, hearing, or movement). Slatin's article offers a host of resources to help you do so.

FOR COLLABORATIVE WORK: CREATING A VISUAL STRUCTURE   **(8a)** ....

Ask students to work in small groups to share information about their use of layout and design features of their word-processing systems and to prepare a brief report for the class on "the top ten best layout and design features available." After the groups report, you can use the information they provide to discuss the aesthetics of document design and to get them thinking, along with you, about which design features are most appropriate — and which ones are inappropriate — for most of their college writing assignments.

On Document Design

In "*Actio:* A Rhetoric of Manuscripts," Robert Connors covers such document design concerns as "Type and Typefaces," "Paper," "Typography and Layout," and some "Minor Considerations." His overview ends with the following reminder regarding the powers — and limits — of any document design:

The rhetoric of manuscripts is a very small part of the entire rhetorical presentation of a writer. At its best, *actio* effaces itself and allows readers to concentrate on comprehension, aware only that the texts they hold are pleasant to the eye and to the touch. The most wonderful manuscript, however, cannot turn a poor piece of writing into a good one or make a vacuous essay meaningful. The best that the suggestions here can do is prevent a good piece of writing from being sabotaged by silly or careless physical presentation. Like speakers, who are scrutinized as soon as they walk out onto the platform, writers are being sized up as soon as their manuscripts fall from a manila envelope or are pulled from a pile. Attention to the tenets of *actio* can make certain that both writer and speaker are able to present their messages in the most effective way. (76)

Paragraph breaks are also an element of *actio*. H. W. Fowler writes, "Paragraphing is also a matter of the eye. A reader will address himself more readily to his task if he sees from the start that he will have breathing-spaces from time to time than if what is before him looks like a marathon course" (434–35). These principles are even more important in online documents, where space is at a premium.

(8c) FOR MULTILINGUAL WRITERS: USING HEADINGS

Research in cognitive psychology has shown that breaking a document into sections through the use of headings helps readers follow and assimilate the text's meaning more easily. This is especially true for multilingual writers who may have difficulty wading through a long, unbroken essay. Encourage your students to incorporate visual design elements such as headings to signal turns in the argument or new sections in the essay.

(8d) TEACHING WITH TECHNOLOGY: USING VISUALS

According to Brian Krebs, the Ninth Circuit Court of Appeals ruled in February 2002 that "while Web sites may legally reproduce and post 'thumbnail' versions of copyrighted photographs, displaying full-sized copies of the images violates artists' exclusive right to display their own works" (par. 1). At stake was a technological technique called "framing" or "inlinking" that imports images and displays them in full size in the new browser window. Such an appropriation of images is not considered "fair use" and thus violates copyright law. Let your students know about this new consequence of using technology to incorporate images in their writing, particularly if they cut and paste images from the Web.

ATTENDING TO DISABILITIES: USING VISUALS   **(8d)**

John Slatin's suggestion for collaborative work provides a way for you to attend to disabilities in your classroom at the same time that you develop all students' writing and production proficiencies. Ask students to assess a group Web page for its visual elements and provide an alternative that would help disabled students access the content. Slatin writes:

> Divide the class into three groups: Art, Charts and Graphs, and News. Assign each group an appropriate image (a work of art, a recent news photo, a chart or graph presenting statistical information, etc.). Then further divide each group into pairs or trios. Each pair or trio should write ALT [alternative] text and a LONGDESC [long description] for the assigned image, and create a Web page that presents the image plus associated text. Students can evaluate each other's descriptions and alternatives, discussing how or whether different kinds of images call for different kinds of textual alternatives. In a subsequent activity, students would incorporate the image and its associated text into a more complex page design that includes navigation links, on-screen text, etc. Students can then discuss how the changing contexts created by these different designs affect their judgment about how to write text alternatives. (par. 28)

FOR COLLABORATIVE WORK: USING VISUALS   **(8d)**

As part of their next writing assignment, ask students to include a legitimate and significant visual of some kind, labeled appropriately, according to the guidelines in section 8d of the *Handbook*. Before allowing your students to hand in the final drafts of their papers, have them exchange these drafts for one final peer response, focusing purely on *actio*. In order to ensure that your students bring in a final typed draft, don't tell them ahead of time that these drafts will be reviewed. Provide each student with a pencil and eraser. Proofreading marks should be made in pencil lightly so that the author of the paper can erase them, if he or she chooses. It is important that your students realize that making or not making the suggested corrections is their choice. If a student finds substantial changes need to be made, then permit him or her to turn the paper in the next day.

··· (8e)

FOR TEACHING: SAMPLE DOCUMENTS

Ask students to bring in various documents that they've received in other classes or gotten through groups they belong to. They may want to break into their groups to analyze the design of each document, deciding what features make for successful or unsuccessful "delivery" of information. They also may want to consider if the document design enhanced a mediocre or an already strong piece of information.

■ **USEFUL READINGS**

Berger, Arthur A. *Seeing Is Believing: An Introduction to Visual Communication.* 2nd ed. Mountain View: Mayfield P, 1998. Berger demonstrates the central role that visual phenomena play in our lives, arguing that our visual experiences are tied to our intellectual and emotional ones.

Connors, Robert J. *"Actio:* A Rhetoric of Manuscripts." *Rhetoric Review* 2 (1983): 64–73. Connors equates manuscript preparation with the last of the five canons of rhetoric. He discusses the rhetorical effects of typefaces, paper, and format.

Fowler, H. W. *A Dictionary of Modern English Usage.* 2nd ed. Rev. and ed. Sir Ernest Gowers. New York: Oxford UP, 1965.

Fox, Roy F., ed. *Images in Language, Media, and Mind.* Urbana: NCTE, 1994. The essays in this book demonstrate and examine the ways in which we create social meaning by interacting with images in areas ranging from teaching to politics to advertising to sexuality. Classroom implications and specific teaching strategies are introduced throughout, with the underlying thesis that "we can no longer separate visual literacy from verbal literacy, that we must treat word and image equally and simultaneously."

Garrett-Petts, Will F., and Donald Lawrence, eds. *Integrating Visual and Verbal Literacies.* Winnipeg, Manitoba: Inkshed, 1996. The essays in this collection offer various approaches to using multimedia literacies in the classroom; the editors contend that as technology makes the combination of image, text, and other media more accessible, the gap between authors and readers of these visual texts will diminish, and the roles of instructor and student will similarly change as classroom and other texts become interactive ones.

Hilligoss, Susan. *Visual Communication: A Writer's Guide.* 2nd ed. New York: Longman, 2002. A short, instructional guide on the mechanics of visual design.

Krebs, Brian. "Court Rules 'Thumbnail' Images OK, Full-Sized Copies Not." *Newsbytes* 7 (Feb. 2002). Rpt. online at <http://www.computeruser.com/news/02/02/09/news3.html>. A brief on the court decision concerning copyright law on the Internet.

Reynolds, John Frederick, ed. *Rhetorical Memory and Delivery: Classical Concepts for Contemporary Composition and Communication.* Hillsdale: Lawrence Erlbaum, 1993. Especially useful for this chapter might be an update of Robert Connors's *"Actio,"* listed on the previous page.

Shriver, Karen. "What Is Document Design?" *Dynamics in Document Design: Creating Texts for Readers.* New York: Wiley, 1997. 1-11. A discussion of terminology for document design.

Slatin, John. "The Imagination Gap: Making Web-based Instructional Resources Accessible to Students and Colleagues with Disabilities." *Currents in Electronic Literacy* 6 (Spring 2002). Online at <http://www.cwrl.utexas.edu/currents/spring02/slatin.html>. Slatin reminds teachers of their legal and ethical obligations to make their Web materials accessible to students with disabilities; he also suggests excellent group activities for raising student awareness of universal design.

Stafford, Barbara Maria, ed. *Good Looking: Essays on the Virtue of Images.* Cambridge: MIT P, 1998. Stafford argues for an "overarching and innovative imaging discipline," one that crosses disciplinary boundaries and continually questions the relations between words and images in all areas of society and all facets of perception. She urges a pragmatic, case-based approach to understanding our cognitive response to imagery, one that recognizes the complexity that emerges along with new and newly converging media technologies.

Stroupe, Craig. "Visualizing English: Recognizing the Hybrid Literacy of Visual and Verbal Authorship on the Web." *CE* 62.5 (May 2000): 607-32. Stroupe questions our ideological preference for the verbal text.

■ **USEFUL WEB SITES**

Graphion's Online Type Museum

http://graphion.com/museum

This site provides information about the history and practice of typesetting, including good advice about indenting, using capitals, and spacing. The site's glossary of typographic terms offers a good starting point for anyone interested in design and layout both in print and online.

Yahoo! Computers and Internet: Graphics

http://dir.yahoo.com/computers_and_internet/graphics

This is a good source for links to clip art and other graphics.

9 ▼ Creating Web Texts

Increasingly, for many of us, the basic document is a Web page or, less frequently, a CD-ROM — what I will call an e-document. . . . Now the challenge is to express [our] dynamic, multidimensional, world in a virtual, multidimensional and dynamic medium. Many of us now inhabit the new virtual world, but we still act and write as though we were permanent residents of Flatland.

– Lawrence M. Hinman, "Escaping from Flatland: Multimedia Authoring"

In his essay "Escaping from Flatland," Hinman goes on to say that the new dynamic, interactive, multimedia-filled Web page has led him to realize that "I no longer write as well as I used to. The medium has changed, and now I realize there are areas of writing in which I am less skilled." Like Hinman, most teachers of writing learned to write a text that was composed solely of words. The last decade, however, has brought the changed medium Hinman talks about, and students are making projector-based presentations, Web pages, CD-ROMs, videos, all sorts of multimedia "writing." While conventions to guide writers in these new forms are evolving, teachers need to become keen observers, taking note of features we find most effective in Web texts and beginning the hard work of creating a pedagogy to encompass them.

At the same time, the development of Web texts should not be limited to student writers. As Sheila Offman Gersch reminds us, we can dramatically revitalize and improve our pedagogy through rhetorically sound Web texts that engage and educate our student audience:

> Teachers . . . can use the Internet to link their students to other classes to work collaboratively to further enrich any topic they are learning. This creates the "shared learning" environment around classroom instruction. (par. 8)

On Hypertext

In "Hypertext and the Rhetorical Canon," Jay David Bolter helps us understand the difference between mere word processing and hypertext, with hypertext never being "finally" delivered, an unusual idea of an ever-in-process product for those of us trained on typewriters. Bolter writes:

> Although word processing remains the most popular use of the personal computer, it is not fully electronic writing. The word processor does demonstrate some of the qualities that the computer can lend to writing: A document in a word processor is flexible, changeable up to the time of printing. But the goal of word processing is still to produce attractive printed output. The flexibility exists only during the process of composition. Once the document is put on paper, it is no more fluid than any other printed text, and the reader of the document still confronts a fixed and finished structure of words. And because the result will be a traditional, fixed structure, writers using the word processor still conceive of their documents in traditional rhetorical terms. With the word processor the writing process has changed, but the product has not. A more significant change occurs when the computer is used both to create and to present electronic text. When a text is written to be read on the computer screen, then both writer and reader can take advantage of the flexibility of the new medium. A text that is meant to be read at the computer no longer needs to have a single, linear presentation. It can instead consist of topical units (paragraphs, sections, chapters) that are related in a variety of ways. This structure of topics is then offered to the reader, who can decide which topics to view and in what order. An electronic text that is in this sense topical and interactive is called a *hypertext*. It is hypertext, not word processing, that fully exploits the computer as a new technology for reading and writing. (97–98)

In *Digital Literacy,* Paul Gilster provides another perspective, commenting on the multimedia capabilities of hypertext:

> What is novel is the ability to connect everything from sound files to animation to moving video to textual documents within a single frame, a so-called page of information. We can do this because computers can digitize these forms of media; to a computer, a file is a file, so that we can connect to a movie clip with the same point-and-click techniques we use to access a text file. When we do this, we move beyond the bounds of pure hypertext into the realm of a far more facile beast called *hypermedia*. The underlying computer functions remain the same, but the kind of information we pull in with our browsers changes. For all practical purposes, in today's Web the terms *hypertext* and *hypermedia* have become synonymous, although we can always call upon the distinction between text and other forms of media when there is need to make a specific point. (132)

(9a)

TEACHING WITH TECHNOLOGY: FEATURES OF WEB TEXTS

Gilster does a fine job of alerting readers to the powerful rhetoric of hypertext, including its central paradox: "it establishes links to banks of information, leading to the assumption that ideas are always backed by evidence. [But] a hypertext discussion can be *manipulated* by the choice of those links. What appear to be inevitable connections to related facts are actually *choices* made by page designers whose views are reflected in their selection of links."

To help your students grasp this principle, ask them to go to a commercial Web site and study its links, reporting back to the class on what those links include, in what ways they are "slanted," and what links are obviously *not* included. Gilster uses the example for Asia Inc. Online at <www.asia-inc.com> to show the ways in which choices regarding page layout and links are overwhelmingly pro-Asia. As a person looking for reliable information on Asian investments, Gilster understandably questions what has been carefully excluded from this site.

(9b)

ATTENDING TO DISABILITIES: PLANNING WEB TEXTS

Like efforts organized to break barriers such as "Whites Only" and "Men Only," the disability rights movement has resulted from people coming together in ways that allow them to compare experiences and forge relationships. Crucial to the movement's success is access to information and communication through technologies such as telecaptioners, TTY devices for telephones, voice-recognition systems, voice synthesizers, screen readers, and computers.
–American History Web Site on Disabilities

In "The Imagination Gap," John Slatin reminds us that we need to teach universal design when instructing students the step-by-step process of creating Web texts:

> None of us would knowingly build a course Web site that students of color, or students who are women, or students who are men, would be unable to use simply by virtue of their racial or ethnic status or their gender. It should be equally unthinkable for us to design Web resources for our classes that are inaccessible to students or colleagues with disabilities simply because of those disabilities. (par. 1)

Slatin suggests the following techniques that you can use in your classroom as you work to create Web texts:

- The Mouseless Week (shifting from mouse to keyboard)
- Week of No Images (Web pages from a blind person's perspective)
- The Great Blow Up (loss of context for those with limited vision)
- The Virtual Keyboard (for those who can't use voice or hands)
- Talking Computer (the Web as an auditory experience)

Slatin concludes that these exercises can help students understand the importance of universal design and accessibility when working with computers. But it can also bring students together to brainstorm the best possible approach — and medium — for their word-processing projects in mediated environments.

FOR TEACHING: PLANNING WEB TEXTS

(9b)

As they plan their Web texts, ask students to fill out a brief form that can help them carry out an ongoing evaluation of their plan:

If John Dewey were alive today, he'd be a webhead.
— PESHE KURILOFF

Title of my Web text or site

Purpose of my Web text or site

The personality I want my Web text to have

Audiences for my Web site

Necessary links for my Web text (and why they are necessary)

FOR COLLABORATIVE WORK: MAPPING WEB TEXTS

(9c)

Ask students to work in pairs or groups of three to lay out or "storyboard" plans for a Web text. Suggest that they use index cards, one to represent the homepage and another for each major page of the text that readers can access from the homepage. For this early planning exercise, ask them to organize the Web site hierarchically — putting the homepage at the top and then arranging the additional pages below. One goal of this exercise is to ask students to show the relationship of each page to the other pages. Finally, ask them to bring their storyboard plan to class for discussion and criticism.

On Designing Web Texts

(9d)

In their book, *Web Style Guide: Basic Design Principles for Creating Web Sites,* Patrick Lynch and Sarah Horton talk extensively about "visual logic," showing how spatial organization of text and graphics on Web pages can "engage readers with graphic impact, direct their attention, prioritize the information they see, and make their interactions with your Web site more enjoyable and efficient." Students can profit from Lynch and Horton's advice by aiming to create a consistent and memorable visual hierarchy that emphasizes important elements and organizes the content in ways that are predictable to most readers. Getting real readers to respond to their site design is thus of great importance, since this kind of user feedback will help in revision of the design.

(9f)

FOR TEACHING: USING VISUALS AND MULTIMEDIA

In the October 1999 special issue of *Syllabus Web: Useful Information on Technology Used to Enhance Education*, the editors discuss the benefits of multimedia and digital content on the Web:

> Today's classrooms have come alive with dynamic animations, simulations, and visualizations that help illustrate complex concepts. Through multimedia, instructors can present material that might be difficult or impractical to bring to the lab or lecture hall. And with more advanced Web technologies, such as Java applications, back-end databases, and streaming media, multimedia content resources can be leveraged online to support campus-based courses or to reach distant learners.

Model the best rhetorical practices of using visuals and multimedia in your teaching. This will inspire students to incorporate dynamic technological visualizations in their own Web texts.

Miriam Schacht, for example, nervous about teaching in a computer-assisted classroom for the first time, asked her students to create multimedia autobiographical Web texts as part of their final writing projects. She used the assignment to model possibilities to the students and turned her "lack of expertise" to pedagogical advantage by modeling the learning process as well. The success of this experiment manifests itself on many levels, as seen in the student projects available through her online article's hypertext.

(9f)

FOR MULTILINGUAL WRITERS: USING VISUALS AND MULTIMEDIA

Loretta Kasper argues in "Print, Film, and Hypertexts" that incorporating multimedia in your pedagogy increases learning for ESL students in three ways: it develops content-area knowledge, enhances linguistic proficiency, and increases overall motivation to learn and work in class.

> At the click of a mouse, hypertext resources present students with a diverse collection of authentic English language texts dealing with a wide array of interdisciplinary topics, and at each Web page link, students have the advantage of reading print texts with the benefit of immediate visual reinforcement

provided by pictures and/or slide shows, facilitating the collaborative effects of print and visual information processing. (408)

FOR TEACHING: CHECKING OUT WEB SITES   **(9g)**

Ask students to bring printouts of two particularly effective and memorable personal homepages to class for comparison and discussion. Then, working in groups of three, students should look for design principles that characterize the most effective homepages. Ask each group to present a report to the class based on their findings.

FOR TEACHING: WRITING WEB TEXTS WITH HTML   **(9h)**

While some software programs now offer the option of saving documents as Hypertext Markup Language (HTML), most instructors of writing working in webbed environments think it is still wise for students to know the basics of HTML. Students should know that HTML is an evolving language and that there are several Web sites that give up-to-the-minute descriptions of changes to HTML. If you want students to experiment with hypertext, or to try designing their own homepage, taking the time to work through the basic HTML tags will pay off.

FOR COLLABORATIVE WORK: POSTING ASSIGNMENTS TO THE WEB   **(9i)**

Ask students to work in small groups to make a list of all the purposes for which they have gone online. (How often do they post assignments? share work? communicate ideas with others?) Use this information as the basis for a class discussion on how the Web affects their everyday lives.

TEACHING WITH TECHNOLOGY: RESOURCES

The Summer 2002 issue of *Kairos* offers an entire host of assignments concerning hypertext and Web texts. Patricia Ventura, for example, in her essay for *Kairos*, asks students to translate a written essay into what she calls a "Websay." Her purpose is to have students "examine the ways in which Web writing both differs from and resembles traditional writing so

Because the monitor serves so many purposes, it seems to me like a public space.
–ROGER EBERT

that you will be able to produce Web projects that take full advantage of this medium." To do so successfully, students need to consider carefully the elements of visual design. Ventura emphasizes that they need to "transform" not "transfer" their documents for the Web. Experiment with a similar exercise in your class before assigning a more complex Web text project.

■ **USEFUL READINGS**

Bolter, Jay David. "Hypertext and the Rhetorical Canon." *Essays on Rhetorical Memory and Delivery.* Ed. Fred Reynolds. Mahwah: Lawrence Erlbaum, 1993. 97–111.

Carbone, Nick. *English Online: A Student's Guide to the Internet and the World Wide Web.* 3rd ed. Boston: Houghton, 2000. This extremely clear and helpful volume is intended as a student's companion to working online. It is also of great help to instructors, especially for its careful explanation of how to enter the Internet and how to create a basic Web page.

Ferris, Sharmila Pixy. "Writing Electronically: The Effects of Computers on Traditional Writing." *Journal of Electronic Publishing* 8.1 (Aug. 2002). Online at <http://www.press.umich.edu/jep/08-01/ferris.html>. Ferris argues that electronic writing is an oral, collaborative process wherein "the reader becomes the author's partner in determining the meaning of the text."

Gersh, Sheila Offman. "Technology's Role in Creating the Shared-learning Environment." *Educator's Outlook* 1 Nov. 2001. Online at <http://www.techlearning.com/db_area/archives/WCE/archives/sheilag.htm>. Gersh details the new collaboration opportunities afforded to teachers, librarians, and students with the increased turn to electronic spaces for pedagogical work.

Gilster, Paul. *Digital Literacy.* New York: Wiley, 1997. Gilster brings his experience as a professional writer to bear in this extremely clear and readable study of the "thinking and survival skills new users need to make the Internet personally and professionally meaningful."

Haas, Christina. *Writing Technology: Studies on the Materiality of Literacy.* Mahwah: Lawrence Erlbaum, 1995. Haas's work examines how writing and technology constitute one another, closely examining the relationship between them. It challenges notions of technological transparency, demonstrating the ways in which writing is transformed by means of its inextricable link with technology.

Hinman, Lawrence M. "Escaping from Flatland: Multimedia Authoring." *Syllabus Magazine* <http://www.syllabus.com/syllmag.html> 13.3 (Oct. 1999). Online at <http://ethics.sandiego.edu/lmh/Papers/Escaping%20from%20Flatland.html>

Johnson, Steven. *Interface Culture: How New Technology Transforms the Way We Create and Communicate.* San Francisco: Harper, 1997. The chapter on "Links" is especially provocative.

Kalmbach, James Robert. *The Computer and the Page: Publishing, Technology, and the Classroom.* Norwood: Ablex, 1997. This book examines publishing as a social and rhetorical act, reflecting on the manner in which increasingly sophisticated technologies have brought more elaborate means of publication into the classroom. Kalmbach offers theoretical and pedagogical analyses of how these evolving social and technological regimes of publication have transformed the composition classroom.

Kasper, Loretta F. "Print, Film, and Hypertexts: A Multimedia Model for Discipline-based ESL Instruction." *TETYC* 26.4 (1999): 406–14. Kasper argues that using multimedia to present discipline-based content improves ESL instruction.

Lessig, Lawrence. *The Future of Ideas: The Fate of the Commons in a Connected World.* New York: Random, 2001. An assessment of how the creativity and innovation of the Internet are increasingly threatened by copyright law.

Lynch, Patrick J., and Sarah Horton. *Web Style Guide: Basic Design Principles for Creating Web Sites.* 2nd ed. New Haven: Yale UP, 2001. Lynch and Horton stress content and interface design for Web sites, with an eye toward rhetorical strategies. The book is a print version of their Web site: <http://info.med.yale.edu/caim/manual>.

Schacht, Miriam. "Converting to the Computer Classroom: Technology, Anxiety, and Web-based Autobiography Assignments." *Currents in Electronic Literacy* 6 (Spring 2002). Online at <http://www.cwrl.utexas.edu/currents/spring02/schacht.html>. One teacher eases her anxieties concerning teaching with technology by creating an autobiographical Web assignment.

Selfe, Cynthia, and Susan Hilligoss. *Literacy and Computers: The Complications of Teaching and Learning with Technology.* New York: MLA, 1994. This book explores the transformation of texts, language, and literacy that has accompanied the increasing use of computer-mediated discourse, particularly in the composition classroom.

Snyder, Illana, ed. *Page to Screen: Taking Literacy into the Electronic Era.* London: Routledge, 1998. This collection explores the "emerging literacies" accompanying the rising use of computers in the composition classroom.

Ventura, Patricia. "The Essay and the Websay." *Kairos* 7.2 (Summer 2002). Online at <http://english .ttu.edu/kairos/7.2/binder.html?sectiontwo/ventura/websay_assignment.htm>. Ventura's assignment details the purpose and necessary steps for transforming a traditional written essay into a Web text. The sample assignment topics provide excellent models for using visual images.

Yagelski, Robert P., and Sarah Powley. "Virtual Connections and Real Boundaries: Teaching Writing and Preparing Writing on the Internet." *Computers and Composition* 13:1 (1996): 25–36. The authors report on a case study of a course they taught collaboratively in Indiana and New York, bringing together high school student writers with undergraduate English majors, to give the university students "hands-on" experience with high school student writing and to provide the high school students with a wider audience for their writing.

■ USEFUL WEB SITES

Advice on Web Site Design

http://info.med.yale.edu/caim/manual/sites/site_design.html

This lengthy and highly detailed discussion of Web site design is part of Yale's Center for Advanced Instructional Media. It provides principles, liberally illustrated, of effective Web page design and includes a tutorial.

American History Exhibit

http://americanhistory.si.edu/disabilityrights/exhibit_technology.html

This Smithsonian Institution Web site explores the significant role of technology in bringing together people with disabilities, particularly with the presence of the Internet since the early 1990s.

Kairos: A Journal of Rhetoric, Technology, and Pedagogy

http://english.ttu.edu/kairos

For essays on working with the Web, see Lawrence Clark's "Staying Human in the Digital Age" (1.2), and the summer 2002 issue on technology, popular culture, and the art of teaching.

Pageresource.com

http://www.pageresource.com

This site provides HTML and javascript tutorials, articles on Web design, and free images.

Syllabus: Technology for Higher Education

http://www.syllabus.com

The Syllabus *Web site provides a repository of articles, columns, and advice on how to use technology to enhance education.*

Web Developer's Virtual Library

http://www.wdvl.com

This site includes tutorials for HTML and javascript, articles on Web authoring and design, and thousands of images and icons.

Making Oral and Multimedia Presentations

Talking and eloquence are not the same: to speak, and to speak well, are two things.
—BEN JONSON

At the same time that oral discourse has been growing in importance in our culture, attention to orality has waned in college courses and in the college curriculum. This situation is, however, now being reversed, as many colleges and universities move to include attention to speaking and to oral presentations in their general education curriculum requirements. As the students we surveyed who have used the *Handbook* told us over and over, they are being asked to give oral presentations in increasing numbers of classes. Students want and need help in responding to these demands.

New trends across the nation to incorporate multimedia presentations in the writing classroom also challenge us as teachers to reconsider our criteria for mastery and assessment in the first-year composition classroom. Alice Trupe raises this very issue in a *Kairos* article:

> The freshman essay and the research paper are vehicles through which students are expected to demonstrate their literacy. . . . Whereas these specialized genres for students have served as the measure of freshman writing ability for a hundred years, transformation of writing courses by computer technology is a recent phenomenon. Composition instructors first welcomed word processing because it facilitated production of the standard freshman essay. However, the move into electronic environments rapidly began to revolutionize classroom practices and genres. Today, the expanding possibilities for writing engendered through desktop publishing, email, Web-based bulletin boards, MOOs, Web page and other hypertext authoring, and presentation software show up the limitations the freshman essay imposes on thought and writing. (par. 2)

Moving from silence into speech is for the oppressed, the colonized, the exploited, and those who stand and struggle side by side a gesture of defiance that heals, that makes new life and new growth possible. It is that act of speech, of "talking back," that is no mere gesture of empty words, that is the expression of our movement from object to subject — the liberated voice.
— BELL HOOKS

Trupe goes on to argue that despite our reliance on new technologies in the writing classroom, we still look to the essay as the "limiting genre that most of us expect first-year writers to master." Consequently, while "we may encourage them to explore the possibilities of interactive computer environments . . . in the final analysis, the test of what students have learned through classroom activities often remains the plain vanilla, five-paragraph essay, since that is what is assessed for a grade" (par. 1–6).

As you design your course syllabus to include a multimedia component and a final presentation, consider how valuable these forms of "writing" will be to students in their future academic and professional careers. It often helps to motivate students by sharing your insight into the applicability of presentation skills. But also consider granting value to their work by readjusting your assessment criteria.

On Multimedia

The advent of the Internet and World Wide Web and the increasing affordability of programs like PowerPoint and DreamWeaver have highlighted the degree to which today's "writing" often combines media. Even before the Web, of course, what often appeared to be in one medium — a speech, let's say — was more accurately *multi*media: a televised speech and even a talk show host's monologue are delivered orally, but they have been previously written. And even the most traditional spoken lectures have long relied on illustrations that may include music, art, and other forms of media.

But these possibilities of multimedia create special challenges for writing instructors who must learn how to discover, and then pass on, the best advice about how to create multimedia presentations that are rhetorically effective. Chapter 10 of the *Handbook* is designed to help you and your students get started on working in and with these new discourses.

(10a)   **FOR MULTILINGUAL WRITERS: CONTRIBUTING TO CLASS DISCUSSIONS**

Most classes impose some form of class participation requirement on all students. But ESL students in particular may not yet be comfortable speaking out in class or sharing their ideas — which may be still evolving — with a group of their peers. As Jim Fredal writes in "Beyond the Fifth

Canon," our culture tends to ascribe certain qualities, values, and skills to people on the basis of their speaking, usually as these are seen to reflect "quality of mind" or "critical thinking" and moral values of relationship, sympathy, egotism, engagement, and so on. But these assumptions are not necessarily valid: great minds are not necessarily always highly articulate or eloquent. Poor speaking can mean lots of things besides poor thinking.

In addition, because speech — especially articulate, measured, orderly, progressive speech — is so highly valued, silence is devalued as a sign of boredom, laziness, confusion, stupidity, or aloofness. It may or may not reflect any of these things. How much one speaks and how often are heavily scripted by cultural expectations, with significant variations for gender, sexual, racial, ethnic, ability, and other differences. These expectations influence our estimations of students' abilities, but we don't think as much about, nor can we review carefully, what our students say in the same way as we can review what they write. Nor can we simply expect them to change in the space of ten (or sixteen) weeks, to match academic expectations (to talk more or in a certain way).

FOR TEACHING: BRIEF ORAL PRESENTATIONS

In "Town Meetings," Gerry Brookes recommends asking students to prepare to speak very briefly (three minutes) on a topic of concern to them. In "town meeting" sessions that occur once a week, two or three students make their presentations. After each one, Brookes says, the class always applauds. Then the teacher poses a series of questions designed to "allow people to suggest alternative points of view, to offer supporting evidence, or to point out misjudgments of audience, without breaking into open disagreement." This kind of controlled response to the presentations, Brookes argues, allows students and instructor to help the speaker even when they disagree passionately about what she or he has said. Brookes recommends writing response notes to each speaker instead of giving formal grades, using the notes as the basis for conferences, and "giving a bit of extra credit if the spoken text is especially good."

As an alternative activity, ask students to prepare two-minute introductions of themselves near the beginning of the term (ideally on the second day of class). After the introductions are over, use the remaining class time to talk about how our oral presentations of ourselves have important impacts. Ask students to think about what was most memorable about these introductions, about what techniques seemed particularly successful, and about what was most threatening about this situation. As a follow-up exercise, ask students to write a journal entry about what conclusions and/or lessons they could draw from the oral introductions about their own strengths and weaknesses as presenters.

.... **(10b)**

FOR TEACHING: CONSIDERING THE ASSIGNMENT, PURPOSE, AND AUDIENCE FOR PRESENTATIONS

Where's your spirit of innovation, of forging on, of damn-the-manual-full-speed-ahead?
— LOU FOURNIER

Before students get started on developing an oral or multimedia presentation, ask them to brainstorm about the assignment. Have them answer the following questions to get their ideas flowing:

- Who is the main audience? What would work best for this audience?
- What, above all, do you want your audience members to take away from the presentation?
- What are your strengths as a writer and a creative individual? public speaking? creative design? humor? clear explication?
- What do you want to learn from the process of creating a presentation? new skills in oral communication, effective ways of using PowerPoint, or practice for poster sessions?
- What should be most memorable in your presentation?
- What risks can you take?

.... **(10c2)**

ATTENDING TO DISABILITIES: USING VISUALS

A man's work is nothing but this slow trek to rediscover, through the detours of art, those two or three great and simple images in whose presence his heart first opened.
—ALBERT CAMUS

Emphasize to students that their visuals should augment the power of persuasion in their oral presentations, not just serve as decoration or distraction. At the same time, raise the issue of attending to disabilities when using visuals. For students who may have vision impairments, visuals may be difficult to see from across the room. If such visuals are produced through technological means, such as on a Web site or through a PowerPoint presentation, there are many alternative methods of communicating that information. Here are two examples:

- Images on posters and handouts can be converted through alternative format production technology and printed as raised images on special paper, allowing a visually impaired person to "feel" the drawing.

- Handouts or poster replicas can be translated into Braille or put on an audio-tape through text-to-speech technology.

FOR COLLABORATIVE WORK: PRACTICING THE ORAL PRESENTATION   **(10c3)**

Students will benefit greatly from working with one another to prepare and practice oral presentations. To help them get started on this work, group them in pairs or sets of three and allow them some class time to talk about their topics, to discuss their deadlines and time constraints, and to set up a schedule. Then ask them to meet out of class to hold group practice sessions. During these sessions, the listener(s) should take notes on three things: what they remember most vividly, what they don't understand, and what they need or want to hear more of. In order to encourage students to work seriously at these sessions, consider awarding some credit for this group work and ask them to write individual summaries of what they did during practice sessions, how the practices helped them, and what might be done to improve future practice sessions.

TEACHING WITH TECHNOLOGY: PEER RESPONSE

You may wish to ask students to evaluate one another's oral or multimedia presentations using an electronic peer-response form. Consider giving them a set of categories or some a rubric to guide their responses. For example, you could ask that they make comments on strategy (adaptation to audience, opening and closing, visual aids); content (supporting materials and language, clarity, line of argument, anticipating and answering objections); organization (overview of main points, signposting, main points); and delivery (eye contact, conversational style, voice quality, gestures).

After each presentation, allow for five minutes of interactive questions and answers. Then ask students to write a short electronic commentary on the presentation and post it to your class's listserv, Web bulletin-board space, or shared electronic list. The benefits of asking students to provide their evaluative comments online are that the speaker can download and print all the comments at once, you avoid having to photocopy and assemble slips of feedback, and all class members can see what others have written and can learn from those peer responses how to rethink their own presentation strategies.

(10d)   On Incorporating Multimedia into Oral Presentations

Great works are performed not by strength but by perseverance.
  –Samuel Johnson

Remind students that "multimedia" does not mean PowerPoint alone. Overheads, posters, handouts, props, and dramatic enactments can all be part of a multimedia presentation. Often students translate "multimedia" as "technology" and don't realize that a powerful presentation can be produced using simply a poster, a carefully constructed handout, or voice and gesture alone. Encouraging students to work on oral and multimedia presentations will also help foster their development as writers in multiple media, and hence to begin to see connections between genres. As James Inman, Rachel Hallberg, and Courtney Thayer argue, we need to ask our students to "imagine new and important connections between technology-rich and non-technological genres of writing" (par 6).

(10d)   FOR COLLABORATIVE WORK: EVALUATING MULTIMEDIA PRESENTATIONS

Ask your students to work together in small groups (of three or four) to evaluate the examples of multimedia presentations in 10d, using the guidelines given there. You might ask one group to concentrate on the slides from the PowerPoint presentation, a second group to examine the transparency, and a third group to evaluate the poster presentation. Then ask each group to report the results of their evaluation to the entire class. As a follow-up exercise, the class might work together to draw up a set of their own tips for creating successful multimedia presentations.

(10d)   FOR TEACHING: TESTING MULTIMEDIA DESIGNS

Professor Kitty Locker reminds instructors that "a design that looks pretty may or may not work for the audience." To see how designs work with actual audiences, Locker suggests asking students to get a reader to "test" the document they are designing, whether it is a homepage, a set of PowerPoint slides, a poster, or some other document that uses multimedia. As the reader uses and reads the document, Locker suggests that the student writer should:

• Ask the reader to "think aloud" while completing the task, saying what he or she is thinking and doing.

- Interrupt the reader at important points in the document, asking what he or she is thinking or feeling.
- Ask the reader to describe what he or she thinks of the document in retrospect.

After completing this exercise, students can bring in their results and work in groups to improve their use of multimedia.

■ **USEFUL READINGS**

Brookes, Gerry H. "Town Meetings: A Strategy for Including Speaking in a Writing Classroom." *CCC* 44 (Feb. 1993): 88–92. This piece contains an especially interesting discussion of how norms and conventions of public speaking reflect cultural values.

Brueggemann, Brenda. *Lend Me Your Ear: Rhetorical Construction of Deafness.* Washington: Gallaudet UP, 1999. Brueggemann's important text redefines "speech" and "orality," critiques what she terms "the will to speech," and presents compelling descriptions and analyses of powerful sign language presentations.

Dragga, Sam. "The Ethics of Delivery." *Rhetorical Memory and Delivery: Classical Concepts for Contemporary Composition and Communication.* Ed. John Frederick Reynolds. Mahwah: Lawrence Erlbaum, 1993. 79–95. Although this essay doesn't deal with oral presentations per se, it offers a particularly cogent discussion of how delivery can be manipulated and perceived. Dragga's discussion of charts and other visuals is also useful for information on the successful and ethical use of visual aids.

Ehninger, Douglas, Bruce E. Gronbeck, Ray E. McKerrow, and Alan H. Monroe. *Principles and Types of Speech Communication.* 14th ed. Boston: Allyn, 2003. This widely used textbook offers good advice on all aspects of public speaking. Particularly valuable is the "Speaker's Resource Book," a "collection of generally short presentations of materials especially relevant to some speaking situations or to particular speakers facing special problems."

Fredal, Jim. "Beyond the Fifth Canon: Rhetorical Constructions of Speech from Homer to Herder." Dissertation. Ohio State University, 1998. In this important study, Fredal uncovers the network of assumptions and ideologies inscribed in the Western world's "will to speech," focusing on Classical Greece and early Enlightenment Europe to illustrate his argument. This work will make all instructors of writing reconsider the definition of "speech" and its relationships to writing and to systems of value.

Garland, James C. "Advice to Beginning Physics Speakers." *Physics Today* (July 1991): 42–45. This is a witty and highly instructive address to science students on how to prepare for and deliver oral presentations.

Haas, Christina. *Writing Technology: Studies on the Materiality of Literacy*. Mahwah: Lawrence Erlbaum, 1995. Haas's work examines how writing and technology constitute one another, closely examining the relationship between them. It also challenges the notions of technological transparency, demonstrating the ways in which writing is transformed by means of its inextricable link with technology.

Hindle, Tim. *Making Presentations*. New York: DK Publishing, 1998. This small guide to communicating effectively offers practical strategies with clear visuals.

Inman, James A., Rachel Fields Hallberg, and Courtney Thayer. "Disney Promotion Poster Analysis: A Post-Technology Assignment." *Kairos* 7.2 (Summer 2002). Online at <http://english.ttu.edu/kairos/7.2/binder.html?sectiontwo/inman>. A discussion of multimedia projects that help students imagine new ways of writing in various technological and nontechnological environments.

Killingsworth, M. Jimmie. "Product and Process, Literacy and Orality: An Essay on Composition and Culture." *CCC* 44:1 (Feb. 1993): 26–39. Killingsworth explores the thesis that "just as the formulators of current traditionalism met the needs of their times—the nineteenth century with its burgeoning culture of literacy—so the advocates of process pedagogy face up to the demands of teaching writing in an age dominated by the nonprint media of mass culture."

Locker, Kitty. "Making Oral Presentations." *Business and Administrative Communication*. 4th ed. Homewood: Irwin, 1997. Although aimed primarily at those interested in business or technical communication, Locker's discussion of how to prepare for and deliver oral presentations provides valuable concrete advice for any student assigned to make an oral presentation.

Moss, Beverly J. "Creating a Community: Literacy Events in African-American Churches." *Literacy across Communities*. Ed. Beverly J. Moss. Creskill: Hampton, 1994. Chap. 5. Moss demonstrates how oral discourse functions in African American churches and relates this use of orality to students' home literacies, which are all too often undervalued in the academy.

Slatin, John. "The Imagination Gap: Making Web-based Instructional Resources Accessible to Students and Colleagues with Disabilities." *Currents in Electronic Literacy* 6 (Spring 2002). Online at <http://www.cwrl.utexas.edu/currents/spring02/slatin.html>.

Trupe, Alice L. "Academic Literacy in a Wired World: Redefining Genres for College Writing Courses." *Kairos* 7.2 (Summer 2002). Online at <http://english.ttu.edu/kairos/7.2/binder.html?sectionone/trupe/WiredWorld.htm>. Trupe explores what it means to write in a computer-mediated environment, examining the rhetorical features of emerging genres and what academic literacy means in a "wired world."

Welch, Kathleen. "Classical Rhetoric and Contemporary Rhetoric and Composition Studies: Electrifying Classical Rhetoric." *The Contemporary Reception of Clas-*

sical Rhetoric: Appropriations of Ancient Discourse. Mahwah: Lawrence Erlbaum, 1990. Chap. 6. Welch reviews the "orality/literacy debate" and relates issues of secondary orality to the contemporary technological revolution.

■ **USEFUL WEB SITES**

College Composition and Communication

http://www.ncte.org/ccc

The Web site for College Composition and Communication *online, with three different graphic interfaces, offers online versions of the journal. The "Related Links" page hosts a wealth of resources for teachers, including links to online journals and organizations.*

Kairos: A Journal of Rhetoric, Technology, and Pedagogy

http://english.ttu.edu/kairos

The Summer 2002 issue's special focus on technology, popular culture, and the art of teaching is particularly enlightening to teachers interested in designing syllabi and assignments for collaborating online and off.

Ohio State University's Fast Facts for Faculty

http://www.osu.edu/grants/dpg/fastfact

This Web site offers excellent advice for designing classes with attention to students with disabilities. Read about the latest technologies, pedagogical approaches, and universal design resources. Sharing this information with all your students will greatly improve the class climate and the quality of students' oral and multimedia presentations.

The Writing Instructor

http://flansburgh.english.purdue.edu/twi

This "networked journal and digital community for writers and teachers of writing" features essays, book reviews, writing activities, and online forms.

PART 3

CRITICAL THINKING
AND ARGUMENT

11 ▼ Analyzing Arguments

> *Responding to culture—clarifying, explicating, valorizing, translating, transforming, criticizing—is what artists everywhere do, especially writers involved in the founding of a new nation.*
>
> – TONI MORRISON

The classical period in Greece was long thought of as being characterized by stable values, social cohesion, and a unified cultural ideal, and thus for many years our conception of classical rhetoric held that it was primarily concerned with argument based on reasonable appeals made within a rational culture.

More recent scholarship has argued that the Western rhetorical tradition has been one of exclusion and agonism, that the classical period was not nearly as complacent and rational a world as earlier scholars thought, and that our view of classical rhetoric was only a partial one. Following some of the ideas of that group of early Greek thinkers known as the sophists, many contemporary rhetoricians view humankind as "symbol-using animals" who live in a fragmented world mediated by and through language. In *A Rhetoric of Motives,* philosopher and critic Kenneth Burke refers to that society when he writes that "rhetoric is concerned with Babel after the Fall" (23) and goes on to substantiate the modern goal of rhetoric as "communication," differing from the traditional goal of combative or coercive "persuasion": "Wherever there is persuasion, there is rhetoric. And wherever there is 'meaning,' there is 'persuasion'" (127).

In *Modern Dogma and the Rhetoric of Assent,* Wayne Booth builds on the work of Burke, positing that good rhetoric is "the art of discovering good reasons, finding what really warrants assent because any reasonable person ought to be persuaded by what has been said" (xiv).

Although good reasons *ought* to guarantee assent, sometimes they do not, for each person finds a reason to believe or not. Sometimes, the reason is not a rational one. However, in *Classical Rhetoric for the Modern Student* Edward P. J. Corbett echoes Aristotle:

> Rationality is humanity's essential characteristic. It is what makes people human and differentiates them from other animals. Ideally, reason should dominate all of people's thinking and actions, but actually, they are often influenced by passions and prejudices and customs. To say that people often respond to irrational motives is not to say that they never listen to the voice of reason. We must have faith not only that people are capable of ordering their lives by the dictates of reason but that most of the time they are disposed to do so. (37)

Speech professors Sonja Foss and Cindy Griffin expand the scope of rhetoric still further — to include forms of discourse that do not involve the intent to change the behavior or beliefs of others and are not solely tied to reason. Their 1993 presentation to the Speech Communication Association offers a new taxonomy that includes rhetorics of conquest, conversion, advice, and invitation. The first three categories involve a conscious intent to persuade that is not present in the fourth.

Invitational rhetoric proposes to create an environment that enables a transformation, should individuals choose to change. The communicative options of invitational rhetoric are (1) modeling, (2) the creation of external conditions for change, and (3) a belief that audience and rhetor are equal, both expert in their own lives.

Students need guidance in exploring the uses of argument, and in challenging the traditional view of argument as only about winning.

TEACHING WITH TECHNOLOGY: RECOGNIZING ARGUMENT   **(11a)** ....

Building on students' familiarity with the Internet, ask them in small groups to identify three of their favorite Web sites. Each group should select two Web sites from the batch to present to the class. Perhaps one Web site is quite obviously an argument. But the second one may be a much more subtle form of persuasion. What is the Web site's message, pitch, or purpose? How is it selling something, convincing the audience to believe something, or making a claim? Project the selected Web sites up on a projector screen for the entire class to analyze. Let the students present the major features of argument in each Web text.

ATTENDING TO DISABILITIES: ANALYZING ARGUMENTS

You might want to begin your class by asking students whether they are auditory, visual, or hands-on learners. Then, rather than relying on the label "learning disabled," emphasize the strengths in a student's learning style and help locate the resources available to maximize that particular approach to learning. Find out whether any students have particular needs that might be served by such aides as screen readers, lecture note-takers, recording devices, video magnifiers, or ergonomic work stations. The on-campus disability resource center often has technology to help compensate for different learning styles and this can be particularly helpful when you are teaching students about analyzing arguments.

For more information on attending to disabilities in the teaching of argument, see the Disability Studies in the Humanities Web site at the end of this chapter.

(11b)

FOR COLLABORATIVE WORK: RECOGNIZING ARGUMENT

In section 11b of the *Handbook* provides pertinent questions that help writers explore and develop a topic. Break the class into groups and have them answer these questions as they relate to "A Curse and a Blessing," the student essay in 11h. These are the kinds of questions that the group will want to use again and again as they write essays and review the essays of the other group members, all through the term.

(11c)

FOR MULTILINGUAL WRITERS: RECOGNIZING CULTURAL CONTEXTS

In *Decoding ESL,* Amy Tucker articulates the problems for our students who are "Trying to Handle Two Languages at Once," her opening chapter. Throughout her book, Tucker tries to take the point of view of our ESL students rather than the more familiar stance of the instructor. And in the manner of Mina Shaughnessy, Tucker helps us see what our students are "trying" to do as well as what they are, indeed, doing. Thus we have both their method and their goal.

Especially pertinent to argumentation in chapters 6 and 7 Tucker discusses the rhetorical preferences of Japanese and Americans, with the Americans being more direct, opinionated, and aggressive. "Some 'Japanese' and 'American' Rhetorical Preferences" and "In Which the Emphasis of Chapter 6 Is Shifted: Some 'American' and 'Japanese' Rhetorical

Preferences" demonstrate the specific ways that Japanese students, for instance, may initially have problems reconciling their native linguistic and behavioral patterns with some of the demands made on them by the syllabi in American college composition courses, which typically include personal narratives, journals, procedural essays, and persuasive or argumentative papers (171).

TEACHING WITH TECHNOLOGY: STASIS THEORY (11d)

Ask students to collaborate using stasis theory in order to examine an argument from a reading in your syllabus. Each student in the group should type up a short paragraph in response to one of the four questions in section 11d of the *Handbook*. Then merge the paragraphs together to form one document. As a group, review the responses and discuss how each question deepens and complicates the analysis of argument. Using a computer, revise the document as a whole to form a collective position. This technological approach also encourages students to consider various perspectives in their writing through responding to the diverse viewpoints of their peers.

FOR COLLABORATIVE WORK: ARISTOTLE'S THREE TYPES (11e)

In order to help students understand Aristotle's basic appeal, assign one essay that contains instances of all three types of appeals and form students into three small groups to analyze the presence of each appeal. Jonathan Swift's famous essay "A Modest Proposal" works particularly well for this activity, and many students may have already encountered the essay earlier in their education. If so, they can then serve as content advisors for their small group, explaining the essay's purpose and meaning.

For collaborative work, ask each group to identify passages that make use of one of the appeals (pathos, ethos, or logos) and to comment on the function and efficacy of each appeal in the essay. Each group should provide a short presentation to the class. You might also ask each group to formulate a contemporary argument equivalent to Swift's essay and create a mock appeal for that topic. How might a contemporary writer or politician employ pathos, logos, or ethos to address world hunger? war? AIDS? poverty? Get students to come up with their own analogies and appeals and then share them with the class.

.... **(11f)**   <u>**FOR TEACHING: THE TOULMIN SYSTEM**</u>

Ask students to analyze Heather Ricker's essay about video games in 13k, reading it now for its implicit argument. Have them analyze the essay using the seven Toulmin categories described in 11f, focusing especially on the assumptions that underlie the writer's claims. Does the essay succeed as an argument? Why, or why not?

.... **(11g)**   <u>**FOR TEACHING: RECOGNIZING FALLACIES**</u>

Writers who rely on manufactured methods of persuasion — distorting evidence, misquoting, misrepresenting opposing views — do not trust their own position on an issue and may not be able to represent that position believably. Encourage your students to rely on the strengths of their personal experience as well as the facts they have selected to support their position on an issue.

Ask the students to bring in ads that *do not* fairly represent a product, or an editorial or a letter to the editor that presents distorted evidence. What are the contexts for the examples? What specifically is slanted or unfair? Then ask the students (1) to write out their responses to the examples and (2) to rewrite the ad or example, according to fair standards. By doing such analyses, your students will sharpen their critical thinking, reading, and writing skills.

After talking about logical appeals, ask your students to look again at the misleading ads, editorials, or columns they brought to class, this time analyzing them for logical appeals. Often unfair text is based on emotional rather than logical or ethical appeals.

■ **USEFUL READINGS**

Belcher, Diane. "An Argument for Nonadversarial Argumentation: On the Relevance of the Feminist Critique of Academic Discourse to L² Writing Pedagogy." *Journal of Second Language Writing* 6 (Jan. 1997): 1 – 21. In this extremely helpful essay for instructors of multilingual writers, Belcher demonstrates the ways in which traditional notions of agonistic argument are *un*helpful to L² learners.

Booth, Wayne. *Modern Dogma and the Rhetoric of Assent.* Chicago: U of Chicago P, 1974. A classic discussion of the art of "good rhetoric."

Burke, Kenneth. *A Rhetoric of Motives*. Berkeley: U of California P, 1969. Burke's emphasis on rhetoric as communicative, not combative, is worth sharing with your students.

Corbett, Edward P. J., and Rosa A. Eberly. *The Elements of Reasoning*. 2nd ed. New York: Longman, 2000. This short, practical summary of common strategies of argumentation — definition, cause and effect, evaluation, proposal — based on classical rhetoric includes chapters on the appropriate arena of argument, on forms of argument, and on logical fallacies.

Corbett, Edward P. J., with Robert Connors. *Classical Rhetoric for the Modern Student*. 4th ed. New York: Oxford UP, 1999. Newly revised, this text still provides a thorough, cogent, and readable exposition of Aristotelian rhetoric and a brief history of the Western rhetorical tradition.

Foss, Sonja, and Cindy Griffin, "Beyond Persuasion: A Proposal for an Invitational Rhetoric." *Communication Monographs* 62 (1995): 2–18. Describing the characteristics of what they term "invitational" — as opposed to agonistic or oppositional — rhetoric, Foss and Griffin urge scholars and instructors to adopt and practice this useful category.

Lamb, Catherine. "Beyond Argument in Feminist Composition." *CCC* 42 (1991): 11–24. Lamb describes teaching a feminist approach to argument, one that emphasizes the use of negotiation and/or mediation in order to resolve a disagreement in a mutually satisfying way.

Lynch, Dennis, Diana George, and Marilyn Cooper. "Agonistic Inquiry and Confrontational Cooperation." *CCC* 48 (1997): 61–85. The authors describe two courses on argument that move beyond traditional disputation and opposition to urge students to explore complexities rather than merely to take sides.

Toulmin, Stephen. *The Uses of Argument*. New York: Cambridge UP, 1958. According to Toulmin, the persuasiveness of our arguments ("claims") depends on both the general principles ("warrants") that underlie our interpretations of data and the reasons we provide for them.

Tucker, Amy. *Decoding ESL*. Portsmouth: Boynton/Cook, 1995. See chapters 6 and 7 on argumentation.

■ **USEFUL WEB SITE**

Disability Studies in the Humanities

http://www.georgetown.edu/crossroads/interests/ds-hum/index.html

The Disability Studies in the Humanities (DS-HUM) Web site, listserv, and syllabus bank provide samples of college course syllabi that either incorporate disability as an issue or center on that subject in the humanities classroom (especially in language, literature, and composition).

12 ⬇ Considering Visual Arguments

The emphasis in composition classrooms on considering visual arguments is becoming more and more prominent in curricula across the country. From analyzing a photograph in the news to interrogating the function of a Web site, students are participating in the "pictorial turn" by moving from passive consumers to active readers and eventually writers of visual media. As Sylvan Barnet and Hugo Bedau remind us, "premises and assumptions tend to remain unstated in visual persuasion; deciphering them requires highly active reading" (93). Whether visual images are found online or in a photo gallery, in a mall or on a monument, in combination with words or on their own, visual culture offers a form of argument that we need to consider in our writing classes.

Much theoretical work in visual culture has been done since W. J. T. Mitchell identified the "pictorial turn" in composition studies. New journals such as *Enculturation* merge visual cultural studies and rhetoric, while the Summer 2002 issue of *Kairos* (an online journal of rhetoric, technology, and pedagogy) hosts a series of articles exploring the intersections of technology, popular culture, and the art of teaching.

Writing is a visual art. If I don't know where to begin, I describe.
– DONALD M. MURRAY

ATTENDING TO DISABILITIES: CONSIDERING VISUAL ARGUMENTS

Teachers who "rely exclusively on word-based pedagogies," Patricia Dunn tells us, are guilty of "setting up a false dichotomy" that "position[s] students against each other rather than against banking-model teaching" and absolves teachers "from having to rethink their epistemological as-

142

sumptions, philosophical goals, or classroom practices" (Bruggemann, White, Dunn, Heiffernan, and Cheu 377). When you construct materials for teaching arguments, think about how using visual arguments for presenting your lessons will expand your students' understanding of the media possible for argumentation. As Dunn explains:

> Granted, a writing class must be about writing. But composition professionals may, unwittingly, be privileging a way of knowing with which we ourselves are most comfortable, perhaps not realizing that our students have other talents we might use even as we teach writing. We may, unwittingly, play a part in disabling some of our best thinkers by overusing one pathway — writing — in the many intellectual tasks leading up to a finished piece: written journals, written peer responses, freewriting, written proposals or outlines, written e-mail discussions, and so on. (Bruggemann, White, Dunn, Heiffernan, and Cheu 379)

On the same note, make sure you model more diverse ways of considering visual arguments by designing your pedagogy with all learners in mind.

FOR COLLABORATIVE WORK: BECOMING ACQUAINTED WITH VISUAL ARGUMENTS

(12b) ....

Ask students to bring in examples of their favorite advertisements from both print sources (such as magazines and campus, and national newspapers) and the Internet. Have each group examine the images in terms of both Aristotle's three types of appeals and Toulmin's elements of argument. How does each image employ pathos, logos, and ethos as a strategy of persuasion? What warrants, claims, and reasons are manifest in the visual argument? What difference does the medium make (print versus Internet; national press versus campus paper; fashion magazine versus independent journal)?

Have each group select two images that work particularly well as visual arguments and present their analysis collaboratively to the class. Then, as a means of reinforcing what was learned, assign students the task of finding another, more subtle visual argument to bring in for the next class.

> *A visual experience is vitalizing. Whereas to write great poetry, to draw continuously on one's inner life, is not merely exhausting, it is to keep alight a consuming fire.*
> – Kenneth MacKenzie Clark

> *In my mind's eye, I visualize how a particular . . . sight and feeling will appear on a print. If it excites me, there is a good chance it will make a good photograph. It is an intuitive sense, an ability that comes from a lot of practice.*
> – Ansel Adams

FOR MULTILINGUAL WRITERS: ANALYZING THE CONTENT OF VISUAL ARGUMENTS

Realize that the argumentative claims and assumptions of a visual argument may not be readily accessible or obvious to all students. Depending

(12c) ....

on their country of origin, students come to visual texts with different perspectives. You can emphasize this difference in the classroom by discussing what happens at the "point of encounter." Find a political cartoon, such as the Mike Luckovich cartoon of Linus reproduced on p. 257 of the *Handbook*, and ask students to write a caption for it. Each student will offer a different visual/verbal combination, one that makes a unique argument. Multilingual writers, however, will offer increased complexity by adding an alternative national lens, one that straddles the border between cultures.

(12c)   **FOR TEACHING: ANALYZING THE DESIGN OF VISUAL ARGUMENTS**

Doreen Piano, in "Analyzing a Web Zine," asks students to "choose a zine of interest to write a rhetorical and cultural analysis." As part of the assignment, students examine "not only textual aspects such as purpose, audience, design and layout, and content but [also] extra-linguistic features such as reception and consumption of the zine" (par. 2). Her purpose is to show students that the visual images help make the Internet "an ethnographic site, a space where people convene and create different kinds of cultures, some that are in opposition to mainstream culture or that present points of view that may not be represented in the media" (par 1).

By emphasizing the point that visual arguments speak to an audience, you can help students apply their analysis of argument skills to visual images. Moreover, they can assess both content and design aspects with an eye to the larger purposes such visual arguments serve.

(12c)   **TEACHING WITH TECHNOLOGY: ANALYZING THE DESIGN OF VISUAL ARGUMENTS**

A great way to get students to appreciate the significance of the design choices of visual arguments is to ask them to manipulate selected images with standard computer programs such as Adobe Photoshop or Paintbrush. What happens when a picture of the human genome is juxtaposed over a baby? a sick patient? a field of identical tomatoes? an industrial smokestack? How does the color scheme affect the power of persuasion in the image? Ask students to explore black and white versus color, sepia versus primary colors. What audiences are addressed by different color schemes, font sizes, and visual tropes?

You might also ask students to write three paragraphs analyzing the effect of each visual manipulation. What have they learned from manipulating images about size, color, placement, font, and composition? Project several examples from the class up on a large screen, and ask the students to read their essays out loud to the class. Then, spend some time getting feedback on both the images and essays from the class as a whole.

Visualization and belief in a pattern of reality, Activates the creative power of Realization.
—A. L. Linall Jr.

■ USEFUL READINGS

Ahern, Jennifer. "Reading/Writing the *X-Files*." *Kairos* 7.2 (Summer 2002). Online at <http://english.ttu.edu/kairos/7.2/binder.html?sectiontwo/ahern>. Ahern's assignment develops students skills as readers, writers, researchers, and editors of visual texts.

Barnet, Sylvan, and Hugo Bedau. *Current Issues and Enduring Questions.* New York: Bedford/St. Martin's, 2002. Chapter 3 provides an excellent discussion of "Visual Rhetoric: Images as Arguments."

Berger, Arthur Asa. *Seeing Is Believing: An Introduction to Visual Communication.* 2nd ed. New York: McGraw, 1998. This primer of visual communication offers helpful chapters on photography, television, and film.

Brooks, Charles, ed. *The Best Editorial Cartoons of the Year.* Gretna: Pelican, 2002. A wonderful resource of political cartoons that students can use in constructing visual arguments.

Brueggemann, Brenda Jo, Linda Feldmeier White, Patricia A. Dunn, Barbara A. Heifferon, and Johnson Cheu. "Visible: Lessons in Disability." *CCC* 52.3 (Feb. 2001): 368–98. A compelling case for thinking beyond "word-based pedagogies."

Corrigan, Dagmar Stuehrk, and Chidsey Dickson. "Ezines and Freshman Composition." *Kairos* 7.2 (Summer 2002). Online at <http://english.ttu.edu/kairos/7.2/ binder.html?sectiontwo/corrigan/description.html>. The authors ask students to analyze and produce an e-zine as a collaborative learning tool.

Hilligoss, Susan. *Visual Communication: A Writer's Guide.* 2nd ed. New York: Longman, 2002. A short guide to visual design, this text suggests ways that students can use computers to produce effective graphic communications.

Messaris, Paul. *Visual Persuasion: The Role of Images in Advertising.* Thousand Oaks: Sage, 1997. An excellent resource book for teaching students how to consider visual arguments in the advertising world all around us.

Mitchell, W. J. T. *Picture Theory: Essays on Verbal and Visual Representation.* Chicago: U of Chicago P, 1994. A classic text by the guru of visual representation theory.

Piano, Doreen. "Analyzing a Web Zine." *Kairos* 7.2 (Summer 2002). Online at <http://english.ttu.edu/kairos/7.2/binder.html?sectiontwo/piano/webzine

home.htm>. Piano offers a practice assignment sequence for analyzing the content and design of Web sites.

Shiflet, E. Stone. "Shifting the Triangle: Critical Thinking through the Mediation of Forensic and Media Discourse." *Kairos* 7.2 (Summer 2002). Online at <http://english.ttu.edu/kairos/7.2/ binder.html?sectiontwo/shiflet>. Shiflet uses the methodology of Paolo Freire to develop students' critical literacy with regard to visual mediations of news events.

Stroupe, Craig. "Visualizing English: Recognizing the Hybrid Literacy of Visual and Verbal Authorship on the Web." *CE* 62.5 (May 2000): 607–32. Stroupe examines the changing professional trends as more institutions question the teaching of both visual and verbal literacies.

■ **USEFUL WEB SITES:**

Kairos: A Journal of Rhetoric, Technology, and Pedagogy
http://english.ttu.edu/kairos
The focus of the Summer 2002 issue on technology, popular culture, and the art of teaching offers excellent articles suggesting strategies for teaching visual arguments.

LD Resource Center Online
http://www.ldresources.com
An important resource for developing pedagogical materials attending to disabilities: read online columns and essays, subscribe to the LD newsletter, keep informed on current happenings and conferences, contact people, find out about educational developments, access both high- and low-tech tools, and link to electronic books and videos.

13

Constructing Arguments

The art of writing has for backbone some fierce attachment to an idea.

–Virginia Woolf

*A*rgumentation, persuasion, rhetoric — these terms may bring to mind images of hostility, manipulation, deception, and of overpowering, overmastering, outmaneuvering. In *A Rhetoric of Motives*, Kenneth Burke postulates that the image of persuasion should not be bellicose, but rather that

> a speaker persuades an audience by the use of stylistic identifications; his act of persuasion may be for the purpose of causing the audience to identify itself with the speaker's interests; and the speaker draws on identification of interests to establish rapport between himself and his audience. (46)

Identification, Burke reminds us, occurs when people share some principle in common — that is, when they establish common ground. Persuasion should not begin with absolute confrontation and separation but with the establishment of common ground, from which differences can be worked out. Such common ground can help students establish their credibility and understand where their audiences are coming from.

When teaching students how to construct arguments, you may wish to reiterate Burke's emphasis on identification and common ground. At the same time, it is helpful to encourage students to advance their own ideas: as Virginia Woolf notes, "fierce attachment to an idea" makes for powerful writing. This balance of identification and originality might be best understood as contributing a new idea to an ongoing conversation. Teaching thesis statements as beginnings of conversations rather than as statements of finality, D. Diane Davis suggests, emphasizes "the encounter" present in all writing.

There are only three things, after all, that a [piece of writing] must reach: the eye, the ear, and what we may call the heart or mind. It is most important of all to reach the heart of the reader.
– ROBERT FROST

ATTENDING TO DISABILITIES: UNDERSTANDING THE PURPOSES OF ARGUMENT

Ask students to recall the many purposes of argument delineated in section 13a of the *Handbook*: to win, convince, reach a decision, explore an issue, and change oneself. Then give students one of the following assignments adapted from a list by Beth Haller of Towson University. All four assignments (which have been modified into argument prompts) deal with awareness of disabilities on campus and in U.S. culture. They can be conducted either by students with disabilities to encourage them to develop their own stances on access or by all class members collectively using the environment around them as material for constructing arguments.

- Have students meet with someone from a local center for independent living to take an "audit" of the campus's compliance with the Americans with Disabilities Act; ask them to argue why noncompliance hurts all community members.
- Through individual or group analysis of ads, TV programs, and movies, ask students to explore the stigmatizing media images of people with disabilities and make an argument on how they can be changed for the better.
- Through interviews with university disability resource centers and academic computing, have students investigate how improved technology for people with disabilities better integrates them into society; ask students to formulate an argument based on their findings.
- Have students evaluate their own attitudes about interactions with people with disabilities or their experiences as people with disabilities; collectively, this group can make an argument for disability etiquette.

FOR COLLABORATIVE WORK: FORMULATING AN ARGUMENTATIVE THESIS

Ask your students to form into small groups and test the following thesis statements for purpose, audience, position, and support:

1. My essay will deal with the issue of recruiting college athletes. My audience is made up of coaches and administrators, and I want to point out that it is their insistence on winning seasons that often causes coaches to resort to unethical recruiting practices.

2. In this essay, I will argue that this university discriminates against people who live off campus and who must drive to school. I know this is true because I am a commuter and can never find a parking spot. If there's a blizzard, the university doesn't close because residence-hall students can walk to class. The university schedules two or three hours between classes for commuter students

An essay is only as good as its thesis.
    – ANONYMOUS

and then doesn't provide them with any place to go except the library, where you can't even get a soda.

How can these statements be improved? Ask each group to provide a revision of one of the statements, working together to formulate a better thesis.

On Formulating Good Reasons

(13d)

In the Western world, rhetoric has long been tied to civic life. Some argue, in fact, that rhetoric as an art grew up as an immediate consequence of the establishment of a democracy in Syracuse, where litigation on claims to property was undertaken by democratic exiles who had been dispossessed. Their claims, going back many years, often required stating and arranging a complicated series of details. Without documents to prove ownership, the litigants were forced to rely on inferential reasoning; without lawyers to plead their cases, they were left to plead their own cases — hence the need for professional advice, and hence Corax's custom-designed art of rhetoric.

Throughout the classical period, Corax's art of inferential reasoning proved to be more persuasive than other forms of testimony. Today, however, jurors place a great deal of emphasis on testimony, while judges and attorneys are often still persuaded by inferential reasoning. In academic writing, we expect both citations of authority and good reasoning.

FOR MULTILINGUAL WRITERS: ESTABLISHING CREDIBILITY
THROUGH ETHICAL APPEALS

(13e)

The multilingual writers in your classes may often come from different cultures or nations where the deliberate establishment of ethos as a persuasive appeal is discouraged. Some students may consider it rude or arrogant to advance their own credibility as experts in an area or as originators of an idea. For these students, emphasize that writers can build respect and credibility not simply by demonstrating knowledge through claims of expertise, but also in more graceful ways, such as by building common ground, appealing to authority, citing evidence uncovered during the research process, and referring to others who have previously participated in the conversation on the topic at hand. If students focus on making connections with their audience and on building identification rather than animosity, then they will develop a more collegial, less blatantly aggressive voice that will have more persuasive power in an argument.

(13e2) FOR COLLABORATIVE WORK: ESTABLISHING COMMON GROUND

Your students will better understand the concept of common ground if you provide them with an opportunity to demonstrate how opposing parties can reach agreement. Divide the class into pairs of students who hold opposing views, and ask each pair to establish a first principle of agreement, their common ground. Use frustrating situations the students experience as well as the following rhetorical situations:

1. Your roommate keeps an annoying schedule. (For example, if an early bird and a night owl are roommates, they may keep antagonistic schedules. Yet when they discuss their unhappiness, both agree that they each need quiet for sleeping and studying and noise for relaxing. They have thus established common ground, a starting point for working out their differences.)
2. Your English instructor doesn't accept late papers.
3. You show your parents your 2.0 average.
4. You'd like permission (and money) to go to Florida during spring break.
5. Your roommate constantly borrows your belongings.
6. You need help with child care or household duties.

(13e3) FOR TEACHING: AUDIENCE AWARENESS

Moor eeffoc — that's "coffee room" backwards, when you look through the glass from the other side. Ask your students to try to see the point of view of the "opposition." When they try to decipher moor eeffoc, they show their willingness to go over to the other side to get a better view of the rhetorical situation. They also demonstrate their sense of audience.

(13f) FOR TEACHING: INCORPORATING LOGICAL APPEALS

Students in Western countries often look to logical appeals as *the* most effective way to persuade an audience. Students from math and science backgrounds, steeped in logical positivism, frequently declare that "hard evidence" such as statistics and "concrete logic" such as rational arguments and syllogisms are the only certain modes for convincing an audience. These students may benefit from reading Darrell Huff's *How to Lie with Statistics* and other texts that analyze how scientific information and statistics are manipulated, selected, and presented to an audience using loaded language and claims to authority. In short, teach students that the most persuasive argument does not merely employ logos, but rather interweaves Aristotle's three appeals in a strategic crafting of knowledge.

Writing is different from speaking. Organize your written thoughts so that you don't have to stud your sentences with asides, sudden additions, curses or last minute entries.
–WILLIAM SAFIRE

FOR TEACHING: USE OF NARRATIVE (13f1)

Judith Gardner of the University of Texas at San Antonio warns that college writers can get into trouble through overdependence on stories and cautions that writing from sources is not telling a story; narrative should be used to support the point, not *be* the point.

I will tell you something about stories, they aren't just entertainment
– LESLIE MARMON SIEKO

FOR TEACHING: CITING AUTHORITY AND TESTIMONY (13f2)

Student writers sometimes rely too heavily on authority figures because they doubt the power of their own strongly held opinions — opinions that might well influence their readers. Encourage your students to cite authorities to support — not substitute for — their own positions on an issue.

While you help your students consider the appropriateness and proportion of their use of authority, ask them to consider Charles Barkley's or David Robinson's authority when they tell students to stay in school. Do students pay any attention to or respect these stay-in-school campaigns? Do they buy hamburgers, athletic shoes, or soft drinks on the advice of the ex-pro-basketball players who advertise them?

Often students overlook the testimony of ordinary people as a means of identifying with their readers; they don't realize that the testimony of someone with firsthand experience lends powerful credibility to an argument. Although Nancy Reagan conducted a very visible "Just say no to drugs" campaign, her credibility was perhaps not as strong as that of an inner-city resident who had witnessed the effects of the drug trade at close range.

(13f3) **FOR TEACHING: ESTABLISHING CAUSE AND EFFECT**

Cause-effect relationships are often complex: what appears at first glance to be the obvious cause of an event turns out to be only a secondary influence, sometimes an influence that obscures the primary cause-effect relationship. For example, one student felt sure that her migraine headaches were brought on by stress, air pressure, and certain food allergies; only after several seizures was she convinced otherwise: she had a small brain tumor. Encourage your students to persevere in finding the real connections between events and their causes.

For practice, ask students to identify the obvious and not-so-obvious connections in the following statements of cause and effect:

1. A large increase in church membership in recent years shows that people are becoming more religious.
2. Older women sometimes fall and break their hips because they don't consume enough calcium.
3. Because of its elderly population, Florida is the best place to buy a gently used car.
4. Republican victories in nearly every presidential election since 1968 show that the country has repudiated social welfare programs.

(13f4) **On Inductive and Deductive Reasoning**

Most of us live our lives according to inductive generalizations: we are aware of the probability that we will miss the heavy traffic if we take a particular route to school each day, that we can stay in the hot sun only so long without getting burned, that we must eat and exercise a specific amount if we are to stay in shape, or that certain foods, animals, and plants provoke an allergic reaction in us. Many such generalizations stem from inductive reasoning: morning traffic is heavy; sun can burn the skin; too many calories make one fat; poison ivy causes a rash.

One of Aristotle's greatest contributions to rhetorical theory was the use of deductive as well as inductive logic: he used the enthymeme, whose essential difference from the syllogism in logic is not so much that one of the premises is left unstated as that the argument is based on premises that are probably true rather than absolutely true and that the opening premise is agreed on by speaker and audience. In his analysis of inductive reasoning, Aristotle put great emphasis on the importance of examples.

On Considering Emotional Appeals

(13g)

Although emotional appeals have traditionally been ignored or devalued as inappropriate to "good" arguments, they are widely used — and widely effective. Indeed, some emotional appeals, including bandwagon and various kinds of flattery as well as boasting and exaggeration, are well-known and highly effective appeals characteristic of African American rhetorical strategy. As Geneva Smitherman puts it in *Talkin and Testifyin,* "Black speakers are flamboyant; flashy; and exaggerative; black raps are stylized, dramatic, and spectacular. . . ." For suggestions on ways of drawing on this rhetorical tradition, see Smitherman's article "'The Blacker the Berry, the Sweeter the Juice': African American Student Writers."

TEACHING WITH TECHNOLOGY: USING SOURCES IN AN ARGUMENT

(13h)

You can help students get started on their own arguments by walking them through a "model" example in the computer classroom. Have students choose one of the following statements and make notes on their computers regarding any personal experience they have that supports or refutes the statements. Then have them use library and online sources to gather as much additional evidence as possible. Finally, ask them to use this information and their notes on personal experience to outline a short essay arguing either for or against the statement.

1. Vegetarians have a lower incidence of heart attacks than meat-eaters.
2. College degrees mean higher incomes.
3. To succeed, college students must resort to various forms of dishonesty.
4. Students should graduate from college if only to be four years older and wiser when they join the job market.
5. Exercise relieves stress.
6. We are returning to the moral standards of the fifties.
7. AIDS is the worst disease the United States has ever known.
8. Student loans, grants, and scholarships are becoming scarce.

Ask students to post their outlines on plasma screens or work together in small groups to gather the potential sources for use in their arguments. Project one or two outlines on a large screen for collective class analysis and revision.

(13i)

FOR COLLABORATIVE WORK: USING VISUALS IN AN ARGUMENT

Divide the class into small groups, and ask your students to find visuals to support an argument for one of the following topics. Have them speculate on what subtopics might be created to support these arguments, write out the working thesis, and then work to construct a set of rough notes for each argument. They should also locate two to three visuals to use as ethical, logical, and emotional appeals for one of the following:

1. banning smoking in all public places
2. two-career marriages
3. "returning" students
4. a topic of current import on campus

(13j)

FOR TEACHING: ORGANIZING AND DESIGNING AN ARGUMENT

Help clarify the five-part classical argument by providing the class with an essay that follows this format. The "My Turn" column in *Newsweek* is a good choice, as are the editorials in city and campus newspapers. Ask your students to analyze the essay, identifying the introduction, background, lines of argument, refutation, and conclusion. As you proceed through this exercise, use the board to outline the thesis statement as well as the five major headings.

You can extend this exercise by asking your students to find an essay on their own that uses this form of argument and to write a short commentary or outline.

Content and form are in a state of dynamic interaction.
— DENISE LEVERTOV

■ USEFUL READINGS

Belcher, Diane. "An Argument for Nonadversarial Argumentation: On the Relevance of the Feminist Critique of Academic Discourse to L² Writing Pedagogy." *Journal of Second Language Writing* 6 (Jan. 1997): 1–21. In this extremely helpful essay for instructors of multilingual writers, Belcher demonstrates the ways in which traditional notions of agonistic argument are *un*helpful to L² learners.

Bridwell-Bowles, Lillian. "Discourse and Diversity: Experimental Writing within the Academy." *CCC* 43 (1992): 349–68. The author explores the ways in which experimental forms, including narrative, can function well in academic writing.

Bruner, Michael, and Max Oelschlaeger. "Rhetoric, Environmentalism, and Environmental Ethics." *Landmark Essays on Rhetoric and the Environment*. Ed. Craig Waddell. Mahwah: Lawrence Erlbaum, 1998. 209–25. Bruner and Oelschlaeger emphasize the importance of pathos, claiming that an argument can only produce social change if it "evoke[s] sentiment." Relying on Richard McKeon's description of transformative rhetoric as "architectonic," they urge artistic rhetoric with the purpose of social change.

Burke, Kenneth. *A Rhetoric of Motives*. Berkeley: U of California P, 1969. Burke's emphasis on rhetoric as communicative, not combative, is worth sharing with your students.

Davis, D. Diane. "Finitude's Clamor; Or, Notes toward a Communitarian Literacy." *CCC* 53.1 (Sept. 2001): 119–45. A compelling alternative to the "adversarial academy" as it manifests itself in the classroom, Davis's article offers a theoretical and scholarly assessment of "communitarian literacy" in contrast to mastery goals in writing instruction, or what Davis calls the rhetoric of assertion.

Haller, Beth. "Integrating Disability Issues into Skills Classes," NCA presentation, Nov. 1998. Online at <http://www.towson.edu/~bhalle/ideas.html>. An excellent list of collaborative ideas for getting students to attend to disabilities and for students with disabilities to argue their own perspectives on issues of access.

Hindman, Jane E. "Special Focus: Personal Writing." *CE* 64.1 (Sept. 2001): 34–108. This collection of short essays on the role and function of personal writing in academic and professional situations opens with an instructive literature review and overview before moving into articles debating the place of the personal in professional research methodologies, in pedagogical settings, and in rhetorical structures within academic writing.

Huff, Darrell. *How to Lie with Statistics*. New York: Norton, 1993. This book is a delightful look at the deceitful presentation strategies and scientific flaws in the media's use of statistics.

Lynch, Dennis, Diana George, and Marilyn Cooper. "Agonistic Inquiry and Confrontational Cooperation." *CCC* 48 (1997): 61–85. The authors describe two courses on argument that move beyond traditional disputation and opposition to urge students to explore complexities rather than merely to take sides.

Smitherman, Geneva. "'The Blacker the Berry, the Sweeter the Juice': African American Student Writers." *The Need for Story: Cultural Diversity in Classroom and Community*. Urbana: NCTE, 1994. Smitherman suggests ways of drawing on the rhetorical tradition that characterizes African American discourse as reliance on emotional appeals.

Spigelman, Candace. "Argument and Evidence in the Case of the Personal." *CE* 64.1 (Sept. 2001): 63–87. Spigelman analyzes arguments for and against the personal in scholarly and student writing, tracing the debates in composition studies, feminist scholarship, and rhetoric. She builds on Aristotelean rhetorical theory to argue that "narrative too offers claims, reasons and evidence for serious analysis and critique" (83).

PART 4

DOING RESEARCH AND USING SOURCES

14 ▼ Preparing for a Research Project

Wisdom begins in wonder.
— SOCRATES

The fifteenth edition of the *New Encyclopaedia Britannica (NEB)* (1987) attributes the dominance of human beings on earth to the "innate ability to communicate and to store, retrieve, and use knowledge so that each generation does not have to relearn the lessons of the past in order to act effectively in the present." Research is the activity that enables us to process, create, and communicate knowledge. But research goes beyond simply gathering data and passing it on. In its most beneficial sense, research is the process of investigating information or data for a purpose: to make decisions about our lives, to understand our world, or to create or advance understanding. Far from being restricted to work on a college "research essay," research informs much of what we do throughout our lives, especially in the age of electronic media. The research carried out for *The St. Martin's Handbook,* in fact, revealed just how much research students today are doing online for *non*school related uses, from tracking the performance of stocks or sports teams to shopping for used cars.

Regardless of the field of study, researching, writing, and learning are interconnected. James Britton's distinction between expressive and transactional writing helps explain this interconnection. We write in order to learn; that is, we think on paper, using writing to process information and to probe ideas. This function of writing, a form of self-expression and exploration, Britton calls *expressive.* It serves the writer; it enables him or her to learn and understand information. We also write to communicate learning. We use language to inform, to persuade, or to help someone else understand. This function Britton calls *transactional* to emphasize the

exchange or transmission of information for an audience's learning purposes. Similarly, Janet Emig views writing as a means of discovery in which
research, writing, and learning are intrinsically connected. She argues that
the notes, outlines, and drafts that comprise the research and writing
process provide a record of the growth of learning.

*We don't receive wis-
dom; we must discover it
for ourselves after a
journey that no one can
take us or spare us.*
–MARCEL PROUST

FOR TEACHING: UNDERSTANDING THE RESEARCH PROCESS

(14a) ⋯⋯⋯⋯⋯⋯⋯

As preparation for a discussion of the nature and process of college-level
research, have students write in their logs about their previous experiences with research, including online research, and research papers.

*Before ideas come to
fruition, they must
germinate. The most
important direct
consequence of an idea
is that it gives rise to
more ideas.*
– ANATOL RAPOPORT

FOR TEACHING: ANALYZING A RESEARCH ASSIGNMENT

(14b) ⋯⋯⋯⋯⋯⋯⋯

Assign a group of students to bring to class three research assignments
from other classes. Then use these as the basis for class discussion of the
purpose, scope, and audience implied in the assignments.

FOR TEACHING: IDENTIFYING THE AUDIENCE

(14c) ⋯⋯⋯⋯⋯⋯⋯

Identifying the audience will likely pose problems for your students. Answering the questions in the text will help them understand that they
must consider the audience when deciding on word choice, tone, strategy,
and presentation.

Point out that one of their responsibilities as researchers and writers is
to make information available and understandable to a variety of audiences. To do so involves making choices about language and development that depend on their analysis of the purpose of the research, the
scope of the project or topic, the specific audience, and so on. For example, the physiologist presenting material on limb regeneration should
judge how much he or she needs to explain the significance of *blastema*
and the relevant aspects of it on the basis of purpose, audience, and scope.
Clearly, colleagues in the writer's field, unlike a general audience, will not
require a preliminary basic working definition of the term *blastema*. On
the other hand, this physiologist would need to define this term and others particular to the field if the essay were written for an audience made
up of readers outside the field.

TEACHING WITH TECHNOLOGY: SCHEDULING A RESEARCH PROJECT

The test of a first-rate intelligence is the ability to hold two opposed ideas in mind at the same time and still retain the ability to function.
– F. SCOTT FITZGERALD

You can provide students with a sample schedule on your course Web page and ask them to download it to their own research files. Alternatively, keep a class timeline on your Web site and update it weekly to show your collective progress in meeting the class research deadlines. Teachers have used technological resources to post a weekly time-check on a course Web page, to offer time-saving tips on the research process and links to time-management workshops on campus, and to set up submission of work in progress through an email discussion forum or electronic bulletin board.

(14c)   **FOR TEACHING: CHOOSING A TOPIC**

After students have read the description of the student's research into guitar styles in section 14a, take time in class and ask them to think of an occasion when a question has puzzled or challenged them. Ask them to jot down ideas about the kind of research they could do to help answer their questions. Then take one or two examples of such questions from the class, put them on the board, and lead the class in a brainstorming session on what kind of research would best help answer these questions. Have them freewrite their ideas and bring in possible topics for the next class.

(14c)   **FOR COLLABORATIVE WORK: GETTING RESPONSES TO YOUR TOPIC**

Have students work in groups of three. Ask them to create some possible research questions on topics of their own choosing. Exchange these with two other groups. Ask the other groups to analyze the topic for the purpose of the research, the audience, the scope, and length limits.

(14d)   **FOR COLLABORATIVE WORK: NARROWING AND FOCUSING A TOPIC**

One way of working toward a manageable topic or question is to have students brainstorm together on a topic. After students have explored a topic using some of the techniques presented in Chapter 3, have them individually explain their interest in a topic, briefly giving some background or other information on it. Open the discussion up to the class, encouraging students to ask questions and to respond to the topic.

By fielding the class's questions and responses, students develop a sense of the possible directions their topics can have. This informal class brainstorming session helps them identify perspectives that interest others in the topic. Limit each session to fifteen minutes, five minutes for the student to present his or her topic, ten minutes for the class to respond and ask questions. At the end of the fifteen minutes, have each student freewrite for ten to fifteen minutes, noting (1) suggestions for focusing, narrowing, or phrasing the research question; (2) a statement on his or her own interest in or possible approach to the topic; or (3) remarks on matters of purpose, audience, scope, or length.

To make the most of the activity, have at least four individual sessions, with no more than two presented in any one class. Then break up the class into groups of four or five to work through this activity. The small group activity gives the entire class practice at working out possible topics.

FOR COLLABORATIVE WORK: INVESTIGATING THE TOPIC (14e)

Have students work in peer-review groups to share their results from Exercise 14.2. Ask each student to take a turn serving as a "designated respondent" and ask a crucial question about another group member's topic. This process of interactive questioning can help students begin to investigate their research areas more deeply and with great investment.

FOR TEACHING: DECIDING ON A PRELIMINARY RESEARCH PLAN (14f)

Scientist and writer Lewis Thomas recommends taking alternate routes to exploring a question or research topic, including going the opposite direction to what seems most natural or just "fiddling around." "Fiddle around," he says, ". . . but never with ways to keep things the same, no matter who, not even yourself." As students begin to formulate a preliminary research plan, encourage them to "fiddle around" as part of the process.

FOR TEACHING: TAKING NOTES AND BEGINNING A RESEARCH LOG (14g)

A research log (or a section of the writing log set off for such a purpose) is a good place to keep track of reading, note-taking, and writing progress, to ask questions, and to attempt tentative syntheses or conclusions. But no less important, it is a good place to write about the blocks, obstacles, or challenges any researcher inevitably faces. Point out these uses to your students and ask that they make several log entries on their research processes. You can use these as the basis for class discussions on how to make research most efficient and productive.

(14g) **ATTENDING TO DISABILITIES: TAKING NOTES AND BEGINNING A RESEARCH LOG**

When providing research log models on a course Web site, remember to take students with disabilities into consideration. This means conforming to standards of universal design. As Patricia Dunn and Kathleen Dunn De Mers explain, "The philosophy of universal design and its principles can help generate multi-modal intellectual pathways to writing pedagogies. As teachers and students put elements of their writing classrooms and studies online, everyone benefits from the site owner's understanding and application of the principles of universal design" (par. 1). Restructuring your pedagogy to make the research process more inclusive and flexible means using the technological tools at your disposal to benefit *all* of your students. Invite students to explore note-taking strategies that signify alternatives to word-focused methods, such as sketching, voice recording, and oral record keeping. Allow students to transfer texts from a database onto a CD for future reference or to transfer written texts into audio files using your institution's disability resource center or technology support staff. Moreover, when you take your students to the library, note if there are any hard-to-reach stacks or library resource areas that may present obstacles to the successful completion of a research project for certain writers.

A prudent question is one-half of wisdom.
–Sir Francis Bacon

(14g) **FOR MULTILINGUAL WRITERS: TAKING NOTES AND BEGINNING A RESEARCH LOG**

Multilingual writers have an expanded range of research materials available to them because of their proficiency in two or more languages. Encourage students to read widely in other languages but to keep careful notes on their research and reading process. You might suggest that if they find a passage they wish to cite, they should record both the original text and their own translation of it in their research logs. Then, on the final paper, they can provide the translated text in the body of their paper and insert a footnote or endnote with the original text and full source information. The words *translation mine* should be placed after the translated passage.

FOR TEACHING: MOVING FROM HYPOTHESIS TO WORKING THESIS   **(14h)** ··

As students work on their research projects, remind them that their focus and working hypotheses will naturally shift. Share with them stories about famous researchers who might serve as role models.

In the following passage, for example, astronomer Carl Sagan describes the excitement of the kind of research in which he is engaged, research that makes you *"really* think" and consequently "experience a kind of exhilaration." Ask students to read Sagan's description carefully. Have they done any research that fits his description? What kind of research would allow them to experience "exhilaration"? How might their own research process develop in this way?

> ... the main trick of [doing research in] science is to *really* think of something: the shape of clouds and their occasional sharp bottom edges at the same altitude everywhere in the sky; the formation of a dewdrop on a leaf; the origin of a name or a word—Shakespeare, say, or "philanthropic"; the reason for human social customs—the incest taboo, for example; how it is that a lens in sunlight can make paper burn; how a "walking stick" got to look so much like a twig; why the Moon seems to follow us as we walk; what prevents us from digging a hole down to the center of the Earth; what the definition is of "down" on a spherical Earth; how it is possible for the body to convert yesterday's lunch into today's muscle and sinew; or how far is up—does the universe go on forever, or if it does not, is there any meaning to the question of what lies on the other side? Some of these questions are pretty easy. Others, especially the last, are mysteries to which no one even today knows the answer. They are natural questions to ask. Every culture has posed such questions in one way or another. Almost always the proposed answers are in the nature of "Just So Stories," attempted explanations divorced from experiment, or even from careful comparative observations.
>
> But the scientific cast of mind examines the world critically as if many alternative worlds might exist, as if other things might be here which are not. Then we are forced to ask why what we see is present and not something else. Why are the Sun and the Moon and the planets spheres? Why not pyramids, or cubes, or dodecahedra? Why not irregular, jumbly shapes? Why so symmetrical, worlds? If you spend any time spinning hypotheses, checking to see whether they make sense, whether they conform to what else we know, thinking of tests you can pose to substantiate or deflate your hypotheses, you will find yourself doing science. And as you come to practice this habit of

thought more and more you will get better and better at it. To penetrate into the heart of the thing — even a little thing, a blade of grass, as Walt Whitman said — is to experience a kind of exhilaration that, it may be, only human beings of all the beings on this planet can feel. We are an intelligent species and the use of our intelligence quite properly gives us pleasure. In this respect the brain is like a muscle. When we think well, we feel good. Understanding is a kind of ecstasy.   – CARL SAGAN, *Broca's Brain*

(14i)   **TEACHING WITH TECHNOLOGY: KEEPING A WORKING BIBLIOGRAPHY**

Students are often hungry to learn practical and successful methods for completing the research process. Suggest to them that they work directly with technology as they begin the research process. When they are exploring library databases online through their dorm computers, they can cut and paste citation information right into a working bibliography. If they find potentially useful quotations or images, they should attach the source information below the copied text. Some students even download articles from large databases such as FirstSearch, Academic Universe, Lexis-Nexis, and Medline, in order to burn a CD-ROM of cited materials. If you require students to hand in photocopies of all works cited and consulted, the use of a CD-ROM can save both time and trees.

■ **USEFUL READINGS**

Belcher, Diane, and George Braine, eds. *Academic Writing in a Second Language: Essays on Research and Pedagogy.* Norwood: Ablex, 1994.

Brent, Douglas. *Reading as Rhetorical Invention: Knowledge, Persuasion, and the Teaching of Research-based Writing.* Urbana: NCTE, 1992. The author provides an excellent overall discussion of research-based college writing.

Britton, James, et al. *The Development of Writing Abilities.* London: Macmillan, 1975.

Clark, J. Milton, and Carol Peterson Haviland. "Language and Authority: Shifting the Privilege." *Journal of Basic Writing* 14.1 (1995): 57–66. Clark and Haviland describe an assignment that shifts linguistic privilege in the classroom in order to facilitate the acceptance of greater linguistic inclusiveness. They describe how, working with magazines written in French, Spanish, and Chinese, students expand their scope and research focus and participate in "genuine collaboration."

Dunn, Patricia, and Kathleen Dunn De Mers. "Reversing Notions of Disability and Accommodation: Embracing Universal Design in Writing Pedagogy and Web Space." *Kairos* 7.1 (Spring 2002). Online at <http://english.ttu.edu/kairos

/7.1/binder2.html?coverweb/dunn_demers/index.html>. Dunn and De Mers argue that as writing teachers and students put their pedagogical work online, they need to incorporate universal design in order to make their work accessible to all learners. Calling Web accessibility a "civil rights issue," the authors offer concrete guidance, Web links, and suggestions for alternative teaching methods to challenge narrow reliance on writing as a mode of learning.

Emig, Janet. "Writing as a Mode of Learning." *CCC* 28 (1977): 122–28. Emig's view of writing as a means of learning informs the interconnection among researching, writing, and learning.

Glenn, Cheryl, Robert Conners, and Melissa Goldthwaite. *The St. Martin's Guide to Teaching Writing.* 5th ed. Boston: Bedford/St. Martin's, 2003. Chapter 4, "Successful Writing Assignments," offers more information on beginning research.

Langer, Judith A. "Learning through Writing: Study Skills in the Content Areas." *Journal of Reading* 29 (1986): 400–406. Langer reports that writing essays encourages content learning more effectively than taking notes and answering questions.

Rodrigues, Dawn. *The Research Paper: A Guide to Library and Internet Research.* 3rd ed. Upper Saddle River: Prentice, 2003. Rodrigues offers students and teachers a walk-through of library and Web search strategies in the context of the research process. The book has a companion Web site at <http://cwx.prenhall .com/bookbind/pubbooks/rodrigues/>.

15

▼ Conducting Research

Knowledge is of two kinds. We know a subject ourselves, or we know where we can find information upon it.

–Samuel Johnson

According to Charles Bazerman, "gathering convincing data is not easy." The method that a researcher uses greatly determines the evidence that supports the research, the conclusions the researcher is able to draw, and ultimately the effectiveness with which the research will influence others to accept its claims. In other words, the way a researcher explores and produces data will affect how an audience responds to the research. Will it be believable? Is it accurate? reasonable and reliable? thorough? careful? appropriate? significant?

Bazerman advises researchers that "method is so central to the understanding and evaluation of the final written product that in many disciplines a writer is obliged to describe as part of the statement the method used to produce and analyze the data. In this way, many articles contain stories of how they were made" (331).

To appreciate the importance of choosing the methods appropriate to different research projects, researchers need to know that methods vary across disciplines and within them, and that they often change with time. For example, in linguistics, many sociolinguists believe that understanding the way words change in meaning is most accurately explained by observing the way words are used in different social contexts. Historical linguists, on the other hand, prefer to explain meaning changes in terms of the historical origins of words and language groups.

The issue of method is especially important today, as many students are conducting research online. They need to understand the disadvantages as well as the advantages of such research methods. The researcher,

All great masters are chiefly distinguished by the power of adding a second, a third, and perhaps a fourth step in a continuous line. Many a man had taken the first step. With every additional step you enhance immensely the value of your first.

–Ralph Waldo Emerson

for instance, is in some ways at the mercy of whatever search engine she is using: what are its principles of exclusion and inclusion? Discussing these difficult issues in class will pay off—for you as well as your students.

FOR TEACHING: UNDERSTANDING DIFFERENT KINDS OF SOURCES   **(15a)**

Have your students list the sources of information they would use to help you decide on which stereo system to buy. They will probably mention their own experiences or their family's experience with a reliable or unreliable system. They will probably mention consumer guides. They'll also likely mention popular stereo magazines or newspaper and television advertisements as well as pertinent Web sites. Have them classify these sources as either primary or secondary and explain their classifications. For example, their own experience is a primary source. The fact that they have owned a particular system for many years and that they have recommended it to relatives and friends who have had trouble-free experiences is a form of raw data. If they mention an article in *Stereo Review* that praises their system, the magazine is a secondary source.

FOR COLLABORATIVE WORK: UNDERSTANDING DIFFERENT KINDS OF SOURCES   **(15a)**

Ask students to work in groups of three and draw up a list of reference sources that would be relevant for the following topics. Then ask them to choose one topic, go to the library, and, using both online and print sources, find the necessary facts. Have them write a brief summary, noting where they found the facts and what strategy they used to do so.

1. The top ten scorers in the WNBA in 2002
2. The articles published on Epstein-Barr syndrome in 1999
3. A description of the elements of deconstructive architecture
4. Information on the 2002 Winter Olympics
5. Reviews of Susan Sontag's book *On Photography*
6. All the critical articles published on Toni Morrison's *Beloved* between 1990 and 1997
7. Information on the life of Gloria Steinem
8. A description of the progress of AIDS research

9. Information on Harry Browne, the Libertarian presidential candidate in the 2000 election
10. The ten most often-cited articles on superconductivity in 2000

(15b)   FOR TEACHING: UNDERSTANDING DIFFERENT KINDS OF SEARCHES

Encourage students to explore the range of search tools available in the library. Spend some time discussing the differences between online library resources that an institution pays for by subscription — such as JSTOR, FirstSearch, Project Muse, Academic Universe, and Lexis-Nexis — and other, less academic and unregulated search engines such as <www.google .com> and <www.yahoo.com>.

(15b)   TEACHING WITH TECHNOLOGY: UNDERSTANDING DIFFERENT KINDS OF SEARCHES

If you are teaching in a technology-enhanced classroom, you can take advantage of the resources available to you by walking through interactive exercises in conducting research with different kinds of searches. Put students into groups of three, and ask them to brainstorm together on the best keywords to use in a database search on the following topics: computer viruses, white-collar crime, contemporary rap, sexual harassment in the military, upcoming NASA missions, the cost of a college education.

Ask each group to go online and collaboratively find the three most promising sources for their topic. Have each group repeat this exercise with an Internet search engine, a subscription database, and the regular online catalog. At the end of class, have each group give a five-minute oral presentation on the benefits and disadvantages of each method. Remember that popular texts found on the Web may not necessarily be bad, depending on the purpose of the search and the nature of the assignment: to analyze the marketing strategies of rap artists, for instance, Yahoo! might produce better results than Lexis-Nexis. Have students write up a short reflection on their investigations and add it to their research files.

(15c)   FOR COLLABORATIVE WORK: STARTING
YOUR RESEARCH AND GATHERING BACKGROUND

Though you will often assign research to be carried out individually, you might ask students to work as a team or group on a project. As one possibility, ask students to work in research teams to gather information for a report on the condition, the level of use, and any needed changes of the bike paths (or commuter parking lots) on campus. Allow a week or so for them to organize their efforts and to decide what kind of observations, interviews, and other data gathering they will need to do. Then ask them to write together a brief summary of how they have proceeded, noting problems they have encountered and projecting ways to solve them.

Encourage your students to benefit from their colleagues' feedback, input, contributions, responses, and constructive criticism when they are, for example, working out an observation schedule. Or encourage them to brainstorm in groups to generate the most purposeful, specific questions for a survey.

On the History of Information Systems   (15d)

When the inventions of writing and paper enabled people to accumulate information, efforts were put into keeping and presenting the new written information. Constructed in about 600 B.C.E., the royal library at Nineveh, capital of the Assyrian empire, may have been among the world's first great libraries. Historians and archaeologists believe that it contained tens of thousands of works on the arts, the sciences, and religion. Its grand achievement of cataloguing all contemporary knowledge made it the early ancestor of today's huge information systems and scientific databases.

FOR TEACHING: USING THE LIBRARY   (15d)

Set up a meeting for your class with the reference librarian (or ask the librarian to attend your class) to discuss the resources in your particular library and how best for students to get access to them. At many schools, the reference librarians are prepared to do a demonstration of online searches for your students as well as provide an overview of the library. Why not plan for a special class session devoted to using the library early in the term?

FOR TEACHING: USING THE WORLD WIDE WEB   (15e)

While most students are now producing their college assignments on computers, fewer are fully comfortable using the Internet and the World

Wide Web. For these reasons, you may want to work through section 15e of the *Handbook* with students. If you can arrange for a workshop to take place in a computer lab, where students could work online together, do so — or ask if someone in the library or at a public computing site could help you set up such a workshop. In addition, some students in your class can probably serve as facilitators. The important thing is to lead students through a simple search, showing them how to apply the "rules" of various search engines and how to evaluate what they find on the Web.

The Web site you seek cannot be located but endless others exist.
  – FOUND ON THE WEB

.... **(15f)**

FOR TEACHING: CONDUCTING FIELD RESEARCH

Students may believe that they will simply "get the facts" when they observe and that they will not or do not bring their own interpretive frames to observation. Students in one of our classes, for instance, had decided to spread out across campus and observe instances of graffiti, taking notes on their observations. This task seemed very straightforward to them. They soon realized, however, that recording the graffiti out of context changed them in significant ways. These graffiti — perhaps scrawled in giant letters sideways on a door — just didn't "mean" the same thing printed neatly in a notebook. Nor did the students record them in the same ways, or even with the same consistency. In this case, the very act of writing down the data changed its context. So the students decided to try to capture something of the spatial orientation and surrounding context of the graffiti by copying the form as well as the content and noting other contextual details. As a result, their data were much richer and more multidimensional than before. You might wish to share this example with students and ask them to talk in class about how they themselves affect the data they gather.

ATTENDING TO DISABILITIES: CONDUCTING FIELD RESEARCH

Students with mobility or hearing/viewing limitations may wish to turn to technological aids to enhance their field research experiences. Vast collections of library resources are now available through university and library Web sites or digitized collections. Interviews with famous scholars or area specialists can now be conducted on the telephone (with special transcribing devices) or through email, foreclosing the need for an in-person meeting. Full-text versions of academic and popular articles can be accessed through library databases, making stack-searching and photocopying a thing of the past. Spend time in class discussing the options available to your students. Consult with your local disability resource center or librarian as well.

FOR MULTILINGUAL WRITERS: CONDUCTING FIELD RESEARCH

Writers from various backgrounds and with expertise in multiple languages may find the research process similar to ethnography work. The process of defamiliarization, which accompanies what Beverly Moss calls "ethnography in composition," can be transformed into a fruitful learning experience for your students if you communicate with them about the unique challenges and opportunities presented by field research.

FOR TEACHING: OBSERVING   **(15f1)**

Suggest that most students assume the role of reporter, using the *who, what, when, where, why,* and *how* questions to note down what they see and hear (see 3a5). At least in the trial run, these questions can help guide students' observation.

FOR COLLABORATIVE WORK: INTERVIEWING   **(15f2)**

Ask students to work in pairs, first preparing tentative interview questions, and then practicing these questions on their partners. Each partner, in turn, provides a critique of the questions. As an alternative, set up one mock interview for your class. Then lead a class discussion on the strengths and weaknesses of the interview.

For additional practice, ask students to choose a professor in a field of study that interests them and interview that person about the research he or she tends to do. Encourage them to draw up a list of questions they would like answered about the kind of research questions asked in that field, the most typical methods of answering them, and the kinds of sources most often used. After the interview, have students summarize in two or three paragraphs what they have learned.

Use their findings for a class discussion on how to conduct an effective interview, on the etiquette of interviewing, and on the ethics of interviewing (whether to change a subject's words to correct a "mistake," for example).

■ **USEFUL READINGS**

Bazerman, Charles. *The Informed Writer: Using Sources in the Disciplines.* 5th ed. Boston: Houghton, 1995. See chapters 11–15 for an extensive, in-depth discussion of the ways different disciplines gather data for research. Bazerman describes the various methods of data gathering in the social and natural sciences and in the humanities and theoretical disciplines.

Bishop, Wendy. "I-Witnessing in Composing: Turning Ethnographic Data into Narratives." *Rhetoric Review* 11 (Fall 1992): 147–58.

Carbone, Nick. *Writing Online. A Student's Guide to the Internet and World Wide Web.* 3rd ed. Boston: Houghton, 2000.

Grobman, Laurie. "'I Found It on the Web, So Why Can't I Use It in My Paper?': Authorizing Basic Writers." *Journal of Basic Writing* 18.1 (1999): 76–90. Grobman argues for the use of Internet sources in writing classrooms as a tool to help basic writers join the "conversation of ideas" and authorize them as members of an academic community.

McCartney, Robert. "The Cumulative Research Paper." *Teaching English in the Two-Year College* 12 (1985): 198–202. This article provides a model for allowing students to conduct research in depth on one topic through several assignments.

Moss, Beverly J. "Ethnography in Composition: Studying Language at Home." *Methods and Methodology: A Sourcebook for Composition Researchers.* Ed. Gesa Kirsch and Patricia Sullivan. Carbondale: Southern Illinois UP, 1992. 153–71.

Schmersahl, Carmen. "Teaching Literary Research: Process, Not Product." *Journal of Teaching Writing* 6 (1987): 231–38. The author provides a sequence of assignments designed to lead students through the stages of a research-based essay.

Spitzer, Michael. "Local and Global Networking: Implications for the Future." *Computers and Writing: Theory, Research, Practice.* Ed. Deborah H. Holdstein and Cynthia L. Selfe. New York: MLA, 1990. 58–70. Spitzer discusses local area networks, mainframe networking, computer conferencing, and electronic libraries. He also suggests activities to introduce students to these resources.

Spradley, James P., and David W. McCurdy. *The Cultural Experience: Ethnography in a Complex Society.* Prospect Heights: Waveland, 1988.

■ **USEFUL WEB SITES**

Bedford/St. Martin's English Research Room

   http://www.bedfordstmartins.com/english_research

   This site collects helpful instruction, tutorials, and links to give students resources and hands-on practice doing research and source-based writing.

Kitty Locker, "Doing Research on the Web"

http://www.cohums.ohio-state.edu/english/people/locker.1/research.htm

Ohio State University's Gateway to Research Information

http://www.lib.ohio-state.edu/gateway/

Program in Writing and Rhetoric, Stanford University, Student Research Resources

http://www.stanford.edu/group/pwr/students/wr_resources/research.html

You can direct your students to Stanford University's online resources for conducting research.

A Student's Guide to Research with the WWW

http://www.slu.edu/departments/english/research/

UCLA College Library: Thinking Critically about WWW Resources

http://www.library.ucla.edu/libraries/college/help/critical

By Esther Grassian of the UCLA College Library, this site lists a number of questions intended to help instructors and students think critically about Web resources.

Widener University: Evaluating Web Resources

http://www2.widener.edu/Wolfgram-Memorial-Library/webevaluation/webeval.htm

This part of the Wolfgram Memorial Library site is devoted to evaluating Web resources and includes a number of useful teaching materials.

16 ⬇ Evaluating Sources and Taking Notes

Every mind must make its choice between truth and repose. It cannot have both.

– RALPH WALDO EMERSON

In ordinary language, we say we have received information when *what we know* has changed. The bigger the change in what we know, the more information we have received. Information, like energy, does work. But whereas energy does physical work, information does logical work. While this view that increased information changes what we know is largely true, it's intellectually disastrous to accept blindly and unquestioningly our information sources. A judicious, practiced researcher learns that not everything she or he reads in journals, magazines, or scholarly books, whether online or off, is true simply because it appears in a text. The truly inquisitive researcher understands that no source is totally beyond dispute.

On the Researcher's Perspective

Many students, especially those in the sciences, will deny that the author's or researcher's perspective influences research. In science, they may claim, researchers look at phenomena objectively, without interpretive bias. Scientists let the facts and data speak for themselves. Though the bias may not be apparent in the analysis of the data, the conclusions cannot avoid some degree of bias. Conclusions result from the interpretive analysis of data.

For a striking example, see Anne Fausto-Sterling's *Myths of Gender: Biological Theories about Women and Men* (New York: Basic, 1987). Fausto-

Sterling, a biologist, demonstrates that many of the questionable distinctions between males and females that scientists have "proven" derive from their research methods and the kinds of questions they have asked. For instance, male superiority in athletic performance can be "proven" when it is measured by muscle strength rather than other criteria such as resiliency or endurance.

FOR TEACHING: UNDERSTANDING WHY YOU SHOULD USE SOURCES

Ask students to look for similar biases in the sources they consult in their research areas. Is there such a thing as an unbiased source? If not, why use sources? What purpose do they serve? Challenge students to consider the merits of evaluating and selecting a number of authoritative sources on their topic to widen the scope of their research. By using a range of carefully chosen perspectives, students can broaden and extend the research questions and offer a new contribution to the ongoing conversation.

Books, like friends, should be few and well-chosen.
–SAMUEL JOHNSON

FOR TEACHING: EVALUATING POTENTIAL SOURCES

(16b)

In "The Web Demands Critical Thinking by Students," Kari Boyd McBride and Ruth Dickstein remind instructors that students no longer get most materials for research writing from traditionally reputable print sources available in the library. Because the Web is awash in all kinds of undifferentiated material — some junk, some masterful, etc. — we have a special obligation to focus on critical reading, writing, and thinking. To carry out this goal, McBride and Dickstein use an exercise asking students to research a topic using a number of different sources — a book, an article, a reference work, a work identified through use of a CD-ROM index, and a Web site. Students then report on one of these resources, "summarizing the information it contains and evaluating the reliability of the author and the plausibility of the argument." While the authors created the exercise to help students think critically about electronic sources, they found that it had a much wider payoff: it has shown students that even encyclopedia articles can be biased and led them to look closely at a writer's sources and to ask what makes an argument authoritative and persuasive, whether in print or online. Why not develop and use a similar exercise with your students?

(16b)

FOR TEACHING: CONSIDERING THE RELEVANCE OF THE SOURCE

Reading through sources with one's research question in mind is the ideal way of reading with focused efficiency. However, students do not always have a research question in mind when they start. If students haven't formulated one, encourage them to look through the table of contents for a perspective or subheading on the general topic. Before they begin to skim through, they might ask themselves a question about the topic based on the table of contents subheadings.

(16b)

FOR MULTILINGUAL WRITERS: EVALUATING
THE CREDENTIALS OF THE PUBLISHER OR SPONSOR

Multilingual writers unfamiliar with publishing houses or incorporated institutions in the United States may want to exchange research logs with a writing partner in order to evaluate the publisher or sponsor of the sources in their collection. This collaboration can provide a fruitful learning experience for both parties, as national differences in access to publication and hierarchies of authority vary from context to context. You can share these differences with the class to broaden the scope for research possibilities: why not include international and translated research materials?

(16b)

FOR TEACHING: READING SOURCES WITH A CRITICAL EYE

Ask students to read the following two passages about the War of 1812, the first from an American encyclopedia and the second from a Canadian history book. Ask students to read each one carefully, and then to answer these questions, noting any differences in the two accounts:

1. What motivated the War Hawks?
2. Who attacked whom at the beginning of the Battle of Tippecanoe?
3. What did the War of 1812 mean in British, American, and Canadian history?
4. Why did the Treaty of Ghent end up restoring the prewar boundaries?

Then have them answer these questions about both passages.

1. What is the perspective, tone, and argument of each passage?
2. How does each passage make clear its point of view?

3. Can you find at least one example in each passage that seems to show how the author's point of view accounts for or affects the interpretation of events?
4. Why do you think each passage takes the view it does?
5. How would you, as a researcher, evaluate and use these sources?

Have students compare their own analysis with those of other students in your class, and be prepared for a full class discussion.

From the *World Book Encyclopedia*

War of 1812

The War of 1812 was in many ways the strangest war in United States history. It could well be named the War of Faulty Communication. Two days before war was declared, the British Government had stated that it would repeal the laws which were the chief excuse for fighting. If there had been telegraphic communication with Europe, the war might well have been avoided. Speedy communication would also have prevented the greatest battle of the war, which was fought at New Orleans fifteen days after a treaty of peace had been signed.

It is strange also that the war for freedom of the seas began with the invasion of Canada, and that the treaty of peace which ended the war settled none of the issues over which it had supposedly been fought.

The chief United States complaint against the British was interference with shipping. But New England, the great shipping section of the United States, bitterly opposed the idea of going to war. The demand for war came chiefly from the West and South, although these sections were not really hurt by British naval policy.

When we add that both sides claimed victory in the War of 1812, it becomes clear that the whole struggle was a confused mass of contradictions. These must be explained and cleared up before we can understand why the democratic United States sided with Napoleon I, the French dictator, in a struggle for world power. . . .

The War Hawks. A group of young men known as "War Hawks" dominated Congress during this period. Henry Clay of Kentucky and John C. Calhoun of South Carolina were the outstanding leaders of the group. Clay was then Speaker of the House of Representatives. Like Clay and Calhoun, most of the War Hawks came from western and southern states, where many of the people were in favor of going to war with Great Britain.

The people of New England generally opposed going to war, because war with Great Britain would wipe out entirely the New England shipping trade which had already been heavily damaged. Another reason New England opposed war was because many New Englanders sympathized with Great Britain in its struggle against the dictator Napoleon.

Many historians believe that a leading motive of the War Hawks was a desire for expansion. The people of the Northwest were meeting armed resistance in their attempt to take more land from the Indians, and they believed that the Indians had considerable British support. An American army was attacked by Indians at the Battle of Tippecanoe in the Wabash Valley in November, 1811, and British guns were found on the battlefield. The Westerners, therefore, were anxious to drive the British out of Canada. Southerners looked longingly at Florida, which belonged to Great Britain's ally, Spain. The South had also suffered a serious loss of markets. But the deciding motive for war seems to have been a strong desire for more territory.

Progress of the War

Declaration of War. On June 1, 1812, President Madison asked Congress to declare war against Great Britain. He gave as his reasons the impressment of United States seamen and the interference with United States trade. He charged also that the British had stirred up Indian warfare in the Northwest. Congress declared war on June 18, 1812. Two days earlier, the British Foreign Minister had announced that the Orders in Council would be repealed, but word of this announcement did not reach America until after the war had begun.

Because President Madison asked for the declaration of war, many Federalists blamed him for the conflict, calling it "Mr. Madison's war." But it was more the War Hawks' war than it was Madison's. . . .

Treaty of Ghent. The British public was tired of war and especially of war taxes. The British Government therefore proposed discussing terms. Commissioners of the two countries met at Ghent, Belgium, in August, 1814.

The British at first insisted that the United States should give up certain territory on the northern frontier, and set up a large permanent Indian reservation in the Northwest. But American victories in the summer and fall of 1814 led the British to drop these demands. A treaty was finally signed on December 24, 1814, in Ghent, Belgium. By its terms, all land which had been captured by either party was to be given up. Everything was to be exactly as it was before the war, and commissions from both of the countries were to settle any disputed points about boundaries. Nothing whatever was said in the treaty about impressments, blockades, or the British Orders in Council, which supposedly had caused the war. The treaty was formally ratified on February 17, 1815.

Results of the War

One important result of the War of 1812 was the rapid rise of manufacturing in the United States. During the war, United States citizens were unable to import goods from Great Britain, and had to begin making many articles for themselves. The war also increased national patriotism, and helped to unite the United States into one nation.

The war settled none of the issues over which the United States had fought. But most of these issues faded out during the following years. In the long period of peace after 1815, the British had no occasion to make use of impressments or blockades. Indian troubles in the Northwest were practically ended by the death of the chief Tecumseh and by the British surrender of Detroit and other posts. The United States occupied part of Florida during the war, and was soon able to buy the rest of it from Spain.

One indirect result of the War of 1812 was the later election to the Presidency of Andrew Jackson and of William Henry Harrison. Both of these men won military fame which had much to do with their elections. Another indirect result was the decline of Federalist power. New England leaders, most of them Federalists, met secretly in Hartford, Conn., to study amendments to the Constitution. Their opponents charged that they had plotted treason, and the Federalists never recovered. . . .

Chief Battles of the War

The War of 1812 was not an all-out struggle on either side. For the British, the war was just an annoying part of their struggle with Napoleon. For many Americans, it was an unjustified attempt to gratify the expansionist ambitions of the South and West.

From *Canada: A Story of Challenge*

Danger on the Western Border

From the Treaty of Versailles in 1783 until the outbreak of a second war with the United States in 1812, the western border of young Canada was never secure. Trouble arose in the lands south of the Great Lakes; in the Ohio country which had been officially granted to the United States in 1783, but which had remained tied to the St Lawrence fur trade. The final consequence was open war. The trouble began almost with the signing of peace in 1783, when Britain quickly came to regret the ready surrender of so much of the West, and sought at least to delay its transfer to the United States.

The chief reasons for delay arose from the fur traders and the Indians who were still the masters of the unsettled Ohio West. The Canadian fur merchants of the St Lawrence drew most of their trade from that country, and they asked that the transfer be postponed for two years until they could adjust their business to this heavy loss. The Indians supplied the major reason, however. They declared that they had been ignored in the Treaty of Versailles and that Britain had handed over their lands, which they had never ceded, to the United States. There was danger that if the West was transferred and opened to American settlement the Indians would, in revenge, attack the thinly held and almost unprotected British settlements in Upper Canada.

Taking advantage of vague wording in the peace treaty, therefore, the British held on to the military and trading posts in the West below the Lakes, giving as their reason the failure of the Americans to carry out the term of the treaty that called for the restoration of Loyalist property. It was a sound reason, but not the chief one for failing to transfer the West.

This situation dragged on into the 1790's, while the Americans feared that the British were arousing the Indians against them, and the British feared that the Indians would become aroused. Dorchester, as governor, darkly expected a new war with the United States, and had some hope of building an Indian state in the Ohio country that would stand between the Americans and the Upper Canadian frontier and help to protect the latter. The Americans, meanwhile, were pressing forward from the region south of the Ohio, and sending forces against the Indians in order to break their hold on the western country. In 1794 one of these expeditions completely defeated the tribes at the battle of Fallen Timbers, and hope of an Indian "buffer state" collapsed. The tribes ceded their lands to the United States. . . .

The rapidly advancing western states of the American union made good use of the growing warlike spirit in the republic. They held that the place to punish Britain was in Canada. Filled with the forceful confidence and expansive drive of the frontier they wanted to add Canada to the American union: a Canada which American frontier settlement had already invaded. Was not Upper Canada by now practically an American state? The "war hawks" of the American West clamoured for an easy conquest. Their chance seemed to arrive in 1811.

In that year the western Indians, being steadily pushed back by advancing American settlement, attempted a last stand. Led by the chief Tecumseh, they formed a league to resist further inroads. The Americans saw this as the threat of a new Pontiac uprising, of savage Indian raids on the frontier. They attacked the Indians, and by their victory at the battle of Tippecanoe, destroyed Tecumseh's league. Yet the American West was not satisfied. It was fully convinced that the British had been behind the Indians, although the Canadian government had actually sought to keep the Indian league at peace. It seemed that the West would only be safe when the British had been driven out of Canada. The war hawks cried for blood, the American frontier wanted new lands to conquer, and the American East was newly aroused by fresh skirmishes over the right of search. The United States declared war in June, 1812, and set out to capture Canada.

The Second Struggle with the Americans

The War of 1812 in British history is only a side-show, not altogether successful, during the huge and victorious contest with Napoleon. In United States history it is a second war of independence, chiefly against the weight of British sea-power. In Canadian history it is above all a land war, a second struggle against American invasion. All these pictures are partly true; and in studying the Canadian version one must bear in mind that it portrays only the War of 1812 as it affected Canada. Yet for Canada the war was vitally important; far more important than it was for Britain, and much more dangerous than it was for the United States. . . .

Thus the war ended late in 1814 in a stalemate, which was probably a good thing for future peace.

It was not completely a stalemate. Britain still held the West and some of the Maine coast, and the British naval blockade was strangling American commerce. But in the peace negotiations the Americans made clear their readiness to go on fighting rather than yield territory. Faced with a revival of Napoleon's power in Europe at that very moment, Britain did not press the point. As a result the Treaty of Ghent of 1814 simply stopped the fighting, restored the pre-war boundaries, and said little about the problems that had caused the conflict.

Nevertheless in the next few years many of these problems disappeared. The question of the right of search ended with the Napoleonic Wars, and vanished in the long years of peace after 1815. The Indian problem declined as American settlement filled in the old West; the tribes had been too weakened by the war to offer any further resistance. The American war-hawks had found Canada no willing mouthful, and the United States was turning away to expand in a new direction, towards the south. . . .

The War of 1812 thus tended to bring British North America together and strengthened the bond with Britain. Any common feelings among the colonists, however, were largely directed against the United States. This anti-American spirit was still a narrow basis on which to build a Canadian nationalism. Anti-Americanism was particularly evident in Upper Canada. Further American settlement was largely prevented there, and American settlers already in the province were in danger of persecution — the Loyalists' case in reverse — if their declarations of British sentiments were not loud enough. Nevertheless, on the whole these reactions to the strain of the War of 1812 were understandable; and not an extreme price to pay for the survival of British North America.   — J. M. S. CARELESS

FOR COLLABORATIVE WORK: INTERPRETING SOURCES   **(16d)**·······················

Ask students to return to the passages about the War of 1812 on pp. 177–81. (If time permits, you might ask that they find two or three other accounts of the same events and copy these for the class as well.) Then ask students to work in small groups to synthesize the data and arguments presented here. When they are satisfied that they have captured the gist of each, ask them to reflect on their syntheses, drawing out implications and points for discussion. Finally, ask them to work together toward an interpretation of these sources that all members of the group can agree on.

.... **(16d)** **ATTENDING TO DISABILITIES: INTERPRETING SOURCES**

In order to ensure the best possible research experience for all of your students, keep in mind the following guidelines from Brenda Jo Brueggemann, associate professor of English and director of Ohio State University's first-year writing program:

- Provide opportunities to review students' research in individual conferences.
- Encourage multimodal approaches to the research process in topic development, organization, source collection, etc. (These should be approaches that involve alternatives to reading- and writing-intensive activities, such as spatial, kinesthetic, and tactile approaches to the subject.)
- Engage students in class discussions about time-on-task and knowing the extent of the subject to be covered.
- Offer in-class opportunities for, and discussions about, prewriting, arrangement, and organization techniques in writing.

Ohio State University's Fast Facts for Faculty Web site, <http://www.osu.edu/grants/dpg/fastfact/writing.html>, gives more examples of multiple types of writing, outlines common problems students have with them, and suggests the best writing practices to help students of varying abilities.

An educated person is one who has learned that information almost always turns out to be at best incomplete and very often false, misleading, fictitious, mendacious—just dead wrong.
–RUSSELL BAKER

.... **(16e)** **FOR TEACHING: TAKING NOTES**

Suggest to students that they use the following process when photocopying or downloading research materials:

1. Photocopy or download only the most important material, after reading and selecting it.
2. Highlight essential passages.
3. Quote, paraphrase, or summarize those passages on note cards.
4. Remember that you may need to ask permission to use material found on the Internet.

.... **(16e)** **TEACHING WITH TECHNOLOGY: TAKING NOTES AND ANNOTATING SOURCES**

Students can save precious time during the research process by taking notes right on a laptop or other computer. Remind students to list the complete information for each source and to provide quotations in full. The cut-and-paste operation of any word-processing program can be extremely helpful in this regard. Moreover, some students now download full-text files to their computers and burn a CD-ROM of works cited to turn in with their final research papers. Suggest to students that they apply a critical eye to sources before downloading in order to avoid having to delete unnecessary files later on. Moreover, evaluating sources while engaging them with technology will allow for students' research agendas to evolve as they read and assimilate source materials.

On Paraphrasing

(16e3)

Paraphrasing is a skill that has twofold value. It helps us communicate, but it also helps us do something else that isn't always readily apparent to students: it helps us in our learning. Because a paraphrase requires us to put someone else's meaning into our own words, we have to understand the meaning of the original. If we have trouble with the paraphrase, our difficulty likely indicates that we don't have an adequate grasp of the original passage. The measure of how well we understand what we've read is the paraphrase (or the summary). In expressing our understanding we are involved in a process of learning.

FOR TEACHING: TAKING PARAPHRASE NOTES

(16e3)

The importance of paraphrasing cannot be overestimated. Make sure to point out to students that:

1. Often a paraphrase may seem to make sense to the writer but it may not to a reader because of the writer's familiarity with the original passage and because the paraphrase is in his or her choice of language.

2. There are at least two purposes of paraphrasing, one to help the writer himself or herself understand, and another to present the information to another person to understand.

3. Much research involves paraphrasing or explaining ideas in the researcher's own words.

4. Having others respond to their writing helps writers learn how to judge and use language for audiences that are different in their levels of understanding and expertise with a subject.

5. The paraphraser is in some ways always in danger of misrepresenting another, or of satirizing or even parodying another, by taking meanings out of context. Thus, like summaries and quotations, paraphrases should be used with care.

(16e3)

FOR COLLABORATIVE WORK: TAKING PARAPHRASE NOTES

Whenever students paraphrase (or summarize), have them compare versions and explain similarities and differences. Collaborating on a second version will help them appreciate not simply where their troubles lie but also the learning effectiveness of collaboratively talking out, working out, and writing out material they are studying.

For additional practice with paraphrasing, divide the class into groups of six, and present them with these instructions: choose for paraphrasing a short passage of about one hundred words from a text, an essay, or an article. Each member of the group should first individually restate the original in his or her own words. Keep in mind that the paraphrase requires a writer to include all major and supporting details. Once they have produced their paraphrases, have them break into three groups of two, and, working together, co-write a paraphrase of the original excerpt. Then they should discuss the similarities or differences of the three versions. Ask the students to try to explain them, especially the differences, focusing on the following guiding questions:

1. Working in pairs, did you disagree over terms and their meaning in the original passage?

2. Was it easy to agree on synonyms or on paraphrases of ideas and concepts?

3. Did you agree on the information to include? to leave out?

4. How similar are the three coauthored versions? Why, or why not?

5. What does trying to agree on a paraphrase tell you about how different people read and interpret a passage? About how they choose to rephrase it?

■ USEFUL READINGS

Brown, M. Neil, and Stuart M. Keeley. *English on the Internet: Evaluating Online Resources.* Upper Saddle River: Prentice, 2001. A detailed and comprehensive guide to finding and evaluating online resources for writing projects.

Carbone, Nick. *Writing Online: A Student's Guide to the Internet and World Wide Web.* 3rd ed. Boston: Houghton, 2000. This useful and clearly written guide can help students get started writing and conducting research online.

Goodwin, Doris Kearns. "How I Caused That Story." *Time* 4 Feb. 2002: 69. Online at <http://www.time.com/time/nation/article/0,8599,197614,00.html>. Goodwin explains how her citations from Lynne McTaggart's book ended up in her publication, *The Fitzgeralds and the Kennedys*, despite her meticulous note-taking techniques: "Though my footnotes repeatedly cited Ms. McTaggart's work, I failed to provide quotation marks for phrases that I had taken verbatim, having assumed that these phrases, drawn from my notes, were my words, not hers." Once her son showed her the footnote function in her word-processing program, she began indicating sources as she inserted notes in her draft—which is an excellent strategy to share with your students.

Harris, Robert A. *Using Sources Effectively: Strengthening Your Writing and Avoiding Plagiarism.* Los Angeles: Pyrczak, 2002. A slim guide of 98 pages, this text helps students confront two key writing issues: unintentional plagiarism and ineffective use of source material.

McBride, Kari Boyd, and Ruth Dickstein. "The Web Demands Critical Thinking by Students." *Chronicle of Higher Education.* 20 Mar. 1996: B6. Online at <http://chronicle .com>.

■ **USEFUL WEB SITES**

Cornell University: Critically Analyzing Information Sources

http://www.library.cornell.edu/okuref/research/skill26.htm

Among the critical reading guides available online, this Web page published by the Cornell Libraries provides a useful set of guidelines to follow in evaluating sources. The page's primary focus concerns assessment of a source's credentials and validity.

Dartmouth College: Sources—Their Use and Acknowledgment

http://www.dartmouth.edu/~sources

This comprehensive online guide to using sources walks students through every step of the process, from questions concerning "Why acknowledge sources?" to five ways to cite sources to an extensive list of FAQs. One of the more accessible and complete online resources.

UCLA College Library: Thinking Critically about WWW Resources

http://www.library.ucla.edu/libraries/college/help/critical

By Esther Grassian of the UCLA College Library, this site lists a number of questions intended to help instructors and students think critically about Web resources.

Widener University: Evaluating Web Resources

http://www2.widener.edu/Wolfgram-Memorial-Library/webevaluation /webeval.htm

This part of the Wolfgram Memorial Library site is devoted to evaluating Web resources and includes a number of useful teaching materials.

17

▼ Integrating Sources into Your Writing

By necessity, by proclivity, and by delight, we all quote.
                                            –Ralph Waldo Emerson

The process of integrating sources into your writing can be similar to hosting a conversation at a stimulating dinner party. As the dialogue unfolds, various participants have the chance to contribute. But the writer remains the moderator, orchestrating the ebb and flow of conversation. Deciding how and when a source should enter this dialogue is a skill developed best through practice, observation of successful models, and attention to rhetorical purpose. Invite your students to begin the conversation, and look to this chapter for advice on how best to guide them through this process.

While teaching integration of sources, do not discount the importance of helpful examples. Stuart Swirsky, in a review of Candace Spigelman's *Across Property Lines: Textual Ownership in Writing Groups*, stresses the way in which models can lead students toward mastery of complex writing processes such as integrating sources:

> As any writing instructor well knows, a co-requisite to becoming a competent writer is to engage in a tremendous amount of careful and critical reading. Perhaps more than anything else, what students really need is more models for writing, models that are readily available in texts. Getting students to do more reading may be as important as getting them to open up to more collaboration in the classroom.

ATTENDING TO DISABILITIES: INTEGRATING SOURCES

Remember that your college or university disability resource center has a wealth of technological aids to help students work on integrating sources. Consider some of the following techniques:

- *Scanners:* Entire books can be scanned into a computer using a high-speed scanner, converted to computer-readable text with OCR software, then printed out in Braille or read aloud via a text-to-speech screen reader.
- *Integrating visuals:* Diagrams and line drawings can be printed as raised images on special paper, allowing a visually impaired person to "feel" the drawing.
- *Viewing sources:* Video magnifiers can enlarge text and pictures for those with visual impairments.
- *Auditory services:* Specialized tape recorders read books-on-tape and FM listening devices offer help for students with hearing impairments or attentional difficulties.

**FOR COLLABORATIVE WORK: DECIDING WHETHER TO
QUOTE, PARAPHRASE, OR SUMMARIZE**   **(17a)** ....

Ask students working in pairs to select an article from a major journal in a field of interest to them. Have them identify each occurrence of paraphrase, summary, or quotation and the function that each serves. These may include:

1. To provide background information
2. To define terms
3. To provide a position for rebuttal
4. To explain quoted material
5. To illustrate a point
6. To show disagreements among sources
7. To cite authorities and, hence, to reinforce claims, statements, or credibility
8. To state a point more precisely, powerfully, or accurately than with a paraphrased version
9. To challenge, resist, or even parody the source

   Once two students have identified the functions, have them exchange their article with another pair. Have them repeat the exercise and then compare versions and findings.

On Working with Quotations   **(17b)** ....

In *A Pedagogy of Possibility,* Kay Halasek — building on the work of Bakhtin and Volosinov — questions traditional ways of teaching quoting as if this practice were ideologically or politically neutral. When we quote, after all, we take another's words out of context, putting them into contiguous relationship with our own words. Such acts of quoting are ordinarily taught as ways to let the quoted person "speak for herself." But to what degree is that actually possible? In addition, when we teach use of quotations as a way to build authority, we implicitly teach students to defer to the authority's quoted words. Halasek wisely suggests that we alert our students to these often invisible aspects of quoting and to show them at least some of the ways in which quotations can be used not to defer to an authority but to resist or even parody that "authority."

(17b)   FOR COLLABORATIVE WORK: WORKING WITH QUOTATIONS

Ask students to bring in the rough draft of five pages of a research essay in progress, making sure to choose pages that include quotations, paraphrases, and/or summaries, and with all signal verbs and phrases underlined or highlighted. Then ask them to work in pairs to examine their use of these verbs and phrases. Can they explain why each signal verb or phrase was chosen and what rhetorical effect it has?

(17d)   On Working with Summaries

Like the paraphrase, the summary is a useful learning and communicating skill. Writing summaries gives students practice identifying and coordinating the main points of a passage. Students don't have to write summaries using their own words, but if they do, if they rephrase the main points of an original passage, they will better understand what they are reading. This practice of rephrasing summarized (and paraphrased) information will also help them work source material into their research projects more easily. For this reason, discourage your students from simply pulling out phrases, sentences, or chunks of the original, and then merely stringing them together.

(17f)   TEACHING WITH TECHNOLOGY: WORKING WITH VISUALS

When teaching students to select and integrate visuals into their writing, be sure to discuss issues of copyright and permissions. Students should carefully note the source of the image. If they are downloading an image from the Web, they need to contact the Web site owner and request permission to use the image as a part of their writing project. If students have found visuals (photographs, charts, ads) from print sources and scanned them into a computer file in order to insert them into their texts, they need to write the owner or publisher and request permission for reproduction of the image.

FOR TEACHING: CHECKING FOR EXCESSIVE USE OF SOURCE MATERIAL **(17g)**

Recall the conversation analogy introduced at the beginning of this chapter. Have students review their drafts and ask themselves: "Am I still the moderator of this conversation? Is my voice clear, compelling, and original? Do I allow my own argument to emerge as foremost in this piece?"

Note that this last question may be difficult for multilingual writers familiar with different kinds of writing conventions. They may feel that emphasizing their own voice is rude or arrogant, or they may feel that they do not have the authority to advance their views. Challenge them to see the emphasis of their own argument as a strategy of ethos, one of the most effective ways for persuading an audience. Indeed, writing instruction aims to build confidence and thereby to develop a compelling and informed voice that can contribute in important ways to the public sphere. As Bill Beattie observes:

Enough! Or too much?
–William Blake

> The aim of education should be to teach us rather how to think, than what to think — rather to improve our minds, so as to enable us to think for ourselves, than to load the memory with thoughts of other men.

■ USEFUL READINGS

Carbone, Nick. *Writing Online: A Student's Guide to the Internet and World Wide Web.* 3rd ed. Boston: Houghton, 2000. This useful and clearly written guide can help students get started writing and conducting research online.

Halasek, Kay. *A Pedagogy of Possibility.* Carbondale: Southern Illinois UP, 1999.

Kennedy, Mary Lynch. "The Composing Process of College Students Writing from Sources." *Written Communication* 2 (1985): 434–56. Based on a protocol analysis of six students writing from sources, Kennedy argues that fluent readers read the sources "with pencil-in-hand," doing more planning, rereading, and note-taking prior to writing than the less-able readers.

Sherrard, Carol. "Summary Writing: A Topographical Study." *Written Communication* 3 (1986): 324–43. In studying paragraph-length summaries written by university students, Sherrard found that most of the summaries were "remarkably mechanical." Summary strategies most favored included omitting text sentences, mapping existing sentences into summary sentences, and combining only those sentences that were next to each other.

Swirsky, Stuart. Rev. of *Across Property Lines: Textual Ownership in Writing Groups*, by Candace Spigelman. *CCC Online* 52.4 (June 2001): 662-66. Online at <http://www.ncte.org/ccc/2/52.4/review.pdf>.

■ **USEFUL WEB SITES**

Library Research Using Primary Sources

http://www.lib.berkeley.edu/TeachingLib/Guides/PrimarySourcesOnTheWeb.html

This annotated list of research collections on the Web is a terrific place for students to start the process of integrating sources. Maintained by the University of California at Berkeley, the page provides descriptions and Web links to digital collections of primary sources in a wide range of disciplines.

Starting Points for Internet Research

http://owl.english.purdue.edu/internet/tools/research.html

This online writing lab page provides an excellent list of Web-based primary source documents organized by discipline and prefaced with a brief guide to Internet research strategies.

18

Acknowledging Sources and Avoiding Plagiarism

Immature poets imitate; mature poets steal.
— T. S. Eliot

Despite T. S. Eliot's pithy wisdom, a mark of intellectual maturity is the recognition of our debt to those whose ideas and insights have fostered the development of our own thinking and whose published and spoken texts have shaped our writing. Encourage your students to think of themselves as part of a larger community of scholars. Have them research the biographies and Web sites of authors whose books they cite; ask them to conceptualize their sources as people whose final texts began as ideas in writing classes and only developed into final form through years of writing, revision, and hard work. Often, when students reconsider sources as the work of writers and researchers who have toiled and struggled as they have, they are more likely to acknowledge sources for the information they glean from them. Recall the conversation analogy on p. 186 of this manual. Ask students to identify each participant by name as he or she enters the text and the conversation unfolds.

On Avoiding Plagiarism

Rebecca Moore Howard, director of the writing program at Syracuse University, challenges us as teachers to rethink our pedagogical approach to teaching proper use of sources:

> In our stampede to fight what *The New York Times* calls a "plague" of plagiarism, we risk becoming the enemies rather than the mentors of our students; we are replacing the student-teacher relationship with the criminal-police relationship. Further, by thinking of plagiarism as a unitary act rather than a collec-

tion of disparate activities, we risk categorizing all of our students as criminals. Worst of all, we risk not recognizing that our own pedagogy needs reform. ("Forget" par. 7)

Her insights are valuable ones; students often don't understand the nuances and complexities of proper citation. As Howard explains, "Encouraged by digital dualisms, we forget that plagiarism means many different things: downloading a term paper, failing to give proper credit to the source of an idea, copying extensive passages without attribution, inserting someone else's phrases or sentences—perhaps with small changes— into your own prose, and forgetting to supply a set of quotation marks" ("Forget" par. 11). Howard suggests that instead of relying on Web sites such as <Turnitin.com> or <Plagiarism.org>, we should develop more interesting and challenging assignments, foster increased dialogue on student drafts, and offer ourselves as an authentically engaged audience for student writing.

Nick Carbone provides a lengthy and insightful discussion of pedagogical approaches to possible plagiarism in his online column, "Technology and Teaching," on the Bedford/St. Martin's TechNotes Web site:

> Turnitin.com was originally founded by John Barrie—a neurobiology graduate student—as Plagiarism.org, which still exists as a marketing arm of Turnitin.com. . . . It assumes the worst about students and the worst about teachers. It assumes students have no honor and need always to be watched and followed electronically, a big brother welcome to academic traditions. It assumes teachers are too beleaguered and inept to design classroom assignments and practices that teach students how to write responsibly. Much of what Turnitin.com proposes to detect can be avoided by careful assignment planning and teaching . . . , by paying better attention early on to students and the work they do. (pars. 5 and 15)

(18a)

FOR TEACHING: UNDERSTANDING WHY YOU SHOULD ACKNOWLEDGE YOUR SOURCES

Take time to provide your students with a bit of historical perspective on acknowledging sources and plagiarism. You might explain the etymology of *plagiarism* and the way in which the demand for originality in writing impelled an ideology of ownership. As Peter Morgan and Glenn Reynolds tell us, it was not until the romantic era that the creation of new material became culturally paramount. In classical times, imitation was not a crime:

The term "plagiarism" came from the word *plagiarius,* which literally meant "kidnapper." It was first used by the poet Martial regarding someone who had "kidnapped" some of his poems by copying them whole and circulating them under the copier's name. But while copying so as to take credit for another's work was wrong, use of another's work to create something of one's own was not. The goal was to take an idea that someone else might have had first, but to improve on it, or its execution. (par. 13)

Help your students see the proper acknowledgment of sources as a professional, economic, and scholarly responsibility—one that respects the livelihoods of other writers—so that they can begin to understand why they need to be vigilant and extremely careful in their note-taking and writing processes.

FOR COLLABORATIVE WORK: KNOWING WHICH SOURCES TO ACKNOWLEDGE (18b)

Have students work in peer-review groups to review each other's drafts for any passages that stand out as unfamiliar and mark them with the highlighter. Often students can help point out to their peers what knowledge is most probably not readily available to them without the help of sources. Peer reviewers can also point out material that is "common knowledge" and doesn't need to be cited.

On Upholding Academic Integrity and Avoiding Plagiarism (18c)

In a lecture called "Why Is Plagiarism Wrong?" given at DePauw University on November 11, 1987, Barry M. Kroll outlined the five different approaches instructors take to discourage plagiarism. The most traditional —and apparently least effective—approach involves *prohibitions.* The instructor simply tells students, typically in moralistic terms, that plagiarism is wrong. Kroll warns us, "Virtually all college students already 'know' that plagiarism is a prohibited act. But despite that knowledge, a significant number of students do not appear to take the prohibition seriously enough to be dissuaded from plagiarizing in their college papers."

The second approach involves *prevention,* an attempt to make it difficult to plagiarize. Some strategies of this approach include assigning different textbooks and paper topics from term to term and not using books for which *Cliffs Notes* exist. Unfortunately, this approach does little to teach students not to plagiarize.

Some instructors and institutions try to deter students from plagiarizing by establishing *penalties* for those caught plagiarizing. This approach gains effectiveness when supported by the institution. However, it turns instructors into police, and most instructors dislike such a role. Such a role tends to undermine instructor-student rapport. More recent software, such as that available at <Turnitin.com>, similarly constructs a policing role for the writing instructor and breaks down the trust necessary for learning. It's much more effective to discuss the rationale for acknowledging sources, give students the benefit of the doubt, and provide excellent models for them to examine.

Education's purpose is to replace an empty mind with an open one.
– MALCOLM S. FORBES

However, some instructors and institutions reject the notion that without penalties cheating would increase. Their remedy for plagiarism is to provide students with *practice* in using source material. This perspective assumes that most plagiarism is caused by unfamiliarity with the conventions of citation, sloppiness and neglect, and insufficient practice in citing sources. Unfortunately, we have ample evidence that students often do plagiarize intentionally.

The fifth approach to plagiarism—and the one that Kroll recommends—consists of teaching the *principles* behind society's attitudes toward plagiarism. In a separate study of how first-year students actually view plagiarism, Kroll discovered that they understood what it was and took it seriously, and that they could explain the wrongness of plagiarism with reference to three principles: fairness to authors; responsibility to one's education; and ownership of ideas. The latter two principles, Kroll argues, are inadequate, and the first incomplete. Kroll found no reference by students to the idea that plagiarism is wrong because it is deception. Yet, Kroll recommends that principle as being the best argument against plagiarism. Such deception is morally unacceptable and is detrimental to the institution, to the community, and to the character of the individual. Moreover, this principle is the basis for the other approaches: "For unless our students understand the reasons that plagiarism is wrong and destructive, they are likely to see our prohibitions as outmoded, to see the practices of careful documentation as merely tedious exercises, and to see the penalties for plagiarism as irrationally punitive."

In the final analysis, plagiarism can be both personally and rhetorically devastating. Whatever the personal consequences, plagiarism inevitably undermines the writer's ethos. The writer who plagiarizes loses all authority, and thus persuasion becomes an impossibility.

In "Plagiarisms, Authorship, and the Academic Death Penalty," Howard raises a number of additional issues that instructors of writing should consider as we examine our own assumptions and preconceptions about the ownership of texts and ideas.

■ USEFUL READINGS

Barks, Debbie, and Patricia Watts. "Textual Borrowing Strategies for Graduate Level ESL Writers." *Linking Literacies: Perspectives on L2 Reading/Writing Connections*. Ed. Diane Belcher and Alan Hirvela. Ann Arbor: U of Michigan P, 2001. The authors present three ideas for teaching "textual borrowing strategies to ESL students at the graduate level": classroom discussion, modeling of practices, and ethnographic approaches.

Bloch, Joel. "Plagiarism and the ESL Student: From Printed to Electronic Texts." *Linking Literacies: Perspectives on L2 Reading/Writing Connections*. Ed. Diane Belcher and Alan Hirvela. Ann Arbor: U of Michigan P, 2001. Bloch's article examines different cultural norms concerning citation and explores the significance of new technologies on writing processes in what he calls "less-developed" countries.

Carbone, Nick. "Turnitin.com, a Pedagogic Placebo for Plagiarism." *Bedford/ St. Martin's Tech Notes: Technology & Teaching*. 5 June 2001. Online at <http:// bedfordstmartins.com/technotes/techtiparchive/ttip060501.htm>. Carbone criticizes the methodology of new software technologies as "the wrong way to teach students about plagiarism, copyright, and intellectual property."

Goodwin, Doris Kearns. "How I Caused That Story." *Time* 4 Feb. 2002: 69. Online at <http://www.time.com/time/nation/article/0,8599,197614,00.html>. Goodwin explains how she unintentionally plagiarized one of her sources; her new technological approach to note-taking offers a concrete strategy you can share with your students.

Hafner, Katie. "Lessons in the School of Cut and Paste." *New York Times* 28 June 2001: E1. Hafner describes the usual signs that a student has lifted a paper off the Web and explains how teachers are now instructing students the consequences of using the Web to unethical ends.

Harris, Robert. *The Plagiarism Handbook: Strategies for Preventing, Detecting, and Dealing with Plagiarism*. Los Angeles: Pyrczak, 2001. With a positive approach to teaching students about academic honesty and appropriate use of sources, Harris emphasizes empathy with students' perspectives and gives concrete strategies for holding productive conversations about this difficult issue.

Howard, Rebecca Moore. "Forget about Policing Plagiarism. Just *Teach*." *Chronicle of Higher Education* 16 Nov. 2001: B24. Online at <http://chronicle.com/weekly/ v48/i12/12b02401.htm>. Howard asserts that new policing technologies such as <Turnitin.com> are indicative of our "mass hysteria" regarding plagiarism. She advocates instead pedagogical reform in terms of better assignments, an authentic audience, and real dialogue about the writing process.

——. "Plagiarisms, Authorships, and the Academic Death Penalty." *College English* 57 (1995): 788–806. Howard argues that plagiarism is widely misunderstood and, as a result, mistaught. Teachers of writing need to acknowledge the extent to which all writers rely on the work of others, and to teach what Howard calls "patchwriting" as a practice students can use as they learn to weave sources (fully credited) into their own texts. It is a thought-provoking review of an issue of ongoing concern to writing instructors.

Kroll, Barry M. "How College Freshmen View Plagiarism." *Written Communication* 5 (1988): 203–21. Kroll describes the results of a study in which 150 first-year college students wrote their explanations of why plagiarism is wrong, rated five standard explanations, and responded to statements about the seriousness and possible consequences of plagiarism.

Levinson, Arlene. "Paper Chase." *Portland Press Herald* 3 Sept. 2001: 2A. A look at the seedy underbelly of term-paper supply companies on the Internet.

Martin, Brian. "Plagiarism: A Misplaced Emphasis." *Journal of Information Ethics* 3.2 (Fall 1994): 36–47. Online at <http://www.uow.edu.au/arts/sts/bmartin/pubs /94jie.html>. Martin examines what he calls "the vast amount of institutionalized plagiarism," such as ghostwriting and nonattribution of authorship, and argues for reducing the stigma of plagiarism in academic contexts.

Masur, Kate. "Papers, Profits, and Pedagogy: Plagiarism in the Age of the Internet." *Perspectives Online* 39.5 (May 2001). Online at <http://www.theaha.org /perspectives/issues/2001/0105/0105new3.cfm>. Masur offers an overview of how students access online Web databases to plagiarize papers.

McNenny, Geraldine, and Duane H. Roen. "Collaboration or Plagiarism — Cheating Is in the Eye of the Beholder." *Dialogue: A Journal for Writing Specialists* 1 (Fall 1993): 6–27.

Morgan, Peter W., and Glenn H. Reynolds. "A Plague of Originality," *Idler* 23 (Jan. 2002). Online at <http://www.the-idler.com/IDLER-02/1-23.html>. This electronic version of chapter 5 of *The Appearance of Impropriety* begins with the ironic observation that the University of Oregon's teaching assistant handbook plagiarized Stanford University's section on plagiarism. The article then provides an eye-opening history of plagiarism and offers a compelling case for considering the ethics of the practice.

Scanlon, Patrick M., and David R. Neumann. "Internet Plagiarism among College Students." *Journal of College Student Development* 43.3 (May–June 2002): 374–85. Professors from the Rochester Institute of Technology have found that students do not plagiarize from the Internet as much as we might think: out of 698 students, only a minority reported cutting and pasting material without citations. More interesting is their finding that statistically speaking, the numbers remain the same for print-based theft as for Web-site theft.

■ USEFUL WEB SITES

Antiplagiarism Strategies for Research Papers

http://www.virtualsalt.com/antiplag.htm

Drawn from his book The Plagiarism Handbook, *Robert Harris delineates strategies of awareness, detection, and prevention.*

Plagiarism and the Web

http://www.wiu.edu/users/mfbhl/wiu/plagiarism.htm

Bruce Leland lists a number of commercial Web sites where students can procure papers and offers concrete strategies for teachers to use in order to confront and avoid plagiarism.

Plagiarism.org

http://plagiarism.org

This subscription-based service allows you to submit student papers for scrutiny and to get reports on whether the work was plagiarized. Feedback can include directions to where on the Web the paper was obtained and charts analyzing how much of a paper was plagiarized.

Tech Notes: Thinking and Talking about Plagiarism

http://bedfordstmartins.com/technotes/techtiparchive/ttip102401.htm

An excellent discussion of alternative approaches to teaching students about plagiarism (rather than policing them), Nick Carbone's page offers excerpts from his own syllabi as well as an invaluable list of links.

Tools for Teaching: Preventing Academic Dishonesty

http://teaching.berkeley.edu/bgd/prevent.html

From her book Tools for Teaching, *Barbara Gross Davis provides concrete steps and general strategies that teachers can use to help prevent academic dishonesty.*

19

Writing for a Research Project

Nothing will work unless you do.
– Maya Angelou

The contemporary idea of "research" for an essay seems not to have gained much currency in college classrooms until the older idea of *all* reading (and especially the keeping of commonplace books) as research began to fade during the nineteenth century. Robert Connors notes that as students could be "counted on less and less for the sorts of commonplace knowledge that the older classical curriculum specialized in, teachers found general assignments worked less and less well. One solution was to ask students to go to the library (a place not easily accessible for most people, even college students, until about 1869 and after) and look up information in books." But this solution only led to more difficulties, notably copying verbatim or "plagiarizing." As a result, according to Connors, "teachers came to turn more and more to assignments that had at least some element of first-person experience." Research could then be used to support this experience, and such assignments grew increasingly common during the 1890s. The first handbook to include a full chapter on the research paper appears to have been Hodges's 1941 *Harbrace Handbook,* and by the 1950s this assignment was firmly entrenched in the college curriculum.

The idea of writing a research-based essay may seem daunting to many students, especially first-year composition students or students who have never written more than a brief response paper. Your job will be as much to motivate, inspire, and lead them through this process as it will be to supervise their research and writing. Most of all, students need encouragement and assurance that they can indeed join the community of scholars.

Every noble work is at first impossible.
– Thomas Carlyle

ATTENDING TO DISABILITIES: REFINING YOUR PLANS   **(19a)**

Realize that students with disabilities may need extra time and support in the completion of a research-based writing project. For students with attention-deficit disorders or other learning impairments, you can offer invaluable assistance with the structure and schedule by providing a syllabus with clearly delineated due dates. However, be flexible if these students have a hard time meeting the course deadlines. Meet with them and collaborate to create a makeup schedule, or allow them extra time to incorporate materials and write the paper. Students with visual impairments may need extra time to access textbooks, library materials, and films. Make sure that your institution has a range of adaptive technologies, such as Braille readers, printer-to-voice conversion software, and voice-to-text production technology.

For many deaf students, English is a second language; these students may need extra tutoring in grammar and mechanics. Provide them with guided notes on your Web site for any lectures on research-based essays, and make sure your Web site is ADA compliant and works with adaptive technology.

**FOR TEACHING: RECONSIDERING YOUR
PURPOSE, AUDIENCE, STANCE, AND WORKING THESIS**   **(19a1)**

To help your students appreciate the value of the questions in 19a1, point out that they help students:

1. Identify their intended audience.
2. Judge whether to define basic terms or to take for granted that their audience already has a basic familiarity with the subject or field. For example, they wouldn't have to define *regeneration* for an audience of senior-level students working in molecular genetics or *apartheid* for senior-level political science students. But in a paper examining *economic disparity* in South Africa that they are writing for a composition class, they might want to define and explain that term fully.
3. Evaluate the sources they will use and how to use them. If the audience is not a specialized one, students will not want to assume that a simple mention of some researcher's claims will give an audience sufficient understanding. If the source involves an advanced level of understanding, and the audience is not a professor or some other well-informed, advanced audience, then sources will have to be carefully explained.

4. Decide on how to present themselves, to identify their relationship to the audience, and to judge how they want to appear to the audience.

5. Consider further how they see their subject. What are they trying to prove? What are they trying to explain? What is their purpose in relation to their potential audience?

6. Reconsider their thesis with the audience in mind. Is the thesis new to the audience? a restatement? a reexamination of something they already assume or accept?

(19a2)

FOR COLLABORATIVE WORK: DEVELOPING AN EXPLICIT THESES

To make fuller use of the thesis statement form in section 19a2, call on a student to present his or her statement to the class. To get things started, ask the writer to clarify or define terms or vague points. Ask the student why he or she has picked the subject. In other words, open the class up to a brainstorming session in which the writer is allowed to answer the class's questions and make clearer the thesis and purpose. In fielding the class's responses, the writer will likely clarify the project in his or her own mind. The writer will see where difficulties lie, where command of the subject is lacking, or where he or she will need to elaborate. The writer may find that the project is too large or may find a way of refining the thesis.

> *I am strongly in favor of intelligent, even fastidious revision, which is, or certainly should be, an art in itself. . . .*
> – JOYCE CAROL OATES

Once you have demonstrated this activity for the whole class, break the students up into groups of two or three and have them work on each other's thesis statements.

(19b)

FOR TEACHING: ORGANIZING INFORMATION

Just as we all have different preferred modalities for learning, we also have different approaches to organizing information. Engage your students in discussion about how they shape their research notes into a draft. Do they begin with a numerical outline? Do they freewrite several pages to discover their direction? Do they group information by subject headings?

(19b)

FOR COLLABORATIVE WORK: ORGANIZING INFORMATION

A new program at Stanford University called "How I Write: Conversations with Faculty" allows students to hear firsthand about the research strategies of senior faculty members across the disciplines. By learning about different strategies for approaching research and producing texts, students become critically aware of their own writing processes. One student, Angela, reflected, "I was glad to find that I wasn't the only one who gets stuck when I write . . . other students and even other professors do, too! I guess it is always a challenge to write something that really expresses what you want to say, and that's why it always take a longer time to revise and revise, until you are satisfied with the writing."

Set up a similar conversation in your own classroom by asking students to interview each other about the writing process. How do they approach the organization of information? Do they need music or food in order to write? How do they work through writer's block? Do they rely on an outline or note cards grouped by subject heading?

FOR TEACHING: OUTLINING   **(19b2)**

The point can't be overemphasized: a full formal outline is devilishly hard to write before one has actually produced at least a revised draft. A working outline is all that students should expect to produce. It can tentatively guide or reflect their planning. Assure your students that an outline is flexible. It mainly serves as a rough plan that enables them to start writing and organizing information. It is subject to revision once they've started writing. This advice rests on the thinking that not until writers put something down on paper can they really judge and plan the appropriateness of the content and format to purpose and audience.

TEACHING WITH TECHNOLOGY: DRAFTING   **(19c)**

Almost all students now compose on a computer. Word processors—with their cut-and-paste function, quick saving capability, and interface with online databases and image banks—make for effective drafting of research-based essays. However, there are practical tips for working with technology that you should bring to the attention of your students:

- Save often and in various formats. You might ask students to use a floppy or CD-ROM for the duration of the writing project in order to back up all of their work. Students can FTP their work up to their home directories on the Internet as well.

- Print out draft versions. Encourage students to print out various stages of their drafting so that there is a record of their writing process. A printed copy can also be a lifesaver if the document file is lost. Moreover, inform students that different kinds of revision and editing changes are made when one can see the entire document versus single lines on a screen. Ask them to reflect on the different kinds of changes they made depending on whether they revised on paper or on a computer screen.

(19c)

FOR COLLABORATIVE WORK: DRAFTING INTRODUCTIONS AND CONCLUSIONS

Have students working in groups of five brainstorm a list of purposes that they think the introduction and conclusion should serve. Ask them to be as specific as possible. Once they've compiled lists, ask them to seek out major journals in various fields and to identify and compare the actual purposes of introductions and conclusions. Here are some possibilities they may come up with:

1. *Introductions*
   State the problem or topic to be explored.
   Give briefly the background or context for the question or topic.
   Get readers interested.
   Give briefly the reason for discussing or researching a topic.

2. *Conclusions*
   Answer the question initially raised in the introduction.
   Confirm the hypothesis.
   Repeat the main idea or point that the article has worked to explain.
   Confirm the importance of the question or subject.
   Suggest areas for further research.

(19e)

FOR TEACHING: REVIEWING YOUR DRAFT

Suggest to students that they copy the questions in section 19e for reviewing drafts into their logs in a prominent place so that they can turn easily to them at any point in the drafting process. The log is a good place to reflect on the current state of any draft they may be working on.

(19e)

FOR MULTILINGUAL WRITERS: REVIEWING AND GETTING RESPONSES TO YOUR DRAFT

For students whose first language is not English, collaborative readings of a draft can greatly enhance their understanding of how a text accomplishes its purpose. Put students into pairs, and ask them to read their drafts out loud to each other. Not only will the auditory expression of the text reveal errors in usage, logic, and organization, but it will also provide multilingual writers with an immediate audience response on the effectiveness of the draft in progress.

FOR TEACHING: REVISING AND EDITING   **(19f)** ··

You might suggest that students use different colored pens or highlighters to work through the various responses they have received on their drafts. In addition, have them respond to the steps in section 19f of the *Handbook* and write a short reflective memo about their revision process. This final step will help them become more aware of their writing strategies and encourage them to apply these steps to future writing endeavors.

TEACHING WITH TECHNOLOGY: PREPARING
AND PROOFREADING YOUR FINAL COPY   **(19h)** ··

Remind students that the spell-check and grammar-check functions on their computers will not always catch every mistake. It's best to proofread the final copy one last time—by reading it out loud, showing it to a dorm tutor or writing center consultant, or scanning the text backwards.

■ **USEFUL READINGS**

Bazerman, Charles. *The Informed Writer: Using Sources in the Disciplines.* 5th ed. Boston: Houghton, 1994. See, especially, his discussion and examples of literature reviews.

Brent, Doug. *Reading and Rhetorical Invention: Knowledge, Persuasion, and the Teaching of Research-Based Writing.* Urbana: NCTE, 1992.

Dickson, Marcia. *It's Not Like That Here: Teaching Academic Writing and Reading to Novices.* Portsmouth: Boynton, 1995. See especially Dickson's cogent discussion of research and writing in chapter 4, "Putting It All Together: Reading, Writing, and Research" (pp. 75–122).

Dinitz, Susan, and Jean Kiedaisch. "The Research Paper: Teaching Students to Be Members of the Academic Community." *Exercise Exchange* 31 (1986): 8–10. The authors suggest that rhetorical concerns — purpose and voice — should be primary concerns for research papers.

I rewrite so much that the first chapter of a book sometimes may be rewritten forty or fifty times. . . . It's this way, see—when a writer first starts out, he gets a big kick from the stuff he does, and the reader doesn't get any; then, after a while, the writer gets a little kick and the reader gets a little kick; and finally, if the writer's any good, he doesn't get any kick at all and the reader gets everything.
    – ERNEST HEMINGWAY

Gay, Pamela. "Dialogizing Response in the Writing Classroom: Students Answer Back." *Journal of Basic Writing* 17.1 (Spring 1998): 3–17. Gay proposes a dialogic approach to teacher commentary on student-written texts wherein students respond to a teacher's comments immediately after receiving them. She also proposes that students write letters to teachers, identifying their goals, strengths, and weaknesses.

Jeske, Jeff. "Borrowing from the Sciences: A Model for the Freshman Research Paper." *Writing Instructor* 6 (Winter 1987): 62–67. This helpful four-part model for writing the research essay encourages students to reflect on the research process itself while they are producing a research project.

McCormick, Kathleen. *The Culture of Reading and Teaching of English.* Manchester: U Manchester P, 1994. See especially chapters 4 and 5, which deal with research-based writing.

Moran, Mary Hurley. "Connections between Reading and Successful Revision." *Journal of Basic Writing* 16.2 (Fall 1997): 76–89. Moran examines the view that reading drafts aloud produces successful writing by attending to the correlation between reading ability and the efficacy of this activity. Her findings—that reading drafts aloud was beneficial to students with adequate or good reading skills but did not make any significant difference in the case of poor readers—have consequences for classroom practices and should encourage teachers to take into consideration the reading-proficiency levels of their students.

■ USEFUL WEB SITES

DO-IT Program: Disabilities, Opportunities, Internetworking, and Technology

http://www.washington.edu/doit

A series of Web pages for students, teachers, administrators, and nonacademic professionals, with instructional pages, links, and resource information.

Ohio State University's Fast Facts for Faculty

http://www.osu.edu/grants/dpg/fastfact/writing.html

This site offers concrete advice and resources for teachers to design their pedagogy with students with disabilities in mind.

20

⬇ Documenting Sources: MLA Style

The style recommended by the association for preparing scholarly manuscripts and student research papers concerns itself with the mechanics of writing, such as punctuation, quotation, and documentation of sources. MLA style has been widely adopted by schools, academic departments, and instructors for nearly half a century.
— MLA Web site

In "The Rhetoric of Citations Systems," Robert Connors traces the origins of contemporary citation forms to manuscript annotation practices, which go all the way back to the beginnings of alphabetical literacy. With the development of movable type in the mid-fifteenth century, however, printers and authors began to develop the formal structures that are now familiar to us as notes and citations. Before 1580, the two familiar kinds of notes, dialogic and reference notes, had become standard. Scholars argued over which notes and what kinds of content were appropriate, but recognizable modern marginal notes had evolved by 1690, and the first footnotes began to appear soon after. During the eighteenth century, citation systems were refined and brought to a high development by such historians as David Hume and, most famously, Edward Gibbon, whose *Decline and Fall of the Roman Empire* remains a touchstone of expert use of both dialogic and reference notes. In the nineteenth century, citation structures evolved further, especially in the sciences, which use annotations for slightly different purposes than do the humanities. During the late nineteenth century, the first citation-style books and pamphlets for authors appeared, and finally, in 1951, the Modern Language Association (MLA) published its first official manual.

Today, citation styles are important to the self-definition of many disciplines, and their forms reflect serious choices for writers and publishers. Indeed, the ideology of citation practices and styles is hotly debated. We suggest that student writers think about the implications of citation styles, what they foreground, and what they erase.

On the Reasons for Documenting Sources

Generally speaking, writers document their sources for four reasons.

1. Careful documentation gives credit for words or ideas to the original writer or speaker, and relieves the writer of any indictment of plagiarism.

2. Documentation lends the writer authority as a researcher. It says to the reader, "I am honest and open to anyone wishing to retrace the steps in my research." Documentation is an important element in the ethos of the writer presenting research. Undocumented (plagiarized) sources—or sources imprecisely documented, even if only slightly—suggest that the writer is careless or even dishonest.

3. Documentation is a courtesy to later writers on the subject who may want to use some of the material. Documentation provides them with directions for finding it.

4. Documentation allows others to follow up on a writer's research in order to test its validity. Not only should writers tolerate such a procedure; they should welcome it. To have others look so carefully at one's work implies that such work is important.

On the History of Documentation

The practice of documenting sources developed out of the larger movement toward bibliography and documentation that has become a hallmark of the twentieth century. Documentation arose out of the increase of information and the growth of information systems.

In ancient times, information storage and retrieval was accomplished for the most part by individuals mnemonically and by societies through rituals. With the rise of literacy came the desire to classify information systematically in the form of writing. The first libraries were built simply to preserve but not to make available their information. That intention really did not begin to change until the late nineteenth century.

Plagiarists are always suspicious of being stolen from.
– Samuel Taylor Coleridge

An important development in the history of documentation was the change during the late Middle Ages and Renaissance in the notion of authorship. Medieval authors did not view their work as necessarily theirs alone; there was little sense of knowledge as somehow owned or its origins as deserving acknowledgment. However, in modern times, authorship became more personalized; writers began to think in terms of "original" ideas and to believe that they had a right to be acknowledged as authors of such ideas.

The invention of the printing press and the great increase in the desire for knowledge during the Renaissance helped increase the flow of information via books and the need for some way to classify such information in order to make it more readily available. Many different and individualized systems of classification and organization of information developed until, in the late nineteenth century, American librarian Melvil Dewey invented the Dewey Decimal System of Classification, which libraries quickly adopted.

The form of such acknowledgment, whether it is MLA style or APA style or any of the many other documentation styles, derives from bibliographical description. Such description is meant to record various characteristics of each book, thereby revealing the uniqueness of each.

FOR TEACHING: MLA FORMAT FOR IN-TEXT CITATIONS   **(20a)**

According to the MLA Web site, there is a particular way to cite electronic texts that have no page numbers. Share the following information from that site with your students:

> In parenthetical references in the text, works on the World Wide Web are cited just like printed works. For any type of source, you must include information in your text that directs readers to the correct entry in the works-cited list (see the *MLA Handbook,* sec. 5.2). Web documents generally do not have fixed page numbers or any kind of section numbering. If your source lacks numbering, you have to omit numbers from your parenthetical references. If your source includes fixed page numbers or section numbering (such as numbering of paragraphs), cite the relevant numbers. Give the appropriate abbreviation before the numbers: "(Moulthrop, pars. 19–20)." (*Pars.* is the abbreviation for *paragraphs.* Common abbreviations are listed in the *MLA Handbook,* sec. 6.4.) For a document on the Web, the page numbers of a printout should normally not be cited, because the pagination may vary in different printouts.

FOR MULTILINGUAL WRITERS: IN-TEXT CITATIONS   **(20a)**

You can address the concerns of multilingual writers by asking them to bring in examples of in-text citations and share them in small groups. Pick examples from student papers, write them on the board for collective review, and then correct the citations as a class. It's helpful to explain the rationale for a particular citation rule as you correct it. At the end of the workshop, leave time for students to ask questions.

(20a) TEACHING WITH TECHNOLOGY: MLA FORMAT FOR IN-TEXT CITATIONS

Try the preceeding exercise in a computer-networked classroom. See Alexandra Barron's online article, "Collaborative Teaching in the Computer Classroom," for ways to "teach MLA documentation to a class without putting students to sleep."

(20b) FOR COLLABORATIVE WORK: MLA FORMAT
FOR EXPLANATORY AND BIBLIOGRAPHIC NOTES

Ask students to exchange copies of their drafts in writing groups and have each student use a highlighter to indicate places in the text that merit an explanatory note. Often, positioning students as the primary audience for a draft will help writers learn when to use explanatory or bibliographic notes.

You can also use a variation of this exercise by asking students to evaluate each note critically. Have students work through the following questions:

• Is the essay's argument hidden in an explanatory note?
• Are there too many notes?
• Do the notes detract from the flow of the essay?
• Should the list of bibliographic references be alluded to in the body of the essay rather than tucked into a note?

(20c) FOR TEACHING: MLA FORMAT FOR A LIST OF WORKS CITED

Spend some time in class discussing the purpose for adhering to the MLA style in the works cited list. Students often view the necessity of learning technical details for MLA style as an onerous task, one without intrinsic merit. But if you remind them that they are participating in a community of scholars and that they need to cite sources as a matter of professional courtesy, then they might be more enthusiastic about learning and following the MLA documentation format.

On the Use of *et al.*

Even though *et al.* has been the preferred MLA option for citing four or more authors, you may want to encourage students to use the second MLA option — that of naming all the authors — because *et al.* leaves all but the first author nameless. As a result, it implicitly devalues collaborative work, suggesting that the only person with any *real* authority is the first author. Yet many who have written collaboratively would agree with Mary Belenky, who argues that such work should count twice as much as that which is singly authored because it is doubly difficult. As a result of these considerations, the authors of this book routinely cite all authors of a work.

TEACHING WITH TECHNOLOGY: MLA FORMAT FOR A LIST OF WORKS CITED   **(20c)** ·······················

Students might complain about the time it takes to format the MLA works-cited list properly. If so, you can tell your class about an excellent software tool called TermPerfect. Students can download a copy for around $10 and use this tool to construct a works-cited list in correct MLA style. They simply enter all the fields, and the program does the rest. You may want to inform students about this tool so that they spend most of their time and attention on the writing of their essays, not necessarily on the finer details of documentation. See the Web site at <www.termperfect .com>.

On Documenting Electronic Sources   **(20c3)** ·······················

Since the publication of the fifth edition of the *MLA Handbook for Writers of Research Papers* in 1999, the MLA has been working to devise a standard style for citing electronic sources. The guidelines provided in Chapter 20 of the *Handbook* adopt these latest MLA guidelines. But several other efforts have been made to adapt MLA style for electronic sources. Janice Walker and Todd Taylor developed a set of guidelines in *The Columbia Guide to Online Style* that can be used for citing electronic sources in *any* of the major styles (MLA, APA, and so on). In addition, building on the work of Walker and Taylor, Andrew Harnack and Eugene Kleppinger have given us *Online!,* which includes guidelines for citing electronic sources based on MLA style.

As these stylistic conventions emerge, our best advice is to help students use *consistent* citation patterns and to alert them to the current debate.

(20d)   **FOR TEACHING: A SAMPLE RESEARCH ESSAY, MLA STYLE**

The outline. Shannan Palma used a key-point working outline as she drafted and redrafted the essay on "Hollywood and the Hero." She produced the formal outline, which appears on pp. 442 – 44 of the *Handbook*, at the point of revising her next-to-last draft, as a means of checking the structure of and logical connections in her essay. She reports that this late outlining always produces better results for her.

The epigraph. Note that Shannan Palma uses the lines of a popular song as an epigraph for her essay. During her drafting, she experimented with using epigraphs for every subdivision of the essay, but eventually decided to drop them because MLA offers no guidelines for them! You may want to discuss the function of epigraphs with your students.

The introduction. After reading the introductory paragraphs (note that Shannan Palma takes *two* paragraphs for her introduction), direct your students to 19a1 and use the eight questions under "Reconsidering your purpose, audience, stance, and working thesis" as a basis for discussing how she establishes her rhetorical stance.

The thesis. Call students' attention to Palma's thesis on p. 442 and then ask them to test it against the questions provided in 19a3.

Paraphrases. Direct students' attention to the discussion of accurate and effective paraphrasing in 16e3. Then ask them to decide how well Shannan Palma has followed the guidelines given there.

Quotations. Refer students to the discussion of direct quotations in 16e2, and then ask them to examine the use of direct quotation in the student essay. What in these quotations is particularly necessary and/or memorable? What other functions do the quotations serve?

In addition, point out the formal features of long quotations, such as rules for indentation, and then reread "Setting off long quotations"

(17b2) with the class, noting that long quotations must be introduced in some clear and explanatory way.

Finally, reread the section on "Integrating quotations smoothly into your text" (17b3) and then discuss how Shannan Palma integrates quotations into her own sentences.

The conclusion. Ask students to refer to "Drafting your conclusion" (19c2). Then ask them to identify the strategies Shannan Palma uses in her conclusion. How effective do they find the conclusion? What alternative conclusions can they offer?

■ **USEFUL READINGS**

Ashton-Jones, Evelyn, and Dene Thomas. "Composition, Collaboration, and Women's Ways of Knowing: A Conversation with Mary Belenky." *Journal of Advanced Composition* 10.2 (Fall 1990): 275–92. An interview in which Mary Belenky describes collaborative work as doubly difficult.

Barron, Alexandra. "Collaborative Teaching in the Computer Classroom." *Currents in Electronic Literacy* 6 (Spring 2002). Online at <http://www.cwrl.utexas .edu/currents/spring02/barron.html>. Barron provides a list of concrete ways to use technology to encourage collaborative learning and the mastery of MLA style.

Bloom, Lynn Z. "Why I (Used to) Hate to Give Grades." *CCC* 48 (1997): 360–71. Bloom offers here an essay that is, as she says, "solidly grounded in current research without any citations." Well worth reading to see how she does it!

Connors, Robert. "The Rhetoric of Citation Systems." Parts 1 and 2. *Rhetoric Review* 17 (Fall 1998): 6–49 and 17 (Spring 1999): 219–46. This lengthy essay recounts the history of citation practices and styles in the first part and discusses "Competing Epistemic Values in Citation" in the second.

Gibaldi, Joseph. *MLA Handbook for Writers of Research Papers.* 5th ed. New York: MLA, 1999. The definitive sourcebook for MLA style.

Harnack, Andrew, and Gene Kleppinger. "Beyond the *MLA Handbook:* Documenting Sources on the Internet." *Kairos* 1 (1996). This article identifies difficulties in using traditional citation styles for Internet sources and recommends alternative models. The same issue includes an interesting and helpful response from Janice Walker, author of the guidelines adopted by the Association for Computers and Writing and of *The Columbia Guide to Online Style.*

Walker, Janice, and Todd Taylor. *The Columbia Guide to Online Style.* New York: Columbia UP, 1998.

■ **USEFUL WEB SITES**

Alliance for Computers and Writing

http://english.ttu.edu/acw

The ACW homepage will introduce you to this group's many activities.

Bedford/St. Martin's English Research Room

http://bedfordstmartins.com/english-research

This online research tutorial offers advice on many steps in the research process, along with links to other research and documentation resources.

Modern Language Association

http://www.mla.org

The MLA's homepage allows you to click on "MLA Style" for more information and updates.

Online! Guide: Using MLA Style to Cite and Document Internet Sources

http://www.bedfordstmartins.com/online/cite5.html

This detailed and accessible online guide to citing Internet sources in MLA style answers many questions students have about specific cases.

TermPerfect

http://www.termperfect.com

TermPerfect, an affordable software solution for students who need to compose a works-cited list, is available online from DigitalStudentware, Inc.

21

▼ Documenting Sources: APA Style

The new, fifth edition provides expanded coverage of technological advances in publishing, as well as the most up-to-date information on APA style guidelines and more in-depth coverage of case studies, tables, and lots more.   –APA Web site

The current *Publication Manual of the American Psychological Association* (APA) has evolved since 1929, when it began as a seven-page article offering general guidelines for stylistic standards, to a book of well over three hundred detail-filled pages. Now followed by writers in a number of fields throughout the social sciences, the APA guidelines aim to foster clear communication and easy reference.

According to the APA Web site, the APA *Publication Manual* is the style manual of choice for many disciplines where effective communication in words and data is fundamental, including psychology, sociology, business, economics, nursing, social work, and criminology. Many of your students majoring in these fields will need to learn and use APA style on a regular basis.

FOR COLLABORATIVE WORK: APA FORMAT FOR IN-TEXT CITATIONS

Send students to the following page at the APA Web site entitled "Citations in Text of Electronic Material." Have students read the guidelines out loud and then work through one another's drafts, helping correct any errors and making the essays conform to APA style.

> To cite a specific part of a source, indicate the page, chapter, figure, table, or equation at the appropriate point in text. Always give page numbers for quotations (see section 3.34). Note that the words *page* and *chapter* are abbreviated in such text citations:

(Cheek & Buss, 1981, p. 332)
(Shimamura, 1989, chap. 3)

For electronic sources that do not provide page numbers, use the paragraph number, if available, preceded by the paragraph symbol or the abbreviation *para*. If neither paragraph nor page numbers are visible, cite the heading and the number of the paragraph following it to direct the reader to the location of the material (see section 3.39).

(Myers, 2000, ¶ 5)
(Beutler, 2000, Conclusion section, para. 1)

–<http://www.apastyle.org/electext.html>

TEACHING WITH TECHNOLOGY: APA FORMAT FOR A LIST OF REFERENCES

Ask students to bring in working bibliographies on diskette and put them on a computer screen for collective assessment and review. Have students consult the APA resource Web site, "APA Reference Examples for Electronic Source Materials" at <www.apastyle.org/elecsource.html>. In small groups, make corrections on the computer where necessary. Then have each group present to the others common errors found in the working bibliographies. Leave time at the end of class to go over any questions.

■ **USEFUL READING**

American Psychological Association. *Publication Manual of the American Psychological Association.* 5th ed. Washington, DC: APA, 2001.

■ **USEFUL WEB SITES**

American Psychological Association
http://www.apa.org
The APA's homepage has much useful information for students — and their instructors!

APA Style: Electronic References
http://www.apastyle.org/elecref.html
A regularly updated Web page providing guidance on citing electronic sources.

APA Style: Frequently Asked Questions

http://www.apastyle.org/faqs.html

The APA's FAQ page provides useful information about APA documentation style.

***Online! Guide*: Using Principles of APA Style to Cite and Document Sources**

http://www.bedfordstmartins.com/online/cite6.html

This detailed and accessible online guide to citing Internet sources in APA style answers many questions students have about specific cases.

22 Documenting Sources: CBE Style

A must for anyone—author, editor, publisher, student, translator, science writer—responsible for writing or publishing scientific material. The book recommends both general and scientific publication style and formats for journals, books, and other types of publications.

—*CBE Manual* Web site

While MLA and APA styles of documentation are widely used in the humanities and social sciences, other disciplines typically use other styles. But like scholars and organizations in the humanities and social sciences, scientists also felt a growing need for a style of documentation that matched their requirements and purposes. Thus the Conference of Biological Editors published its first manual of scientific citation styles in 1960. Now widely used in the sciences, CBE style is currently recommended by the Council of Biology Editors and its newer incarnation, the Council of Science Editors.

Major revisions and changes are underway for the new seventh edition of *Scientific Style and Format* (better known as the *CBE Manual*). Since the Council of Science Editors Style Manual Committee will be previewing these changes as they become available, you can follow the developments online at the CBE Web site, <www.cbe.org/pubs_ssf_7th.shtml>.

■ **USEFUL READINGS**

Biology and Natural Sciences

Council of Biology Editors. *Scientific Style and Format: The CBE Manual for Authors, Editors, and Publishers.* 6th ed. New York: Cambridge UP, 1994.

Geology

Suggestions to Authors of the Reports of the United States Geological Survey. 7th ed. Washington: GPO, 1991.

Mathematics

A Manual for Authors of Mathematical Papers. 8th ed. Providence: American Mathematical Soc., 1989.

Medicine

American Medical Association Manual of Style. 9th ed. Baltimore: Williams, 1998. This comprehensive guide to publication in the medical sciences includes chapters on preparing an article for publication, ethical and legal considerations, style terminology, quantification and measurement, and technical information.

Patrias, Karen. *National Library of Medicine Recommended Formats for Bibliographic Citations.* Bethesda: National Library of Medicine, 1991. See chapter 12, pp. 101–61, on electronic formats. See also <http://www.nlm.nih.gov/pubs/formats/internet.pdf> for the 2001 addendum on Internet sources.

■ **USEFUL WEB SITES**

Online! Guide: Using Principles of CBE Style to Cite and Document Sources

http://www.bedfordstmartins.com/online/cite8.html

This detailed and accessible online guide to citing sources in CBE style answers many questions students have about specific cases.

Scientific Style and Format: The CBE Manual for Authors, Editors, and Publishers

http://www.cbe.org/pubs_ssf.shtml

The main Web page for the CBE Manual, *maintained by the Council of Biology Editors Style Manual Committee, includes links to previews of the forthcoming seventh edition, particularly formats for bibliographic citation of Internet sources.*

23 Documenting Sources: Chicago Style

[T]he one essential reference for all who work with words—writers, editors, proofreaders, indexers, copywriters, designers, and publishers. Almost 200 pages longer than its predecessor, this edition reflects nearly every significant change in style, usage, procedure, and technology. It is easier to use, richer in illustrative examples, and informed everywhere by the presence of computers in publishing, from manuscript preparation to editing, typesetting, indexing, design, and printing.

–The Chicago Manual of Style, 14th ed.

First published in 1906, *The Chicago Manual of Style* became the touchstone for use of footnote styles. Now in its fourteenth edition (1993), this classic reference work provides consistent and systematic advice about punctuation, design, and typography as well as about documentation. It is still a standard.

■ USEFUL READINGS

General Reference

Howell, John Bruce. *Style Manuals of the English-speaking World.* Phoenix: Oryx, 1983.

Law

The Bluebook: A Uniform System of Citation. 17th ed. Cambridge: Harvard Law Review Assn., 2000.

Linguistics

LSA Bulletin, December issue, annually.

■ **USEFUL WEB SITES**

The Chicago Manual of Style Online: Frequently Asked Questions

http://www.press.uchicago.edu/Misc/Chicago/cmosfaq/

As a supplement to the hardcopy, this Web site provides an extensive list of questions and answers grouped by keyword.

Ohio State University Libraries: *Chicago Manual of Style* Form Guide

http://www.lib.ohio-state.edu/guides/chicagogd.html

A very accessible guide to help students work through the Chicago guidelines.

Online! Guide: Using Principles of Chicago Style to Cite and Document Sources

http://www.bedfordstmartins.com/online/cite7.html

From the Web site of Online! *this detailed online guide to citing sources in Chicago style answers many questions students have about specific cases.*

PART 5

USING LANGUAGE EFFECTIVELY

24 ▼ Writing to the World

As we see more diversity both in our classrooms and in our professional circles, we need to reevaluate what it means to "write to the world." How can we teach students to communicate across cultures and with various audiences, using appropriate evidence and structures, and with an eye toward what it means to "write well" in a particular context or community? Perhaps the best lesson we can teach our students is that all language use is embedded in multiple contexts and gains meaning in and through those contexts. Thus what is utterly persuasive in one context fails miserably in another; what is elegant in one is tacky in another; what is clear and well organized in one may be anything but in yet another.

Scholars of contrastive rhetoric have been trying to teach us these lessons for a long time. The Sapir-Whorf hypothesis, for instance, proposes a kind of linguistic relativism that recognizes the intricate relationship between language and culture—but we have yet to apply this hypothesis to teaching U.S. students how to write well. The early work of Robert Kaplan, arguing that language and writing are culturally embedded and that varying languages are characterized by different patterns of organization, logic, and so on, gained widespread attention, including charges of essentialism. Today Kaplan's early work is still relevant, and it has been expanded by a number of others who are helping teachers understand writing as a cultural activity. Ideally, our students would all learn to engage in contrastive rhetorical analysis in order to understand their own preferences for particular writing patterns and styles as well as those of others. Chapter 24, "Writing to the World," asks students to begin this important work.

On Writing to the World

This concept of world writing draws on the powerful work of Maria Lugones. In "Playfulness, World Traveling, and Loving Perception," Lugones uses the term "world traveling" and says, "The reason I think that traveling to someone's 'world' is a way of identifying with them is because by traveling to their 'world' we can understand *what it is to be them and what it is to be ourselves in their eyes*" (17).

On Reconsidering What Seems "Normal"   **(24b)**

Disability scholar Lennard J. Davis has shown that the terms *normal* and *normality* didn't enter English usage until 1857. These terms, Davis tells us, were mobilized in Western Europe and the United States by pioneers in the fields of statistics and eugenics to signify "constituting, conforming to, not deviating or differing from, the common type or standard, regular, usual" (24). As educators in composition, we can make our students aware of the historical baggage associated with the term *normal* and work instead for a more global, open acceptance of difference in both the writing we require and the standards we teach.

ATTENDING TO DISABILITIES: RECONSIDERING WHAT SEEMS "NORMAL"   **(24b)**

Realizing that appropriate behavior, discourse, and conventions are culturally and community bound, you might encourage a discussion of "normalcy" on the first day. Try engaging your students in a critical analysis of the social norms perpetuated by the media, advertising, popular movies, and magazines. Design your lesson plan with the following questions from Johnson Cheu in mind:

> What are students' preconceptions about disability, and how should their literacies regarding disability influence pedagogy and curriculum?
>
> How does a teacher validate students' "uneasy" feelings and experiences surrounding disability yet assist them in finding their own way of engaging with the subject matter? (Brueggemann, White, Dunn, Heifferon, and Cheu, 387)

Teach students that being a world writer means expanding one's conception of the world to include all participants. Let your students with disabilities share their perspectives on encountering obstacles to learning with other students so that together, we can begin to change the social norms that constrict our understanding of what seems normal.

(24b)

FOR COLLABORATIVE WORK: RECONSIDERING WHAT SEEMS "NORMAL"

Ask students to work in groups of three to answer the following questions. Ask each group to draw up a report of their findings and present it to the class.

1. What do you think are the "good manners" of writing? That is, how do you show politeness in writing?
2. In general, what kind of evidence is most persuasive to you, and why?
3. What styles and tones in writing appeal to you most? Which carry the most authority? Which work best in college?

(24c)

FOR COLLABORATIVE WORK: LISTENING FOR MEANING

Paul Kei Matsuda and Tony Silva offer a classroom exercise focused on raising awareness and understanding of cultural differences. In this "cultural profile" exercise, students form groups of three, with each student representing a different cultural group. Students interview one another, trying to learn all they can about cultural practices that differ from their own. In Matsuda's and Silva's own classes, students have discussed such issues as arranged marriage in Japan and India, the status of women in Indonesia, and the use of physical punishment by teachers in Korea. Students identified "dissonances" between their own and others' cultural practices and then interviewed each other again, trying to gain a better understanding of the particular practice in its local culture.

(24c)

FOR TEACHING: LISTENING FOR MEANING

Ask students to pay careful attention, during two classes and at least one out-of-class activity (a conversation at home, a trip to a concert or movie), to what they seem to be listening for. What kinds of things "stick" in their minds? What are their purposes for listening? Are they listening with an eye toward making a comment or response themselves? learning something new? changing their minds? something else? Ask students to make notes in their writing logs about what they notice and to bring the logs to class for discussion. (You might consider taking a set of notes for yourself since you probably have highly developed strategies for listening.) By encouraging students to attend to their own modes of listening and then to explain those modes to others in the class, this activity should make for lively discussion — and perhaps for more effective listening.

On Considering Your Authority as a Writer   **(24d)**

Helen Fox, author of *Listening to the World: Cultural Issues in Academic Writing*, reminds us that language and power are closely related. Noting that North American business style dominates the world, Fox says "the ethnocentrism of the powerful is more significant, in a global environment, than the ethnocentrism of weaker countries. According to the 1999 United Nations Human Development Report, global communication occurs mainly in English and mainly in the richer countries. The same report reveals that while English is used in roughly 80 percent of Web sites, fewer than one in ten people in the world speaks this language." Such statistics point up the importance of teaching students to examine their own inevitable ethnocentrism — without somehow feeling guilty about it — and to understand their own linguistic values and preferences in light of that knowledge.

FOR MULTILINGUAL WRITERS: PEER RESPONSE

In classes with students from many different cultures, peer response can pose special challenges. Matsuda and Silva refer to a study conducted by George Brain, who found that multilingual students often commented on not feeling "comfortable" in their classes: "During peer review of papers in groups, these students felt that the [native English-speaking (NES) students] were impatient with them, and one student said that he overheard a[n] [NES] student complain to the teacher about her inability to correct the numerous grammatical errors. . . ." If you have used peer response, you will know that students can make quick and often incorrect judgments about others. To solve this problem, spend some time at the beginning of the class modeling effective peer-review strategies. If possible, ask a group of former students (as culturally mixed as possible) to come into class and present a peer-response session for your current students.

(24e) TEACHING WITH TECHNOLOGY: CONSIDERING YOUR AUDIENCE'S EXPECTATIONS

Another way to study and learn the differences in audience expectations across the globe is to use the Internet. Ask students to locate three Web pages on the same topic posted in different countries. Then have them conduct a rhetorical analysis of each Web page's formal properties, strategies of address, use of argumentative diction, and placement of images. Ask them to post their reflections on the differences among national audiences to your class discussion list. Alternatively, have students work collaboratively and create their own Web page analyzing the differences in audience expectations.

Writing . . . keeps me from believing everything I read.
    –GLORIA STEINEM

This exercise works particularly well for multilingual writers. Loretta Kasper argues that "as ESL students become more comfortable surfing the Internet, they discover that it is a vast resource that can be used to develop not only content area knowledge, but also linguistic proficiency" (408).

(24f) TEACHING WITH TECHNOLOGY: CONSIDERING WHAT COUNTS AS EVIDENCE

Ask students to keep an electronic journal on their computers concerning their awareness of differences in film and visual texts. Have them watch a movie that will help them learn about what counts as evidence in a culture other than their own. *Smoke Signals,* for example, a filmic translation of Sherman Alexie's collection of stories *The Lone Ranger and Tonto Fist Fight in Heaven,* was written, directed, and acted by American Indians and offers cultural representations based on their own, rather than another culture's, points of view. Julie Dash's *Daughters of the Dust,* which uses film strategies and figures drawn from African culture, might make another good choice. After you and the class draw up a list of films, ask students to view one of their choosing and to make an entry in their electronic journals about what they learned from the film in terms of "evidence" or proof, organization, style, and so on. They can also post their responses to the class discussion list and begin a dialogue online about evidence across cultures.

(24g, h) ## On Organization and Style

We can identify a number of historical reasons that led to preferences for verbally elaborate style and structure in some European countries (such as Spain) and for "plain talk" and explicit structures in England and the United States. Some scholars trace this development of preferences to the utilitarian movement, whereas others argue that it is related to the growing power of democracy. In any case, it is clear that such linguistic preferences are culture-specific.

■ USEFUL READINGS

Davis, Lennard J. *Enforcing Normalcy: Disability, Deafness, and the Body*. London: Verson, 1995. This pioneer in disability studies examines the historical uses and social implications of the terms *normal* and *normality*.

Fox, Helen. *Listening to the World: Cultural Issues in Academic Writing*. Urbana: NCTE, 1994. Using personal stories and experiences of students to inform her thinking, Fox discusses the difficulty that "minority" students have in learning to write according to American academic conventions.

Kaplan, Robert B. "Cultural Thought Patterns in Intercultural Education." *Language Learning* 16: 1–20.

Li, Xiao-Ming. *"Good Writing" in Cross-Cultural Context*. Albany: SUNY P, 1996. In an ethnographic account of teachers' perceptions of good writing in China and America, Li builds a dialogue between expert teachers in the two countries in order to show that "good writing" is a complex interaction between student texts and the teachers who read and judge that writing.

Lugones, Maria. "Playfulness, World Traveling, and Loving Perception." *Hypatia* 2 (1987): 17.

Matsuda, Paul Kei, and Tony Silva. "Cross-Cultural Composition: Mediated Integration of U.S. and International Students." *Composition Studies* 27 (1999): 15–30.

Severino, Carol, Juan C. Guerra, and Johnella E. Butler, eds. *Writing in Multicultural Settings*. New York: MLA, 1997. This collection addresses the challenges presented by the racial, ethnic, gender, class, religious, age, and physical-ability differences among college writing students. See, especially, the essays by Juan Guerra and Ulla Connor.

25 ⬇ Considering Others: Building Common Ground

The thought of Kenneth Burke informs much contemporary work in rhetoric and composition, and it certainly informs the *Handbook* in general and this chapter in particular. Burke's key term is *identification*:

> A is not identical with his colleague B. But insofar as their interests are joined, A is *identified* with B. Or he may *identify himself* with B even when their interests are not joined, if he assumes that they are, or is persuaded to do so. . . . To identify A with B is to make A "consubstantial" with B.
>
> . . . Here is perhaps the simplest case of persuasion. You persuade a man only insofar as you can talk his language by speech, gesture, tonality, order, image, attitude, idea, *identifying* your ways with his. (20, 55)

Burke's concept of identification underlies the advice in this chapter, which is meant to remind student writers of the many ways that language can promote — or destroy — identification. Ironically, given the extensive attention Burke devotes to identification, his own texts exclude half of humankind with their consistent use of the generic *he* and *man*.

Of course, you don't have to look far to see *dis*-identification at work. We overheard a fourteen-year-old exclaim to his aunt: "I am *not* a 'kid' anymore, so please stop calling me that!" The nephew objected to a label he found both inaccurate and disrespectful, one that clearly built no common ground, no source of identification, between him and his aunt. Ask students to think of situations when they've struggled to find just the right words to avoid offending someone: what salutation to use instead of "Dear Sir" when they are not sure who will read the letter, for instance, or how to describe an eighty-year-old without calling him or her "old," or what besides "mailman" to call someone who delivers your mail — especially when that person is *not* a man. These are choices student writers must make every day in trying to build common ground and communicate with others.

FOR TEACHING: DIVERSITY IN THE CLASSROOM

One good way to get the class to start thinking about differences and common ground is to ask students to look around the classroom and try to describe the class in writing. After all, generations of college students have found themselves in classes filled with people both like them and different from them. Here is Eudora Welty, describing her first year (1926) at Mississippi State College for Women:

> There I landed in a world to itself, and indeed it was all new to me. It was surging with twelve hundred girls. They came from every nook and corner of the state, from the Delta, the piney woods, the Gulf Coast, the black prairie, the red clay hills, and Jackson — as the capital city and the only sizeable town, a region to itself. All were clearly differentiated sections, at that time, and though we were all put into uniforms of navy blue so as to unify us, it could have been told by the girls' accents, by their bearings, the way they came into the classroom and the way they ate, where they'd grown up. This was my first chance to learn what the body of us were like and what differences in background, persuasion of mind, and resources of character there were among Mississippians — at that, among only half of us, for we were all white. I missed the significance of both what was in, and what was out of, our well-enclosed but vibrantly alive society.
> – EUDORA WELTY, *One Writer's Beginnings*

Take time to have students read this passage and then talk about where they've come from — their ages, ethnicities, hometowns, religions, and so on. Use the discussion to help them focus on their *own* diversity.

On Common Ground and Educational Opportunity

Mike Rose, in his extraordinary book *Lives on the Boundary,* talks about the sorts of sensitivity that will be necessary to build the common ground that will enable many people to be well served by our schools.

> We are in the middle of an extraordinary social experiment: the attempt to provide education for all members of a vast pluralistic democracy. To have any prayer of success, we'll need many conceptual blessings: A philosophy of language and literacy that affirms the diverse sources of linguistic competence and deepens our understanding of the ways class and culture blind us to the richness of those sources. A perspective on failure that lays open the logic of error. An orientation toward the interaction of poverty and ability that undercuts simple polarities, that enables us to see simultaneously the constraints poverty places on the play of mind and the actual mind at play within those

A writer lives in awe of words, for they can be cruel or kind, and they can change their meanings right in front of you. They pick up flavors and odors like butter in a refrigerator.
–JOHN STEINBECK

constraints. We'll need a pedagogy that encourages us to step back and consider the threat of the standard classroom and that shows us, having stepped back, how to step forward to invite a student across the boundaries of that powerful room. Finally, we'll need a revised store of images of educational excellence, ones closer to egalitarian ideas — ones that embody the reward and turmoil of education in a democracy, that celebrate the plural, messy human reality of it. At heart, we'll need a guiding set of principles that do not encourage us to retreat from, but move us closer to, an understanding of the rich mix of speech and ritual and story that is America. (238)

(25a)   **FOR TEACHING: REMEMBERING THE GOLDEN RULE**

To help students see that writing has powerful effects, ask them to write about a time when someone — a friend, parent, teacher, employer — wrote or said something about them that affected the way they thought or felt about themselves, that labeled them in some way that led to disidentification and misunderstanding. Then ask them to write about a time when their words had an important effect on someone else. Use these entries as a starting point for class discussion about the power of language.

(25a)   **FOR MULTILINGUAL WRITERS: REMEMBERING THE GOLDEN RULE**

Students whose first language is not English are often familiar with the power of language as both a tool of respect and as a tool that inflicts harm. Ask your students to relay their experiences with the class in order to forge identifications across differences. Do multilingual speakers have to combat damaging assumptions about their countries of origin or intellectual abilities?

(25b)   **FOR TEACHING: WATCHING FOR STEREOTYPES**

Give students a few paragraphs from Jonathan Swift's *A Modest Proposal* and ask them to identify language that stereotypes certain groups — the Irish, women, or Americans, for example. Then ask them to consider such stereotyping in relation to Swift's *satiric purpose*. Particularly in the case of satire, such labeling may serve to argue for exactly the opposite of what it seems to be saying. In such cases, do the students find such stereotypes offensive — or useful? Ask them to look at contemporary political satire and to address the same questions about it.

TEACHING WITH TECHNOLOGY: REVISING SEXIST LANGUAGE   **(25b1)**

Ask students to read the opening of the Declaration of Independence and to consider what groups of citizens are made invisible by the document's language.

> When in the Course of human events, it becomes necessary for one people to dissolve the political bands which have connected them with another, and to assume among the powers of the earth, the separate and equal station to which the Laws of Nature and of Nature's God entitle them, a decent respect to the opinions of mankind requires that they should declare the causes which impel them to the separation. — We hold these truths to be self-evident, that all men are created equal, that they are endowed by their Creator with certain unalienable Rights, that among these are Life, Liberty and the pursuit of Happiness. — That to secure these rights, Governments are instituted among Men, deriving their just powers from the consent of the governed.

Following class discussion, ask students to post an entry on your electronic discussion board on the term *sexist language*. Ask them to try to define the term and to offer examples of terms that are or may seem to be sexist. These computer entries should then be used to initiate a class dialogue.

On Nonracist Language   **(25b2)**

In a 1991 article by Daniel Goleman, the *New York Times* reported on an experiment done by Smith College psychologist Dr. Fletcher Blanchard that led him to conclude that "a few outspoken people who are vigorously anti-racist can establish the kind of social climate that discourages racist acts." After asking 144 Smith College students for their reactions to a racist incident on campus, Dr. Blanchard found that students who heard others making racist remarks were more willing to make racist remarks themselves. These findings suggest that the peer group in the writing classroom could serve as an effective mechanism for encouraging students to consider the effect their language could have on others.

(25b2)

FOR TEACHING: USING PREFERRED TERMS

You may want to get students working toward the exercise on *Handbook* p. 520 by asking them to write a paragraph or two about their own ethnic heritage. Some may want to talk with parents or grandparents about their own ethnicity. Such research would form the basis for class discussion and for a writing assignment about "where I come from."

In addition, you may want to ask students to spend a few minutes asking "what's in a name?" and discussing the terms used to refer to their own ethnic group and, perhaps, their own names. Some students may not know, for instance, that Booker T. Washington long ago wrote that former slaves must change their slave names and that this impetus is related to the practice of taking names that reflect African or Islamic influence: Malcolm Little to Malcolm X and then to Malik Al-Shabazz; Cassius Clay to Muhammad Ali; Lew Alcindor to Kareem Abdul-Jabbar. What names might students choose to reflect their own ethnicity? What terms do they prefer to use when referring to their own ethnic group, and why?

(25b2)

FOR TEACHING: RACE AND ETHNICITY

Ask students to read the following excerpt from Carol Lee Sanchez's description of the language that white culture has used to characterize Native Americans. Have students contrast these stereotypes with the Native American perspective of themselves, their way of life, and the white culture that threatens them. Who is Sanchez's audience in this article? How does she build common ground with readers? Are students persuaded by her arguments?

If you want to talk with somebody you have to arrive at the same language somehow. And/but talking the same language cannot and must not mean "my language and not yours" or "your language and not mine." It means finding a way to understand, not to change or to eclipse or to obliterate but to understand each other.
—JUNE JORDAN

On the negative side, to be Indian is to be thought of as primitive, alcoholic, ignorant (as in "Dumb Indian"), better off dead (as in "the only good Indian is a dead Indian" or "I didn't know there was any of you folks still left"), unskilled, non-competitive, immoral, pagan or heathen, untrustworthy (as in "Indian-giver") and frightening. To be Indian is to be the primary model that is used to promote racism in this country.

How can that happen, you ask? Bad press. One hundred and fifty years of the most consistently vicious press imaginable. Newspapers, dime novels, textbooks and fifty years of visual media have portrayed and continue to portray Indians as savage, blood-thirsty, immoral, inhuman people. When there's a touch of social consciousness attached, you will find the once "blood-thirsty," "white-killer savage" portrayed as a pitiful drunk, a loser, an outcast or a mix-blood not welcomed by, or trusted by, either race. For fifty years, children in this country have been raised to kill Indians mentally, subconsciously through the visual media, until it is an automatic reflex. That shocks you? Then I have made my point. . . .

The Indian Way is a different way. It is a respectful way. The basic teachings in every Tribe that exists today as a Tribe in the western hemisphere are based on respect for all the things our Mother gave us. If we neglect her or anger her, she will make our lives very difficult and we always know that we have a hardship on ourselves and on our children. We are raised to be cautious and concerned for the *future* of our people, and that is how we raise our children — because *they* are *our* future. Your "civilization" has made all of us very sick and has made our mother earth sick and out of balance. Your kind of thinking and education has brought the whole world to the brink of total disaster, whereas the thinking and education among my people forbids the practice of almost everything Euro-Americans, in particular, value.

ATTENDING TO DISABILITIES: PHYSICAL ABILITY

(25b3)

As a culture, how reliant are we on metaphors of mobility, visibility, and ability? You can discuss ways of building common ground that attend to disabilities by asking students to examine common patterns of speech or colloquial expressions. Johnson Cheu, for instance, normalizes wheelchair mobility by using the following expression:

> Some time after the class was over, one of the students stopped me as I was rolling on campus. (Brueggemann 390)

Brenda Jo Brueggemann and colleagues point out some of these common expressions and remind us that we need to be aware of varieties of language that inclusively transform the way our culture demarcates people as able-bodied or "dis-abled":

> Another concern lies in the metaphor of visibility . . . in the very ways that the language we and our students use is laden with metaphors of ability. Not that we would want to police the propriety of sight equaling insight; the political power gained with "visibility" in our culture; the importance of "hearing others' voices"; the meaning of "throwing our own voices," "turning deaf ears," or coming up with "lame ideas." To do so would pretty much have emptied out the 1999 CCCC's program book, which was overladen with these very metaphors. (369)

Ask students to create innovative linguistic expressions for their own experiences of mobility, ability, vision, and hearing.

Disability studies . . . invite us all to at least consider the able-bodied agenda lurking in the way we make meaning through so many crippling metaphors, in the way we compose and communicate that disables even as it might be attempting to "enable."

– BRENDA JO BRUEGGEMANN

(25b3) **On Other Kinds of Differences: Sexual Orientation**

Students should be aware that people whose sexual orientation is not strictly heterosexual constitute a significant minority of our world and inhabit all walks of life. They should also be aware that, as with many other labels, the terms used to describe sexual orientation are in flux. *Sexual orientation* itself is the term preferred by many who view sexuality as genetically determined or as the result of very early socialization (or as some combination of the two). *Sexual preference,* on the other hand, is preferred by many who see sexuality as primarily a matter of personal or political choice.

It is also worth noting that style sheets for most organizations recommend using the term *gay* only as an adjective; *homosexual* and *lesbian* are used as both adjectives and nouns.

FOR COLLABORATIVE WORK: HATE SPEECH AND THE FIRST AMENDMENT

Because campus speech codes often ban slurs and epithets, they are most usually referred to as "Hate Speech Codes." And when these speech codes are enforced, they usually fire up controversies about what exactly constitutes "hate speech" as well as what kinds of speech violate First Amendment rights.

Form students into groups to investigate the campus speech codes at your college, reporting to the rest of the class on their content as well as instances of when — if ever — they have been enforced. How have the codes been applied in the past? What were the results? How were violations of the codes solved or resolved? Are there situations on your campus now that merit application of the campus speech codes?

■ **USEFUL READINGS**

Ball, Arnetha, and Ted Lardner. "Dispositions toward Language: Teacher Construction of Knowledge and the Ann Arbor Black English Case." *CCC* 48 (1997): 469–99. Ball and Lardner explore the effects of language-based stereotypes and offer important ways to teach beyond these stereotypes for all instructors interested in inclusive writing instruction.

Brueggemann, Brenda Jo. "On (Almost) Passing." *College English* 59 (1997): 647–60. The author explores her "coming out as a deaf person" and traces the effect of this rite of passage on herself, her teaching, and her writing.

Brueggemann, Brenda Jo, Linda Feldmeier White, Patricia A. Dunn, Barbara A. Heifferon, and Johnson Cheu. "Becoming Visible: Lessons in Disability." *CCC* 52.3 (Feb. 2001): 368–98. Calling for increased awareness of disability in composition studies, the authors argue that such an awareness can productively disrupt notions of "writing" and "composing" at the same time it challenges "normal"/"not normal" binaries in the field.

Burke, Kenneth. *A Rhetoric of Motives*. Berkeley: U of California P, 1969.

Carpenter, Carol. "Exercises to Combat Sexist Reading and Writing." *CE* 43 (1981): 293–300. Carpenter describes three activities designed to explore the implications of sexism while building reading and writing skills.

Davis, Lennard. "Deafness and Insight: The Deafened Moment as a Critical Modality." *College English* 57 (1995): 881–900. In this wonderfully provocative essay for teachers of writing, Davis examines the notion of "disability" in order to uncover the "epistemological bases and dialectical relations inherent in any notion of aesthetics."

Frank, Francine Wattman, and Paula A. Treichler. *Language, Gender, and Professional Writing: Theoretical Approaches and Guidelines for Nonsexist Usage*. New York: MLA, 1989. This book addresses the issue of linguistic sexism in scholarly and professional writing, presenting relevant ideas and research and a set of guidelines for nondiscriminatory usage.

Goleman, Daniel. "New Ways to Battle Bias: Fight Acts, Not Feelings." *New York Times* 16 July 1991: B1+.

Keating, Ann Louise. "Interrogating 'Whiteness': (De)Constructing 'Race.'" *College English* 57 (1995): 901–18. Keating argues that teachers must complicate existing concepts of race—both by "exploring the many changes that have occurred in all apparently fixed racial categories and by informing students of the political, economic, and historical factors shaping the continual reinvention of 'race.'"

Mairs, Nancy. "Body in Trouble." *Waist-High in the World: Life among the Nondisabled*. New York: Beacon, 1997. The author of the now-classic "On Being a Cripple" and *Carnal Acts* writes with particular insight and passion about living with and beyond disabilities.

Matthews, Anne. "Brave, New 'Cruelty Free' World." *New York Times* 7 July 1991. A teacher of nonfiction writing at Princeton University, Matthews satirizes current expressions that, in attempting to be "cruelty-free," actually deny or trivialize difficult human conditions.

A Media Guide to Disability. East Hartford: Connecticut Developmental Disabilities Council, 1985. <http://www.state.ct.us/ctcdd/mediaguide.html>. This is a discussion of language most often used in professional literature and most preferred by people with various disabilities.

Moss, Beverly J., and Keith Walters. "Rethinking Diversity: Axes of Difference in the Writing Classroom." *Theory and Practice in the Teaching of Writing: Re-thinking the Discipline*. Ed. Lee Odell. Carbondale: Southern Illinois UP, 1993. 132–85.

Nilsen, Aileen Pace. "Winning the Great 'He'/'She' Battle." *CE* 46 (1984): 151–57. Nilsen uses examples from manuscripts submitted for publication to illustrate the complexities involved in using "inconspicuous sex-fair language." Based on an analysis of these examples, she offers four principles for instructors and students who lack the sometimes considerable skill necessary for writing in a gender-neutral manner.

Okawa, Gail Y. "Diving for Pearls: Mentoring as Cultural and Activist Practice among Academics of Color." *CCC* 53.3 (Feb. 2002): 507–32. This discussion of Geneva Smitherman and Victor Villanueva, two senior scholars of color, shows that mentoring is far more than an academic exercise and helps build a multiethnic/multiracial professoriate in our discipline.

Rose, Mike. *Lives on the Boundary*. New York: Penguin, 1989.

Stockton, Kathryn Bond. "Reading Details, Teaching Politics: Political Mantras and the Politics of Luxury." *College English* 64.1 (Sept. 2001): 109. Stockton examines the repetition of received cultural norms in teaching and scholarship.

Considering Varieties of Language

26

> [I]f you want to really hurt me, talk badly about my language. Ethnic identity is twin skin to linguistic identity — I am my language. Until I can take pride in my language, I cannot take pride in myself.
>
> – Gloria Anzaldúa

Linguist Walt Wolfram has done a great deal to explicate and map varieties of English and to demonstrate that such variations are not only extensive but also strongly influenced by a number of factors, including region or geographical location, social status, ethnicity, age, and gender. "Cutting across and intersecting with these variables," Wolfram says, "are the dimensions of formality of style and occasion of use of the language." In spite of the work of such scholars, and because the language is constantly changing, we still have only a limited picture of the current diversity within English. Instructors of writing will benefit from learning what we can about *all* the varieties of English that inform our students' literate practices.

In "English in Our Language Heritage," Shirley Brice Heath explains that a number of languages played important roles in the early life of this country, and that the use of different languages was encouraged. Only in the late nineteenth century, according to Heath, did political and ideological forces move to champion monolingualism. Today, as this chapter demonstrates, the United States is once again using — and appreciating — multiple languages.

Keith Walters, in an essay on "Dialects," provides an excellent discussion of "the nature of language and dialect and the role they are likely to play in the construction of individual and group identity in a multicultural society that prides itself on a democratic way of life." He goes on to say that:

> Teaching students about . . . the many dialects of American English will surely not rid the country of prejudice, but it might be a first step in helping those

Is it that we think the brain too small a place to hold more than one language at a time?
– DELL HYMES

237

whose native dialect differs from that of the academy appreciate the tasks they are engaged in as they strive to acquire Standard English. It would likewise help those from mainstream backgrounds appreciate the challenge some of their classmates face. Surely, it would help prepare future citizens to live in a society characterized by increasing linguistic diversity.

(26b)   ## On Using Standard Varieties of English

In *The Language Instinct*, Steven Pinker demystifies any questions speakers of so-called standard English might have about varieties of the English language, particularly about African American English Vernacular, one of the most widely used languages in the United States. Responding to the labeling of such English as a "non-logical mode of expressive behavior," Pinker writes:

> If the psychologists had listened to spontaneous conversations, they would have rediscovered the commonplace fact that American black culture is everywhere highly verbal; the subculture of street youths in particular is famous in the annals of anthropology for the value placed on linguistic virtuosity. Indeed, . . . a number of ethnic varieties of English display linguistic virtuosity and power. In addition to African American vernacular English, Walt Wolfram lists Italian, Jewish, Irish, German, Puerto Rican, Chicano, American Indian, and Vietnamese Englishes as of interest to scholars and teachers. Students in your class may be familiar with still other ethnic varieties of English.

In *Speak Standard, Too—Add Mainstream English to Your Talking Style*, Mary I. Berger encourages her students to speak standard English whenever they are "out there" and to speak their home dialect at home. Her advice is controversial, especially given what many linguists feel is the political nature of such switching and shifting. Geneva Smitherman tells us in *Talkin' and Testifyin': The Language of Black America* that we expect only the "colonized" person to make linguistic shifts, and she writes:

> An individual's language is intricately bound up with his or her sense of identity and group consciousness. In the history of man's inhumanity to man, it is clearly understandable why the conqueror forces his victim to learn his language, for as black psychiatrist Frantz Fanon said, "every dialect is a way of thinking." Certainly this principle has been operative in the history of colonized people where the colonizer's language and culture occupy a position superior to that of the colonized, even among the oppressed persons themselves. (The fact that America was once a colony of England goes a long way toward explaining why British English still commands such great pres-

A standard language is a dialect with an army and a navy.
– Old one-liner among sociolinguists

tige in this country — despite the real communication barrier it poses for most Americans. Fanon would label this the "colonized mentality" of White America. . . .

In the American context, the negative attitude toward black speech is but a variation on this same theme. Historically, Black English has been the usage pattern associated with plantation figures like Uncle Remus and Uncle Tom. Contemporaneously, it is the dialect associated with black urban "ghetto" types. . . . Since the Civil War, and in the twentieth century especially, upward mobility for Black Americans has come to mean the eradication of black language (and black culture) and the adoption of the linguistic norms of the white middle class. . . . Moreover, some blacks contend that being bidialectal not only causes a schism in the black personality, but it is also like saying black talk is "good enough" for blacks but not for whites. (171–73)

On Using Ethnic Varieties of English   (26c)

In recent years, the debate over "standard English" — as well as over "English only" — has become increasingly virulent, as we saw in the uproar over Ebonics, a term coined well over twenty years ago. Instructors of writing need to be aware of these debates and to help their students think and talk through the issues involved. The Useful Readings and Web site listed at the end of this chapter provide many resources.

On Using Occupational Varieties of English   (26d)

No occupations in recent years have brought more new vocabulary and patterns into English than those surrounding the computer industry. Unless readers keep up, in fact, they may find themselves having a harder and harder time following instances of this particular occupational variety of English. Here is a fairly simple example:

The Presentation Manager programmers in Redmond, who had been having Nerfball fights with their Windows counterparts every night for months, suddenly found themselves melded into the Windows operation. A cross-licensing agreement between the two companies remained in force, allowing IBM to offer subsequent versions of DOS to its customers and Microsoft the right to sell versions of OS/2, but the emphasis in Redmond was clearly on DOS and Windows, not OS/2. "Our strategy for the 90s is Windows — one evolving architecture, a couple of implementations," Bill Gates wrote. "Everything we do should focus on making Windows more successful."

— ROBERT X. CRINGELY, *Accidental Empires*

Some of this occupational vocabulary is no doubt familiar — *Windows*, *DOS*, *Microsoft*, for example. Less well-known by the person on the street is *OS/2*, however; and *cross-licensing* may be unfamiliar. In addition, what exactly Gates means by "architecture" or "a couple of implementations" is not clear from the context of this passage alone. Instead, the reader must bring some knowledge of this particular occupational dialect to the text in order to comprehend it. Your students will be able to provide additional examples of occupational varieties of English — perhaps from the areas of film, video, and music.

Ask your students to gather some examples of occupational language — from their own workplaces, from their professors, or from the language of a field they know well — and then use the examples as the basis for a parody of that language. Use these parodies for class discussion of occupational varieties of English.

(26c)   **FOR TEACHING: USING REGIONAL VARIETIES OF ENGLISH**

John Algeo recommends using a quiz like the following one to introduce students to the subject of regional variation in English:

Match each lettered term with its numbered meaning:

a. Coney Island butter	1. sandstorm
b. Boston dollar	2. burro
c. Adam's ale	3. razorback hog
d. Albany beef	4. downpour
e. Arizona cloudburst	5. mustard
f. Arkansas dew	6. penny
g. Carolina racehorse	7. sturgeon
h. Colorado mockingbird	8. water

(key: a – 5, b – 6, c – 8, d – 7, e – 1, f – 4, g – 3, h – 2)

Impassable and impossible distances were measured by the distance from "Hog to Kick 'em Jenny." Hog? Kick 'em Jenny? Who knew until I was . . . grown that these were two little reefs in the Grenadines, between Grenada and Carriacou.
— Audre Lorde

Algeo says that students in any level class can make up similar quizzes, exercises that could lead to a survey of oral language use among their families and friends — and provide rich material for class discussion of regional variation in English.

Following this exercise, you might ask students to bring to class some examples of a regional variety of language they know well, to demonstrate the use of these words or phrases in context and to explain the nuances of their meanings.

FOR COLLABORATIVE WORK: USING VARIETIES OF ENGLISH	**(26c–e)**

Exercise 26.1 could be done very effectively in small groups, particularly the task of analyzing the purpose and audience for the passage. Groups can then present their revised versions, and the conclusions they drew about them, to the class as a whole.

FOR MULTILINGUAL WRITERS: BRINGING IN OTHER LANGUAGES	**(26f)**

Following Gloria Anzaldúa's lead, students may wish to integrate other languages in their papers. Such interweaving can be an extremely successful rhetorical strategy. Share with your students examples of imbricated texts that work well by bringing in many varieties of language.

FOR TEACHING: USING VARIETIES OF LANGUAGE IN ACADEMIC WRITING	**(26g)**

In his "Mr. Language Person" columns, Dave Barry often mixes the language of a hypothetical English instructor with his own brand of outrageous examples:

Q. What are the rules regarding capital letters?

A. Capital letters are used in three grammatical situations:

1. At the beginning of proper or formal nouns.

   Examples: Capitalize "Queen," "Tea Party" and "Rental Tuxedo." Do *not* capitalize "dude," "cha-cha" or "boogerhead."

2. To indicate a situation of great military importance.

   Example: "Get on the TELSAT and tell STAFCOM that CONWIMP wants some BBQ ASAP."

3. To indicate that the subject of the sentence has been bitten by a badger.

   Example: "I'll just stick my hand in here and OUCH!"

■ **USEFUL READINGS**

Algeo, John. "DARE in the Classroom." *Language Variation in North American English*. Ed. A. Wayne Glowka and Donald M. Lance. New York: MLA, 1993. 140–43. One essay in a collation that covers theories of vernacular, regional, ethnic/social, gender, and historical variations of English.

Berger, Mary I. *Speak Standard, Too—Add Mainstream English to Your Talking Style.* Chicago: Orchard, 1994.

Brueggemann, Brenda Jo, Linda Feldmeier White, Patricia A. Dunn, Barbara A. Heifferon, and Johnson Cheu. "Becoming Visible: Lessons in Disability." *CCC* 52.3 (Feb. 2001): 368–98. Calling for increased awareness of disability in composition studies, the authors argue that such an awareness can productively disrupt notions of "writing" and "composing" at the same time it challenges "normal"/"not normal" binaries in the field.

Campbell, Kermit E. "The Signifying Monkey Revisited: Vernacular Discourse in African American Personal Narratives." *Journal of Advanced Composition* 14.4 (Fall 1994): 463–73. Campbell argues that signifying is a means of affirming "cultural identity and community in the face of the imposition of cultural dominance and oppression," that vernacular and academic discourses share large numbers of similarities, and that including vernacular discourse in writing pedagogy "would bring the African American experience from the margins to the center of the academic community where it belongs."

Coleman, Charles F. "Our Students Write with Accents—Oral Paradigms for ESD Students." *CCC* 48 (Dec. 1997): 486–500. Coleman provides important information for instructors on the practices that shape the writing of some English as a Second Dialect students.

"Commentary." *Black Caucus Notes.* Urbana: NCTE, 1997. This reprint of a document written twenty years ago carefully outlines the position of African American linguists and educators on the Ebonics issue.

Delpit, Lisa. *Other People's Children: Cultural Conflict in the Classroom.* New York: New P, 1995. An expansion of two influential essays that appeared in the *Harvard Educational Review,* this book offers an important reassessment of the "process movement" in composition. In it, Delpit argues that in some ways the methods employed in progressive education deny rather than give access to the skills that many African American students want and need.

Farr, Marcia, and Harvey Daniels. *Language Diversity and Writing Instruction.* Urbana: NCTE, 1986. This is an excellent discussion of variation and diversity in U.S. English. The authors argue that what we call "standard English" is really one particular variety of English, along with African American English Vernacular, Hispanic-influenced English, and other ethnic and regional varieties. The book ends with concrete recommendations for teaching linguistically diverse students.

Ferguson, Charles A., and Shirley Brice Heath, eds. *Language in the USA.* Cambridge: Cambridge UP, 1981. Multiple varieties and dialects of English and the role that class, gender, race, occupation, and nationality play on such variety are covered by the authors.

Fu, Danling. *My Trouble Is My English: Asian Students and the American Dream.* Portsmouth: Boynton, 1995. This is a personal account of the writer's struggle to come to terms with the ways in which standard English helps both to empower and to oppress.

Galindo, D. Letticia. "Bilingualism and Language Variation among Chicanos in the Southwest." *Language Variation in North American English.* Ed. A. Wayne Glowka and Donald M. Lance. New York: MLA, 1993. 199–218.

Gilyard, Keith. *Let's Flip the Script: African American Discourses on Language, Literature, and Learning.* Detroit: Wayne State UP, 1996. This series of essays explores the politics of language teaching and the linguistic legacies of racism.

Heath, Shirley Brice, and Leslie Mangiola. *Children of Promise: Literate Activity in Linguistically and Culturally Diverse Classrooms.* Washington, DC: NEA, 1991.

Kachru, Braj B., ed. *The Other Tongue: English across Cultures.* 2nd ed. Urbana: U of Illinois P, 1992. This collection of essays on English in a global and multicultural context includes essays on nonnative Englishes, on American English, on culture and discourse, and on teaching world Englishes.

Kreiner, Leslie, and Alan Merikel. "The Bilingual Model: Encouraging Diversity in the Writing Classroom." *Teaching English in the Two Year College* 22 (Dec. 1995): 284–92.

Labov, William. *The Study of Nonstandard English.* Champaign: NCTE, 1970. A classic study in which Labov dispels a number of myths about "nonstandard" English and demonstrates that such nonstandard dialects are in fact self-contained and rule-governed systems worthy of serious study.

Lunsford, Andrea A. "Toward a Mestiza Rhetoric: Gloria Anzaldúa on Composition and Postcoloniality." *A Journal of Advanced Composition* 18 (1998): 1–29. In this interview, Anzaldúa speaks at length about the importance of using a variety of languages (sometimes without translation) in her writing.

Marback, Richard. "Ebonics: Theorizing in Public Our Attitudes toward Literacy." *CCC* 53.1 (Sept. 2001): 11–32. Marback argues that responses to the Oakland Ebonics resolution miss the significance of the resolution; he focuses on attention to attitudes and literacy education in a racially divided democracy.

McKay, Sandra Lee, and Sau-Ling Cynthia Wong, eds. *Language Diversity: Problem or Resource?* Boston: Heinle, 1988. Following a discussion of historical perspective on language diversity, the authors of the essays in this collection focus on the language situations of Americans of Mexican, Puerto Rican, Cuban, Chinese, Filipino, Korean, and Vietnamese ancestry.

Moss, Beverly J., ed. *Literacy across Communities.* Cresskill: Hampton P, 1994. This collection includes five essays on literacy practices among Chicago Mexicanos, in Philadelphia's Hmong community, in Navajo print culture, among young African American males, and in African American churches, and a concluding reflection on broadening our understanding of nonmainstream literacies.

Pinker, Steven. *The Language Instinct.* New York: Harper, 1995.

Pough, Gwendolyn D. "Rhetoric: Black Students Writing Black Panthers." *CCC* 53.3 (Feb. 2002): 466–86. Pough examines black student's responses to Black Panther party documents and how those documents moved the students toward change.

Smitherman, Geneva. *Talkin' and Testifyin': The Language of Black America*. Boston: Houghton, 1977.

Tannen, Deborah. "The Oral/Literate Continuum in Discourse." *Spoken and Written Language: Exploring Orality and Literacy*. Ed. Deborah Tannen. Norwood: Ablex, 1982.

——. *You Just Don't Understand: Women and Men in Conversation*. New York: Ballantine, 1990; *That's Not What I Meant! How Conversational Style Makes or Breaks Relationships*. New York: Ballantine, 1987; and *Talking from 9 to 5*. New York: Morrow, 1994. These books provide fascinating evidence of differences between the ways men and women converse and interact.

TuSmith, Bonnie. "The Englishes of Ethnic Folk." *College English* 58 (1996): 43–57. TuSmith argues that English instructors are responsible for teaching not only standard English but also other Englishes "without conveying the message that these systems are inferior." To illustrate one strategy for doing so, TuSmith looks closely at Milton Murayana's 1975 novel *All I Asking for Is My Body*.

Villanueva, Victor. *Bootstraps: From an American Academic of Color*. Urbana: NCTE, 1993. Villanueva discusses his own literacy histories and offers a number of insights about multilingual students in monolingual schools. Of special interest is chapter 5, "*Inglés* in the Colleges."

Walters, Keith. "Dialects." *Encyclopedia of English and Language Arts*. Ed. Alan Purvec. Urbana: NCTE, 1994. Walters discusses the role of language variety on identity.

Wolfram, Walt. *Dialects and American English*. Englewood Cliffs: Prentice, 1991. Wolfram includes an extensive discussion of what dialects are and how they arise, and a thorough exploration of regional, social, ethnic, and gender-based variations in U.S. English; chapters 10 and 11 on "Standard English and Education" and "Dialect and Testing" are especially important for instructors of writing.

■ **USEFUL WEB SITE**

Center for Applied Linguistics

http://www.cal.org/ebonics

This Ebonics information page offers links, an annotated bibliography, and multiple resources.

Considering Diction

27

The difference between the right word and the almost right word is really a large matter — 'tis the difference between lightning and the lightning bug.
— MARK TWAIN

What Mark Twain calls the difference between the "right" and the "almost right" word is a matter of *diction,* which derives from the Latin word for "say" and means literally how one says or expresses something. In speaking of someone you work with, for example, you might choose one or more of the following words: *accomplice, ally, associate, buddy, cohort, collaborator, colleague, comrade, co-worker, mate, partner, sidekick.* As these examples suggest, such choices of diction are always highly contingent on purpose, audience, and situation. Reconsidering these elements of every writer's rhetorical situation may be one good way to introduce a discussion of diction.

FOR TEACHING: CHOOSING WORDS CAREFULLY   **(27a)**

To give students practice in considering diction, have them write a paragraph about something they might want to do at school — change their major, spend their junior year abroad, take a semester off, or something else. Have them first use familiar words, assuming their audience to be someone close — parents, spouse, good friend. Then ask them to rewrite their paragraphs to address their academic advisor, using a more formal diction. Finally, suggest that they analyze each paragraph to identify the elements that create familiar or formal diction.

On Slang   **(27a1)**

In "The Blab of the Pave," her *New York Times* book review of *The City in Slang,* Elizabeth Hawes tells us:

Slang is by nature urban; it is "the blab of the pave" as Walt Whitman celebrated it, the informal language of reporters, policemen, songwriters and street kids — "hooligan," "plug ugly," "hooker" and "taxi." Like the city, it becomes richer with diversity.

Technically, *slang,* a word that cropped up in the 18th century, can be distinguished from *cant,* the idiom of criminal and low life, and *argot,* the jargon of professional and social classes. But in practice, slang embraces all of these modes and is, by that fact, a cross-cultural, multi-ethnic distillation of voices. American slang, which diverged from British slang after independence, has its own special provenance. As H. L. Mencken concluded in his scholarly study *The American Language,* English slang seems to reside in doubling consonants or in the addition of "-er" to words, like "brekker" for breakfast, while its American counterpart concocts phrases like "lounge lizard" and "rubberneck." With the possible exception of the French, Americans have produced more slang than any other people and have put it to heavier daily use. And of all Americans, New Yorkers have waxed the most eloquent about metropolitan life.

More recently, linguist Steven Pinker says:

As for slang, I'm all for it! Some people worry that slang will somehow "corrupt" the language. We should be so lucky. Most slang lexicons are preciously guarded by their subcultures as membership badges. When given a glimpse into one of these lexicons, no true language-lover can fail to be dazzled by the brilliant wordplay and wit: from medical students *(Zorro-belly, crispy critter, prune),* rappers *(jaw-jacking, dissing),* college students *(studmuffin, veg out, blow off),* surfers *(gnarlacious, geekified),* and hackers *(to flame, core-dump, crufty).* When the more passé terms get cast off and handed down to the mainstream, they often fill expressive gaps in the language beautifully. I don't know how I ever did without *to flame* (protest self-righteously), *to dis* (express disrespect for), and *to blow off* (dismiss an obligation), and there are thousands of now-unexceptional English words like *clever, fun, sham, banter, mob, stingy, bully, junkie,* and *jazz* that began life as slang. It is especially hypocritical to oppose linguistic innovations reflexively and at the same time to decry the loss of distinctions like *lie* versus *lay* on the pretext of preserving expressive power. Vehicles for expressing thought are being created far more quickly than they are being lost.

(27a3)   **FOR TEACHING: RECOGNIZING DOUBLESPEAK**

To combat the proliferation of public doublespeak, the National Council of Teachers of English published the *Quarterly Review of Doublespeak* and each year presented an Orwell Award (for honesty in public discourse) and

a Doublespeak Award (for the most egregious example of doublespeak).
You may want to bring some issues of the *Review* to class for discussion.
Here is a "winner" of the 1993 Doublespeak Award:

> A second-place award was voted to former president George Bush. President
> Bush pardoned six former holders of high government office who played
> major roles in the Iran-Contra affair. These officials had secretly engaged in
> acts specifically forbidden by law, including dealing in arms with a terrorist
> state, failure to obtain Congressional approval for arms sales to another state,
> and transferring arms to the Nicaraguan Contras. After these illegal acts were
> exposed, some of these officials lied under oath and destroyed evidence of
> their crimes. In his pardon [of them], President Bush called the people who
> committed these crimes "patriots" and said their legal troubles were simply
> a matter of a "criminalization of policy differences." By "patriots" President
> Bush seems to mean government officials who act secretly in the service of a
> President committing acts specially forbidden, and who, if they get caught by
> Congress, lie and cover up for each other and the President. By "policy dif-
> ferences" President Bush seems to mean selling arms to Iran and giving arms
> to the Nicaraguan Contras, as well as lying to a grand jury and to Congress
> and destroying evidence. But according to President Bush, breaking these
> laws is simply a "policy difference" and those who break such laws are "pa-
> triots."   *– Quarterly Review of Doublespeak* XX (Jan. 1994): 2

*We have too many high
sounding words, and too
few actions that
correspond with them.*
– Abigail Adams

FOR COLLABORATIVE WORK: RECOGNIZING DOUBLESPEAK   **(27a3)**

David Sprunger of Concordia College has created an entire Web site devoted to what he calls "Language Lite: A Gallery of Linguistic Trivia."
Share with your students his page on Doublespeak Proverbs, reproduced
below:

Doublespeak Proverbs

If you can translate these camouflaged (but familiar) witticisms, you have a
talent for making clear writing out of mud.

Scintillate, scintillate asteroid minific.

Members of an avian species of identical plumage congregate.

Surveillance should precede saltitation.

It is fruitless to become lachrymose over precipitately departed lacteal fluid.

Freedom from incrustations of grime is contiguous to divinity.

The stylus is more potent than the claymore.

It is fruitless to indoctrinate a super-annuated canine with innovative
maneuvers.

The temperature of the aqueous content of an unremittingly ogled cooking container does not reach 212 degrees Fahrenheit.

Male cadavers are incapable of yielding testimony.

Individuals who make their abode in vitreous edifices would be advised to refrain from catapulting petrous projectiles.

A plethora of individuals with expertise in culinary techniques vitiates the potable concoction produced by steeping comestibles.

Exclusive dedication to necessary chores without interludes of hedonistic diversion renders John a heptudinous fellow. (http://www.cord.edu/faculty /sprunger/e315/dbltk.html)

(27b)

FOR TEACHING: UNDERSTANDING DENOTATION AND CONNOTATION

Read aloud the following excerpt from *Dust Tracks on a Road,* Zora Neale Hurston's account of growing up in the South. As you read, your students may want to jot down the denotative and connotative language Hurston uses to describe the bittersweet flavor of being African American, being female, and being thrust ahead by a loving mother. After you have finished reading, your students can identify which of Hurston's language use was her academic language, and which was her home language.

If I could fasten the mind of the reader upon words so firmly that he would forget words and be conscious only of his response, I felt that I would be in sight of knowing how to write narrative. I strove to master words, to make them disappear, to make them important by making them new, to make them melt into a rising spiral to emotional stimuli, each greater than the other, each feeding and reinforcing the other, and all ending in an emotional climax that would drench the reader with a sense of a new world. That was the single aim of my living.
— Richard Wright

[She] gave me my first glimmering of the universal female gospel that all good traits and leanings come from mother's side.

Mama exhorted her children at every opportunity to "jump at de sun." We might not land on the sun, but at least we would get off the ground. Papa did not feel so hopeful. Let well enough alone. It did not do for Negroes to have too much spirit. He was always threatening to break mine or kill me in the attempt. My mother was always standing between us. She conceded that I was impudent and given to talking back, but she didn't want to "squinch my spirit" too much for fear that I would turn out to be a mealy-mouthed rag doll by the time I got grown. Papa always flew hot when Mama said that. I do not know whether he feared for my future, with the tendency I had to stand and give battle, or that he felt a personal reference in mama's observation. He predicted dire things for me. The white folks were not going to stand for it. I was going to be hung before I got grown. Somebody was going to blow me down for my sassy tongue. Mama was going to suck sorrow for not beating my temper out of me before it was too late. Posses with ropes and guns were going to drag me out sooner or later on account of that stiff neck I toted. I was going to tote a hungry belly by reason of my forward ways. My older sister was meek and mild. She would always get along. Why couldn't I be like her? Mama would keep right on with whatever she was doing and remark, "Zora is my young'un, and Sarah is yours. I'll be bound mine will come out more than conquer. You leave her alone. I'll tend to her when I figger she needs it." She meant by that that Sarah had a disposition like Papa's, while mine was like hers.

What words or phrases are most memorable? Are they academic or slang? specific or deliciously vague? In what ways does Hurston balance general and specific diction?

FOR COLLABORATIVE WORK: BALANCING GENERAL AND SPECIFIC DICTION   **(27c)**

Moving from general to specific language often involves describing something so that it can be seen, heard, felt, experienced.

1. We had a good time.
2. We were bored and had nothing to do.
3. Their tiredness showed.
4. We weren't content to just sit there, frustrated, impatient, and annoyed.

Divide the class into groups, and ask them to expand each of these brief sentences into a paragraph. Ask them to work on showing the reader the good time or the frustration and annoyance. Suggest questions such as the following to help them develop the sentences into concrete descriptions. For example, to develop *We had a good time,* you might have them ask:

> What were you doing?
> With whom?
> How did you do it?
> What did it involve?

You can also ask them to apply the same questions to *Their tiredness showed.*

FOR TEACHING: GENERAL AND SPECIFIC DICTION   **(27c)**

Ask students to read the following passage carefully and identify the balance of abstract and concrete and of general and specific diction.

> Migraine is something more than the fancy of a neurotic imagination. It is an essentially hereditary complex of symptoms, the most frequently noted but by no means the most unpleasant of which is a vascular headache of blinding

severity, suffered by a surprising number of women, a fair number of men (Thomas Jefferson had migraine, and so did Ulysses S. Grant, the day he accepted Lee's surrender), and by some unfortunate children as young as two years old. (I had my first when I was eight. It came on during a fire drill at the Columbia School in Colorado Springs, Colorado. I was taken first home and then to the infirmary at Peterson Field, where my father was stationed. The Air Corps doctor prescribed an enema.) Almost anything can trigger a specific attack of migraine: stress, allergy, fatigue, an abrupt change in barometric pressure, a contretemps over a parking ticket. A flashing light. A fire drill. One inherits, of course, only the predisposition. In other words I spent yesterday in bed with a headache not merely because of my bad attitudes, unpleasant tempers and wrongthink, but because both my grandmothers had migraine, my father has migraine and my mother has migraine.   –JOAN DIDION, "In Bed"

(27d)   **FOR TEACHING: USING FIGURATIVE LANGUAGE**

To show your students that the use of figurative language occurs in our everyday reading and writing, encourage them to look at magazines, articles, and books that they read outside the classroom in their leisure time. Roger Angell's *Season Ticket: A Baseball Companion,* a collection of essays published in the *New Yorker* between 1983 and 1987, contains wonderful examples of simile, for example. Joel Conarroe, in a review in the *New York Times Book Review,* praises Angell: "This is a meticulous writer with an eye for the telling simile, the domestic image that can bring an observation vividly to life." Conarroe mentions Angell's description of "a slumping team" going through September "like an ember in a snowbank" and of Steve Carlton's three-quarter-speed slider that "drops out of the strike zone like a mouse behind the sink."

(27d)   **On the Power of Metaphor**

The bare-bones definition of *metaphor* as an "implicit comparison" hardly does justice to this most important figure. In fact, many language theorists view metaphor as the very grounding of language, which is, in fact, always referring, always deferring. Even a concrete word like *chair* is metaphorical, standing in as it does for some specific object, "figuring" it in the mind of the hearer in certain ways. Students need to understand how deeply metaphorical all language is, and to understand the power of metaphor in shaping our thoughts. One good way to begin might be to take some examples from Lakoff and Johnson's now-classic 1980 study, *Metaphors We Live By,* which demonstrates in vivid detail how deeply metaphor is embedded in thinking.

FOR TEACHING: METAPHORS AND SLANG

(27d)

Share these metaphorical definitions of *slang* with your students. Ask them to decide which one they like best and why, and then create their own metaphorical definitions of *slang* or of some other abstraction — *beauty, truth, justice, hunger,* and so on.

1. [Slang] is always strong. . . . Cut these words and they would bleed; they are vascular and alive; they walk and run. — RALPH WALDO EMERSON

2. Slang is the speech of him who rolls the literary garbage carts on their way to the dump. — AMBROSE BIERCE

3. Slang is language that takes off its coat, spits on its hands, and gets to work. — CARL SANDBURG

4. Slang: words with their shoes off. — PATRICK HARTWELL

5. Slang is adventure and experiment in words. — MARY AUGUSTA JORDAN

6. [Slang is] the grunt of the human hog (Pignoramus intolerabilis). — AMBROSE BIERCE

7. [Slang is] the poetry of everyday life. — S. I. HAYAKAWA

FOR TEACHING: EFFECTIVE SIMILES, METAPHORS, AND ANALOGIES

(27d)

Ask your students to evaluate the effectiveness of similes, metaphors, and analogies in the following sentences and to revise any that are mixed or clichés.

1. These children were brought up to eat, drink, and sleep tennis.

2. In presenting his alibi, the defendant chose the alley he was going to bowl on — and the jury wouldn't swallow it.

3. The president's economic plan is about as useful as rearranging the deck chairs on the *Titanic.*

4. The narrative was heavy as lead — it just flowed on and on and on.

5. For as long as I can remember, my mother has been the backbone for my father's convictions.

Clichés are the last word *in bad writing, and it's* a crying shame *to see all you* bright young things *spoiling your* deathless prose *with phrases as* old as the hills. *You must* keep your nose to the grindstone, *because the* sweet smell of success *only comes to those who* march to the tune of a different drummer.
— JANET BURROWAY

(27d)

FOR COLLABORATIVE WORK: CLICHÉS AND MIXED METAPHORS

Ask students to work together in groups of three to five to complete the preceding exercise on similes, metaphors, and analogies. In the case of identifying mixed metaphor and cliché especially, two (or more) heads are better than one. You also may want to ask students to write brief explanations of what they found wrong in the sentences and of how their revisions remedy the problems.

(27d)

FOR MULTILINGUAL WRITERS: ANALOGIES

For multilingual writers who may have a difficult time with the cultural nuances of diction, take time to review the following list of exaggerated analogies and the cultural connotations that produce the humor in each case. Read each sentence out loud, and then discuss what makes each analogy a parody.

- "The ballerina rose gracefully en pointe and extended one slender leg behind her, like a dog at a fire hydrant." (Jennifer Hart, Arlington)
- "The revelation that his marriage of thirty years had disintegrated because of his wife's infidelity came as a rude shock, like a surcharge at a formerly surcharge-free ATM." (Paul J. Kocak, Syracuse)
- "The dandelion swayed in the gentle breeze like an oscillating electric fan set on medium." (Ralph Scott, Washington)
- "It was an American tradition, like fathers chasing kids around with power tools." (Brian Broadus, Charlottesville)
- "He was deeply in love. When she spoke, he thought he heard bells, as if she were a garbage truck backing up." (Susan Reese, Arlington)
- "She was as easy as the *TV Guide* crossword." (Tom Witte, Gaithersburg)
- "She grew on him like she was a colony of *E. coli* and he was room-temperature Canadian beef." (Brian Broadus, Charlottesville)
- "The young fighter had a hungry look, the kind you get from not eating for a while." (Malcolm Fleschner, Arlington)

I write out loud, hearing the music that gives writing meaning. I can write the first draft with the screen turned off. I write by ear.
– DONALD M. MURRAY, Boston Globe

Language is not an abstract construction of the learned, or of dictionary-makers, but is something arising out of the work, needs, ties, joys, affections, tastes . . . .
– WALT WHITMAN

(27d)

FOR TEACHING: EXTENDED ANALOGIES

Ask students, perhaps working in groups, to try their hands at an extended analogy, perhaps using this one from Jeff Jarvis's 1994 *TV Guide* review of *Frasier:*

Frasier has learned to play its characters as Leonard Bernstein played an orchestra: masterfully. Kelsey Grammer as Frasier is a blustery bassoon; David Hyde Pierce as brother Niles, a squeaky oboe; John Mahoney as grumpy Dad, a big, bad drum; and Jane Leeves as Daphne, with her beguiling accent, a sweet clarinet. Each week, with precise timing and harmony, these players give us wonderful comic concerts.

Fear not: The musical metaphor ends here. But the point remains: Creating a sitcom can be an art — and a difficult one.

TEACHING WITH TECHNOLOGY: REVISING FOR DICTION

Ask students to bring selections from their own work to class, choose several to project up on a computer screen, and ask the class as a whole to discuss the diction of each piece. How would students describe the dominant impression given by the selection? How would they characterize its register? Which words seem most effective and memorable — and why? Are there any instances in which they might revise the diction for different effect?

Revise the selections collaboratively, using the keyboard and inputting students' suggestions.

■ USEFUL READINGS

Altick, Richard D., and Andrea A. Lunsford. *Preface to Critical Reading.* 6th ed. New York: Holt, 1984. See chapter 1 for a discussion of the uses of connotation in advertising, political persuasion, and literature.

Coe, Richard M. "Beyond Diction: Using Burke to Empower Words — and Wordlings." *Rhetoric Review* 11.2 (Spring 1993): 368-77.

Corbett, Edward P. J., with Robert Connors. *Classical Rhetoric for the Modern Student.* 4th ed. New York: Oxford UP, 1999. Corbett's discussion of ethical and emotional appeals provides a sound rationale for the importance of diction.

Lakoff, George, and Mark Johnson. *Metaphors We Live By.* Chicago: U of Chicago P, 1980.

Orwell, George. "Politics and the English Language." *Shooting an Elephant and Other Essays.* New York: Harcourt, 1974. The essay provides a discussion of appropriate verbs and nouns, pretentious diction, and meaningless words.

Perry, Theresa, and Lisa Delpit, eds. *The Real Ebonics Debate: Power, Language, and the Education of African American Children.* Boston: Beacon, 1998. This collection of writings, by distinguished scholars and writers on the definitions and implications of Ebonics for the education of African American students, offers an

Why shouldn't we quarrel about a word? What is the good of words if they aren't important enough to quarrel over? Why do we choose one word more than another if there isn't any difference between them?
– G. K. CHESTERTON

insightful analysis of the complex and political nature of language as well as its inextricable relation to race and class in the United States.

Pinker, Steven. *The Language Instinct: How the Mind Creates Language.* New York: Harper, 1995.

Skorczewski, Dawn. "'Everybody Has Their Own Ideas': Responding to Cliché in Student Writing." *CCC* 52.2 (Dec. 2000): 220–39. While writing instructors often identify clichés as the weakest spots in student writing, Skorczewski argues that looking at students' uses of cliché in context can teach us about their knowledge base and ways of communicating.

Stark, Ryan J. "Clichés and Composition Theory." *A Journal of Composition Theory* 19.3 (1999): 453–64. Stark makes the compelling case for the cliché as a rhetorical device to establish common ground.

Williams, Joseph M. *Origins of the English Language: A Social and Linguistic History.* New York: Macmillan, 1975. See pp. 204–207 for a discussion of slang as a source of change in word meaning. Williams cites interesting historical instances of slang.

▼ Using Dictionaries

28

I was reading the dictionary. I thought it was a poem about everything.

— STEVEN WRIGHT

The dictionary, as we know it, is comparatively modern. To the medieval scholar, a dictionary was a collection of "dictions" or phrases put together for the use of pupils studying Latin — the social elite. The earliest dictionaries in English (Robert Cawdray's *A Table Alphabetical* of 1604 is the first) consisted of *hard words*. Through the seventeenth and eighteenth centuries, dictionaries steadily increased in size as lexicographers gradually moved toward the principle of including all words, not just hard words, in dictionaries. By the time Samuel Johnson composed his dictionary, he could assume that he had to include all words in his dictionary. Johnson's contribution was his systematic inclusion of illustrative quotations to demonstrate proper usage. Noah Webster's *American Dictionary of the English Language* built on Johnson's use of quotations by including selections from the Founding Fathers of the Republic and by insisting on American spellings. In 1961 *Webster's Third International Dictionary of the English Language* caused an outcry because the editors, departing from Webster's practice, decided to let usage determine correctness rather than impose an external authority. In contrast to the prescriptive dictionaries of Johnson and Webster, most modern dictionaries tend to be descriptive.

FOR TEACHING: THE IMPORTANCE OF DICTIONARIES

Consider demonstrating the keen usefulness of dictionaries by bringing in a couple of legal contracts — say from life insurance companies. Reading

WORDS . . . are the wildest, freest, most irresponsible, most unteachable of all things. Of course, you can catch them and place them in alphabetical order in dictionaries. But words do not live in dictionaries; they live in the mind . . . all we can say about them, as we peer at them over the edge of that deep, dark and only fitfully illuminated cavern in which they live — the mind — all we can say about them is that they seem to like people to think and to feel before they use them, but to think and to feel not about them, but about something different.

— VIRGINIA WOOLF

these materials calls for a sharp eye and a very clear knowledge of what each word means. Materials describing one such plan, for example, contain the following terms: *semiannual, net cost, underwrite, waiver, conversion, incontestability,* and *incapacitated.* Ask your students to define each of these words, without — and then with — the help of a dictionary. Which ones would they want to make sure they really understood before signing a contract?

(28a)   **FOR TEACHING: EXPLORING THE DICTIONARY**

To extend the ways students use dictionaries, devise assignments that require students to use a dictionary to complete the assignment. One such assignment might be an extended definition of a term (for example, *wife*), either of your own or of the students' choice. To have students define the term fully, you might require that they include all uses of the term, from formal to slang. You might also require that students examine how the term has changed over time (for example, *guy*), or you might require students to examine how the meaning of a certain word changes from country to country and region to region *(grill* and *barbeque).* The various requirements demand that students examine a variety of sources.

For additional practice, ask your students to copy the definitions of a word of their choice from three unabridged dictionaries: *Oxford English Dictionary, Webster's Third New International Dictionary of the English Language,* and *The Random House Dictionary of the English Language.* Assign a short essay (250 – 500 words) that describes the changes in meaning their word has undergone. If you assign a word, make sure that the definitions include enough material for the length of the assignment you expect. If the students choose their own words, take care to emphasize that they need to choose a word with enough information listed about that word. Ask students to eliminate the need for extensive citations and to help build a file of words and definitions.

(28b)   **FOR COLLABORATIVE WORK: DISTINGUISHING AMONG DICTIONARIES**

Break the class into small groups, and either assign a word to each group or allow the group to pick a word they find interesting. Each person in the group should investigate the definition and usage of the word in one of the dictionaries, usage books, or thesauruses in the following list. The group members are responsible for presenting as rich a definition as possible for the word they researched and for reporting on the kind of dictionary they used. The "product" of the research can take the form of a written report, but an oral presentation is often more valuable and interesting, particularly if the words the students choose contain surprises for them.

Here is a list of potential sources (not including the ones listed in the *Handbook*).

Brewer's Dictionary of Phrase and Fable. 16th ed. New York: Harper, 2000.

Chapman, Robert L. *Dictionary of American Slang.* 3rd ed. New York: Harper, 1998.

Hall, John R. *A Concise Anglo-Saxon Dictionary.* Toronto: U of Toronto P, 1984.

Lighter, Jonathan E., and John J. O'Connor. *Random House Historical Dictionary of American Slang.* 2 vols. New York: Random House, 1997.

Matthews, Mitford M. *A Dictionary of Americanisms on Historical Principles.* Chicago: U of Chicago P, 1951.

Partridge, Eric. *A Dictionary of Slang and Unconventional English.* 8th ed. New York: Routledge, 2002.

Wentworth, Harold, and Stuart B. Flexner. *Dictionary of American Slang.* 2nd ed. New York: Crowell, 1975.

FOR TEACHING: DISTINGUISHING AMONG DICTIONARIES   **(28b)**

Here are the *Webster's Third* entries for *unique* as an adjective and as a noun. The adjective entry lists the meaning "unusual, notable" and provides examples of the use of *most unique* but does not discuss the controversy over this usage. At the end of the entry, the notation *syn* refers to the entries for *single* and *strange,* where the shades of meaning that distinguish *unique* from its synonyms are explained. The phonetic symbols differ slightly from those in either the *OED* or the abridged dictionaries.

Ask your students to look up *unique* in several other dictionaries, such as those listed above. In addition, suggest that they look up the same word in Fowler's *Modern English Usage,* in Bergen Evans and Cornelia Evans's *Dictionary of Contemporary American Usage,* and in Margaret M. Bryant's *Current American Usage* and write a brief description of how these works agree and disagree on the usage of *unique.*

¹**unique** \yü'nēk, '⌄,⌄\ *adj, sometimes* -ER/-EST [F, fr. L *unicus* sole, single, unique, fr. *unus* one + *-icus* -ic — more at ONE] **1 a :** being the only one : SOLE ⟨earning money whose ~ object could be nothing but Cyril's welfare —Arnold Bennett⟩ ⟨has thus preserved the original and often ~ records —G.B. Parks⟩ ⟨you are a miracle, a wonder, a mystery . . . one single ~ and inimitable living thing —J.C.Powys⟩ **b** *of a book* **:** known to exist in no other copy **2 :** being without a like or equal : single in kind or excellence : UNEQUALED ⟨they stand alone, ~, objects of supreme interest —A.B.Osborne⟩ ⟨as historian he knows that events, like persons, are ~ —J.M. Barzun⟩ ⟨remains singularly himself, a ~ lyrist of the first water —I.L.Salomon⟩ ⟨an almost ~ experience —Havelock Ellis⟩ ⟨tendencies present in our contemporary world which make our own times somewhat ~ —M.B.Smith⟩ ⟨story of his life is considerably more ~ than most autobiographies —Dorothy C. Fisher⟩ ⟨the more we study him, the less ~ he seems —Harry Levin⟩ — sometimes used with *to* ⟨the problem of what to do with surplus women is by no means ~ to our own society — Ralph Linton⟩ or *with* ⟨by no means ~ with the song sparrow —*Nature Mag.*⟩ **3 :** UNUSUAL, NOTABLE ⟨possessed ~ ability in the raising of funds —C.F.Thwing⟩ ⟨the wife of a career diplomat has a ~ opportunity to observe the world political scene —Ray Pierre⟩ ⟨a frankness ~ in literature —David Daiches⟩ ⟨~ peace and privacy —R.W.Hatch⟩ ⟨cheap, nourishing, and a ~ dining experience —T.H.Fielding⟩ ⟨the most ~ characteristic of that environment —R.A.Billington⟩ ⟨she's the most ~ person I ever met —Arthur Miller⟩ ⟨the most ~ theater in town —*advt*⟩ **4 :** capable of being performed in only one way ⟨the factorization of a number into its prime factors is ~⟩ **syn** see SINGLE, STRANGE
²**unique** \"\ *n* -S **:** something (as a specimen, thing, circumstance, or person) that is unique : the only one of its kind ⟨mistaking the ~ for the typical —W.J.Reilly⟩ ⟨the zest of the collector for possession of a ~ —Roy Bedichek⟩ ⟨a display of glass, including undercoated ~s —*Danish Foreign Office Jour.*⟩ ⟨the phoenix, the ~ of birds —Thomas De Quincey⟩

For another exercise, ask your students to look up the entry *strange* in *Webster's New Dictionary of Synonyms* and read it carefully. Then ask them to write a brief summary of what the entry has to say about the relationship of *unique* to *strange*. Finally, have them look up *strange* in *The New Roget's Thesaurus,* and compare that entry with the one in *Webster's.*

On Language Change

A reminder that language changes, no matter how the dictionaries might guide us:

> Those who have been persuaded to think well of my design, require that it should fix our language, and put a stop to those alterations which time and chance have hitherto been suffered to make in it without opposition. With this consequence, I will confess that I have flattered myself for a while; but now begin to fear that I have indulged expectations which neither reason nor experience can justify. . . . [M]ay the lexicographer be derided, who being able to produce no example of a nation that has preserved their words and phrases from mutability, shall imagine that his dictionary can embalm his language, and secure it from corruption and decay, that it is in his power to change sub-

lunary nature, and clear the world at once from folly, vanity, and affectation. With this hope, however, academies have been instituted, to guard the avenues of their language, to retain fugitives, and to repulse intruders; but their vigilance and activity have hitherto been vain; sounds are too volatile and subtle for legal restraints; to enchain syllables, and to lash the wind, are equally the undertakings of pride, unwilling to measure its desires by its strength.

— SAMUEL JOHNSON, Preface to his 1755 Dictionary

FOR COLLABORATIVE WORK: CONSULTING SPECIALIZED DICTIONARIES   (28c)

Ask your students to bring their dictionaries to class. Read some of the following Ambrose Bierce definitions from *The Devil's Dictionary* to them. Then ask your students to find the correct use of the term that Bierce satirizes. Finally, ask your students to write a short analysis of Bierce's specialized dictionary. What makes each definition parodic?

Here are some examples from Bierce:

corporation, n. An ingenious device for obtaining individual profit without individual responsibility.

edible, adj. Good to eat, and wholesome to digest, as a worm to a toad, a toad to a snake, a snake to a pig, a pig to a man, and man to a worm.

impiety, n. Your irreverence toward my deity.

lawyer, n. One skilled in circumvention of the law.

Occident, n. The part of the world lying west (or east) of the Orient. It is largely inhabited by Christians, a powerful sub-tribe of the Hypocrites, whose principle industries are murder and cheating, which they are pleased to call "war" and "commerce." These, also, are the principle industries of the Orient.

positive, adj. Mistaken at the top of one's voice.

radicalism, n. The conservatism of tomorrow injected into the affairs of today.

■ USEFUL READINGS

Baugh, Albert C., and Thomas Cable. *A History of the English Language.* 5th ed. Upper Saddle River: Prentice, 2001. See items 170, "Dictionaries of Hard Words"; 197, "Johnson's Dictionary"; and 246, "Noah Webster and an American Language."

Johnson, Samuel. "Preface to a Dictionary of the English Language." *Samuel Johnson: Rasselas, Poems, and Selected Prose.* 3rd ed. Ed. Bertrand H. Bronson. New York: Holt, 1971. Johnson describes his goals, the problems he encountered, and the limitations of the work.

▼ Enriching Vocabulary

29

Words are all we have.
– SAMUEL BECKETT

In one of the great heroic tales in English literature, Beowulf faces a series of difficult challenges. In the face of them, he calls not for weapons or for superhuman strength. Instead he says, quite simply, "I will unlock my word hoard." Beowulf regards his word hoard—his vocabulary or language—as his greatest strength. Indeed, in the history of Western culture, the connection between language and creative power has been very close, as in the biblical act of creating the world by naming it.

Today, we are called on not only to draw on our own "word hoards" but to learn new words all the time, to add to our vocabularies in significant ways. Doing so can sometimes lead to a good laugh (unintended or not) when we don't quite know the meaning of a term. The famous baseball player Dizzy Dean was known partly for his tendency to make such mistakes. Once after he injured his leg sliding into second base, the trainer announced with a serious expression that it looked as if the leg was fractured. "Fractured, hell!" Dean is reported to have exclaimed: "The damned thing's broken!" In this case, Dean probably figured out the meaning of "fractured" pretty quickly. Why not ask your students to bring in a couple of words they've recently learned, along with two or three other new words they've heard but don't know the meanings of? Then use these to lead a class discussion on building vocabulary.

I am less interested in what the definition is. You might argue technically, are we in a recession or not. But when there's this kind of sluggishness and concern—definitions, heck with it.
– GEORGE BUSH SR.

FOR TEACHING: CHARTING THE HISTORY OF ENGLISH

(29a) ⋯⋯⋯⋯⋯⋯⋯⋯

Old or Middle English may look remote to students, but if you read a Middle English text aloud, they will be surprised at how much they pick up. Provide your students with a copy of one of Chaucer's *Canterbury Tales,* and read part of it to them. Ask them to underline any words they cannot understand, and as a class, attempt to define these words. Here is a section from the Wife of Bath's Prologue:

> Lo, here the wyse king, dan Salomon
> I towe he hadd wyves mo than oon.
> As wolde God it level ful were to me
> To be refressed half so ofte as he!
> Which yifte of God hadde he for alle his wyvis!
> No man hath switch, that in this world alyve is.

(29a)
On Charting the History of English: New Words

Studying how the English colonists in the New World confronted many new places, plants, animals, and experiences reveals how speakers of English have always developed new words. The colonists provided new names for new things in four ways.

1. By borrowing directly from another language, usually one of the Native American languages. Native Americans spoke 350 different languages. The largest number of loan words came from the Algonquin languages. *Wigwam* is an example.
2. By translating foreign words (usually Native American) and phrases into English. An example is *war path*.
3. By using an English word to serve as a label for something new. *Corn* and *robin* refer to different objects in England than they do in North America.
4. By coining a new word entirely, although such coinages were rare. The *bobwhite* and the *whippoorwill* received names meant as imitations of the sounds they made. And *backwoods* is another colonial coinage.

Language continues to change. The process of adapting language to fit current needs never stops. Your students and their coinages are best seen as part of this process.

(29a)
On Charting the History of English: Language Borrowing

English owes its hybrid nature to the various invasions of Britain—that is, to the fact that the earliest native peoples and their language, the Celts, and the later dominant peoples, the three Germanic tribes (the Jutes, the Angles, and the Saxons) intermixed with each other and other peoples invading the country. The Romans, who ruled Britain for almost four hundred years, contributed *castra,* the Latin word meaning "camp." It is evident in the names of such places as *Lancaster* and *Winchester.* Also, Latin words were brought over to Britain by the German invaders, whose language had borrowed them previously; *win* ("wine"), *ancor* ("anchor"), *weall* ("wall"). The Anglo-Saxons gave us the earliest ancestors of many modern English words, such as *hus* ("house"), *wulf* ("wolf"), and *faeder* ("father"). They also gave the country its permanent name, *Englaland* ("England"), the "land of the Angles." The Danes, who invaded Britain in the ninth century, added *skull, sky, band, egg, want,* and *low.* And they gave us our personal pronouns for the third person, *they, their,* and *them.* A tremendous number of new English words and new spellings originated with the Norman Invasion in 1066. *Service, castle, chancellor, army,* and *literature* all came from Norman French originally.

Renaissance scholars deliberately borrowed many Greek and Latin words. Also, many Greek and Latin prefixes, suffixes, and roots of words were borrowed and combined with other borrowings to form whole new words.

English continues to be a very acquisitive language, borrowing from almost every language it comes in contact with. From Spanish, we have *canyon, cafeteria,* and *taco.* From German, we borrowed *protein* and *bratwurst.* From Italian, we have *malaria,* but also *pasta* and *studio.* From Slavic, we have *robot* and *vampire.* From Arabic, we adopted *genie, candy, safari,* and *assassin* (originally meaning "hashish eater"). From Hebrew, we borrowed *amen, Sabbath,* and *Satan.* From Yiddish, we borrowed *kosher* and *matzo.* From Persian, we got *spinach, lilac,* and *bazaar.* From Sanskrit, we have *swastika* and *yoga.* From Hindustani, we got *dungaree, pajamas, jungle,* and *loot.* From Chinese, we adopted *tea* and *ketchup.* From Japanese, we borrowed *zen* and *karate.*

FOR TEACHING: BUILDING YOUR VOCABULARY   **(29d)**

In *Classical Rhetoric for the Modern Student,* Edward P. J. Corbett notes that Samuel Johnson and Oliver Goldsmith identified themselves in their writing by stylistic choices, such as diction. Johnson's is described as "philosophical, polysyllabic, Latinate"; Goldsmith's as "concrete, familiar, colloquial."

Consider using examples of writing, either from these authors or from legalese and rock lyrics, to point out how building vocabulary can restrict or free writers.

(29d)

FOR COLLABORATIVE WORK: BUILDING YOUR VOCABULARY

Ask your students to form into groups and record inventive uses of vocabulary. To get them started, read some of Tom Wolfe's prose, such as "Pornoviolence" (the title coins a new word), "Hugh Hefner" (in which he coins the word *statusphere*), or "Las Vegas (What!) Las Vegas (Can't Hear You! Too Noisy) Las Vegas!!" (in which Wolfe names the signs on the strip: "Boomerang Modern, Palette Curvilinear, Flash Gordon Ming Alert Spiral, McDonald's Hamburger Parabola, Mint Casino Elliptical, Miami Beach Kidney"). Paul Fussell's "Notes on Class" uses the following terms to identify his classifications of society: "Top Out-of-Sight; Upper [class]; Upper Middle/Middle; High-Proletarian; Mid-Proletarian; Low-Proletarian/Destitute; Bottom Out-of-Sight," and a floating class "Class X."

Douglas Coupland coins new words in the margins of *Generation X* to describe some twenty-somethings and their cultural dilemmas, including the McJob, poorochondria ("hypochondria derived from not having medical insurance"), tele-parablizing ("morals used in everyday life that derive from TV sitcom plots"), and down-nesting ("the tendency of parents to move to smaller, guest-room-free houses after the children have moved away so as to avoid children aged 20 to 30 who have boomeranged home").

Words are with us everywhere. In our erotic secrecies, in our sleep. We're often no more aware of them than our own spit, although we use them oftener than legs. So of course in the customary shallow unconscious sense, we comprehend the curse, the prayer, and the whoop.
– WILLIAM H. GASS

(29d)

FOR MULTILINGUAL WRITERS: BUILDING YOUR VOCABULARY

Ask students to choose a language to investigate: the language of rap, the language of parents, the language of doctors. As part of their investigation, ask students to draw up a "vocabulary," complete with definitions and examples, for the language they choose. A few years ago, a compendium of the language of first-year students would probably have included words like *chill* (short for *chill out*, which means to cool it or calm down) and *yo* (a glottal vibration meant to indicate either "Give me your attention" or "Yes, you have my attention").

Wrestling with words gave me my moments of greatest meaning.
– RICHARD WRIGHT

(29d)

FOR TEACHING: BUILDING YOUR VOCABULARY

Students can build word power by trying to think of words to substitute for the italicized ones in the passages in the reading exercise at the end of 29d. You can use these potential substitutes (*erased*, say, for *eradicated*) to

The man who doesn't read good books has no advantage over the man who can't read them.
– MARK TWAIN

reflect on nuances of connotation and on why a writer may have chosen one particular word over another.

■ USEFUL READINGS

Heath, Shirley Brice. *Ways with Words*. Cambridge: Cambridge UP, 1983. See chapter 9, "Learners as Ethnographers," for more information about students as "investigative reporters."

Herndon, Jeanne H. *A Survey of Modern Grammars*. New York: Holt, 1976. See pp. 146–47 for a discussion of competence and performance, *la langue* and *la parole*.

Mencken, H. L. *The American Language*. 4th ed. New York: Knopf, 1999. See "The Expanding Vocabulary," "The Making of New Nouns," and "American Slang."

30 ▼ Attending to Spelling

My spelling is Wobbly. It's good spelling but it Wobbles, and the letters get in the wrong places.
—A. A. MILNE

Students ask us all the time—"why do we need to attend so meticulously to spelling?" Our answer might be rooted in classical rhetoric, for what's at stake with spelling errors is the very ethos of the writer. As Larry Beason found out in his study of reader's impressions of orthographic errors, mistakes matter—immensely: "In the nonacademic workforce, errors can affect people and events in larger ways. . . . Whether we believe it to be the optimum situation or not, errors have an impact on the writer's image and communicability. Error avoidance, I submit, should have a presence in the composition curriculum—but without overpowering it" (60). Similarly, in research conducted for an earlier edition of the *Handbook,* Andrea Lunsford and Robert Connors found that spelling errors were the most common mistakes made by student writers. These findings suggest that spelling cannot—and should not—be overlooked by writing instructors.

The public unfortunately believes that the majority of students are bad spellers, but in fact, the results of recent research contradict this notion. For instance, Ede Kidder and Karl Taylor conclude that spelling errors generally decline from the first through the eighth grades. Only the "wrong words" category, primarily homonyms, increases. Their conclusion corroborates that of Lunsford and Connors, who found that the most frequent spelling errors involved problems with homonyms. As with other writing errors, spelling errors tend to fall into patterns which, once discovered, can be corrected.

On English Spelling

In 1066, England was invaded for a fourth time. The Normans from France were led by William the Conqueror, and they overran the island in just a year. They declared their language, Norman French, to be the official language, and for the next two hundred years or so, business, education, and government were all conducted in French. English was considered barbaric. However, the government could not—and didn't even bother to try to—control the language of the masses. Therefore, English continued to be spoken by most people in their daily lives.

As with the Norse invasion earlier, the Normans influenced the lexicon of the English language. In *The Origins and Development of the English Language,* Thomas Pyles and John Algeo point out that French spelling conventions were borrowed along with French vocabulary. They also note that "some of the apparent innovations in Middle English spelling were, in fact, a return to earlier conventions" (139). For instance, *th* was reintroduced. "Other new spellings were true innovations" (139); *g* entered English orthography for the first time.

Eventually the Normans' influence waned, and French was spoken less and less. English began to reappear in education, in business affairs, and in government documents. By the fifteenth century, English had once again been taken up by imaginative writers. For example, Chaucer's *Canterbury Tales* was written in English.

Never in the history of the English language was spelling more uniform than it is today. Spelling conventions during the Middle Ages and early Renaissance were very relaxed. No prescriptions existed for spelling uniformity—not even within the same text. Orthographic conventions "were used with a nonchalance that is hardly imaginable in the era of the printing press" (Pyles and Algeo 142). A person might even spell his or her own name in different ways. "Shakespeare," for instance, was spelled *Shakespeare, Shakespear,* and *Shake-spear,* and the "correct" spelling is still being argued.

Of course, most writers spelled words more or less consistently, and people communicated with one another without great confusion. It is difficult to tell whether some spelling inconsistencies were products of the writers themselves or of the printers taking advantage of instability in spelling in order to easily "justify" a line. In spite of all the variety, Baugh and Cable tell us that "by 1550 a nucleus of common [spelling] practice" existed. In fact, the sixteenth century marked a distinct change in attitude toward spelling. Changing cultural values marked this period, and in their search for stability, scholars focused on stabilizing English spelling.

Throughout the sixteenth and seventeenth centuries, numerous attempts to standardize (and, in many cases, reform) spelling were made. The earliest one, *An A. B. C. for Children,* appeared sometime before 1558.

As their language evolves, children use longer, more complicated [syntactic] structures and more sophisticated vocabulary. As they begin to use less familiar words and to employ different structures, they make errors of all types, from comma splices to misspellings. Error, then, is a sign of growth.
– EDE B. KIDDER and KARL K. TAYLOR

Most of these attempts tried to develop an alphabet that corresponded to pronunciation.

The most important of these treatises is *Elementarie* (1582) by Richard Mulcaster, who saw the futility of trying for an exact, scientific correspondence between spelling and pronunciation. Whether Mulcaster's work really influenced the stability of spelling or simply reflected that stability as it developed naturally is impossible to say, but English spelling did develop along the lines he called for.

(30a)

FOR TEACHING: THE MOST COMMONLY MISSPELLED WORDS

President Andrew Jackson once exclaimed in exasperation, "It's a damn poor mind that can think of only one way to spell a word!" This comment is just as true today as it was during Jackson's era. A short drive along an interstate, for example, turned up the following examples of "more than one way to spell a word": *Kountry Kitchen, Kutz for Mutz, Phat Phil's Phone Phood.* Ask students to keep an eye out for fanciful or amusing "alternative" spellings. Gather their findings and use them to discuss what purposes the writer might have had for such spellings. One reason is often copyright!

On Recognizing Homonyms

(30b)

It's good style to use simple spelling whenever you have a choice. . . . But don't use spellings that may annoy some readers, like nite, tho, thru.
— RUDOLPH FLESCH

In the *Harper Dictionary of Contemporary Usage,* William and Mary Morris make an interesting distinction among homographs, homonyms, and homophones. *Homographs* are words spelled alike but pronounced differently (e.g., *tears* we shed and *tears* in a cloth). *Homonyms* are words spelled alike and pronounced alike (e.g., *bear* the animal, and *bear* meaning "carry"). *Homophones* are words spelled differently but pronounced alike *(peace* and *piece).* Normally, we just refer to all three under the label *homonym.*

(30b)

FOR MULTILINGUAL WRITERS: RECOGNIZING ENGLISH SPELLING

Noah Webster, the most influential individual in the history of American spelling, published his dictionary in 1828. But before that, he published a speller, a grammar, and a reader. All his works aimed to "standardize"

U.S. English. Not only did he want to standardize our spelling, but he also sought to "Americanize" English in the United States. He excised the *u* from (British) English words spelled with the *-our* ending, words such as *colour, labour, favour,* etc. And he was responsible for the American practice of using *-er* rather than *-re* to end many words: *theater, center, sepulcher,* and so on. The use of *-se* in place of *-ce* has also been attributed to Webster (*defense, offense,* and so on), as has dropping the *k* in words like *almanack, musick,* and *publick.*

Fortunately both my wife and my mother-in-law seem to love digging up mistakes in spelling, punctuation, etc. I can hear them in the next room laughing at me.
– SHERWOOD ANDERSON

FOR TEACHING: IMPROVING SPELLING

The findings of recent research have important implications for spelling instruction and suggest that traditional methods of such instruction do not suffice.

Traditionally, instructors have marked orthographical errors and told students to look up misspelled words in the dictionary. But Mina Shaughnessy claims that just pointing out misspellings without helping students understand them and revise them sends the message that such misspellings cannot be revised, that the student is a "'born' misspeller." If the student continues to spell as he or she hears without regard to semantic connections, he or she will continue to misspell.

Also, traditional spelling instruction has taken the form of drills, unrelated to the student's other writing. But spelling instruction is not an end in itself. As Kidder and Taylor point out, "Learning how to spell will not necessarily improve reading or speaking, but it is essential for writing and is reinforced when practiced in real writing situations" (237). Spelling drills are of little value, unless students use the words themselves in their own writing.

On Linking Spelling and Pronunciation

(30c) ································

One of the most controversial areas in the study of spelling remains the relationship of orthography to pronunciation. The Roman alphabet cannot phonetically represent the English language; for instance, the alphabet possesses only five vowel symbols, while the language has eleven, not including diphthongs and [r] modifications. Some language reformers call for refashioning spelling to conform to pronunciation. Yet good, practical reasons exist for differentiating the lexical and phonetic aspects of language.

Wilson Follett notes that pronunciations differ with dialects. Therefore, choosing the phonetic representation of words as a measure for spelling becomes a political decision as much as anything else.

William J. Stevens cites the problem of homonyms spelled alike under the above reform. We could not differentiate among *to, too,* and *two.*

More important, Carol Chomsky argues that spelling corresponds less to surface features of the language (i.e., pronunciation) than to the underlying meanings of words. Spelling, she claims, retains lexical connections between words, connections that might be lost in pronunciation shifts. For instance, *nation* retains its semantic affiliation with *nationality* through their sharing of the same semantic core, represented orthographically as *nation,* despite a different pronunciation of that core. On the other hand, such a connection does not exist between *nation* and *notion.* They share a common ending but not a semantic core. While variations in pronunciation, instigated by phonological rules such as the shifts in phonological stress with the addition of suffixes, may occur, semantic connections are retained through the spelling of the two words.

(30d)   **FOR TEACHING: TAKING ADVANTAGE OF SPELLING RULES**

You can use the teaching of spelling rules to your advantage. Dorothy Thompson argues that short periods of spelling instruction are more effective than longer periods. Ann Dobie suggests no more than fifteen or twenty minutes per class time.

Consider the following practice for each student's final draft:

1. Circle all misspelled words in the paper.
2. Ask the student to correct the misspelling himself or herself.
3. Ask the student to bring in two other related words and identify the shared core.

FOR COLLABORATIVE WORK: EDITING FOR SPELLING

Many "spelling" errors are actually errors of proofreading—or the lack thereof. We all commit "typos," but they indicate nothing more than our imperfect humanity, and they are easily corrected during spell-checking and proofreading. Genuine spelling errors are, of course, a different story. However, the reader has no way to distinguish between the two. Therefore, proofreading becomes a vitally important activity for the writer. To encourage students to proofread more carefully, you might consider the following practice.

Before taking up the final draft of the first paper, divide the class into groups of two or three. Have them exchange papers and check for words that they think might be misspelled. On a separate sheet of paper, they should note the page number and paragraph number, the misspelled word, and what they believe is the correct spelling of that word. After the papers have been returned to the authors, allow them time to go through their papers and make the corrections. They should be aware that there is no guarantee that their proofreaders are correct 100 percent of the time. The writers themselves must make the final choice about the spelling. Along with the paper, the separate sheet with the proofreader's notes on the spelling should be handed in. When grading this first paper, don't count off for any corrected spelling but do record the originally misspelled words pointed out by the proofreader.

Do the same for following papers, but call special attention — whether through grading sanctions or by a reminder to the student — to misspellings that are repeated from earlier work.

I could be typing kifiu joew.mv jiw *and enjoy it as much as typing words that actually make sense.*
– STEVE MARTIN

No doubt you are as alarmed as I by the tragic decline in America's language skills. If 10 people read the following sentence — "Two tanker trucks has just overturned in Alaska, spilling a totel of 10,000 gallons of beer onto a highway" — two would find an error in subject-verb agreement, two would find an error in spelling, and six would find a sponge and drive north.
– MIKE NICHOLS

FOR TEACHING: CORRECTING SPELLING IN DRAFTS

Although spelling can be very important in the creation of ethos for the writer, too much emphasis on spelling in the classroom might eventually paralyze some writers. It is important to emphasize to your students that spelling correction is a late-draft revision activity rather than an early-draft revision activity. Writers should not be concerned with spelling during early drafts that they know will be revised; they should get down on paper their ideas and the organization of those ideas before they need to be concerned with spelling. However, if student writers are bothered by the fact that they know some of the words are misspelled, between writing drafts they should go through the text of the last draft, marking all the words the spelling of which they are unsure about. Then, before the next draft, they can look them up and write them out in their writing logs as a special reminder of troublesome words.

FOR TEACHING: USING YOUR SPELL CHECKER

In addition to using the spell-checker feature on their word-processing program, ask students who compose or type their papers on computers to use the "Search" feature to check for homonym problems.

Instruct them to choose the homonyms and frequently confused words that they are unsure about (see the lists in section 30b). Search for these in a draft, using the automatic feature. When the search stops at each instance of the word they are concerned about, they should double-check their use of it with the explanations from the *Handbook* and with a dictionary.

FOR TEACHING: BUILDING ON VISUALIZATION AND MEMORY CUES

Readers store the visual memory of words in their minds and can often spell them correctly by "seeing" them. Students can make use of this fact by attending to the spelling of new or unfamiliar words as they read, making a conscious mental "note" of how the word looks correctly spelled. Once they start paying attention to spelling as they read, they will probably marvel at how well they generally spell: the point of "Spelling and Pronunciation — Hints for Internationals."

> I take it you already know
> Of tough and bough and cough and dough?
> Others may stumble but not you,
> On hiccough, thorough, laugh and through
> Well done! And now you wish, perhaps,
> To learn of less familiar traps?
>
> Beware of heard, dreadful word
> That looks like beard and sounds like bird,
> And dead: it's said like bed, not bead —
> For goodness' sake don't call it "deed"!
> Watch out for meat and great and threat.
> (They rhyme with suite and straight and debt.)
>
> A moth is not a moth in mother
> Nor both in bother, broth in brother,
> And here is not a match for there
> Nor dear and fear for bear and pear,
> And then there's dose and rose and lose —
> Just look them up — and goose and choose,

And cork and work and card and ward,
And font and front and word and sword,
And do and go and thwart and cart —
Come, come, I've hardly made a start!
A dreadful language? Man alive,
I'd mastered it when I was five.

On Visualization and Memory Cues   **(30g)** ....

Working with colleagues John Logan and Tamara Lindsey, [Mary] Olson surveyed the early literacy experiences and spelling practices of 174 fourth- to
eighth-graders, all finalists in the 1986 national spelling bee. The researchers
specifically wanted to know how these young people learned to spell new
words, hard-to-remember words, and words that cannot be sounded out.
      Simply put, gifted students improve their spelling abilities by seeing the
word mentally, saying it aloud, and learning its meaning.
                                               – PERRY BUFFINGTON, *Sky* (Aug. 1991): 75 – 76

■ USEFUL READINGS

Anderson, Kristen F. "Using a Spelling Survey to Develop Basic Writers' Linguis-
      tic Awareness: A Response to Ann B. Dobie." *Journal of Basic Writing* 6 (1987):
      72 – 78.

Baugh, Albert C., and Thomas Cable. *A History of the English Language.* 5th ed. Upper
      Saddle River: Prentice, 2002. The authors cover the whole history of the lan-
      guage, including excellent sections on spelling.

Beason, Larry. "Ethos and Error: How Business People React to Errors." *CCC* 53.1
      (Sept. 2001): 33 – 64. Through quantitative research on fourteen businesspeople,
      Beason offers a rhetorical analysis of errors in terms of how textual transgres-
      sions lead readers to produce judgments of character and consequently con-
      struct "a negative ethos of the writer." An enlightening article for both teachers
      and students to read, Beason's research suggests that errors impede more than
      communication; they endanger a writer's credibility and character.

Chomsky, Carol. "Reading, Writing, and Phonology." *Harvard Education Review*
      40 (May 1970): 287–309.

Davis, Betty J. "Fanciful Spellings as a Reflection of Pronunciation in Advanced
      ESL Composition Students." *Journal of the American Society of Geolinguistics* 13
      (1987): 107–23. A discussion of spelling errors in relationship to pronuncia-
      tion.

Dobie, Ann B. "Orthographical Theory and Practice, or How to Teach Spelling."
      Journal of Basic Writing 5 (1986): 41 – 48.

——. "Orthography Revisited: A Response to Kristen Anderson." *Journal of Basic Writing* 7 (1988): 82–83.

Follet, Wilson. *Modern American Usage: A Guide.* 1966. New York: Hill, 1998.

Kidder, Ede, and Karl Taylor. "The Development of Spelling Skills from First Grade through Eighth Grade." *Written Communication* 5 (Apr. 1988): 222–44.

Morris, William, and Mary Morris. *Harper Dictionary of Contemporary Usage.* New York: Harper, 1975.

Olson, M. W., J. W. Logan, and T. P. Lindsey. "Early and Current Reading and Spelling Practices of Gifted Spellers." *Reading Psychology* 10 (1989): 189–201.

Pyles, Thomas, and John Algeo. *The Origins and Development of the English Language.* 4th ed. New York: Harcourt, 1993. The fourth edition of this history of the language contains a good deal of information on spelling.

Shaughnessy, Mina. *Errors and Expectations.* New York: Oxford UP, 1977. See chapter 5 on spelling.

Stevens, William J. "Obstacles to Spelling Reform." *English Journal* 54 (1965): 85–90.

Thompson, Dorothy. "Spelling's Day in the Sun." *Instructor* 85 (1976): 16.

PART 6

SENTENCES: MAKING GRAMMATICAL CHOICES

31 ⬇ Constructing Grammatical Sentences

> *. . . when the rules of Grammar are skillfully taught, any language can be more easily understood, more surely learnt, and longer kept in the memory.*
> — CHRISTOPHER COOPER

Although closely related, rhetoric and grammar have traditionally maintained themselves as separate disciplines. Rhetoric, nearly as old as Greek culture itself, formed the basis of the *trivium,* the Greek educational system that also included grammar and dialectic (philosophical logic). For some 1,700 years, from late antiquity to the Middle Ages, the *trivium* remained the centerpiece of education, keeping grammar allied with rhetoric. But today, grammar is more closely connected with other fields of language study — with linguistics, composition studies, and stylistics — that make constant reference to grammatical terms. The relationship of grammar to composition studies has always been controversial: how to teach grammar in writing courses — indeed, whether to teach it at all — remains a topic much disputed. Few teachers have been willing to dispense entirely with instruction in grammar; most teach it without any conclusive evidence that teaching grammar in any way improves the writing of students. In his impressive meta-analysis, *Research on Written Composition,* George Hillocks reports that "[n]one of the studies reviewed . . . provides any support for teaching grammar as a means of improving composition skills" (138). Yet we continue to teach our students about grammar, perhaps because we feel that, to be the most effective writers, they need to learn certain grammatical conventions. As William Irmscher writes in *Teaching Expository Writing,* "The relation of grammar and writing is one of the enduring controversies of English studies" (16).

Grammatically, should of *is a predatory admonition; as such, it is always used as part of a herpetological phrase.*
—DAVE BARRY

Never a day without a line. —HORACE

On the Origins of Language and Its Grammar

The first Greek grammarian, Plato, debated theories of the origin of language and of the correlation between thought and language in the *Cratylus* (385 B.C.E.). Moreover, he examined the concepts of *truth* and *falsehood* to see if they could be translated into and transmitted by any particular grammatical structure. For example, the following sentences are perfectly grammatical — and false:

> The Ohio State University football team likes to lose games.
>
> Hillary Rodham Clinton is a doctor interested in health care reform.
>
> Learning to write is always easy.

Although Plato successfully and permanently separated judgments regarding grammatical structure and *truth,* using examples like the preceding ones, no grammarian has yet been able to dislodge the specious connection between grammatical correctness and morality. In *Grammar and Good Taste: Reforming the American Language,* Dennis E. Baron argues that the association of grammatical correctness with moral virtue and social prestige in the United States grew out of patriotic attempts during the post-Revolutionary period to distinguish American English from British English. He goes on to note that this association of grammar and morality fostered the anxiety over grammatical correctness that the public still feels today.

Plato's most important contribution to grammar, the division of sentence into nominal (*onoma*) and verbal (*rheme*) components, has remained the primary grammatical distinction underlying syntactic analysis and word classification in all linguistic description; all grammatical approaches divide sentences into two parts, subject and verb. Later, in the *Rhetoric,* Aristotle added a third grammatical category of function words (*syndesmoi*) that includes conjunctions, articles, and pronouns. Plato's categories remain full parts of speech because they have meaning in isolation; Aristotle's function words, though, have only grammatical meaning.

> *Like everything metaphysical, the harmony between thought and reality is to be found in the grammar of language.*
> – LUDWIG WITTGENSTEIN

On Understanding the Basic Grammar of Sentences

(31a)

When students face grammar lessons, they often feel that their language has become suddenly foreign — that they don't know any grammar. Oh, but they do. They completely mastered the grammar of their native tongue long ago. They may be comforted to know that there is a difference between what they know about their language — their *competence* — and how they use their language — their linguistic *performance*. Unlike certain "speaking" animals, which can only imitate what they have heard before, your students know the rules for combining the elements of their native language — words, ideas, and sentences — and have the *competence* to say things that have never been said before and to create purposeful and meaningful discourse. If one of your students says, "Yesterday, I seen a horrible fight," you know exactly what she means. Her *competence* is perfect, though her *performance* — by the standards of academic English at least — may not be. She makes sense. But if she says, "A yesterday saw fight I horrible," you have trouble understanding her. The words themselves are correct, but not the grammar. Your student will be able to tell you that the second string of words is ungrammatical and that it doesn't make sense. Her *competence* with her language, her knowledge of grammar, gives her this ability.

(31b1–2)   **FOR TEACHING: RECOGNIZING VERBS AND NOUNS**

A verb is the key to a sentence: the starting point for any translation, the pivot of action, the movement. We tend to emphasize verbs in our teaching because so few writers use them effectively, and those who do, produce lively, often powerful, prose. We usually begin to learn a language, however, by building up our repertoire of nouns — in much the way Helen Keller, who was blind and deaf, rose to a new level of consciousness when she learned her first word, a noun, with the help of Annie Sullivan. Read aloud to the class the following excerpt from *The Story of My Life* in which Keller relates that magical event, and then use it to lead a class discussion of the power of nouns *and* verbs:

> We walked down the path to the well-house, attracted by the fragrance of the honeysuckle with which it was covered. Someone was drawing water and my teacher placed my hand under the spout. As the cool stream gushed over one hand, she spelled into the other the word *water,* first slowly then rapidly. I stood still, my whole attention fixed upon the motion of her fingers. Suddenly I felt a misty consciousness as of something forgotten — a thrill of returning thought; and somehow the mystery of language was revealed to me. I knew then that "w-a-t-e-r" meant the wonderful cool something that was flowing over my hand. That living word awakened my soul, gave it light, hope, joy, set it free! . . . I left the well-house eager to learn. Everything had a name, and each name gave birth to a new thought. As we returned to the

house every object which I touched seemed to quiver with life. That was because I saw everything with the strange, new sight that had come to me. . . .
[M]other, father, sister, teacher were . . . words that were to make the world blos-
som for me. . . .

FOR COLLABORATIVE WORK: RECOGNIZING ADJECTIVES AND ADVERBS   (31b4–5)

Have students work in groups to transform the following ordinary statements into powerful messages — expanding them with adjectives and
adverbs. Then, have them share their messages with the rest of the class.

1. Candidates travel across the nation.
2. The spider went up the waterspout.
3. A stir was audible in the hall.
4. Fifi gets angry.
5. The prisoner dozed off and was wakened.
6. The boy entered the line.

On Prepositions   (31b6)

Besides connecting nouns and pronouns to other words, prepositions
also have important semantic dimensions, serving as the most important
words in certain sentences.

Watch that crazed killer *behind* you.

Tie that artery *below* his ear.

Until the late Middle Ages, relationships among words were indicated
by inflectional endings. But by 1300, when only the possessive (-'s) and
plural (-s) endings remained, prepositions were used to signal relationships. Chaucer was the first to use the preposition *during* (c. 1385), while
the *Piers Plowman* poet was the first to use the prepositions *concerning* and
except (c. 1377).

FOR TEACHING: RECOGNIZING CONJUNCTIONS   (31b7)

To give your students practice in thinking about the relationships between words and ideas, you may want to present them a conjunction-less

passage, asking them to insert the appropriate conjunctions. With the italicized conjunctions left out, present the following passage:

> *If* my mother was in a singing mood, it wasn't so bad. She would sing about hard times, bad times, *and* somebody-done-gone-and-left-me times. *But* her voice was so sweet *and* her singing-eyes so melty I found myself longing for those hard times, yearning to be grown without "a thin di-i-ime to my name." I looked forward to the delicious time *when* "my man" would leave me, *when* I would "hate to see that evening sun go down . . ." 'cause *then* I would know "my man has left this town." Misery colored by the greens *and* blues in my mother's voice took all of the grief out of the words *and* left me with a conviction that pain was *not only* endurable, it was sweet.   – TONI MORRISON, *The Bluest Eye*

Attempting to learn conjunctions by their grammatical categories can be confusing. Some students may respond better when they are presented with the following semantic categories of conjunctions (and transitional phrases):

1. *To express agreement between items* — and, also, likewise, both . . . and, similarly, not only . . . but also
2. *To express additional items* — besides, furthermore, moreover, and, also (in addition)
3. *To express disagreement between items* — but, yet, however, instead, anyway, nevertheless, still (in spite of that)
4. *To express alternative items* — or, nor, either . . . or, neither . . . nor
5. *To express causations* — for, so, since, because, therefore, thus
6. *To express various time relations* — when, often, before, while, as, until, finally, meanwhile, next, now, then
7. *To express certainty* — certainly, indeed, undoubtedly (to be certain, without a doubt)
8. *To express possibility or qualifications* — if, if . . . then, until, although, before, besides, unless, otherwise (on the other hand)
9. *To express parenthetically* — besides, incidentally
10. *To express specificity* — namely (that is to say)

(31c)   On Recognizing the Parts of a Sentence

In reaction to the purely formal, static quality of the terms *subject* and *predicate,* various linguists developed a theory linking the binary form of the sentence with the functions of those major divisions. As described by

William J. Van de Kopple in "Something Old, Something New: Functional Sentence Perspective":

> In brief, for Functional Sentence Perspectivists a sentence conveys its message most effectively if its two major parts, the topic and comment, perform specific semantic and communicative tasks. In English, the topic usually includes the grammatical subject and its adjuncts. The comment usually includes the verb and objects or carries primary sentence stress.
>
> For each part the theorists posit slightly different but often corresponding communicative functions. They claim that the topic should express either the theme of the sentence, the elements with the least communicative dynamism, . . . the least important information, or the old information. They assert that the comment should express either information about the theme, the elements with the most communicative dynamism, the most important information, or the new information.

FOR TEACHING: RECOGNIZING SUBJECTS AND PREDICATES   **(31c1–2)**

Share the following poem with your students, asking them to identify the *subject* and *predicate* of each line and of the last two lines:

We'll begin with a box, and the plural is boxes.
But the plural of ox should be oxen, not oxes.
The one fowl is a goose, but two are called geese,
Yet the plural of moose should never be meese.
You may find a lone mouse or a whole set of mice,
Yet the plural of house is houses not hice.
If the plural of man is always called men,
Why shouldn't the plural of pan be called pen?
If I speak of a foot and you show me your feet,
And I give you a boot, would a pair be called beet?
If one is a tooth and a whole set is teeth,
Why should not the plural of booth be called beeth?
Then one may be that, and three would be those,
Yet hat in the plural wouldn't be hose.
And the plural of cat is cats and not cose.
We speak of a brother and also of brethren,
But though we say Mother, we never say Methren.
Then the masculine pronouns are he, his, and him,
But imagine the feminine she, shis, and shim.
So English, I fancy, you all will agree,
Is the funniest language you ever did see.

Clear in the poem are some of the inconsistencies of the English language, inconsistencies of plurality that have grown out of our long and colorful language history. Just as fashions inevitably change — more drastically and rapidly in some areas than others, over time, and because of foreign influences — so inevitably does language. Perhaps the most profound reflection of constant language change is the common assumption held by most of us that the language we speak is "standard," while that spoken by many others is "nonstandard."

The version found in most printed materials and spoken in most public arenas is often referred to as edited American English. But that is *not* to say that is the one "standard" dialect. Speakers of American English offer many variations, many dialects, and many registers, which the *Handbook* explores in Chapter 26.

(31c1–2)

FOR COLLABORATIVE WORK: RECOGNIZING
COMPLETE SUBJECTS AND PREDICATES

Have students bring a double-spaced copy of a paragraph from any current draft and, for each sentence, identify the complete subject and predicate, the type of verb (linking, transitive, or intransitive), and all objects and complements. They may find it most productive to work in small groups to test their choices.

(31c2)

On Recognizing Transitive and Intransitive Verbs

Verbs that take an object are *transitive,* from the Latin *transire,* "pass over." Transitive verbs cannot express their meaning without passing over to a complement.

> We *bounced* our *ball* in Waterford Galley.
>
> We *bounced* our *ideas* off one another.
>
> We *bounced* the *pickpocket* out of the restaurant.

Intransitive — that is, "not passing over" — verbs are capable of expressing themselves without a complement to complete their meaning.

> Oz *has spoken.*
>
> Jorge *slunk* past the mission.
>
> The ball *bounced* over my head.

Sometimes, transitive verbs take an indirect object as well as a direct object, as in:

Christiana gave Alfred (*i.o.*) a black eye (*d.o.*).

Aurelia sent Joe (*i.o.*) a Christmas card (*d.o.*).

These classifications, transitive and intransitive, vary from one sentence to another, depending on how a particular verb is used. A few words (*ignore*) are only transitive, while others (*reign, die*) are only intransitive.

Dictionaries label verbs as *v.t.* (transitive verb) or *v.i.* (intransitive verb), according to use.

TEACHING WITH TECHNOLOGY: RECOGNIZING AND USING PHRASES   (31c3)

Have students select any full page from a current draft and identify all the types of phrases (participial, gerund, infinitive, appositive, absolute, and prepositional) they have used. Then have them type up an electronic post describing the range and pattern of phrasal constructions they have employed and setting out a plan to improve their use of phrases. Ask one class member to respond to the post, highlighting a particular phrase by cutting and pasting it into the reply.

FOR COLLABORATIVE WORK: RECOGNIZING AND USING PHRASES   (31c3)

Have students share the results of their survey of the kinds of phrases they use. Then have students work together to expand or revise selected sentences from one another's drafts to incorporate new types of phrases, and discuss the effects of their revisions.

FOR TEACHING: USING PHRASES   (31c3)

Consider using sentence-combining techniques to reinforce the effective compression that can be achieved with absolute and appositive phrases. For instance, *I jumped into the car and took off, the tires screeching in protest* combines at least three simpler sentences:

I jumped; (I jumped) into the car.

I took off.

The tires were screeching in protest.

Write these sentences on the board and work with your students to delete repetitive elements and form a combined sentence with an absolute element. You can do the same exercise to achieve an appositive phrase:

> Maya Angelou will appear on campus tonight.
>
> Maya Angelou is a celebrated novelist and (Maya Angelou is a celebrated) essayist.

(31d) On Classifying Sentences

In a series of essays, Francis Christensen demonstrated a way to map sentences and paragraphs according to levels of generality and modification. According to Christensen, *periodic* sentences are those that delay or postpone announcing the general main clause until the very end, leading into the topic with supporting or modifying details. This kind of sentence forces a reader to hold the subject in mind until the very end and keeps syntactic tension high. In the hands of skilled writers, periodic sentences can keep readers alert for what is to come and make the main idea, when it finally does appear, all the more impressive.

Although structures using various degrees of periodicity can be very effective in challenging and interesting readers, they do not constitute the most frequently used pattern in Modern English. Rather, the *cumulative* structure, which adds details after the main clause or announcement of the topic, is the more dominant. Christensen writes in "A Generative Rhetoric of the Sentence":

> The main clause, which may or may not have a sentence modifier before it, advances the discussion; but the additions move backwards, as in this clause, to modify the statement of the main clause or more often to explicate or exemplify it, so that the sentence has a flowing and ebbing movement, advancing to a new position and then pausing to consolidate it, leaping and lingering as the popular ballad does. (156)

Because the main clause is presented at or near the beginning of the sentence, cumulative structures do not require readers to hold the subject in suspense until the end. In one sense, then, these sentences may be easier to read than periodic ones, yet the skillful writer can position the most important piece of information at the end. But Christensen warns in *Notes toward a New Rhetoric* that "the cumulative sentence in unskilled hands is unsteady, allowing a writer to ramble on, adding modifier after modifier, until the reader is almost overwhelmed, because the writer's central idea is lost."

Using exclusively periodic or cumulative sentences, of course, would be very monotonous. And so the best writers mingle structures — short and long, periodic and cumulative — though never forgetting that the most important ideas naturally deserve the most prominent positions.

FOR TEACHING: CLASSIFYING SENTENCES   **(31d)**

Before your students turn in their papers, ask them to classify by type each of the sentences in their papers. (You may want to review with them the definitions and constructions of each sentence type.) Then ask them to tally each type (simple, compound, complex, compound-complex, cumulative, periodic). They should use the results to answer the following questions, possibly in their writing logs:

What kinds of sentences do you use most often?

Do you use all kinds of sentences or rely on just a couple?

What effect does your choice of sentence structures have on your prose?

Do you recognize or know how to construct all the sentence types?

If any students express interest in doing so, you may want to give them an opportunity to revise these papers before they hand them in.

FOR COLLABORATIVE WORK: REVISING SENTENCES

Ask students to work in groups on the following sentence-combining exercises. They should combine each group of sentences into a single sentence, transforming some individual sentences into phrases to expand and shape the basic sentence. Then they should try to produce at least two versions of each combined sentence. Example:

The paint is peeling.
The roof is leaking.
The house is in a crummy neighborhood.
The house will never sell.

That paint-peeling, roof-leaking dump will never sell, especially in a crummy neighborhood.
With peeling paint and a leaking roof, that house in that crummy neighborhood will never sell.

1. It was a crisp morning in early spring.
   A man walked through the city park.
   He was alone.
   The trees and plants were newly budding.

2. We climbed a tree.
   The tree was gnarly.
   The cherries on the tree were sweet.
   The tree stood in Jess's backyard.
   We climbed all summer long.

3. Only two people were in the library.
   A man with gray hair was slightly sleepy.
   A young woman was in the library.
   She wore jeans.

4. Anna is a Snow Princess in the Marysville Winter Parade.
   Anna feels proud.
   Anna feels excited.
   The snow is falling furiously.

5. New York City is a great place to visit.
   New York City is a prohibitively expensive place to live.

6. Jaron was at the Easter egg hunt.
   Jaron found several eggs.
   The eggs were hidden.
   The eggs were tucked beneath a dogwood tree.

■ **USEFUL READINGS**

Baron, Dennis E. *Grammar and Good Taste: Reforming the American Language.* New Haven: Yale UP, 1982.

Christensen, Francis. "A Generative Rhetoric of the Sentence." *CCC* 14 (1963): 155–61. The idea for expanding sentences by adding and manipulating modifying phrases derives largely from Christensen, who maintains that students can achieve syntactic fluency by adding modifiers at the beginning, middle, and end of their sentences. He focuses on the cumulative sentence and demonstrates how writers can add final free modifiers to main clauses in order to expand sentences.

———. *Notes toward a New Rhetoric.* New York: Harper, 1978.

D'Eloia, Sarah. "The Uses—and Limits—of Grammar." *Journal of Basic Writing* 1 (Spring/Summer 1977): 1–20. In addition to her insights into the relationship between grammar and writing instruction, the author offers excellent classroom pedagogy.

Hartwell, Patrick. "Grammar, Grammars, and the Teaching of Grammar." *CE* 47 (1985): 105–27. Rpt. in *The St. Martin's Guide to Teaching Writing*. 5th ed. Hartwell examines the definitions and purposes of the various grammars.

Hillocks. George. *Research on Written Composition*. Urbana: NCTE, 1986.

Hunter, Susan, and Ray Wallace, eds. *The Place of Grammar in Writing Instruction: Past, Present, Future*. Portsmouth: Boynton, 1995. This compelling collection of essays provides what the editors describe as a reevaluation of grammar in terms of "discussions of 'standard' English and dialects, research on dialect-switching, attitudes toward error and students' right to their own language, academic discourse, and varieties of literacy, language acquisition, orality and literacy, and class struggle." See, especially, R. Baird Shuman's "Grammar for Writers: How Much Is Enough?" and Cheryl Glenn's "When Grammar Was a Language Art."

Irmscher, William. *Teaching Expository Writing*. New York: Holt, 1979.

Noguchi, Rei. R. *Grammar and the Teaching of Writing: Limits and Possibilities*. Urbana: NCTE, 1991. Noguchi streamlines the teaching of grammar by focusing on the writing problems most responsive to grammar-based instruction, by drawing on students' unconscious understanding of their native language, and by relating grammar to style, content, and organization.

O'Hare, Frank. *Sentence Combining: Improving Student Writing without Formal Grammar Instruction*. Urbana: NCTE, 1973.

Pyles, Thomas, and John Algeo. *The Origins and Development of the English Language*. 4th ed. Boston: Heinle, 1993. Systematic and textbook-like, this book gives emphasis to American English.

Van de Kopple, William J. "Something Old, Something New: Functional Sentence Perspective." *Research in the Teaching of English* 17 (Feb. 1983): 85–99.

Weaver, Constance. *Grammar for Teachers: Perspectives and Definitions*. Urbana: NCTE, 1979. Although Weaver may be less confident about the use and importance of grammatical vocabulary for students, she claims that "the teacher needs a fairly solid background in grammar in order to work with students" (90).

Williams, Joseph. *Style: Ten Lessons in Clarity and Grace*. 6th ed. New York: Addison Wesley, 2002. Williams provides methods for both streamlining and enriching sentences.

32  Understanding Pronoun Case

A kind of duet—she as oboe, he as contrabassoon, and full of obbligato digressions. — RICHARD EDER

When a pronoun follows a pronoun's nature, a pronoun substitutes for a noun; the noun then becomes the pronoun's antecedent.

Thanks to the existence of pronouns, we are able to avoid such redundancy and write, instead:

> When a pronoun follows its nature, it substitutes for a noun that becomes its antecedent.

The most highly inflected parts of speech in present-day English, pronouns are nearly as complex and informational as their Latinate counterparts. Compare:

> As Dennis delivered Dennis's inaugural address, Dennis nervously looked out into the freezing crowd only to see Dennis's mother smiling beatifically at Dennis.

> As *he* delivered *his* inaugural address, Dennis nervously looked out into the freezing crowd only to see *his* mother smiling beatifically at *him*.

Although *Dennis* is the antecedent of *he, his,* and *him,* the pronoun form changes. English pronouns are specific in terms of person, gender, and number. In fact, our pronouns often carry as much information as their antecedents. *I, you,* and *he* tell us about person; *he, she,* and *it* tell us about gender; *I, we, she,* and *they* tell us about number.

FOR MULTILINGUAL WRITERS: CASE, NUMBER, AND GENDER OF PRONOUNS

If you have students who speak languages other than English, ask them to explain the pronoun system of those languages, in terms of case, number, and gender.

FOR COLLABORATIVE WORK: USING THE THREE CASES   (32a)

The following passage comes from "University Days," James Thurber's classic essay about his years as a student at Ohio State University. Most of its pronouns have been removed. Have students work together to put a correct pronoun in each blank. (You may also have them label each one as subjective, objective, or possessive case.)

Another course that I didn't like, but somehow managed to pass, was economics. _____ went to that class straight from the botany class, which didn't help _____ to understand either subject. _____ used to get them mixed up. But not as mixed up as another student in _____ economics class who came there direct from a physics laboratory. _____ was a tackle on the football team, named Bolenciecwcz. At that time Ohio State University had one of the best football teams in the country, and Bolenciecwcz was one of _____ outstanding stars. In order to be eligible to play it was necessary for _____ to keep up in _____ studies, a very difficult matter, for while _____ was not dumber than an ox _____ was not any smarter. Most of _____ professors were lenient and helped _____ along. None gave _____ more hints in answering questions or asked _____ simpler ones than the economics professor, a thin, timid man named Bassum. One day when _____ were on the subject of transportation and distribution, it came Bolenciecwcz's turn to answer a question. "Name one means of transportation," the professor said to _____. No light came into the big tackle's eyes. "Just any means of transportation" said the professor. Bolenciecwcz sat staring at _____. "That is," pursued the professor, "any medium, agency, or method of going from one place to another." Bolenciecwcz had the look of a man _____ is being led into a trap. "You may choose among steam, horse-drawn, or electrically propelled vehicles," said the instructor. "I might suggest the one which _____ commonly take in making long journeys across land." There was a profound silence in which everybody stirred uneasily, including Bolenciecwcz and Mr. Bassum. Mr. Bassum abruptly broke this silence in an amazing manner. "Choo-choo-choo," _____ said, in a low voice, and turned instantly scarlet. _____ glanced appealingly around the room. All of _____, of course, shared Mr. Bassum's desire that Bolenciecwcz should stay abreast of the class in economics, for the Illinois game, one of the hardest and most important of the season, was only a week off. "Toot, toot, too-toooooooot!" some student with a deep voice moaned, and _____ all looked encouragingly at Bolenciecwcz. Somebody else gave a fine imitation of a locomotive letting off steam. Mr. Bassum himself rounded off the little show. "Ding, dong, ding, dong," _____ said, hopefully. Bolenciecwcz was staring at the floor now, trying to think, _____ great brow furrowed, _____ huge hands rubbing together, _____ face red.   –JAMES THURBER, "University Days"

Answers

(Besides the unkind stereotypes of student athletes, Thurber also resorts to generalizations about the student's ethnicity, acceptable fodder for humor some fifty years ago.)

Another course that <u>I</u> didn't like, but somehow managed to pass, was economics. <u>I</u> went to that class straight from the botany class, which didn't help <u>me</u> to understand either subject. <u>I</u> used to get them mixed up. But not as mixed up as another student in <u>my</u> economics class who came there direct from a physics laboratory. <u>He</u> was a tackle on the football team, named Bolenciecwcz. At that time Ohio State University had one of the best football teams in the country, and Bolenciecwcz was one of <u>its</u> outstanding stars. In order to be eligible to play it was necessary for <u>him</u> to keep up in <u>his</u> studies, a very difficult matter, for while <u>he</u> was not dumber than an ox <u>he</u> was not any smarter. Most of <u>his</u> professors were lenient and helped <u>him</u> along. None gave <u>him</u> more hints in answering questions or asked <u>him</u> simpler ones than the economics professor, a thin, timid man named Bassum. One day when <u>we</u> were on the subject of transportation and distribution, it came Bolenciecwcz's turn to answer a question. "Name one means of transportation," the professor said to <u>him</u>. No light came into the big tackle's eyes. "Just any means of transportation," said the professor. Bolenciecwcz sat staring at <u>him</u>. "That is," pursued the professor, "any medium, agency, or method of going from one place to another." Bolenciecwcz had the look of a man <u>who</u> is being led into a trap. "You may choose among steam, horse-drawn, or electrically propelled vehicles," said the instructor. "I might suggest the one which <u>we</u> commonly take in making long journeys across land." There was a profound silence in which everybody stirred uneasily, including Bolenciecwcz and Mr. Bassum. Mr. Bassum abruptly broke this silence in an amazing manner. "Choo-choo-choo," <u>he</u> said, in a low voice, and turned instantly scarlet. <u>He</u> glanced appealingly around the room. All of <u>us</u>, of course, shared Mr. Bassum's desire that Bolenciecwcz should stay abreast of the class in economics, for the Illinois game, one of the hardest and most important of the season, was just a week off. "Toot, toot, too-toooooooot!" some student with a deep voice moaned, and <u>we</u> all looked encouragingly at Bolenciecwcz. Somebody else gave a fine imitation of a locomotive letting off steam. Mr. Bassum himself rounded off the little show. "Ding, dong, ding, dong," <u>he</u> said, hopefully. Bolenciecwcz was staring at the floor now, trying to think, <u>his</u> great brow furrowed, <u>his</u> huge hands rubbing together, <u>his</u> face red.

.... **(32a)**   **FOR TEACHING: USING THE THREE CASES — SECOND-PERSON PRONOUNS**

The pronoun *you* gives no information other than number — second person. Except for context, there is no way to tell if *you* is singular or plural, masculine or feminine. Such was not always the case. Until the thirteenth century, English used different forms of second-person pronouns: the *th*-forms, indicating singular (*thee, thy, thou*); and the *y*-forms, indicating plural (*ye, you, your*).

With the influence of the French language, the *th*-forms came to denote intimacy and were used with close friends, family, and children; the *y*-forms, to denote a measure of formality or respect, were used with everyone else. These two forms corresponded with the *tu* and *vous* forms of French.

Who would succeed in the world should be wise in the use of pronouns. Utter the You twenty times, when you once utter the I.

– JOHN HAY

FOR TEACHING: THE POSSESSIVE CASE

(32a3) ·······················

Ask students to insert a correct possessive pronoun in the blank in each sentence. Example:

<u>My</u> eyes ached after studying for ten hours.

1. Your parents must be pleased about _____ going back to college.
2. Ken's dinner arrived quickly, but Rose waited an hour for _____.
3. We agreed to pool _____ knowledge.
4. Even many supporters of Lincoln opposed _____ freeing the slaves.
5. _____ responsibility should it be to teach moral values?

Answers

1. your
2. hers
3. our
4. his
5. Whose

I, pro. In grammar it is a pronoun of the first person and singular number. Its plural is said to be We, *but how there can be more than one* myself *is doubtless clearer to the grammarians than it is to the author of this incomparable dictionary.*
  ME, pro. The objectionable case of I. The personal pronoun in English has three cases, the dominative, the objectionable and the oppressive. Each is all three.
  –AMBROSE BIERCE, THE DEVIL'S DICTIONARY, 1911

On Using *Who, Whoever, Whom,* and *Whomever*

(32b) ·······················

Students may enjoy Mencken's discussion of the "shadowy line" between sound usage and barbarism:

> The schoolmarm . . . continues the heroic task of trying to make her young charges grasp the difference between *who* and *whom*. Here, alas, the speechways of the American people seem to be again against her. The two forms of the pronoun are confused magnificently in the debates in Congress, and in most newspaper writing, and in ordinary discourse the great majority of Americans

avoid *whom* diligently, as a word full of snares. When they employ it, it is often incorrectly, as in *"Whom* is your father?" and *"Whom* spoke to me?" Noah Webster, always the pragmatic reformer, denounced it as usually useless so long ago as 1783. Common sense, he argued, was on the side of *"Who* did he marry?" Today such a form as *"Whom* are you talking to?" would seem very affected to most Americans; they might write it, but they would never speak it. . . . A shadowy line often separates what is currently coming into sound usage from what is still regarded as barbarous.   – H. L. MENCKEN

■ **USEFUL READINGS**

Haussamen, Brock. *Revising the Rules: Traditional Grammar and Modern Linguistics.* Dubuque: Kendell/Hunt, 1994. See chapters 6, 7, and 8 for more on "Pronoun Agreement," "Pronoun Case and Restrictiveness," and "He and They."

Hayes, Christopher G. "A Brief Writing Assignment for Introducing Non-Sexist Pronoun Usage." *TEYTC* 28.1 (Sept. 2000): 74–77. Hayes describes a narrative writing assignment that helps demonstrate to students how and why sexist language can limit thinking, sometimes injuriously.

33 Using Verbs

After the verb "to Love," "to Help" is the most beautiful verb in the world.   —Bertha von Suttner

English has the most varied and flexible verb forms of all the modern languages: its six tenses can fall in the indicative, subjunctive, or imperative mood; its verbs can be in active or passive voice, in present, continuous, or emphatic form, in completed or progressive aspect. English verbs can stand alone or work together, or they can transform themselves into nouns and adjectives.

Such plasticity arose from Scandinavian, German, and French influences. In fact, Old English verbs were Germanic in nature: they distinguished between only two simple tenses, present and past, and signified all other information (number, person, gender, mood, voice) by inflectional endings. Old English verbs were more often strong than weak, or more often *irregular* than *regular: strong verbs (sing, sang; bind, bound; choose, chosen)* have the power to indicate tense by transforming their medial vowels, not by merely adding a feeble *-ed* inflectional ending *(kick, kicked, kicked).*

The Norman Invasion greatly influenced Middle English, infusing it with the vocabulary and grammar of the French- and Latin-speaking ruling class. One significant influence was the linguistic regularization of the verbs: more than half of the strong (irregular) verbs became weak (regular), using *-ed* inflectional endings rather than internal transformation to indicate tense. This impulse to regularize verbs was checked by the rise of English on the social scale and the stabilizing effect of printing. Now, even the native-born English speaker must memorize the strong or irregular verb forms.

Whenever the literary German dives into a sentence, that is the last you are going to see of him until he emerges on the other side of his Atlantic with his verb in his mouth.

—Mark Twain

FOR TEACHING: EVERYDAY VERBS

Restaurant menus are often a good source of verbs in action. One famous place in Boston offers, for instance, to bake, broil, pan-fry, deep-fry, poach, sauté, fricassee, or scallop any of the fish entrees on its menu. To someone ordering — or cooking — at this restaurant, the important distinctions lie entirely in the verbs.

Have students choose some kind of text they read regularly — the sports section, perhaps, or a cookbook, or a piece of their own writing — and have them look at the verbs. Then ask them to note down some interesting examples and use them to discuss the power of everyday verbs at work.

FOR MULTILINGUAL WRITERS: AFRICAN AMERICAN VERNACULAR VERB FORMS

Toni Cade Bambara uses verb forms characteristic of African American English Vernacular in many of her stories. Ask students to read the concluding paragraph to "Gorilla, My Love" and then to see what happens to the rhythm of the prose if "standard" verb forms are substituted throughout.

> "You a lying dawg," I say, when I meant to say treacherous dog, but just couldn't get hold of the word. It slipped away from me. And I'm cryin and crumplin down in the seat and just don't care. And Grandaddy say to hush and steps on the gas. And I'm losing my bearins an don't even know where to look on the map cause I can't see for cryin. And Baby Jason cryin too. Cause he my blood brother and understands that we must stick together or be forever lost, what with grownups playin change-up and turnin you round every which way so bad. And don't even say they sorry.

FOR TEACHING: VERB FORMS

Ask students to edit the following sentences so that all verb forms are appropriate for standard academic English. (Some of the sentences do not require any change.) Example:

seems   *make*
Although Joe *seem* in control, his actions *making* me wonder.

1. When the dance begin, a man in costume appears.
2. The man have long fingernails and a mask.
3. All of the people in the village participate in the ceremony.

4. The doctor works two nights a week at a clinic.
5. A hot shower always relax me.
6. The thought of nuclear war be terrifying to most people.
7. New mothers often be suffering from depression.
8. He don't know whether to try again or to give up.
9. The deposit refunded if the customer don't buy the equipment.
10. Mayor Burns running for reelection this fall.

Answers

1. begin → begins
2. have → has
3. correct
4. correct
5. relax → relaxes
6. be → is
7. be suffering → suffer
8. don't → doesn't
9. is refunded; don't → doesn't
10. is running

On Verb Forms

By today's standards, even Shakespeare sometimes chose the "incorrect" verb form:

Then, Brutus, I have much mistook your passion.	– *Julius Caesar*
Have you chose this man?	– *Coriolanus*
When they are fretten with the gusts of heaven.	– *Merchant of Venice*

On Using Auxiliary Verbs   **(33a)** ·······························

The term *auxiliary* comes from the Latin *auxiliaris,* meaning "help." Hence, auxiliary verbs help to make some form of another verb. In *is eating,* the auxiliary verb *is* helps to make a form of the verb *eat;* in *have seen* and *will have brought,* the auxiliary verbs *have* and *will have* help to make forms of *see* and *bring,* respectively.

Your students should be aware that other words sometimes intervene between the auxiliary and the main verb as in *I have already given you the money.*

(33a)

TEACHING WITH TECHNOLOGY: USING AUXILIARY VERBS

To practice and highlight the use of modals and auxiliaries, ask students to post an entry to your online discussion forum about hopes and dreams, a stream-of-consciousness list of what could or should be, or what could, should, or might have been.

The exercise will work best if students write on several hopes rather than focusing on just one. (By focusing, they may shift tenses and stop using the modal auxiliaries that you will soon be calling to their attention.) Then ask them to exchange their writing logs, read one another's entries, and mark the auxiliaries. Discuss their effective and their questionable uses of auxiliaries.

(33b)

FOR TEACHING: USING IRREGULAR VERBS

Because everyone has a tendency to regularize, or generalize, the English language, even native speakers need to memorize the irregular verb forms. Until we incorporate those irregular forms of our language, we overgeneralize the regular forms. As children, we overgeneralize both the plural form (*dogs, mouses,* and *sheeps*) and the verb form (*hummed, runned, shaked,* and *catched*). You may want to review these verb paradigms with your students.

For additional review, write the present tense of ten or twelve irregular verbs on the chalkboard and call on volunteers to provide the past-tense and past-participle forms. Then have your students write entries in their writing logs, using only verbs from the list on *Handbook* pp. 620–23. Ask several of the students to read their work aloud, noting the irregular forms they have used properly.

For a final class exercise using a recent piece of writing, have your students identify the kinds of verbs they used: auxiliary, modal auxiliary, regular, and irregular. Ask the students to choose a portion of text and make all the verbs (except the verb *be* and auxiliary verbs) monosyllabic, then recopy the same piece replacing all the verbs with polysyllabic ones of similar meaning. As they read to themselves or aloud, can they hear a difference in style and tone, simply from the change in verbs? Is one version stuffier? clearer? more academic? reader friendly?

FOR COLLABORATIVE WORK: USING REGULAR AND IRREGULAR VERBS **(33b)**

After the class has divided into groups, have the students compose two sentences for each of twelve verbs either of your own choosing or from the list on *Handbook* pp. 620–23. In one sentence they should use the past-tense form; in the second they should use the past-participle form.

These exercises will help your students recognize the comparative differences in usage and sense between the two forms. At the same time, the students will also develop an ear for which auxiliaries sound best with which past participles.

Let the students share their sentences with the rest of the class so they can see the range of possible combinations.

FOR TEACHING: USING *LIE, SIT, RISE* **(33c)**

As a mnemonic device, you might point out to students that, in each of these three troublesome pairs, the *i* word (*lie, sit, rise*) is the intransitive one. For a quick review exercise, have your students complete each of the following sentences with a form of either *raise* or *rise*.

1. She suddenly (*rose*) up and spoke.
2. Yeast causes bread to (*rise*).
3. We all know to (*raise*) our hand before we speak in class.
4. Some say that Jesus (*raised*) Lazarus from the dead.

On Verb Tense **(33d–g)**

The concept of tense can be especially confusing to those students who try to correlate it directly with actual time. Grammatical tense gives us the mechanical forms of verbs, forms that follow definite rules of construction, but it does not always represent actual time in the past, present, or future.

For example, *present tense* can indicate an action or existence taking place in the present, past, or future:

His feet hurt. (taking place right now — present)

Water boils at 212°F. (a fact in the past, present, future)

My roommate drinks iced tea every morning. (habitual action — past, present, future)

We are having turkey for Thanksgiving. (intended future action)

Huckleberry Finn is a resourceful, sensitive boy. (historical present, giving vividness to a past event)

I hear that Jaime spoke to the new students. (*hear* gives the past action a present connection)

In *Revising the Rules,* Brock Haussamen explains how the *aspect* of a verb enriches our understanding of its *tense:*

> The grouping of tenses in today's handbooks reflects the understanding of verbs as it stood at about the middle of the nineteenth century. Since that time, while the handbook descriptions have remained frozen, linguists have broken away from the paradigm of past, present, and future and have taken the discussion of the meaning of verb forms into new realms. . . . Nineteenth-century linguists adopted the word *aspect* (from the Latin for the ways things appear from a certain point of view) to refer to such features of verbs as completion, duration, and repetition — and temporal features not related to past, present, or future, in other words. (35)

(33d–g)   **FOR MULTILINGUAL WRITERS: USING VERB TENSES**

Because speakers of African American English Vernacular, Chinese, and Spanish often omit -*s,* -*ed,* and -*ing,* you may want to review the following chart with them:

I learn / am learning / learned
you learn / are learning / learned
s/he learns / is learning / learned

we learn / are learning / learned
you learn / are learning / learned
they learn / are learning / learned

(33f)   **On the Future-Tense Forms**

In the early seventeenth century, the rules of English usage were codified according to the Latin model by John Wallis, who prescribed that *shall* and *will* could not be considered synonymous. Simple future expectation was to be indicated by *shall* in first person and by *will* in second or third person:

> I *shall* meet Jens in the morning, then we *shall* review his money-market account.
>
> Although you *will* gasp when you see her tattoo, Delphine *will* be delighted that you noticed.

According to Wallis (and all prescriptivists since), determination, desire, willfulness, or promise on the part of the speaker is represented by just the opposite paradigm — *will* in the first person and *shall* in second or third person:

> Tomorrow, I *will* return and defeat you.
>
> Of course, we *will* go to the funeral, whatever the weather.
>
> You *shall* remain in my will, no matter whom you marry.
>
> Before they return to the Republic of China, Meimei is determined that both she and Sheng *shall* finish medical school and their internships.

Despite the three-hundred-year crusade to establish this distinction, most English speakers have successfully expressed futurity and determination without it.

FOR TEACHING: USING THE FUTURE-TENSE FORMS   **(33f)** ································

Students claim that they never use the word *shall* in any locution, that *shall* is rare, hence "formal." Ask your students to think a minute about the use of *shall*. What examples can they offer? Which uses seem most natural to them? "*Shall* questions," which imply a certain amount of jointness, and "*shall* injunctions" are not so rare as the class might think. Consider the following examples:

> *Shall* I pick you up at six?
>
> What *shall* we drink? (first person — request)
>
> You *shall* not take the name of the Lord in vain.
>
> You *shall* regret your evil ways. (second person — moral injunction)
>
> The vendor *shall* maintain the equipment in good repair.
>
> The athlete *shall* maintain a 2.5 grade point average. (third person — legal or commercial usage; specifications or requirements)
>
> Who *shall* decide when doctors disagree? (third person — literary usage)

FOR TEACHING: USING VERB TENSES IN SEQUENCE

The sequence-of-tense principle governs the relationship between the verbs in main and accompanying subordinate clauses.

Verbs in *natural sequence* indicate a natural, logical time relation between the actions they represent. In "Bob *believes* that you *are* telling the truth," both actions take place simultaneously. Whereas, in "Celia *believes* that you *swiped* her candlesticks," the first verb reflects on a past-tense verb. And in "Tina *guarantees* that Mick *will sing* with her tonight," the first and second verbs represent present and future tenses, respectively and naturally.

Verbs in *attracted sequence* harmonize without regard to the actual time represented. Main verbs in *past tense* and *past perfect tense* followed by indirect discourse and clauses of purpose call for attracted sequence:

Myra *said* that Rolf *was* slim and handsome. (He has not suddenly become fat and ugly.)

Myra *asked* if Rolf *was* also smart. (He remains brilliant.)

Adam *strangled* the serpent so that he *could live* without temptation. (purpose)

Eve *entered* an assertiveness training course so she *could learn* to be forceful. (purpose)

A main verb in any other tense followed by a clause of purpose attracts the present tense:

Helen *is joining* a health club so she *can get* in shape. (purpose)

She *will enter* the Boston marathon so she *can compete.* (purpose)

Certain verbs (for example, *expect, suppose, thought, knew*) and predicate adjectives (*evident, certain, sure*) also call for attracted sequence:

We *expected/supposed/thought/knew* Chloë *would make* a grand entrance.

It was *evident* that Michele *was* happily pregnant.

Fritz was *sure/certain* you *would plead* innocent.

Ask your students to look at their most recent piece of writing—an essay or a writing log entry—and note how they naturally balanced the sequence of tenses in their prose.

FOR TEACHING: USING THE SUBJUNCTIVE   **(33h)** ··············

In *A Room of One's Own,* Virginia Woolf employs the subjunctive mood:

> [I]t is unthinkable that any women in Shakespeare's day *should have had* Shake-speare's genius. For genius like Shakespeare's is not born among laboring, un-educated, servile people. It was not born in England among the Saxons and the Britons. It is not born today among the working classes. How, then, *could* it *have been* born among women whose work began, . . . almost before they were out of the nursery, who were forced to it by their parents and held to it by all the power of law and custom? Yet genius of a sort *must have existed* among women as it *must have existed* among the working classes.

Discuss how Woolf's use of the subjunctive affects the tone and mean-ing of this passage. How does this mood help her make an ironic point?

FOR COLLABORATIVE WORK: TENSE, VOICE, MOOD

If the diversity of verbal forms (tense, voice, and mood) overwhelms your students, encourage them to appreciate how these forms help them convey meaning accurately and flexibly. Assure them that what the forms are called is less important than how they are used for spe-cific purposes. Whenever possible, point out and discuss how your stu-dents' purpose in writing dictates the choice of a particular verbal treat-ment.

For this practice session, divide the class into small groups and have the students exchange recent essays or passages they have written. Can they identify the writer's use of tense, voice, and mood? You can move from group to group, helping them see these forms of verbs at work in their own writing.

FOR TEACHING: REVIEWING VERBS

The following poem is a famous example of nonsense verse, one that plays games with words—and freely invents words. Read the poem aloud to your students and then ask them to identify all the verbs, whether or not the verbs are actual English words. Use this exercise as a way to judge what your students know about verbs.

'Twas brillig, and the slithy toves
    Did gyre and gimble in the wabe;
All mimsy were the borogoves,
    And the mome raths outgrabe.
"Beware the Jabberwock, my son!
    The jaws that bite, the claws that catch!
Beware the Jubjub bird, and shun
    The frumious Bandersnatch!"

He took his vorpal sword in hand:
    Long time the manxome foe he sought—
So rested he by the Tumtum tree,
    And stood awhile in thought.

And as in uffish thought he stood,
    The Jabberwock, with eyes of flame,
Came whiffling through the tulgey wood,
    And burbled as it came!

One, two! One, two! And through and through
    The vorpal blade went snicker-snack!
He left it dead, and with its head
    He went galumphing back.

"And hast thou slain the Jabberwock?
    Come to my arms, my beamish boy!
O frabjous day! Callooh! Callay!"
    He chortled in his joy.

'Twas brillig, and the slithy toves
    Did gyre and gimble in the wabe;
And mimsy were the borogoves,
    And the mome raths outgrabe.
          –LEWIS CARROLL, "Jabberwocky"

■ USEFUL READINGS

Aitchison, Jean. *Language Change: Progress or Decay.* 3rd ed. Cambridge, Engl.: Cambridge UP, 2001. Written from a sociolinguist's perspective, this work explains the implementation, causes, and developmental features of language change. The entire discussion is accessible and straightforward; chapter 3 specifically discusses verb forms and the inherent causes of their change.

Bailey, Guy. "A Perspective on African-American English." *American Dialect Research.* Ed. Dennis R. Preston. Philadelphia: John Benjamins, 1993. 287–318. A particularly informative discussion of verbs appears on pp. 296–307.

Baugh, John. *Black Street Speech: Its History, Structure, and Survival.* Austin: U of Texas P, 1983. Baugh provides a useful discussion of invariant *be* and future perfective *be done.* See, especially, Chapter 6.

Chappell, Virginia A., and Judith Rodby. "Verb Tense and ESL Composition: A Discourse Level Approach." *On TESOL '82: Pacific Perspectives on Language Learning and Teaching; Teachers of English to Speakers of Other Languages.* Ed. Mark A. Clarke and Jean Handscombe. Washington, DC: TESOL Publications, 1983. 309–20.

Comrie, Bernard. *Aspect: An Introduction to the Study of Verbal Aspect and Related Problems.* Cambridge, Engl.: Cambridge UP, 1976. This is a study of aspect, which differs from tense in that it refers to the duration or continuation of an action in time, rather than its occurrence in relation to the present moment.

Fasold, Ralph W. *Tense Markings in Black English: A Linguistic and Social Analysis.* Washington, DC: Center for Applied Linguistics, 1978. The author offers a thorough explanation of verb forms in African American English Vernacular.

Haussamen, Brock. *Revising the Rules.* Dubuque: Kendall/Hunt, 1994.

Labov, William. *Language in the Inner-City: Studies in the Black English Vernacular.* Philadelphia: U of Pennsylvania P, 1972. This landmark work includes a discussion of verb forms in African American English Vernacular.

Smitherman, Geneva. *Talkin and Testifyin: The Language of Black America.* Detroit: Wayne State UP, 1986. This book contains a discussion of the aspectual verb system in African American English Vernacular; see, particularly, Chapter 2, "It Bees Dat Way Sometime."

Williams, Joseph M. *Origins of the English Language: A Social and Linguistic History.* New York: Free P, 1975. 265–74. Williams describes and traces the historical development of the two aspects: progressive *(He was imitating his mother)* and perfect *(He has fixed the car).*

——. *Style: Ten Lessons in Clarity and Grace.* 6th ed. New York: Addison-Wesley, 2002. The writer provides advanced discussion of the stylistic virtues of active and passive voice.

34
▼ Maintaining Subject-Verb Agreement

The subject always agrees with the verb, except on those occasions when the subject does not agree.
— GUSTAVE FLAUBERT

The English language, even in its earliest stages, is extremely redundant: such redundancy is a type of "agreement" in terms of person, number, gender, and tense. One needs only the most basic facility with language to make meaning out of the following passage, written in Modern English:

> The wolf stood in the pit, so hungry that he was crazy. He was really cursing the one who brought him there.

Look how much help we get with tense; *stood, was, was cursing*. We are provided with three times the information, the agreement, we need to know that this passage is in past tense. Now, look at the information telling us that there is only one wolf: *wolf* has no plural marker (*-s*); the *was* and *was cursing* are in the third-person singular form, and the pronouns referring to the wolf are singular (*he* and *him*).

From the source of the above passage, *The Fox and the Wolf*, we can see the redundancy or agreement that even in A.D. 1200 wove a safety net for the reader:

> þe wolf in þe putte stod,
> A fingret so þat he ves wod.
> Inou he cursede þat þider him broute!   (11. 257–59)

Here, we are given the same three clues, in verb forms that look vaguely familiar, that the passage is in past tense: *stod, ves, cursede;* and nearly the same information regarding the singleness of the wolf: *wolf* (without the plural marker *-s*); and the singular verb *ves*.

On Agreement

In "Agreement," an important section of *Errors and Expectations,* master diagnostician Mina Shaughnessy writes:

> The idea of agreement—that is, of certain words in sentences being formally linked to others so as to reinforce or repeat some kinds of meaning rather than others—is common to many languages. What is arbitrary in each language is what that language chooses to reinforce. Standard English, for example, is laced by forms that reinforce number . . . a time frame . . . gender and person. (136)

One of the most common student errors, error of agreement grows out of all the possibilities for agreement in our language. Shaughnessy saw such errors as "exercises in competence" and knew that students who have trouble with agreement need to become *habituated* in, to develop an "ear for," the conventions of their language.

If your students seem puzzled by the concept of agreement, or by the term itself, remind them that subjects and verbs are at work in almost every statement they make and that they make them "agree" effortlessly most of the time. Show them several sentences from a recent newspaper to illustrate, such as these three from a sports page:

Guzman powers another blistering ball over the plate.

The Yanks move on to Milwaukee tomorrow.

The duel of the no-hitters *continues* into the eighth.

Then ask students either to listen or to read for one day with special attention to subjects and verbs and to bring in a list of interesting sentences for a class discussion of agreement.

FOR MULTILINGUAL WRITERS: MAINTAINING SUBJECT-VERB AGREEMENT

If your students speak languages in addition to English, ask them to explain the agreement necessary in those languages. Spanish, for example, extends agreement to the gender and number of adjectives. African American English Vernacular, French, and many other languages call for negative concord whereas English rejects it; Chinese languages do not use agreement, depending instead on word order to relate words in sentences.

FOR TEACHING: AGREEMENT

Traditionally, sentence diagraming has been the way students identified the subject and verb of a sentence. Although such close syntactical analysis will help *some* students determine subject-verb or pronoun-antecedent agreement, most of our students just don't have the technical command of grammar to diagram or parse a sentence.

To help your students develop their ear for agreement, ask them to bring in or create sentences that seem confusing. Then ask them to come up with ways of determining the information that separates the subject from the verb. For example, try these sentences orally with your students:

1. To see so many people here *is*/are gratifying.
2. The problems with the house is/*are* overwhelming.
3. Every one of the details *was*/were perfect.
4. It *is*/are the fault of the citizens.
5. Pizza with pepperoni, mushrooms, and green peppers *is*/are delicious.

The following sentences contain compound and collective-noun subjects. For additional practice, have your students edit them for subject-verb agreement.

1. Every week, Sharma, Julio, and Richard attends/*attend* a group total of fifty hours of school.
2. Crosby, Stills, Nash, and Young *was*/were one of the hottest groups in the early seventies.
3. Neither the president nor his administration *claims*/claim to know anything about an arms shipment.
4. Mike and his friends is/*are* going to decorate your yard with crepe paper after the game.
5. The composition class plan/*plans* to celebrate Valentine's Day at the professor's house.
6. The professor or her assistant *is*/are always in the office.
7. The couple *vow*/vows to have and to hold until death.

Here are three additional exercises on agreement that will provide practice for your students. Have students edit the following sentences for subject-verb agreement.

1. The best thing about college *is*/are the vacations.

2. Panning up and down staircases *was*/were a frequent feature of Hitchcock's films.

3. In this context, the word *values is*/are vague.

4. *The Letters of Henry James* provide/*provides* interesting and important, if sometimes ambiguous, information about the nineteenth-century author.

5. It *is*/are a melancholy object to those who *walk*/walks through this great town or *travel*/travels in the country, when they *see*/sees in the streets, the road, and cabin doors, crowded with beggars of the female sex, followed by three, four, or six children, all in rags and importuning every passenger for an alms. These mothers, instead of being able to work for their honest livelihood, is/*are* forced to employ all their time in strolling to beg sustenance for their helpless infants, who, as they *grow*/grows up, either *turn*/turns thieves for want of work, or leaves/*leave* their dear country to fight for the Pretender of Spain, or *sell*/sells themselves to the Barbados.   – JONATHAN SWIFT, "A Modest Proposal"

Have students edit the following sentences for verb agreement. In addition, ask them to note carefully linking verbs, inverted-word order, and titles.

1. You need to know that both of them *appeal*/appeals to me.

2. Everybody in both classes *was*/were ready.

3. Some is/*are* here; others is/*are* not.

4. Every one of the details *was*/were perfect.

5. I like instructors who *smile*/smiles.

6. *The 39 Steps* demand/*demands* moviegoers' rapt attention.

Have students underline the appropriate verbs in parentheses in the following passage about the Iks, a tribe in Uganda.

The solitary Ik, isolated in the ruins of an exploded culture, (*has*/have) built a new defense for himself. If you (lives/*live*) in an unworkable society, you can make up one of your own, and this (*is*/are) what the Iks (has/*have*) done. Each Ik (*has*/have) become a one-man tribe on its own, a constituency.

Now everything (*falls*/fall) into place. This is why they do (seems/*seem*), after all, vaguely familiar to all of us. We've seen them before. This is precisely the way groups of one size or another, ranging from committee to nations, (behaves/*behave*). It is, of course, this aspect of humanity that (*has*/have) lagged behind the rest of evolution, and this is why the Ik (*seems*/seem) so primitive. In his absolute selfishness, his incapacity to give anything away, no matter what, he (*is*/are) a successful committee.   – LEWIS THOMAS, "The Iks"

·· **(34d)**

___
FOR TEACHING: COLLECTIVE NOUNS AND AGREEMENT
___

Encourage your students to think critically about collective nouns as wholes or parts. Write this topic sentence on the board: *The jury disagree/disagrees on a number of details.* Then ask your students to decide whether to treat *jury* as singular or plural, according to the following context:

> After examining both sides of the case for over seven hours, only one member thinks for certain that the defendant is "not guilty." Three other jurors, however, cannot decide at all. In view of this stand-off, the jury leader has no choice but to insist that the entire jury review the case and evidence yet one more time.

■ **USEFUL READINGS**

Kolln, Martha. *Rhetorical Grammar.* 4th ed. New York: Longman, 2001.

Shaughnessy, Mina. *Errors and Expectations.* New York: Oxford UP, 1977.

35

Maintaining Pronoun-Antecedent Agreement

Of all that is good, sublimity is supreme. Succeeding is the coming together of all that is beautiful. Furtherance is the agreement of all that is just. Perseverance is the foundation of all actions. — LAO-TZU

The use of a plural pronoun with an indefinite antecedent has a long history in educated usage:

Everyone in the house were in their beds. — HENRY FIELDING

A person can't help their birth. — WILLIAM THACKERAY

It's enough to drive anyone out of their senses. — GEORGE BERNARD SHAW

This lineage notwithstanding, such usage is now apt to be considered incorrect by many readers. However, because it provides a simple solution to many problems of sexist usage, it is becoming more and more widely accepted in academic and formal writing.

On Making Pronouns Agree with Collective Noun Antecedents

(35b)

The adjectives *every* and *each* and the pronouns *everyone, no one, anyone,* and *anybody* are generally regarded as singular, regardless of the sentence construction. These words cause difficulty for students, not so much because of their indefiniteness, but because of the agreement problem inherent in third-person singular nouns and verbs: should agreement be reached in number or gender?

In the following sentence, should you pair *every* with *his* and perpetuate sexist language? Or should you pair the singular *every* with the plural *their,* a practice that is falling into general usage?

Every driver takes *his/her/its/their* lives into *his/her/its/their* own hands.

There is nothing more likely to start disagreement among people or countries than an agreement.
                    —E. B. WHITE

Long afterward,
Oedipus, old and
blinded, walked the
roads. He smelled a
familiar smell. It was the
Sphinx. Oedipus said, "I
want to ask one
question. Why didn't I
recognize my mother?"
"You gave the wrong
answer," said the
Sphinx. "But that was
what made everything
possible," said Oedipus.
"No," she said. "When I
asked, What walks on
four legs in the morning,
two at noon, and three
in the evening, you
answered, Man. You
didn't say anything
about woman." "When
you say Man," said
Oedipus, "you include
women too. Everyone
knows that." She said,
"That's what you
think."
    – MURIEL RUKEYSER
.... (35d)

Or should you recast the entire sentence into the plural?

All drivers take *their* lives into *their* own hands.

Current convention prefers the singular for *everybody* even when a contextual and commonsense analysis shows that *everybody* refers to more than one person.

On Saturday mornings, *everybody* meets at Shauna's place before heading to the ball diamond. Beth, Cindi, and Robert always show up first. Aneil and Matt usually arrive last.

FOR TEACHING: PRONOUN-ANTECEDENT AGREEMENT

Ask students to think for a moment of a memorable object—a toy, a dog-eared favorite children's book, anything they can remember well—and to write a paragraph or two describing the object: what it looks like, how they used it, how they feel about it. Then ask them to look over the descriptions, identifying all pronouns. Finally, ask them (in small groups, perhaps) to check to see that each pronoun has a clear antecedent.

FOR TEACHING: CHECKING FOR SEXIST PRONOUNS

Ask students to look for other examples of writing in newspapers, magazines, or on the Web that uses pronouns to refer to both men and women, similar to the example from de Toqueville's *Democracy in America* given on p. 649. Suggest that they look for both sexist and nonsexist examples, and have them bring their examples to class for discussion. You might want to read a few of them aloud and then put one sexist example up on the board for the class to revise.

■ USEFUL READINGS

Baron, Dennis. *Grammar and Gender*. New Haven: Yale UP, 1986. Baron offers a critical history of the relationship between sexism and the development of the English language; chapter 10 focuses on attempts to solve the problem of pronoun agreement with the third-person singular.

Hayes, Christopher G. "A Brief Writing Assignment for Introducing Non-Sexist Pronoun Usage." *TETYC* 28.1 (Sept. 2000): 74–77. Hayes describes a narrative writing assignment that helps demonstrate to students how and why sexist language usage can limit thinking, sometimes injuriously.

Nilsen, Aileen Pace. "Winning the Great 'He'/'She' Battle." *CE* 46 (1984): 151–57. Nilsen uses an examination of manuscripts submitted to *English Journal* to demonstrate the complexities of using "sex-fair" language. She then offers four principles intended to guide such usage.

Schwartz, Marilyn. *Report of the Task Force on Bias-Free Language of the Association of American University Presses.* Bloomington: Indiana UP, 1995. This AAUP report gives the association's official recommendations on how to produce "bias-free" writing, paying special attention to nonsexist discourse.

36

▼ Using Adjectives and Adverbs

The adjective is the banana peel of the parts of speech.

–CLIFTON PAUL FADIMAN

In early English, many adverbs were formed from adjectives by adding *e*: *bright,* the adjective, became *brighte,* the adverb. In time, the *e* was dropped, but the adverbial use was kept. Hence by analogy, many adjectives (such as *excellent*) that could not form adverbs by adding *e* were simply used as adverbs. Shakespeare freely used such constructions:

Which the false man does *easy.* — MACBETH *2.3.143*

Thou didst it *excellent.* — TAMING OF THE SHREW *1.1.89*

Grow not *instant* old. — HAMLET *1.5.94*

'Tis *noble* spoken. — ANTONY AND CLEOPATRA *2.2.99*

And he used both forms of the adverb side by side:

She was *new* lodged and *newly* deified. — LOVER'S COMPLAINT *84*

In function, adjectives and adverbs alike modify other parts of speech, and their differences in spelling and pronunciation have been conflated in the linguistic tendency toward regularization. Like the English of Shakespeare's day, many informal varieties of English often make no distinction between an adjective and an adverb in constructions such as *Come quick!* and *The moon shines bright* that omit the *-ly* adverb suffix. In their enthusiasm to use standard academic or "correct" English, some speakers even add the *-ly* suffix to words that function as adjectives, such as in *I feel <u>badly</u> that you've lost your job.* Since *feel* is a linking verb, the speaker should use the adjective *bad* rather than the adverb *badly.*

On Overusing Adjectives and Adverbs

Many well-known writers on style, heirs of Hemingway and Orwell, counsel in the strictest terms against any but the most "necessary" adjectives and adverbs. William Zinsser calls the overuse of modifiers "clutter" and advises writers to "strip every sentence to its cleanest components":

> . . . Every word that serves no function . . . [and] every adverb that carries the same meaning that's already in the verb, . . . weaken the strength of a sentence.

According to Zinsser in *On Writing Well,* carefully chosen nouns and verbs resonate with connotative meaning. These words rarely need modifiers: *friend* does not need *personal; mope* does not need *dejectedly.*

On the other hand, Francis Christensen, in "A Generative Rhetoric of the Sentence," argues that a mature and interesting prose style lies in the use of adjectives and adverbs, which enables students to express complicated thoughts in complicated ways.

And on still *another* hand, in her chapter on "Vocabulary" in *Errors and Expectations,* Mina Shaughnessy describes the vocabulary features of three groups of writers (basic, intermediate, and advanced), including their use of adjectives and adverbs. Basic writers commonly use only a few, already-overused adverbs (*too, very, really, quite, hardly*) and just twenty-one or so adjectives. Intermediate writers, she claims, use *-ly* adverbs (*adequately, fluently,* for example) and adjectives more "informative" than *good, bad, important;* these include *hostile, honest, monstrous, impatient.* Shaughnessy encourages instructors to work with writers of all levels, building their academic vocabulary in three ways: learning about words, learning words, and learning a sensitivity to words.

Adjectives often carry indispensable shades of meaning. In basketball, for example, there's an important difference between a *slam dunk* and an *alley-oop dunk,* a *flagrant foul* and a *technical foul,* a *layup* and a *reverse layup.* Consider as well the distinction between *talk* and *trash talk,* or *color commentary* and *play-by-play commentary.* In each case, the difference is in the adjectives. Ask your students to look in the newspaper for examples of adjectives that carry significant meaning in a sport or other activity that they know well. Of the adjectives they find, ask them to identify which ones add vividness to the writing and which ones add essential information.

Anything that needs an adjective, be it civics education, or socialist education, or Christian education, or whatever-you-like education, is not education, and it has some different goal. The very existence of modified "educations" is testimony to the fact that their proponents cannot bring about what they want in a mind that is free. An "education" that cannot do its work in a free mind, and so must "teach" by homily and precept in the service of these feelings and attitudes and beliefs rather than those, is pure and unmistakable tyranny.
— RICHARD MITCHELL

FOR COLLABORATIVE WORK: USING ADJECTIVES   **(36a–b)**

The following sentence uses adjectives effectively to paint a picture of beauty in motion:

> *Tall, powerful, barefoot, graceful, soundless,* Missouri Fever was like a *supple black* cat as she paraded serenely about the kitchen, the *casual* flow of *her* walk beautifully *sensuous* and *haughty.*   — TRUMAN CAPOTE, *Other Voices, Other Rooms*

Have students break into their groups and write imitations of Capote's sentence, using as the focus of their descriptions a pet, a person they know, or a performing artist (dancer, musician, or actor) they have seen. Have them compare sentences among their groups and then select one they find particularly powerful to share with the best sentences from the other groups.

By using Capote's sentence as a model, they will be able to internalize his syntax while they experiment and discover the semantic possibilities of adjectives.

(36a–b)   **TEACHING WITH TECHNOLOGY: USING ADJECTIVES**

Suggest that students do a version of the preceeding For Collaborative Work exercise on their own. Have them locate two or three other sentences that use adjectives effectively — perhaps from popular music or a film they know well — and post them on your course's electronic listserv. Then have them try generating their own sentences using them as models.

(36c)   **On *Well* and *Good***

The use of *well* and *good* to describe physical health is confusing, especially since many English speakers consider the two words synonymous: "Don't you feel good?" "Don't you feel well?"

Used as an adjective, *well* expresses relief from sickness, while the adjective *good* expresses a more general sense of well-being. When *good* is used after such linking verbs as *be, feel, seem, smell, sound,* and *taste,* it qualifies the subject of the verb.

(36d)   **On Using Comparatives and Superlatives**

Not the product of a set of rules, the common irregular adjectives and adverbs originated from different Old English words. For example, *good* came from the Old English *god,* which is related to the German *gut.* Both words are derived from the Indo-European root *ghedh-,* "unite, join together, be suitable." *Better* and *best* come from the Old English *betera* and *betst,* both of which are derived from the Indo-European *bhad-,* "good."

Bad is not derived from the Old English word for bad or evil, *yfel*. Instead, it comes from the Old English *baedan*, "compel, afflict." *Worse* and *worst* come from their Old English synonyms, *wiersa* and *wyrsta*.

On Double Comparatives   (36d3)

In *The American Language,* H. L. Mencken points out that some double comparatives may actually have a logic to their usage: "more better," for instance (463). One day we feel better than the day before; the next day, we feel completely well. Hence, we can report that we are "even better" or "still better" or, colloquially, "more better."

FOR TEACHING: INCOMPLETE COMPARISONS   (36d4)

Ask students to rewrite the following incomplete comparisons, making them clear and explicit by providing a situation and a revised, complex form:

1. You're taller!
2. No, you're more than I am.
3. She's happier.
4. They cheat more.
5. Mine are the most.
6. Mostly red ones.

On Using Nouns as Modifiers   (36e)

"The long compound noun phrase" is a common stylistic habit, according to Joseph Williams. In *Style: Ten Lessons in Clarity and Grace,* Williams provides perfect examples of overnominalization:

> The frequent use of *nominalizations* instead of verbs results in the *frustration* of reader *expectations.* Their *expectation* is of the *appearance* of characters as subjects and their *actions* as verbs. (50)

Although piling up nominalizations is both acceptable and considered economical in some scientific and technical circles, it has the potential for ambiguity and confusion. In Williams's term, it is "graceless." To unpack such phrases, he says, begin with the last noun and reverse the order, turning the packed phrase into a string of prepositional phrases. Better yet is to look for verbs that have been nominalized such as *misdiagnosis;* used as verbs, those words can put new life into a sentence. Watch, too, for possessive nouns that can be rewritten as prepositional phrases.

FOR COLLABORATIVE WORK: USING ADJECTIVES AND ADVERBS

Have students bring their responses to "Reading with an Eye for Adjectives and Adverbs" to class, and put them up on the board. Ask for comments about what the adjectives and adverbs add in each case. Ask students to suggest synonyms that might be substituted, and consider the effectiveness of the different versions. Try removing the adjectives and adverbs altogether, and consider the result. Finally, ask students which version they prefer, and why.

■ **USEFUL READINGS**

Curme, George O. *English Grammar.* 1947. New York: HarperPerennial, 1991. This book contains a traditional grammarian's explanations and examples of the common kinds and forms of adjectives and adverbs.

Christensen, Francis. "A Generative Rhetoric of the Paragraph." *CCC* 16 (Oct. 1965): 144–56.

——. "A Generative Rhetoric of the Sentence." *CCC* 14 (1963): 155–61.

Lee, Donald W., ed. *English Language Reader: Introductory Essays and Exercises.* New York: Dodd, 1963. This collection includes essays on grammar, history of the language, dictionaries, and other language-related topics. The final section discusses the various definitions of *adjective.*

Mencken, H. L. *The American Language.* 2nd ed. New York: Knopf, 1921.

Shaughnessy, Mina P. *Errors and Expectations.* New York: Oxford UP, 1977. See chapter 6, "Vocabulary."

Williams, Joseph. *Style: Ten Lessons in Clarity and Grace.* New York: Addison, 1997.

Wolfram, Walt. *Dialects and American English.* Englewood Cliffs: Prentice, 1991. See, especially, chapter 4, "Regional Dialects."

Zinsser, William. *On Writing Well: An Informal Guide to Writing Nonficiton.* 5th ed. New York: HarperCollins, 1995.

PART 7

SENTENCES: MAKING CONVENTIONAL CHOICES

37

▼ Maintaining Clear Pronoun Reference

Two speakers immersed in conversation can be somewhat ambiguous about their pronoun references because they are speaking in an immediate context. They can rely more on their physical signals and close proximity than on their actual syntax. Each listener has opportunities to interrupt and question anything that seems unclear, or to look perplexed.

The audience of a public speech and the reader of written discourse, however, have little chance to interrupt or question the speaker or author. The rules of etiquette and the varying degrees of formality produce this distance and its demand for clarity of references. Members of an audience rarely interrupt a speaker to ask a question. Readers rarely telephone authors to clarify their pronoun references.

A piece of oratory or writing often creates its own context that clarifies potentially confusing pronoun references. Take, for example, the last sentence of the preceding paragraph: *Readers rarely telephone authors to clarify their pronoun references.* Taken out of context, *their* could confuse us, but we know that only authors create pronoun references—a fact made clear in the context.

On the Importance of Pronouns

In their book *Frequency Analysis of English Usage,* W. Nelson Francis and Henry Kucera studied the frequency with which words appear in edited American English. Pronouns are among the most frequently used words, as the following chart indicates:

Word	Rank
he	7
it	11
they	13
I	15
we	23
she	24
you	30
who	35

The authors also note that personal, reflexive, singular pronouns (*myself, herself, himself*) occur much more frequently in imaginative prose than in informative prose. Conversely, plural forms of these reflexive personal pronouns (*ourselves, themselves*) occur much more frequently in informative prose than in imaginative prose. While Francis and Kucera offer no explanation for this relationship, pronoun use seems to indicate that imaginative prose tends to focus on individuals, while transactional or informative prose tends to focus on groups of people.

FOR TEACHING: MATCHING PRONOUNS CLEARLY TO ONE ANTECEDENT   **(37a)** ················

Ask students to spend five minutes interviewing two friends or classmates about the courses they are currently taking. Have them take notes and try to get down the interviewee's exact words. Then have them write up a brief summary of their interviews. Have them note how they have used pronouns in their summaries — and make sure that each pronoun refers accurately to the person they intend.

FOR TEACHING: EVERYDAY PRONOUN REFERENCE

If your students are not familiar with the term *pronoun reference,* remind them that they use the concept every day, particularly in conversation. In fact, speakers of English rely constantly on clear pronoun reference.

A driver we know recently faced this challenge:

Mechanic:	So what's the problem?
Driver:	On rainy days, it really acts weird.
Mechanic:	It won't start on rainy days?

Driver:	Sometimes it won't start. But there are other problems too. All those little lights on the dashboard light up at once. That white needle goes all the way over, and the little gauge there jiggles around nervously.
Mechanic:	Hmmm. Does it crank?
Driver:	The little gauge?
Mechanic:	The car. The engine.

This conversation shows pronoun reference in use. The one breakdown in communication occurs because the driver assumes that the mechanic's question — "Does it crank?" — refers to the last thing the driver mentioned — "the little gauge." The mechanic, however, is using *it* to refer to *the car,* not the gauge. Have students think of times when unclear pronoun reference has made for confusion.

On Pronouns and Deixis

In *Linguistics for Students of Literature,* Elizabeth Traugott and Mary Louise Pratt explain pronoun reference in terms of *deixis,* the process of anchoring in the "spatio-temporal perspective of the speaker." More explicitly, deixis allows us to understand a communicative act as an interaction among elements in the universe of discourse. Each communicative act, then, be it speaking, writing, listening, reading, or even watching and observing, involves an interaction among (1) the writer/speaker; (2) the reader/listener; (3) the written, spoken, or visual text; and (4) the referent of that text — the four components of the universe of discourse.

We tend to rely on deictic pronouns because we have a clear, context-bound sense of their reference. Confusion occurs only when our audience (readers or listeners) doesn't share our vantage point, or when it cannot or does not reconstruct the position or perspective of the speaker or hearer.

> *You* did so *do it.*
>
> *I did* nothing of *the sort.*
>
> *She* saw *you* leave *there.*
>
> *That* is *what she* thinks *she* saw, but *she did*n't.
>
> Well, *I'*m not standing for any more of *this treatment.*

The italicized words exemplify deixis, for they make sense in a reliable or reconstructible context. (Why not ask your students to use deixis to create a context for the above exchange?)

The issue of pronoun reference is one of clarity and effective communication. Writers, who are rarely present or available to clarify any confusion, must write so that their readers do not have to second-guess them.

■ USEFUL READINGS

Francis, W. Nelson, and Henry Kucera. *Frequency Analysis of English Usage.* Boston: Houghton, 1982.

Haussamen, Brock. *Revising the Rules: Traditional Grammar and Modern Linguistics.* 2nd ed. Dubuque: Kendell/Hunt, 1997. See the chapters on "Pronoun Agreement," "Pronoun Case and Restrictiveness," and *"He* and *They."*

Traugott, Elizabeth, and Mary Louise Pratt. *Linguistics for Students of Literature.* San Diego: Harcourt, 1980.

Williams, Joseph M. *Style: Ten Lessons in Clarity and Grace.* 6th ed. New York: Addison-Wesley, 2002. See, especially, the discussion of summative modifiers.

38 🔻 Recognizing Shifts

The shifts a speaker/writer makes — in language, dialect, grammar, punctuation, and spelling — can be thought of in several ways, from "merely an error" to practical social switching to accommodating a political agenda. In the most traditional sense, shifting is seen as an error, often not a very significant error. Currently, however, sociolinguists see shifts as changes in language that can be politically and rhetorically responsive to the setting and to the audience.

Isabella Halsted tells us that errors are simply mistakes that we are all capable of, given the wrong circumstances: lack of sleep, deadline pressure, unfamiliarity with formal standard English:

> Like the soot on the pane, Error is something that gets in the way of the clear vision. . . . Error on all levels is distracting, annoying, obstructive. Error is inexcusable ultimately, yes, [but] not because it is Wrong *per se*. . . . In plain pragmatic terms, the absence of Error is useful, but when our students take pains to avoid it — by writing short sentences, by sticking to one tense, by writing as little as possible — I doubt very much that they do so in order to better communicate with a reader, but rather to play safe, to avoid the red marks.

Errors in shift are relatively minor: they rarely obstruct communication, amounting to nothing more than stumbling blocks. Mina Shaughnessy says, for example, that pronoun shifts "usually go unnoticed by the writer until someone points them out" (113), for the writer usually believes the sentence is written correctly.

On the other hand, really dramatic or outrageous shifts are a staple of comedians and humor writers. Here is columnist Dave Barry: "I would have to say that the greatest single achievement of the American medical establishment is nasal spray." Part of Barry's humor comes from his tendency to shift tone, from the serious (the American medical establishment) to the banal (nasal spray).

FOR TEACHING: RECOGNIZING SHIFTS

One way to approach errors like those described in this chapter is to have your students read about them, do exercises, and attempt to find them in their own work. Or you can wait until the error appears, then ask the student to read the erroneous sentence(s) aloud. In "The Study of Error," David Bartholomae suggests that students will often orally correct written errors without noticing the correction. Not only does the reading-aloud technique reveal their competence but it also allows you a dramatic way to reveal the error to them.

FOR COLLABORATIVE WORK: UNNECESSARY SHIFTS IN MOOD   **(38b)** ....

Help your students identify mood by using the following passages from Martin Luther King Jr.'s "I Have a Dream" speech. Put the students in small groups and have them analyze each passage.

Indicative: used in making a statement of fact.

It is obvious today that America has defaulted on this promissory note insofar as her citizens of color are concerned. Instead of honoring this sacred obligation, America has given the Negro people a bad check; a check which has come back marked "insufficient funds." But we refuse to believe that the bank of justice is bankrupt. We refuse to believe that there are insufficient funds in the great vaults of opportunity of this nation. So we have come to cash this check—a check that will give us upon demand the riches of freedom and the security of justice.

Imperative: expresses a command or an entreaty.

Go back to Mississippi, go back to Alabama, go back to South Carolina, go back to Georgia, go back to Louisiana, go back to the slums and ghettos of our northern cities, knowing that somehow this situation can and will be changed. Let us not wallow in the valley of despair.

Subjunctive: makes a conditional statement, expresses a wish, or indicates doubt and uncertainty.

I have a dream that one day every valley shall be exalted, every hill and mountain shall be made low, the rough places will be made plain, and the crooked places will be made straight, and the glory of the Lord shall be revealed, and all flesh shall see it together.

(38c) On Voice

Voice comes from the Latin *vox,* meaning "voice" or "sound." In 1382, John Wyclif became the first to use *voice* as a grammatical label in English. Students may need some extra help in understanding the grammatical sense of voice.

(38d) On Unnecessary Shifts in Person and Number

Mina Shaughnessy suggests that problems in pronoun shifts stem from the writer's "unstable sense of the writer-audience relationship, with the shift to 'you' signifying a more direct sense of audience" (113). She identifies three additional general sources of pronoun-shift errors: (1) students' tendency "to reduce complexity without impairing communication"; (2) the problem of remembering which pronouns have been used; and (3) the problem of learning the differences among descriptive, narrative, and analytic writing.

(38a, d) FOR TEACHING: UNNECESSARY SHIFTS IN PERSON AND TENSE

To illustrate how shifts in person (and in tense) can be used effectively, read aloud Martin Luther King Jr.'s "I Have a Dream" speech. Make a special point of focusing on paragraphs 7, 8, and 11–18, discussing King's rhetorical purpose.

(38d) TEACHING WITH TECHNOLOGY: UNNECESSARY SHIFTS IN PERSON

Because many students have been told never to use *I* in their papers, they frequently alternate between *I* and *you* within a single piece of writing.

I went to the fair and couldn't find any of *my* friends. So *I* was really bored. *You* want to be with *your* friends, but *you* can't find them, and *you* don't see anyone *you* know to ride the ferris wheel with. So *I* went to the beer garden, ordered a beer, sat down, and waited to see if *I* would see anybody *I* know.

To help make students aware of their shifts in pronoun, ask them to high-light or boldface all their uses of *I* and *you* in one of their essays. Then ask them to exchange essays by switching computers and let their partner help them find appropriate alternatives to any shifts. Post a few selected papers up on a projector to show revisions to the entire class.

On Unnecessary Shifts between Direct and Indirect Discourse

(38e)

Indirect discourse is often preceded by the word *that,* and both pronouns and verb tenses are often different from those used in direct discourse. Generally, if the introducing verb is past, it doesn't affect the verb in a di-rect quotation. However, a signal verb in past tense will ordinarily shift the verbs in indirect discourse one step back into the past.

> *Direct discourse*
>
> The president said, "I *have* no knowledge of those events."
>
> *Indirect discourse*
>
> The president said that *he had* no knowledge of those events.

When questions appear in direct discourse, they are followed by a ques-tion mark (*The instructor confronted us, asking "What do you think you are doing?"*). When reported in indirect discourse, questions often include *who, if, why, whether, what,* or *how* — and they omit the question mark (*The instructor confronted us, asking __what__ we thought we were doing.*).

On Confusing Shifts in Tone

(38f)

Tone denotes the way a writer's attitude toward a subject or audience comes across to an audience. Just as tone of voice in speaking may be ir-ritating, harsh, or soothing, the tone of a piece of writing may be humor-ous, bitter, ironic, patronizing, passionate, or angry. Tone affects the at-titude of readers just as tone affects listeners. A word like *terrific,* for example, can suggest enthusiasm, frustration, or sarcasm, depending on the speaker's tone.

Shifts in tone and diction can be effective. In the following excerpt, a parody of college catalogs, the diction shifts from formal, sometimes technical, language to much less formal, colloquial language, and finally to slang.

> Economic Theory: A systematic application and critical evaluation of the basic analytic concepts of economic theory, with an emphasis on money and why it's good. Fixed coefficient production functions, cost and supply curves and non-convexity comprise the first semester, with the second semester concentrating on spending, making change, and keeping a neat wallet. The Federal Reserve System is analyzed, and advanced students are coached in the proper method of filling out a deposit slip. Other topics include: Inflation and Depression — how to dress for each. Loans, interest, welching.
> — WOODY ALLEN, "Spring Bulletin"

(38f)   **FOR TEACHING: CONFUSING SHIFTS IN TONE**

Read the following passage to your class, and then ask students to write a short paragraph describing the tone and including specific references. Then ask students with differing opinions about the tone to read the passage aloud, demonstrating the tone they think suits the words. The drama begins to unfold with the arrival of the corpse at the mortuary.

> Alas, poor Yorick! How surprised he would be to see how his counterpart of today is whisked off to a funeral parlor and is in short order sprayed, sliced, pierced, pickled, trussed, trimmed, creamed, waxed, painted, rouged and neatly dressed — transformed from a common corpse into a Beautiful Memory Picture. This process is known in the trade as embalming and restorative art.
> — JESSICA MITFORD, "Behind the Formaldehyde Curtain"

(38f)   **FOR COLLABORATIVE WORK: SHIFTS IN TONE AND DICTION**

To illustrate shifts in tone, you may want to provide your class with copies of both Lincoln's Gettysburg Address and Mencken's "Gettysburg Address in Vulgate." To highlight the change in tone, read them aloud. Then ask the class to identify the phrases and words Mencken uses in place of Lincoln's terms. Discuss how the connotations of words control the "meaning" of a piece of writing.

To give students practice in identifying tone, break them into groups, asking each group to describe the characteristics of one Gettysburg Address. You can use Lincoln's version, Mencken's, and the five versions reprinted in *Preface to Critical Reading*, 6th ed., by Richard D. Altick and Andrea A. Lunsford ([New York: Holt, 1984], 104–107).

FOR MULTILINGUAL WRITERS: CONFUSING SHIFTS IN TONE AND DICTION   **(38f)** ································

Encourage students to record examples of shifts in tone and diction — including ones that are either intentionally or unintentionally humorous. Some students may enjoy fashioning deliberately humorous sentences containing such shifts, modeled after the examples by Woody Allen on p. 326, above, and Dave Barry in the box on p. 666 of the *Handbook*. Parodying English language instructors will help students learn faster.

■ **USEFUL READINGS**

Bartholomae, David. "The Study of Error." *CCC* 31 (1980): 253–69. Rpt. in *The Writing Teacher's Sourcebook*. 4th ed. Ed. Edward Corbett, Nancy Myers, and Gary Tate. New York: Oxford UP: 1999.

Berger, Mary I. *Speak Standard, Too — Add Mainstream English to Your Talking Style*. Chicago: Orchard, 1994.

Halsted, Isabella. "Putting Error in Its Place." *Journal of Basic Writing* 1 (Spring 1975): 72–86.

Mangelsdorf, Kate, Duane H. Roen, and Victoria Taylor. "ESL Students' Use of Audience." *A Sense of Audience in Written Communication*. Ed. Gesa Kirsch and Duane H. Roen. Newbury Park: Sage, 1990. 231–47. The authors consider the audience expectations of ESL writers/speakers and the ways that ESL students can come to reconsider the needs of their intended audience.

Shaughnessy, Mina. *Errors and Expectations*. New York: Oxford UP, 1977.

Smitherman, Geneva. *Talkin and Testifyin: The Language of Black America*. Detroit: Wayne State UP, 1986. See, especially, chapter 6, "Where It's At: Black-White Language Attitudes."

39 ⬇ ▼ Identifying Comma Splices and Fused Sentences

While we certainly pause as we speak in order to mark off our thoughts or to add emphasis, we do not "speak" punctuation. In fact, excited conversation usually contains "comma splices," which then appear in dialogue to represent the rhythms of speech. For example:

> "What about Tom?"
> "We can tell your father and Billy that Tom's mother called, he was sick, his grandmother died, anything, just so we don't have to bring him with us."
> — THOMAS ROCKWELL, *How to Eat Fried Worms*

The comma splices in this dialogue are effective because they convey the speech patterns of two ten-year-old boys.

As this example suggests, comma splices and fused sentences appear frequently in literary and journalistic writing, for, like many other structures commonly identified as "errors," each can be used to powerful effect. In the following passage, the comma splices create momentum and build to a climax:

> Golden eagles sit in every tree and watch us watch them watch us, although there are bird experts who will tell you in all seriousness that there are NO golden eagles here. Bald eagles are common, ospreys abound, we have herons and mergansers and kingfishers, we have logging with percherons and belgians, we have park land and nature trails, we have enough oddballs, weirdos, and loons to satisfy anybody. — ANNE CAMERON

In the second sentence, six independent clauses are spliced together with commas. The effect is a rush of details, from the rather oddball birds to the oddball people and finally to the "loons," a word that can apply to either birds or people.

In their attempts to recapture the "stream of consciousness," both James Joyce and William Faulkner experimented freely with comma splices and fused sentences. Molly's soliloquy in Joyce's *Ulysses* is one of the most famous of these attempts:

> why cant you kiss a man without going and marrying him first you sometimes love to wildly when you feel that way so nice all over you you cant help yourself I wish some man or other would take me sometime when hes there and kiss me in his arms theres nothing like a kiss long and hot down to your soul almost paralyses you[.]

Joyce deliberately used comma splices and fused sentences for purpose and effect.

When student writers use comma splices or fused sentences (which are almost never appropriate in academic writing), they usually do so unknowingly. When they combine two independent clauses without appropriately signaling the combination, they produce a *comma splice* (often called a *comma fault*) or a *fused sentence* (often called a *run-on sentence*). Student writers often defend their *comma splices* in terms of their closely connected ideas or logical progression.

> Anna came in from the tennis court absolutely famished, she opened the freezer, took out the chocolate mocha ice cream, and dug in.

Because it indicates how the two independent clauses are to be separated, the *comma splice* above is easier to read than the following *fused sentence:*

> Anna came into her room to find her cat prancing around on her dresser her jewelry box was lying sideways on the floor her jewelry all sprawled out.

Although these sentence-level "errors" often indicate closely connected ideas, they just as often reflect hurried writing or typing and little or no proofreading.

FOR TEACHING: SEPARATING THE CLAUSES INTO TWO SENTENCES **(39a)** ··

If you provide your students with practices for differentiating among conjunctions, they will be better able to write effective and meaningful sentences. Supply them with the following fused sentences and ask them to make revisions:

> The apple cider was steaming hot, we sipped it eagerly, it took the chill out of us.

They will likely come up with revisions like these:

1. Because/Although/Even though the apple cider was steaming hot, we sipped it eagerly. It took the chill out of us.
2. The apple cider was steaming hot. Even so, we sipped it eagerly because it took the chill out of us.
3. The apple cider was steaming hot, but/yet/and we sipped it eagerly for it took the chill out of us.

Each of these combinations results from and indicates a particular meaning.

(39b)
FOR TEACHING: LINKING THE CLAUSES WITH A COMMA AND A COORDINATING CONJUNCTION

Give students the following sentences, and ask them to explain their revision choices, carefully accounting for the context of each revision:

The clock struck 2:00 A.M. We continued talking.

(39c)
FOR TEACHING: LINKING THE CLAUSES WITH A SEMICOLON

Ask students to revise the following passage adapted from Jessica Mitford's "Behind the Formaldehyde Curtain" to eliminate sentence-level errors by using the semicolon.

The religious service may be held in a church, it may be held in the chapel of the funeral home, the funeral director vastly prefers the latter arrangement. Not only is it more convenient for him but it affords him the opportunity to show off his beautiful facilities to the gathered mourners. After the clergyman has had his way, the mourners queue up to file past the casket for a last look at the deceased, the family is never asked whether they want an open-casket ceremony, in the absence of their instruction to the contrary, this is taken for granted, well over 90 per cent of all American funerals feature the open casket—a custom unknown in other parts of the world, foreigners are astonished by it.

FOR COLLABORATIVE WORK: READING WITH AN EYE FOR SPECIAL EFFECTS

Ask your students to read this passage by Gertrude Stein and then write a short paragraph describing the effects Stein achieves with her comma splices. As a class, share your insights in a discussion. Then ask your students to rewrite the passage to achieve different effects, such as short, choppy sentences or a stream-of-consciousness narration.

> Think of all the detective stories everybody reads. The kind of crime is the same, and the idea of the story is very often the same, take for example a man like Wallace, he always has the same theme, take a man like Fletcher he always has the same theme, take any American ones, they too always have the scene, the same scene, the kind of invention that is necessary to make a general scene is very limited in everybody's experience, every time one of the hundreds of times a newspaper man makes fun of my writing and of my repetition he always has the same theme, always having the same theme, that is, if you like, repetition, that is if you like repeating that is the same thing, but once started expressing this thing, expressing any thing there can be no repetition because the essence of that expression is insistence, and if you insist you must each time use emphasis and if you use emphasis it is not possible while anybody is alive that they should use exactly the same emphasis.

FOR TEACHING: READING WITH AN EYE FOR SPECIAL EFFECTS

To help your students better understand the role of context in determining the acceptability of comma splices or fused sentences, bring in texts from outside the classroom as sources of exercises. Advertisements, for example, are a prime source of comma splices and sentence fragments, though ideas are rarely left without closure long enough to become fused sentences. Song lyrics are another good source. Ask your students to identify and revise the sentence-level errors in the advertisements or lyrics, and discuss the lack of punctuation. (They do not need to be punctuated according to academic standards; often, the function of the advertisement is to present images rather than explanations; lyrics often depend on tone, pitch, rhythm, and stress to achieve meaning.)

■ **USEFUL READING**

Weathers, Winston. "Grammars of Style: New Options in Composition." *Freshman English News* 4 (Winter 1976): 1–4. Weathers points out that although instructors think they are giving students a wide range of stylistic options, they are, in fact, subscribing to a rather limited "grammar of style." He offers a description of marginalized styles that teachers should consider, including a style he calls the "labyrinthine sentence."

40

Recognizing Sentence Fragments

Many instructors simply ban fragments outright. However, certain students will discover in their reading and writing just how effectively fragments can be used. In their research, Charles R. Kline Jr. and W. Dean Memering quote fragments from a number of "formal" writings.

> "They then determined the number of these unrelated words and the sequence of words. 'The more words recalled, the less memory used to store the sentence. The fewer words recalled, the more memory used to store the sentence.'"
> – NOAM CHOMSKY, "Language and Mind"

> "Emily Dickinson's poems . . . are more authentically in the metaphysical tradition than Emerson's are. Not, however, that many of his values were not hers also — especially where they concerned the integrity of the mind and the sufficiency of inner resources."
> – F. O. MATTHIESEN, *American Renaissance*

Here is another example, this time from Virginia Woolf:

> The history of England is the history of the male line, not of the female. Of our fathers we know always some fact, some distinction. They were soldiers or they were sailors; they filled that office or they made that law. But of our mothers, our grandmothers, our great-grandmothers, what remains? *Nothing but a tradition.* One was beautiful; one was red-haired; one was kissed by a Queen. We know nothing of them except their names and the dates of their marriages and the number of children they bore.
> – VIRGINIA WOOLF, "Women and Literature"

"Nothing but a tradition." This fragment brings drama to Woolf's statement, arresting readers' attention in a way that a complete sentence would not, giving added emphasis to the word *nothing* and thus to Woolf's point.

What distinguishes these "professional" fragments from those of our students? Often nothing. Consider viewing student papers as professional texts in the making. Allow that fragments can be acceptable on rhetorical or stylistic grounds. Unacceptable fragments are those that (1) lack a close

A writer is not someone who expresses his thoughts, his passion or his imagination in sentences but someone who thinks sentences. A Sentence-Thinker.
– ROLAND BARTHES

relationship to other sentences, (2) create noncontinuous thought, or (3) confuse the reader.

FOR TEACHING: REVISING PHRASE FRAGMENTS **(40a)**

As rhetorical devices, sentence fragments should not be overused lest they lose their effect. But, first of all, students need to be able to recognize unacceptable sentence fragments, those discontinuous ones that confuse the reader. Introduce the ineffective fragment to them by speaking to them in fragments: "Today. Chapter 40. Frequently used. Understand?" Naturally, your students won't know what you mean and will try to get more information from you. Write what you said on the board. Eventually, your students will tell you that your statements are incomplete. Then drop your mask and announce that they've just given you the definition of "sentence fragment." Ask them to complete your statements.

Once students demonstrate their ability to recognize and revise unacceptable fragments, introduce the concept of acceptable "nonsentences." On the board, write this famous quote from Mark Twain: "Man is the only animal that blushes. Or needs to." Ask your students to "correct" this fragment, no doubt an easy task for them: "Man is the only animal that blushes or needs to." Some of your students may be bothered by this revision and may suggest other forms of punctuation in an attempt to recapture the emphasis lost in the revision, while others may be content. You may want to ask what is wrong with the original. Is it confusing? Does the second part connect with the preceding sentence? Were they bothered or confused when they first read it?

From here, you can explain the difference between acceptable and unacceptable fragments, emphasizing the criteria of clarity and continuity. Point out that fragments of any kind should be used rarely and that acceptable fragments do not validate those that should be corrected.

FOR TEACHING: IDENTIFYING FRAGMENTS **(40a–c)**

Sentence fragments can be particularly effective not only in narrative, where they call up the rhythms of speech, but also in *description*. Note the following passage from Keith Gilyard's *Voices of the Self: A Study of Language Competence*. In this passage (part of which also appears in Reading with an Eye for Fragments on p. 682 of the *Handbook*), Gilyard uses verbal and noun phrase fragments to describe his route to church on Sundays, as well as to describe the church itself:

> On Sundays, for religion, we went up the hill. *Skipping along the hexagon-shaped hill in Colonial Park.* . . . *Leaning forward for leverage to finish the climb up to the church.* I was always impressed by this particular house of the Lord. *Tremendous gray and white cinder blocks. Polished maple pews in the main service room. Red carpet, stained windows, and gigantic organ pipes.* . . . And Pops was up in the front row with the rest of the deacons. *A broad-shouldered frame in a gray or blue suit.* (24)

Ask your students to bring in similar examples of fragments and identify their type (and purpose); this additional practice will help them better identify these structures.

(40a–c)

FOR COLLABORATIVE WORK: REVISING FRAGMENTS

Ask students to bring to class any essays in which they find fragments. Choose several fragments, and put them on the board for class discussion. Ask students to identify the missing element in each and then, after supplying necessary context from the essay, to decide on the *best* means of revision.

■ USEFUL READINGS

Gilyard, Keith. *Voices of the Self: A Study of Language Competence.* Detroit: Wayne State UP, 1991.

Kline, Charles R., Jr., and W. Dean Memering. "Formal Fragments: The English Minor Sentence." *Research in the Teaching of English* 11 (Fall 1977): 97–110. Rpt. in *Rhetoric and Composition: A Sourcebook for Teachers and Writers.* Ed. Richard L. Graves. Upper Montclair: Boynton, 1984. 148–61. Kline and Memering report that in their analysis of fifty books and magazines representing educated adult writers they found a wide variety of sentence fragments — none of which resulted in confusing or incoherent prose. They conclude that fragments that function effectively should be considered "minor sentences," and they offer a few general rules for the use of such sentences.

Noguchi, Rei R. *Grammar and the Teaching of Writing: Limits and Possibilities.* Urbana: NCTE, 1991. Noguchi streamlines the teaching of grammar by focusing only on those problems that are amenable to instruction and by taking advantage of what all native speakers of English already know; chapter 5 deals specifically with fragments.

41 Placing Modifiers Appropriately

Modifiers—adjectives, adverbs, and the various kinds of phrases and clauses used as adjectives and adverbs—enrich writing by making it more concrete, vivid, and memorable. Writers want to take full advantage of them, as Ann Petry does in the following sentence:

> She wore the kind of clothes he liked, simple, unadorned and yet completely feminine, white gloves on Sundays, small black leather pocketbooks, carefully polished shoes, pretty small hats, a feather the only gay note on her best felt hat, and the seams in her stockings always straight.   – ANN PETRY, *The Narrows*

You might point out to students that this sentence could have stopped after the first clause: "She wore the kind of clothes he liked." Everything that follows is built on modifiers; they bring the sentence to life and help readers picture the clothes she wore.

Note also, perhaps, that modifiers must be carefully placed and must refer clearly and unambiguously to some word or words in the sentence. In the preceding sentence, for example, *completely* modifies *feminine*; if it were placed elsewhere in the sentence, we would have a different statement: "completely unadorned and yet feminine," perhaps. And look at the difference if *only* were placed somewhere else: white gloves "only on Sundays," for instance—or even "only white gloves on Sundays"!

FOR TEACHING: IDENTIFYING MODIFIERS   (41a–c) ·····································

Ask students to study the following paragraph, in which Maya Angelou relies heavily on modifiers to describe herself at an awkward age:

> I was too tall and raw-skinny. My large extroverted teeth protruded in an excitement to be seen, and I, attempting to thwart their success, rarely smiled. Although I lathered Dixie Peach in my hair, the thick black mass crinkled and

kinked and resisted the smothering pomade to burst free around my head like a cloud of angry bees.

– MAYA ANGELOU, <i>Singin' and Swingin' and Gettin' Merry Like Christmas</i>

Then ask students to think for a few minutes about some of the awkward stages they remember going through, brainstorming a bit by completing these thoughts: "I was too . . ." or "What I remember most about being fifteen was . . ." Have them spend ten minutes or so writing a brief description about themselves, underlining the words they recognize as modifiers, then revising the passage by eliminating them all. Finally, ask them to compare the two versions and think about what modifiers add to their writing.

(41a–c)   **On Placing Modifiers Appropriately:** *Only*

Columnist James J. Kilpatrick offers this humorous and enlightening demonstration of just how many ways the modifier *only* could be placed. He starts with the sentence "She told me that she loved me."

> Let us count the ways:
> <u>*Only*</u> *she told me that she loved me.* No one else has told me that.
> *She* <u>*only*</u> *told me that she loved me.* She did not provide any evidence of her love — she only told me about it.
> *She told* <u>*only*</u> *me that she loved me.* Not the gabby type.
> *She told me* <u>*only*</u> *that she loved me.* Pretty closemouthed. She had nothing more to say.
> *She told me that* <u>*only*</u> *she loved me.* The lady is claiming exclusive rights.
> *She told me that she* <u>*only*</u> *loved me.* She doesn't adore me, worship me, idolize me. She only loves me.
> *She told me that she loved me* <u>*only*</u>. Ahhhh!   – JAMES J. KILPATRICK

More recently, *Parade Magazine* received a letter from a reader asking the following question — and providing her own answer:

> There's only one word that can be placed successfully in any of the 10 numbered positions in this sentence to produce 10 sentences of different meaning (each sentence has 10 words): (1) *I* (2) *helped* (3) *my* (4) *dog* (5) *carry* (6) *my* (7) *husband's* (8) *slippers* (9) *yesterday* (10).
> What is that word?   – Gloria J., Salt Lake City, Utah

The word is "only," which makes the following 10 sentences:

1. Only *I* helped my dog carry my husband's slippers yesterday. (Usually the cat helps too, but she was busy with a mouse.)
2. I only *helped* my dog carry my husband's slippers yesterday. (The dog wanted me to carry them all by myself, but I refused.)
3. I helped only *my* dog carry my husband's slippers yesterday. (I was too busy to help my neighbor's dog when he carried them.)
4. I helped my only *dog* carry my husband's slippers yesterday. (I considered getting another dog, but the cat disapproved.)
5. I helped my dog only *carry* my husband's slippers yesterday. (I didn't help the dog eat them; I usually let the cat do that.)
6. I helped my dog carry only *my* husband's slippers yesterday. (My dog and I didn't have time to help my neighbor's husband.)
7. I helped my dog carry my only *husband's* slippers yesterday. (I considered getting another husband, but one is enough.)
8. I helped my dog carry my husband's only *slippers* yesterday. (My husband had two pairs of slippers, but the cat ate one pair.)
9. I helped my dog carry my husband's slippers only *yesterday*. (And now the dog wants help again; I wish he'd ask the cat.)
10. I helped my dog carry my husband's slippers yesterday only. (And believe me, once was enough — they tasted *terrible*.)

Finally, here is James Thurber's take on *only:*

> Where to use *only* in a sentence is a moot question, one of the mootest questions in all rhetoric. The purist will say the expression "He only died last week" is incorrect, and that it should be "He died only last week." The purist's contention is that the first sentence, if carried out to a natural conclusion, would give us something like this: "He only died last week; he didn't do anything else; that's all he did." It isn't a natural conclusion, however, because nobody would say that. . . . The best way is often to omit *only* and use some other expression. Thus . . . one could say: "It was no longer ago than last Thursday that George L. Wodolgoffing became an angel."   – James Thurber

On Revising Misplaced Modifiers   (41a)

Although misplaced, disruptive, and dangling modifiers affect the reader differently, they all create ambiguity within a sentence. Misplaced and disruptive modifiers often lead to confusing or garbled sentences. Dangling modifiers leave the reader guessing to which word or phrase the modifier belongs.

For many, clarity is an unchallenged ideal. Indeed, when assembling a new barbecue grill or mountain bike we want clear, unambiguous instructions. Many advertisements, however, *deliberately* create ambiguity, conflating the product being advertised with another desirable image. For example, an advertisement for a television set that uses the caption "PLAY TIME" suggests vigorous physical activity, while in fact promoting an activity — watching televison — that is anything but physical or vigorous. The ambiguous use of the word *play* evokes both the physical activity and the programs that will play on the television itself. And the reader has little trouble understanding and synthesizing that ambiguity, indeed probably doesn't even notice it.

Although it is most clear to place a modifier either directly before or after the words it modifies, there are exceptions. For an example, see the sample sentences on *Handbook* p. 683. Sometimes, the writer's *emphasis* or *sense of rhythm* or *intention* determines the syntactic placement of the modifier in a sentence.

Misplaced modifiers usually lead to confusion, but sometimes they lead to amusing double entendres as well. Consider, for example, the following Associated Press description of England's Prince Andrew as "the son of Queen Elizabeth and a Royal Navy helicopter pilot." Whether deliberate (for effect) or inadvertent, these little beauties crop up from time to time. Several months later, the AP reported that Princess Anne was the daughter of Queen Elizabeth and a noted equestrian performer. A Florida newspaper reported that the "37-year-old daughter of Queen Elizabeth II and her horse finished fourth in the National Hunt at Hereford."

(41a–c)   **FOR TEACHING: REVISING MISPLACED, DISRUPTIVE, AND DANGLING MODIFIERS**

You may want to share the following examples of misplaced, disruptive, and dangling modifiers with your students:

1. Retrieving the duck, Kevin knew he could become a trainer.
2. I ate a hamburger wearing my tuxedo.
3. Soft and mushy, Albert baked a banana cake.
4. Big and noisy, Tom ran for his life away from the street gang.
5. Hanging from the telephone pole, Sally could not retrieve her kite.
6. Big after-Christmas shirt sale for men with sixteen necks.

You might also have students work in small groups to see if they can deliberately generate some funny or ludicrous examples of their own.

On Revising Dangling Modifiers   **(41c)** ....

We have not always been so strict about enforcing the incorrectness of dangling modifiers. In *Modern American Usage,* Wilson Follett points out that in the eighteenth century, any modifier was acceptable as long as it referred to a noun either present or implied in the sentence. Follett quotes from the *Old Farmer's Almanac:*

> Sheridan was once staying at the house of an elderly maiden lady who wanted more of his company than he was willing to give. Proposing, one day, to take a stroll with him, he excused himself on account of the badness of the weather. (117)

Follett tells us that "it was the maiden lady that did the proposing; she is present only in the preceding sentence, and only in a very subordinate construction. But the passage does not violate the canons of Sheridan's generation or the next." He goes on to explain that after around 1880, such constructions began to be cited as errors, as they are today. Nevertheless, experienced adult writers continue to use, and to get by with using, such constructions. Although "dangling" remains the most common label for these constructions, Follett believes it to be a misnomer, indicating an attachment that is not really there, and would have us use, instead, a word such as *adrift, unanchored, unmoored, unlinked, floating, disconnected, loose,* or *unattached.*

Cornelia and Bergen Evans tell us that the rule against the dangling modifer must sometimes be broken. In *A Dictionary of Contemporary American Usage,* they discuss two types of participial phrases that are exceptions. First of all, some participles are often used independently either as prepositions or conjunctions: *concerning, regarding, providing, owing to, excepting,* and *failing.* Frequently, an unattached participle is meant to apply indefinitely to anyone or everyone, as in *Facing north, there is a large mountain on the right* and *Looking at the subject dispassionately, what evidence is there?* Constructed any other way, these idiomatic statements would seem unnatural and cumbersome.

(41c)

TEACHING WITH TECHNOLOGY: REVISING DANGLING MODIFIERS

In your computer classroom, have students revise each of the following sentences to eliminate the dangler (1) by providing a subject that tells who or what is being modified, and (2) by rewording. (Sentence 3 is correct.)

1. Diving into the lake, Bev's head struck the raft.
2. To be considered for a teaching job, your references must be top-notch.
3. Listening to the CD, we forgot our worries.
4. Found guilty, the judge dismissed him.
5. At the age of two, my dad took me and my mom with him to Texas.

(41a–c)

FOR TEACHING: REVISING MODIFIERS

Ask students to revise the following passage to eliminate any misplaced, disruptive, or dangling modifiers.

One day last December, before going to class, a blizzard forced the administration to, for the first time anyone could remember, announce that all classes would be until further notice suspended. After leaving the dorm, the first thing that we noticed was the silence. The snow that had been falling all night steadily covered the ground. Being the last day of the semester, we weren't very worried about classes, so we "arranged," with another dormitory, a snowball fight. While building up a stock of good snowballs near Lord Hall, our jackets began to get oppressively warm. Eventually, we peeled down to shirt sleeves, ready for a fight. The central lawn became the battleground for the great Stoke-Lord Snowball Fight, where the Stoke Hall people finally set up their forts. Our piles of snowballs almost reached the tops of our forts, which were well-packed and handy to be picked up and thrown. At last both sides were ready, and the first snowball flew through the air from the "Stoke stack." The bombardment was for a while fierce and deadly. I learned that when throwing a snowball, the standing position is very risky, getting a hard one in the mouth. Finally, having almost thrown all of our snowballs, the Stoke charge was met and resisted. The timing was measured with great accuracy, being sure not to countercharge until we saw that Stoke was low on snowballs. Then we all ran toward the enemy carrying three or four snowballs each and routed them.

■ **USEFUL READINGS**

Evans, Cornelia, and Bergan Evans. *A Dictionary of Contemporary American Usage.* New York: Random, 1957. 354–55.

Follett, Wilson. *Modern American Usage.* New York: Hill, 1966.

Williams, Joseph M. *Style: Ten Lessons in Clarity and Grace.* 6th ed. New York: Addison-Wesley, 2002. See, especially, "Some Problems with Modifiers," where Williams discusses dangling and misplaced modifiers.

42 ⬇ Maintaining Consistent and Complete Grammatical Structures

In "The Uses — and Limits — of Grammar," Sarah D'Eloia explains "syntactically tangled sentences" as inconsistent and incomplete sentences that confuse the reader and that cannot be rhetorically justified in normal prose. Often these garbled sentences are the results of experiments in "logical and grammatical subordination, differential relation, and equivalence" (228), which students write for several reasons: (1) not knowing the "right" word or syntactic structure, the student may turn to the familiar (but inappropriate); (2) the student tries to juggle a number of subordinations at once; (3) unsure of the choice, the student may allow the alternatives to "contaminate" his or her decision; (4) the student lacks the academic self-confidence necessary to produce syntactically complex structures; (5) the student is unaware of the benefits that come with revision. Unfortunately, some of the most outgoing and sociable students lack confidence in academic situations: they do not believe their knowledge or opinions warrant development; their syntax is often tentative and qualifying. Worse, many of these students believe that "real" writers get it right the first time. When Mina Shaughnessy's writing students saw the messy pages of Richard Wright's novel *Native Son,* they concluded that Wright was not a good writer — he made too many mistakes.

If you ask students to listen carefully to the conversations around them, they will hear inconsistent and incomplete grammatical structures, particularly in lively or heated discussion. For instance:

> "The Bulls are . . . They must be the best team in . . . not in the league even . . . in the country."
>
> "Wait till the Jazz take them. Because you know Malone and Stockton, they make magic happen, in a SWEEP."

In the flow of informal conversation, such structures pose few problems for speakers and listeners. But they do pose problems for writers.

FOR COLLABORATIVE WORK: MAKING GRAMMATICAL PATTERNS CONSISTENT   **(42a)** ....

We want our students to be able to produce clear and consistent texts, yet we ask them to appreciate texts — canonized essays and stories — that often do not incorporate those same qualities. Critically acclaimed writer Toni Cade Bambara, for instance, frequently uses sentence structures that resist classroom standards. Ask your students to listen for purpose and effect as you read aloud the following passage from "My Man Bovanne," a story of a woman and a blind man at a benefit dance. Then ask them to work in groups to revise the passage according to standard academic English. Did they improve the text? interfere with it? What were the specific effects of their revisions?

> But right away Joe Lee come up on us and frown for dancin so close to the man. My own son who knows what kind of warm I am about; and don't grown men all call me long distance and in the middle of the night for a little Mama comfort? But he frown. Which ain't right since Bovanne can't see and defend himself. Just a nice old man who fixes toasters and busted irons . . . and changes the lock on my door when my men friends get messy. Nice man. Which is not why they invited him. Grass roots you see. Me and Sister Taylor and the woman who does heads at Mamies and the man from the barber shop, we all there on account of we grass roots. And I ain't never been souther than Brooklyn Battery and no more country than the window box on my fire escape. And just yesterday my kids tellin me to take them countrified rags off my head and be cool. And now can't get Black enough to suit 'em. So everybody passin saying My Man Bovanne. . . . And him standin there with a smile ready case someone do speak he want to be ready. So that's how come I pull him on the dance floor and we dance. . . .

On Making Subjects and Predicates Consistent   **(42b)** ....

The mismatch of the linking verb *be* and clauses opening with *when* or *because* is often termed *faulty predication*. Linking verbs of course link a subject with a subjective complement, which renames or modifies the subject: *Sports courtesy is maturity in fast action. Sports courtesy is important to team players.* When a student uses *when* after *is,* he or she introduces an adverbial element, which no longer renames or modifies the subject, but modifies the verb: *Sports courtesy is when players treat one another with fairness and consideration.*

One of the best explanations of *reason . . . is because* can be found in Wilson Follett's *Modern English Usage.* Follett tells us that when we make *reason* the subject of a sentence, we tend to substitute *because* for *that*. Such a switch "besides being a breach of idiom, is an obvious redundancy: *because = for the reason that*" (275). Hence, *the reason is because* paraphrases as *the reason is for the reason that*.

(42c) ## On Using Elliptical Structures Carefully

Elliptical structures omit certain *understood* words. For instance, when your students ask you when you plan to pass back their papers and you answer "Tomorrow," you have left out the understood words, "I will pass back your papers." And when you say to them, "If in doubt about the comments I've made on your papers, please see me," you've left out the understood information: "If *you are* in doubt." One student may say to another, "You'll probably get an A, but I won't (get an A)."

Although dependent on context, elliptical structures are the most convenient way to avoid repetition while providing conciseness and movement in speech and writing.

(42c) ### FOR TEACHING: USING ELLIPTICAL STRUCTURES CAREFULLY

To better acquaint your students with the concept of ellipsis, you may want to turn to George Curmé's *English Grammar*, which provides a list of different kinds of ellipses — the stylistic and syntactic omission of key words and phrases. Curmé explains the following kinds of omissions:

Clauses of comparison

That teacher cares for her students as a mother (cares for) her children.

Conditional sentences

She could easily win the contest (if she tried).

Clauses of exception

Nobody knew her except/but I (knew her).

Imperatives

Heads, eyes front. (Turn your heads and eyes to the front.)

Independent propositions

He cooks better than you do (better than you cook).

FOR TEACHING: MAKING COMPARISONS COMPLETE   **(42e)** ·······································

"Incomplete" comparisons are common in spoken discourse. In practice, *A person who drives drunk is more dangerous* will probably make sense to most of your students; context will supply the missing information, or your students will effortlessly fill in the missing information. Ask your students if they can create a context for the incomplete comparisons in section 42e of the *Handbook*.

■ **USEFUL READINGS**

Curmé, George. *English Grammar.* New York: Harper, 1947. See Curmé's coverage of the ellipsis.

D'Eloia, Sarah. "The Uses—and Limits—of Grammar." *Journal of Basic Writing* 1 (Spring/Summer 1977): 1–20.

Follett, Wilson. *Modern American Usage.* New York: Hill, 1966.

PART 8

SENTENCES: MAKING STYLISTIC CHOICES

43 ⬇️ Constructing Effective Sentences

*I had begun, at long last, in midlife, to love sentences, glorifying in those
I read in various genres and working hard to make some "comely and
muscular" ones of my own.*   – CYNTHIA OZICK

How do writers create effective sentences? One way is by carrying out what philosopher Kenneth Burke calls "the arousal and fulfillment of desire," his definition of "form." In "Lexicon Rhetoricae," Burke goes on to describe five verbal forms:

1. *Syllogistic progressive form,* whereby the reader is advanced (by the text) step by step in cause-and-effect fashion, as in a mystery story;

2. *Qualitative progressive form,* whereby the reader connects one quality to an earlier quality; the reader recognizes the rightness of one event to follow another, as in the death of Juliet after Romeo;

3. *Repetitive form,* which involves the restatement of a theme with new details, as in the exemplifications of size discrepancy in *Gulliver's Travels;*

4. *Conventional form,* whose appeal is that of form *per se,* as in a sestina, a sonnet;

5. *Minor form,* which involves the natural appeal of the various figures of speech, such as metaphor, simile, synecdoche.

Any form at whatever level of discourse, from the phrase and the sentence to the paragraph and the entire work, may inhabit any of these types. A writer may purposely suggest fulfillment of any of these formal appeals and then surprise the reader—by denying it.

Substituting the more mundane *expectations* for Burke's provocative term *desire* can illustrate better to students just what he means in terms of the sentence: an effective sentence is one that creates or appeals to certain expectations and then fulfills them — or startles, amuses, or alarms readers by *not* fulfilling them. Here is one good example:

> I sometimes think of the reader as a cat, endlessly fastidious, capable, by turns, of mordant indifference and riveted attention, luxurious, recumbent, and ever poised.   – PATRICIA HAMPL, "Memory and Imagination"

This sentence fulfills expectations by following up on the image of the reader as cat with words such as "fastidious" and "luxurious." In addition, the sentence is structured so as to pull readers along, saving its most powerful cat-like image for the end: "ever poised."

On the other hand, the following sentence aims to surprise readers by *breaking* expectations:

> He was a tall, dark, handsome creep.

On the Definition of *Sentence*

What is a sentence? In *A Dictionary of Modern English Usage,* H. W. Fowler claims that modern writers "show greater freedom than was once customary" and that the word *sentence* has "broken the bounds" once set for it (546). He lists ten definitions for *sentence,* the first seven "popular," the eighth and ninth grammatical, and the tenth a combination of the two.

1. A group of words followed by a pause and revealing an intelligible purpose.
2. A group of words which makes sense.
3. A combination of words which is complete as expressing a thought.
4. A collection of words of such kind and arranged in such manner as to make complete sense.
5. A meaningful group of words that is grammatically independent.
6. A complete and independent unit of communication, the completeness and independence being shown by its capability of standing alone, i.e., of being uttered by itself.
7. A group of words, or in some cases a single word, which makes a statement, or a command (or expression of wish), or a question or an exclamation.
8. A number of words making a complete grammatical structure.
9. A combination of words that contains at least one subject and one predicate.

10. A set of words complete in itself, having either expressed or understood in it a subject or question or command or exclamation; if its subject or predicate or verb (or more) is understood, it is an elliptical sentence.

FOR TEACHING: CONSTRUCTING EFFECTIVE SENTENCES BY IMITATION

Ask students to try their hand at imitating Hampl's sentence on p. 349 and to bring their imitations to class. Then duplicate some or all of them, read them aloud, and use them to stimulate class discussion of and appreciation for powerfully constructed sentences. You might also wish to ask students to match the imitations to the models, clause for clause, phrase for phrase, as a means of identifying structural elements in sentences.

(43a)   **FOR TEACHING: EMPHASIZING MAIN IDEAS**

Use Burke's theory of form in the classroom and ask your students to generate examples of each type. Not all of their examples will come from books or stories; some may come from movies, television programs, or music videos, compelling examples that will help the entire class understand. However, make sure that each example emphasizes a main idea.

(43a2)   **FOR COLLABORATIVE WORK: USING CLIMACTIC ORDER**

To demonstrate climactic order, ask your class to suggest a topic (such as the qualities of a good friend, a good car, or a popular campus restaurant). Brainstorm the topic, creating a list of associations on the board. Then ask students to write a one-sentence statement summarizing their ideas about the topic. Ask students to read their statements and comment on possible reasons for ordering their subtopics the way they did. You may want to take this opportunity to point out that climactic order reflects the relative importance the writer attaches to ideas.

(43a2)   **FOR TEACHING: USING CLIMACTIC ORDER**

Ask students to imitate the climactic form of the *Handbook* example: *Soap operas offend our ears, assault our eyes, and damage our brains.* Then after reading aloud the following sentences and examining their climactic order, ask students to write imitations.

1. I have in my own life a precious friend, a woman of 65 who has lived very hard, who is wise, who listens well, who has been where I am and can help me understand it; and who represents not only an ultimate ideal mother to me but also the person I'd like to be when I grow up.   –Judith Viorst

2. To assign unanswered letters their proper weight, to free us from the expectations of others, to give us back to ourselves — here lies the great, the singular power of self-respect.   –Joan Didion

3. She loved the flat, she loved her life, she loved Herbie.   –Dorothy Parker

4. I came, I saw, I conquered.   –Julius Caesar

FOR TEACHING: BEING CONCISE   **(43b)**

To demonstrate that being concise may not always be preferable, discuss with your class the opening paragraph of Charles Dickens's *A Tale of Two Cities,* followed by a revision by someone using the style-and-diction-checking computer program Workbench. Read both versions aloud, and then get the class to decide which makes a more effective opening for the novel.

It was the best of times, it was the worst of times, it was the age of wisdom, it was the age of foolishness, it was the epoch of belief, it was the epoch of incredulity, it was the season of Light, it was the season of Darkness, it was the spring of hope, it was the winter of despair, we had everything before us, we had nothing before us, we were all going direct to Heaven, we were all going direct the other way — in short, the period was so far like the present period, that some of its noisiest authorities insisted on being received, for good or for evil, in the superlative degree of comparison only.   –Charles Dickens

He can compress the most words into the smallest ideas of any man I ever met.
– Abraham Lincoln

The times were the best and worst, wise and foolish. The era was one of belief and disbelief, light and darkness, hope and despair. Before us lay everything and nothing. We were all going direct to heaven or straight to hell. The period was so much like today that its loudest critics could describe it only in superlatives.   –Workbench

If you would be pungent, be brief.
– Southey

FOR TEACHING: SIMPLIFYING SENTENCE STRUCTURE   **(43b4)**

Read aloud the following paragraph from a mystery novel by Amanda Cross (the heroine, Kate Fansler, is mapping out her mystery-solving

plan), and then ask your students to revise it using the simplest grammatical structures. Finally, ask them to compare versions and to decide
which ones they like best and why.

> She felt, nonetheless, as she stood indecisively in the hall, like a knight who has
> set off to slay the dragon but has neglected to ask in what part of the world the
> dragon may be found. It was all very well to decide upon action, but what ac-
> tion, after all, was she to take? As was her habit, she extracted notebook and
> pen and began to make a list: see Janet Harrison's room, and talk to people who
> knew her in dormitory; find out about ten and twelve o'clock patients; find out
> who person in picture Janet Harrison had was (lists always had a devastating
> effect on Kate's syntax).   – Amanda Cross, *In the Last Analysis*

FOR COLLABORATIVE WORK: REVISING SENTENCES

Ask students to work in small groups to read over Emily Lesk's essay in 3f,
paying attention to the sentences. Then have them choose a paragraph
and evaluate its sentences in terms of emphasis and conciseness. Ask them
to try to find a paragraph that they think might be made more emphatic
or more concise and to revise accordingly. Finally, have each group report its findings to the whole class.

■ USEFUL READINGS

Burke, Kenneth. "Lexicon Rhetoricae." *Counter-Statement*. 1931. Berkeley: U of Cal-
    ifornia P, 1968. 123–83. Burke explores the appeal to the reader of various cat-
    egories of forms.

Connors, Robert J. "The Erasure of the Sentence." *CCC* 52.1 (Sept. 2000): 96–128.
    Connors traces the history of sentence rhetorics, showing composition stud-
    ies as a subfield of English and arguing that prior to 1980 studies indicate
    that sentence rhetorics were effective in producing "mature" writing. We have
    lost that benefit as a result of English theoretical perspectives on composition
    pedagogies.

Fowler, H. W. *A Dictionary of Modern English Usage*. 2nd ed. Rev. and ed. Sir Ernest
    Gowers. New York: Oxford UP, 1965.

Laib, Nevin. "Conciseness and Amplification." *CCC* 41 (1990): 443–59. Laib argues
    that carried to excess, conciseness can lead to "bluntness, opacity, and under-
    development" and suggests that teachers of writing should encourage "pro-
    fuseness" as well. According to Laib, "Elegant variation is an essential art of de-
    velopment, emphasis, and explanation."

Lanham, Richard. *Style: An Anti-Textbook.* New Haven: Yale UP, 1977. Lanham argues for the teaching of style, not of clarity. He writes that "instruction in composition builds on a single premise — clarity — and that premise is false."

Williams, Joseph M. *Style: Ten Lessons in Clarity and Grace.* 6th ed. New York: Addison-Wesley, 2001. In "Managing Endings for Emphasis," Williams demonstrates ways of shifting emphasis to the end of sentences; in Lesson Ten he offers advice on how to achieve elegant structures.

44 ▼ Creating Coordinate and Subordinate Structures

It is when I struggle to be brief that I become obscure.

– HORACE

Current pedagogical theory — and popular lore — tends to value clarity and conciseness. Yet, composition researchers tell us that complex sentences indicate a writer's syntactic maturity. Are we sending our students mixed messages, then? No. The two concepts are not necessarily contradictory: beginning writers often need practice in clarity and conciseness to make meaning; more mature writers can use those same qualities to grace more complex sentence structures.

The notion that subordination and complex sentence structures indicate sophistication of thought and language ability, or maturity in the writer, needs some qualification, if only historical. In Old and Middle English, subordination was not expected, nor was it used to measure a writer's skill. In *Classical Rhetoric for the Modern Student*, Edward P. J. Corbett tells us that "the history of the prose style of most Western languages reveals a gradual evolution from a paratactic syntax — stringing together a series of coordinate structures without conjunctions — to the most sophisticated of sentence patterns, subordination."

In *Teaching English Grammar*, Robert C. Pooley cites passages from the King James Version (KJV) of the Bible as examples of the predominance of coordination over subordination in earlier English, but without acknowledging that that particular translation reflects the sentence structure of the original Hebrew, not English. John B. Gabel and Charles B. Wheeler tell us that "in general [Hebrew] lacks our great variety of words that indicate logical connections between clauses and phrases. In Hebrew, sentence units tend to string out one after another in boxcar fashion and to be hooked together by means of a single, all-purpose connective that is usually translated 'and' in the KJV" (*The Bible as Literature: An Introduction*

[New York: Oxford UP, 1986]). For example, Genesis 19:1–3 repeats the connective seventeen times in Hebrew: in the KJV, it appears as "and" sixteen of those times.

> (1) And there came two angels to Sodom at even; and Lot sat in the gate of Sodom: and Lot seeing *them* rose up to meet them; and he bowed himself with his face toward the ground; (2) And he said, Behold now, my lords, turn in, I pray you, into your servant's house, and tarry all night, and wash your feet, and ye shall rise up early, and go on your ways. And they said, Nay; but we will abide in the street all night. (3) And he pressed upon them greatly; and they turned in unto him, and entered into his house; and he made them a feast, and did bake unleavened bread, and they did eat.

On *Parataxis* and *Hypotaxis*

Parataxis is Greek for "placing side by side." Paratactic clauses, phrases, or sentences are arranged independently (a coordinate, rather than a subordinate construction), often without the customary connectives. In the following passage from *A Farewell to Arms,* Ernest Hemingway leaves the causal connections up to the reader:

> There were wet dead leaves on the road from the rows of bare trees and men were working on the road, tamping stone in the ruts from piles of crushed stone along the side of the road between the trees.

Although many beginning writers use parataxis, few use it with Hemingway's skill. Hence, their prose, which balances overtly equal relationships, often elicits simple, spliced, or fused sentences.

Hypotaxis is Greek for "subjection." Hypotactic prose makes clear the dependent or subordinate relationships. In "Travail," H. L. Mencken makes clear causal and logical relationships:

> It is no wonder that schoolboys so often turn for stimulus from their teachers to their fellows. The fact, I believe, is largely to blame for the juvenile lawlessness that prevails in America, for it is the relatively daring and lawless boys who stand out from the mass, and so attract their weaker brethren. . . . On the female side they have the instincts of duennas, and on the male side they seldom rise above the levels of scoutmasters and Y.M.C.A. secretaries.

Students who write in paratactic style (and who are writing comma splices and fused sentences) are often thinking in hypotactic style. Ask them to make their connections aloud.

(44a)

FOR TEACHING: USING COORDINATION

Students tend to have little problem understanding coordination, dependent as many are on a few all-purpose connectors such as *and* or *but*. Because some students overuse coordination, you may want to emphasize their striking a balance among coordinated, subordinated, and simple constructions.

In *Style: Ten Lessons in Clarity and Grace,* Joseph Williams cites another problem connected with coordination: lost connections. When the grammatical coordination of a sentence becomes too long, the reader cannot follow its internal connections. He uses the following sentence as an example:

> "Teachers should remember that students are vulnerable people, insecure and uncertain about those everyday, ego-bruising moments that adults ignore, *and that they do not understand that one day they* will become as confident and as secure as the adults that bruise them." (194)

According to Williams, placement of that italic clause is troublesome because it is not close enough to its source of coordination. And he offers two possible revisions: repetition of a key phrase or starting a new sentence. "Every teacher ought to *remind* himself daily that his students are vulnerable people, . . . and to *remind himself* that his students do not understand . . ." or ". . . adults no longer concern themselves with. Teachers should remind themselves that their students do not understand." Note that the second revision uses nonsexist language.

(44a)

FOR COLLABORATIVE WORK: USING COORDINATION

Ask students to break into their groups and identify the coordinate elements of the following passage, taken from Joyce Carol Oates's *Black Water.* What is the effect of the coordinate elements? Each group might want to rewrite the passage, using subordination to create a different effect — from the point of view, perhaps, of the driver of the car, who had escaped watery death.

> He was her friend. He was no one she knew but he was her friend, *that* she knew. In another minute she would remember his name.
>
> It was a car that had trapped her, she was jammed somehow in the front seat of a car but the space was very small because the roof and the dashboard and the door beside her had buckled inward pinning her legs and crushing her

right kneecap held as if in a vise and her ribs on that side were broken but the pain seemed to be held in suspension like a thought not yet fully acknowledged scarcely any sensation at all so she knew she would be all right so long as she could lift her head free of the seeping black water that smelled of raw sewage and was cold, colder than you could imagine on such a warm midsummer night.

FOR TEACHING: USING COORDINATION FOR SPECIAL EFFECT

(44a)

Consider sharing the following excerpt from William Gass's *Habitations of the Word* to demonstrate how the coordinating conjunction *and* can be used for special effect:

"Ands"

are most essential for excess. They are perfect if you want to make big piles or imply an endless addition. One "and" may make a tidy pair, closing a couple like a lock: *War and Peace,* ham and eggs, *Pride and Prejudice.* Add another, however, and the third "and" will begin to alter the earlier ones the same miraculous way the squashed and flattened condition designated by "mashed" is lent the fully contrasting sense of "heaped" simply by putting it near the word "potato." No one is any better at this energetic mounding than the Dickens of *Dombey.* Here is part of a long passage describing the ruination of a neighborhood by some new-laid railroad tracks. It implies he is not telling us the half of it:

> There were frowzy fields, and cow-houses, and dunghills, and dust-heaps, and ditches, and gardens, and summerhouses, and carpet-bearing grounds, at the very door of the railway. Little tumuli of oyster shells in the oyster season, and of lobster shells in the lobster season, and of broken crockery and faded cabbage in all seasons, encroached upon its high places. Posts, and rails, and old cautions to trespassers, and backs of mean houses, and patches of wretched vegetation, stared it out of countenance.

On Using Subordination

(44b)

In *Errors and Expectations,* Mina Shaughnessy describes subordination in terms of the demands it makes on the student writer:

> If the dependent unit comes first in the sentence, the writer must suspend the independent unit in his mind while he qualifies it (as with introductory adverbial phrases and clauses). If the dependent unit comes between the subject and predicate of the base sentence (as with a relative clause after the subject), the writer must hold the main subject in his mind while he writes out the subject

and predicate of the qualifying clause, and then he must return to the predicate of the base sentence. These operations require a memory for written words and grammatical structures that the inexperienced writer may not have. He hears what he says easily enough, but he does not as easily recall what he has written once his hand has moved on to another part of the sentence, and unlike the experienced writer, he is not in the habit of reviewing what he has written but instead moves headlong, as a speaker might, toward the open line, often forgetting the constraints he has set for himself a few words back.

Students react to these demands in different ways, of course. Some will shy away from the complexity and rely as much as possible on simple and compound structures. Others, motivated by a perceived need to write academic-sounding discourse, will produce what Shaughnessy calls "ruptured" or garbled sentences. Shaughnessy offers several options for the instructor: drills and grammatical explanations, sentence-combining exercises, and other types of exercises. But she concludes that the most improvement may occur when the student commits herself to communicating with her reader, despite "the exasperating literalism of the medium" (89).

Traditionally, instructors have assumed that grammar reflected logical thinking — that use of subordination should include subordinate ideas, with the most important ideas going in the main clause, and that coordination juxtaposed two ideas of equal rank. Linguists, however, hold that grammar is not necessarily logical. In "Coordination (Faulty) and Subordination (Upside Down)," James Sledd writes that "the traditional theory of clauses is simply untenable." Subordinate ideas can and often do show up in main clauses, and main ideas can appear in subordinate clauses, as in the opening sentence of this note.

(44b)

FOR TEACHING: USING SUBORDINATION TO DISTINGUISH MAIN IDEAS

Have your students combine each of the following sets of sentences into one sentence that uses subordination to signal the relationships among ideas. Here is an example:

I was looking over my books.

I noticed that *Burr* was missing.

This book is a favorite of my roommate's.

While I was looking over my books, I noticed that *Burr,* one of my roommate's favorite books, was missing.

1. I walked into the shelter.

   Men, women, and children were slumped against the wall.

   Shopping carts containing families' belongings lay on their sides.

2. Barbra Streisand announced her first concert tour in years.

   Ticket sales were advertised.

   Fans lined up as many as forty-eight hours in advance.

3. We had dug a seventy-foot ditch.

   My boss would pour gravel into the ditch.

   I would level the gravel with a shovel.

4. *Working* was written by Studs Terkel.

   It is an important book.

   It examines the situation of the American worker.

5. The scenery there is beautiful.

   The mountains have caps of snow.

   The lakes are deep and full of fish.

   The pastures are green.

   It is an ideal spot to spend spring break.

Answers

1. Walking into the shelter, I saw men, women, and children slumped against the wall, their belongings lying in overturned shopping carts.

2. When ticket sales were advertised for Barbra Streisand's first concert tour in years, fans lined up as many as forty-eight hours in advance.

3. After my boss poured gravel into the seventy-foot-long ditch we had dug, I leveled the gravel with a shovel.

4. *Working*, an important book by Studs Terkel, examines the situation of the American worker.

5. The snow-capped mountains, green pastures, and deep, fish-filled lakes make the park a beautiful and ideal spot to spend spring break.

FOR COLLABORATIVE WORK: USING SUBORDINATION **(44b)**

Ask students to use the analysis from "Thinking about Your Own Use of Coordination and Subordination" (on *Handbook* p. 712) as the basis for a peer-group discussion of (1) what they have learned about their own use of subordination and coordination, and (2) what plans or goals they have for using the two syntactic structures more effectively.

■ USEFUL READINGS

Corbett, Edward P. J. *Classical Rhetoric for the Modern Student.* 4th ed. New York: Oxford UP, 1999.

Lanham, Richard A. *Analyzing Prose.* 2nd ed. New York: Continuum, 2002. Lanham attacks the dominant theory of prose style, which values clarity, brevity, and sincerity. Instead, he calls for the use of a variety of different styles, depending on the desired rhetorical effects.

Pooley, Robert C. *Teaching English Grammar.* New York: Appleton-Century-Crofts, 1957.

Shaughnessy, Mina. *Errors and Expectations.* New York: Oxford, 1977.

Sledd, James. "Coordination (Faulty) and Subordination (Upside Down)." CCC 7 (1956): 181–87.

Traugott, Elizabeth Closs, and Mary Louise Pratt. *Linguistics for Students of Literature.* San Diego: Harcourt, 1980. See "Recursive Property of Language" for a transformational-linguistics perspective on coordination and subordination. Traugott and Pratt call subordination and coordination "linguistic creativity," or the ability to create complex sentences out of simple sentences by applying the generative principles of "recursiveness" (154–55).

Williams, Joseph M. *Style: Ten Lessons in Clarity and Grace.* 6th ed. New York: Addison-Wesley, 2002. Williams offers advice for the control of "sprawling" sentences, the result of a main clause connected to too many subordinate clauses.

Winterowd, Ross. "The Grammar of Coherence." CE 31 (1970): 328–35. Transformational grammar does not fully explain the coherence of units of discourse. Seven transitional relations account for coherence: coordinate expressed (*and*); obversive (*but*); causative (*for*); conclusive (*so*); alternative (*or*); inclusive (the colon); and sequential (*first . . . second*).

45

Creating and Maintaining Parallel Structures

All successful rhetoricians recognize the power of parallel structures. The rhetorician Gorgias (c. 420 B.C.E.) was noted for his use of parallelism and antithesis. In his encomium (a formal expression of enthusiastic praise) to Helen, he declares:

> Speech is a powerful lord which by means of the finest and most invisible body effects the divinest words: it can stop fear and banish grief and create joy and nurture piety.

By contemporary standards, Gorgias's style is considered artificial and contrived — partially because of what we perceive as excessive parallelism.

In spite of the modern tendency to dislike excessive ornamentation of any kind, the appeal of parallel structures may be inherent in human psychology, or so argues Richard L. Graves in "Symmetrical Form and the Rhetoric of the Sentence." Graves notes that symmetry is everywhere — from our own physiology and self-expression to our art and architecture. Kenneth Burke, too, suggests that the concept of symmetry may be one of "the innate forms of the mind," along with comparison/contrast and repetition (46).

Echoing tradition, Joseph Williams notes received wisdom: coordinate elements only of the same grammatical structure — clause and clause, predicate and predicate, prepositional phrase and prepositional phrase. Yet Williams concedes that the rule is often broken, on the grounds that clarity — not grammatical structure — measures the success or failure of parallel structures. Parallelism involves more than initially meets the eye. For instance, instead of looking at *She is tall, tanned, and very handsome* as a set of parallel adjectives, we might regard it as a combination of three separate but parallel sentences: *She is tall. She is tanned. She is very handsome.*

In combining these sentences, the writer suppresses the repeated subject-verb cluster *She is,* expecting the reader to provide it mentally. When students see the source of parallel structures, they become more sensitive to their own parallel constructions.

(45a–b)   **FOR TEACHING: USING PARALLEL STRUCTURES**

The following examples of parallel structures can be used to supplement those in the text:

> Why is second base so important? Because when an easy grounder or a high pop-up is hit to that position, and you kick it away, or misjudge it and let it bounce on your head, the whole team gets demoralized. The shortstop comes over and says, Too bad the school bus didn't clip you this morning. The first baseman slaps his leg and laughs. The pitcher gives you the finger in front of everybody.   – LAURENCE SHEEHAN, "How to Play Second Base"

> The dog has got more fun out of Man than Man has got out of the dog, for the clearly demonstrable reason that Man is the more laughable of the two animals. The dog has long been bemused by the singular activities and the curious practices of men, cocking his head inquiringly to one side, intently watching and listening to the strangest goings-on in the world. He has seen men sing together and fight one another in the same evening. He has watched them go to bed when it is time to get up, and get up when it is time to go to bed. He has observed them destroying the soil in vast areas, and nurturing it in small patches. He has stood by while men built strong and solid houses for rest and quiet, and then filled them with lights and bells and machinery. His sensitive nose, which can detect what's cooking in the next township, has caught at one and the same time the bewildering smells of the hospital and the munitions factory. He has seen men raise up great cities to heaven and then blow them to hell.   – JAMES THURBER, "A Dog's Eye View of Man"

As an additional example, ask students to consider the following passage. Read it aloud, and ask students to try to identify the parallel structures.

> Let the word go forth from this time and place, to friend and foe alike, that the torch has been passed to a new generation of Americans — born in this century, tempered by war, disciplined by a hard and bitter peace, proud of our ancient heritage — and unwilling to witness or permit the slow undoing of those human rights to which this nation has always been committed, and to which we are committed today at home and around the world.   – JOHN F. KENNEDY, Inaugural Address

What is the aural effect of the parallelism? Help your students break down each sentence into its root sentences, so they can see how beautifully those sentences are combined.

TEACHING WITH TECHNOLOGY: USING PARALLEL STRUCTURES   (45a–b)

Have your students post a comment to your online discussion board concerning their analysis of the Kennedy passage. Then use the log entries as the basis for class discussion.

FOR COLLABORATIVE WORK: USING PARALLEL STRUCTURES WITH PAIRS   (45b)

Songwriters, like poets and other professional users of language, become exceptionally aware of the effects of parallelism (and of many other stylistic devices). In fact, a look at the songs from any generation will provide you with examples of parallelism. You might consider sending your students out to find examples of various types of parallel structures that appear in pairs. Have them look at essays, novels, poems, songs, jingles, advertisements, and lectures. Then use their findings for class discussion and for practice in creating parallel structures of their own.

FOR TEACHING: USING PARALLEL STRUCTURES FOR EFFECT—*CHIASMUS*   (45d)

The following sentence exemplifies *chiasmus,* the device in which the elements of a first clause, phrase, or sentence are inverted in the second clause, phrase, or sentence:

Humankind must put an end to war, or war will put an end to humankind.

Used sparingly, this rhetorical flourish is effective. When such rhetorical/poetic techniques are taught, they can be introduced as a form of style. Teaching these techniques is related to the teaching of schemes and tropes, so popular in classical rhetoric. Other famous examples of *chiasmus* include the following:

Ask not what your country can do for you, but what you can do for your country.   – JOHN F. KENNEDY

Let us never negotiate out of fear. But let us never fear to negotiate.   – JOHN F. KENNEDY

FOR TEACHING: IMITATION OF PARALLEL STRUCTURES

In preparation for a class discussion, ask students to bring to class their imitations *and* their revisions of their own paragraphs from "Thinking about Your Own Use of Parallelism" (*Handbook* p. 718). Then divide the imitations and revisions into groups of five and ask students to work in groups to choose the one or two *most effective* uses of parallelism and to be prepared to report the reasons for their decisions to the rest of the class.

■ **USEFUL READINGS**

Burke, Kenneth. "The Poetic Process." *Counter Statement.* 1931. Berkeley: U of California P, 1968.

Graves, Richard L. "Symmetrical Form and the Rhetoric of the Sentence." *Essays on Classical Rhetoric and Modern Discourse.* Ed. Robert J. Connors, Lisa S. Ede, and Andrea A. Lunsford. Carbondale: Southern Illinois UP, 1984. 170–78. Graves identifies four major categories of parallelism: the repetition of key words, the use of opposite words (antithesis), repetition of grammatical elements, and various combinations of these three categories.

Lindemann, Erika, and Daniel Anderson. *A Rhetoric for Writing Teachers.* 4th ed. New York: Oxford UP, 2001. See chapter 10 on teaching sentences, especially the discussion of sentence combining, background for understanding syntactic parallelism, repetition, and reduction.

46 Varying Sentence Structures

All my books literally come to me in the form of a sentence, an original sentence which contains the entire book. — RAYMOND FEDERMAN

Gifted writer, journalist, and literary, social, and political critic, H. L. Mencken rarely limited his reviews to content: he enjoyed immensely writing reviews of style as well. In 1921, Mencken wrote a column on former newspaper editor Warren G. Harding, making clear that not even the president of the United States was safe from Mencken's iconoclastic sensibilities. Using the simplest of sentences and sustained repetition, Mencken writes a powerful and memorable review of Harding's style:

> He writes the worst English that I have ever encountered. It reminds me of a string of wet sponges; it reminds me of tattered washing on the line; it reminds me of stale bean soup, of college yells, of dogs barking idiotically through endless nights. It is so bad that a sort of grandeur creeps into it. It drags itself out of the dark abyss of pish, and crawls insanely up to the topmost pinnacle of posh. It is rumble and bumble. It is flap and doodle. It is balder and dash.

Student writers can take a cue from Mencken, trying their hands at a sustained insult—all in good fun, though!

On Varying Sentence Structures

Several techniques have been developed to help teach students to vary sentence structures, with sentence combining being perhaps the most well known and thoroughly studied. A lesser-known technique is Richard Larson's strategy of writing an essay on the board or overhead over several days, correcting and talking about the stylistic choices he makes as he writes. A third way to draw students' attention to varying sentence structures is Edward P. J. Corbett's method of stylistic analysis.

Whatever method you choose, remember that stylistic choices about sentence structures depend upon the larger context of each individual sentence, the intended audience, and the purpose for writing.

(46a)

FOR TEACHING: VARYING SENTENCE LENGTH

Very short "capsule" reviews usually contain varied sentence structures, perhaps to keep readers' attention with a snappy, fast-paced description. A *Newsweek* column included the following brief review:

> *Thelma & Louise* looks like an *Easy Rider* for women. A good idea. But this isn't going to have men lining up in droves or cheering for more.

The writer of this review varies sentence length by using a three-word fragment between two longer sentences and varies openings as well, beginning one sentence not with the subject but with *but*. This variety helps make the brief synopsis easy to read and remember.

Ask students to study some "capsule" reviews in a magazine or newspaper (or on television), noting the variety of sentences used and bringing a few examples to class to compare with those found by classmates. Together, try to draw conclusions about the effect of sentence variety on readers.

(46a)

FOR COLLABORATIVE WORK: VARYING SENTENCE LENGTH

Distribute the following paragraph. Ask half of your students to recast the information in the passage into a series of long sentences. Ask the other half to recast it into a string of short sentences. How do they compare? Reading the revisions aloud will help students "see" the difference.

> As I said this I suddenly beheld the figure of a man, at some distance, advancing towards me with superhuman speed. He bounded over the crevices in the ice, among which I had walked with caution; his stature, also, as he approached, seemed to exceed that of a man. I was troubled; a mist came over my eyes, and I felt a faintness seize me; but I was quickly restored by the cold gale of the mountains. I perceived, as the shape came nearer (sight tremendous and abhorred!) that it was the wretch whom I had created. I trembled with rage and horror, resolving to wait his approach and then close with him in mortal combat. He approached; his countenance bespoke bitter anguish, combined with disdain and malignity, while its unearthly ugliness rendered it almost

too horrible for human eyes. But I scarcely observed this; rage and hatred had at first deprived me of utterance, and I recovered only to overwhelm him with words expressive of furious detestation and contempt.

– MARY SHELLEY, Frankenstein

FOR COLLABORATIVE WORK: VARYING SENTENCE LENGTH   **(46a)**

Have students, working in pairs or in groups of three, choose a topic of interest to all the members and then write passages of at least twenty-five short sentences (shorter than twelve words). After they have traded passages with another group or pair, ask each group to combine some of the twenty-five sentences into longer sentences, while retaining some short sentences for emphasis.

Naturally, each group will combine sentences differently, so you might want to take an opportunity to explain their choices and reasons for combining some sentences while keeping others short.

TEACHING WITH TECHNOLOGY: VARYING SENTENCE LENGTH   **(46a)**

Consider the following paragraphs that include both long and short sentences used effectively. After your students have identified the variety of sentences according to length and type, ask them to post to your online discussion group an imitation of these paragraphs on a topic of their own, such as participating in sports, giving birth, winning an award, or attending a concert. Then ask them to respond to two or three other posts and comment on the variations in sentence length. You can also select several posts to project up on a computer screen for collaborative review and discussion.

> Champion of the world. A Black boy. Some Black mother's son. He was the strongest man in the world. People drank Coca-Colas like ambrosia and ate candy bars like Christmas. Some of the men went behind the Store and poured white lightning in their soft-drink bottles, and a few of the bigger boys followed them. Those who were not chased away came back blowing their breath in front of themselves like proud smokers.
>
> It would take an hour or more before the people would leave the Store and head for home. Those who lived too far had made arrangements to stay in town. It wouldn't do for a Black man and his family to be caught on a lonely country road on a night when Joe Louis had proved that we were the strongest people in the world.   – MAYA ANGELOU, "Champion of the World"

(46b)

On Varying Sentence Openings

In *Classical Rhetoric for the Modern Student,* Edward P. J. Corbett lists eleven sentence openers—all of which any beginning writer can learn to use in effective combination.

1. Subject—*John* broke the window. *The high cost* of living will offset . . .
2. Expletives—*It* is plain that . . . *There* are ten Indians. Exclamations: *Alas, Oh*
3. Coordinating conjunction—*And, But, Or, Nor, For, Yet, So*
4. Adverb word—*First, Thus, Moreover, Nevertheless, Namely*
5. Conjunctive phrase—*On the other hand, As a consequence*
6. Prepositional phrase—*After the game, In the morning*
7. Verbal phrase—participial, gerundive, or infinitive phrase
8. Adjective phrase—*Tired but happy, we* . . .
9. Absolute phrase—*The ship having arrived, we* . . .
10. Adverb clause—*When the ship arrived, we* . . .
11. Front-shift (inverted word order)—*That expense we could not bear. Gone was the wind. Happy were they to be alive.*

(46b)

FOR TEACHING: VARYING SENTENCE OPENINGS

Consider sharing with your students the following passage. Point out to them the ways Rodriguez varies his sentence openers, including his use of dependent clauses.

> Three months passed. Five. A half year. Unsmiling, ever watchful, my teachers noted my silence. They began to connect my behavior with the slow progress my brother and sisters were making. Until, one Saturday morning, three nuns arrived at the house to talk to our parents. Stiffly they sat on the blue living-room sofa. From the doorway of another room, spying on the visitors, I noticed the incongruity, the clash of two worlds, the faces and voices of school intruding upon the familiar setting of home. I overheard one voice gently wondering, "Do your children speak only Spanish at home, Mrs. Rodriguez?" While another voice added, "That Richard especially seems so timid and shy."
>
> – RICHARD RODRIGUEZ, "Aria: A Memoir
> of a Bilingual Childhood"

FOR COLLABORATIVE WORK: SENTENCE OPENINGS AND DEPENDENT CLAUSES   **(46b)**

Ask your students to exchange their latest piece of writing in a peer-review group, and analyze all the declarative sentences according to sentence openers. How many (and what percentage of) sentences begin with one of the eleven options in the preceding list? Students may want to analyze a professional essay as well and then compare their results.

FOR TEACHING: SENTENCE OPENINGS AND DEPENDENT CLAUSES   **(46b3)**

Some students have considerable trouble punctuating dependent clauses, especially introductory dependent clauses. They often turn them into sentence fragments by separating them from the main clause with a period. Outlined here is one possible method for helping students overcome this problem.

> I worked all summer at the car dealership. Although I really wanted to go to baseball camp.

1. You may want to point out the problem in meaning for the reader — the false or due expectation. (Coming after a period, the *Although I really wanted* clause makes us think that another sentence is coming.)

2. Then ask students to supply an alternative, relying on their competence to provide a solution. (They may want to erase the period and make the *A* of *Although* a lowercase letter. Or they may add more information to the *Although* clause: *Although I really wanted to go to baseball camp, I needed to earn money, not spend it.*)

3. You can use this opportunity to suggest other alternatives that clarify or reiterate the meaning conveyed by the kernel sentence ([1] *Although I really wanted to go to baseball camp, I worked all summer at the car dealership.* [2] *I worked all summer at the car dealership although I really wanted to go to baseball camp instead.* [3] *I worked all summer at the car dealership. Although I really wanted to go to baseball camp, I needed to earn money, not spend it.*)

FOR TEACHING: VARYING SENTENCE TYPES   **(46c)**

For quick reference, here are examples of each of the four grammatical types:

Simple

Later, Susan arrived.

Compound

People tried to reassure me, but they could not understand my fear.

Complex

While we walked over to the picnic, we talked about the problem of being roommates.

Compound-complex

I told her about the courses I enjoyed most, and she told me about her current reading, including *The Sheep Look Up.*

(46c1)   **FOR TEACHING: VARYING SENTENCES BY GRAMMATICAL TYPES**

Consider using Edward P. J. Corbett's system from *Classical Rhetoric for the Modern Student* for studying the grammatical types of sentences that students use. First, make sure that your students can name and distinguish between different kinds of grammatical sentences. Next, consider using the following chart to ask them to compare their own writing with a professional example of the same type or perhaps with another student's in the class. Finally, discuss the results as a class.

1. Total number of sentences in essay:
2. Total number of simple sentences:
3. Percentage of simple sentences:
4. Total number of compound sentences:
5. Percentage of compound sentences:
6. Total number of complex sentences:
7. Percentage of complex sentences:
8. Total number of compound-complex sentences:
9. Percentage of compound-complex sentences:
10. Write down the sequence of grammatical types in two or three consecutive paragraphs.

You might also want to copy and distribute examples of writing that differ widely in number of simple sentences or number of compound-complex sentences.

On Varieties of English Sentences

Some fields explicitly avoid variation in sentence structure and length. Many technical writers, and particularly those who write manuals that will be translated into numerous languages, must follow stringent rules for sentence structure and length. Technical writers working for Hewlett-Packard, for example, are required to adhere strictly to subject-verb-object order in all sentences and to keep all sentences to fifteen words at most. Have a class discussion about discipline- and profession-specific types of sentences.

■ **USEFUL READINGS**

Corbett, Edward P. J., with Robert Connors. *Classical Rhetoric for the Modern Student*. 4th ed. New York: Oxford UP, 1999. The author offers copious advice about analyzing sentence style.

Larson, Richard. "Back to the Board." *CCC* 29 (1978): 292–94. Larson offers a further explanation of his composing technique.

Lindemann, Erika, and Daniel Anderson. *A Rhetoric for Writing Teachers*. 4th ed. New York: Oxford UP, 2001. See, especially, the historical survey of sentence-combining research — from Hunt and O'Hare to Daiker and Morenberg.

47 ⬇ Creating Memorable Prose

If we use common words on a great occasion, they are the more striking, because they are felt at once to have a particular meaning, like old banners, or everyday clothes, hung up in a sacred place.

— GEORGE ELIOT

Like the clothes we wear, the words we choose and the way we use them bring memorable qualities to our language. Nowhere are such choices more evident in daily life than in music. Every songwriter knows the importance of creating lyrics and rhythms that listeners will remember.

Rap music demands careful attention to stylistic choices, for its lyrics must be concise as well as memorable. Here's an example from Queen Latifah and Monie Love's "Ladies First."

> I'm conversating to the folks who have no whatsoever clue
> So listen very carefully as I break it down for you
> Merrily, merrily, merrily, merrily, hyper, happy, overjoyed
> Pleased with all the beats and rhymes my sister has employed
> Slick and smooth, throwing down, the sound totally a yes
> Let me state the position: Ladies first, yes?
>
> Yes!

Ask students to look at the words and structures that the writer here has chosen in order to make the lyrics memorable: the active verbs ("listen"), the inversion of normal word order ("no whatsoever clue"), the powerful use of repetition ("Merrily, merrily, merrily, merrily"), and especially the three "yes's" that drive home both the rhythm and the point. What do they find most memorable about this particular rap?

Once your students begin to compare particularly memorable passages, you will be on the way to encouraging them to create memorable writing of their own.

FOR TEACHING: CHARACTERISTICS OF MEMORABLE PROSE

A Tale of Two Cities can offer a starting point for students to identify memorable prose.

> It was the best of times, it was the worst of times, it was the age of wisdom, it was the age of foolishness, it was the epoch of belief, it was the epoch of incredulity, it was the season of Light, it was the season of Darkness, it was the spring of hope, it was the winter of despair, we had everything before us, we had nothing before us, we were all going direct to Heaven, we were all going direct the other way—in short, the period was so far like the present period, that some of its noisiest authorities insisted on being received, for good or for evil, in the superlative degree of comparison only.
> – CHARLES DICKENS, *A Tale of Two Cities*

Following class discussion, ask students to bring in their own examples of memorable prose.

FOR COLLABORATIVE WORK: CHOOSING STRONG VERBS

(47a)

Ask students to bring a section of a newspaper to class. Direct their attention to the headlines, and ask them to make a list of the headlines that they think are the most effective. Divide the class into small groups of three to five, and ask them to read their lists of headlines and identify strong verbs and nouns. Next, ask students to rewrite the headlines with weak verbs and nouns. Finally, ask one member of each group to read the following: (1) a few of the headlines that the group felt used strong verbs and nouns, and (2) some of the weak headlines and the group's revisions of those weak headlines.

FOR TEACHING: CHOOSING STRONG VERBS

(47a)

In the midst of a relatively lifeless early draft of a student essay on the Chernobyl nuclear disaster, the reader suddenly comes across the following sentences:

> The force of the blast toppled the reactor's thousand ton lid. It shattered the sides and roof of the building as if they were glass. Tons of uranium dioxide fuel and other products used in the fission process detonated. The explosion sent heat, debris, and radiation nearly five kilometers into the sky.

The passage is not so different from the rest of the essay that we suspect plagiarism, but the strong verbs (and nouns) are striking and bring an otherwise dull essay alive momentarily.

Memorable writing can occur at all levels. Whole passages such as the one above may occur, or single words may jump out of an otherwise desert of weak, forgettable prose. Pointing out what's good in a piece provides the student writer with a model, however brief, for later writing and boosts a student's self-esteem, something that may very well stimulate his or her commitment to writing.

(47a)   **TEACHING WITH TECHNOLOGY: CHOOSING STRONG VERBS**

Often, students will err on the side of choosing verbs that are *too* strong to be appropriate for the audience, purpose, or genre of their writing task. One way to approach this topic with humor is to share an excerpt from the Purple Prose division of the Bulwer-Lytton Fiction Contest. Post the excerpt on your online discussion board or on a computer screen in class, and then have students respond to it by commenting on the author's choice of prose. Here, for is example, is a recent winning entry penned by David Hirsh of Seattle:

> Rain, violent torrents of it, rain like fetid water from a God-sized pot of pasta strained through a sky-wide colander, rain as Noah knew it, flaying the shuddering trees, whipping the whitecapped waters, violating the sodden firmament, purging purity and filth alike from the land, rain without mercy, without surcease, incontinent rain, turning to intermittent showers overnight with partial clearing Tuesday.

You might also ask students to compose their own parodies of memorable prose by exaggerating their choice of verbs. Share excerpts of these in a PowerPoint presentation in order to get a discussion going about the nuances of composing effective prose.

(47a2)   **On Nominalization**

Joseph Williams offers five cases of *useful* nominalization:

1. Nominalizations can be subjects referring to previous sentences: These arguments all depend on a single unproven claim.

2. Nominalizations can name what would be the objects of their verbs: I do not understand *her meaning.*

3. *The fact that* typically can be reduced to a more succinct nominalization: *My denial of* [replacing *The fact that I denied*] his accusations impressed the jury.

4. Some nominalizations serve as a conventional shorthand, referring to a well-established concept: *Taxation without representation* was not the central concern of the American *Revolution.*

5. A nominalization at the end of the first sentence of a paragraph can introduce a topic to be developed later: "There is no need, then, for argument about the *existence,* the inevitability, and the *desirability* of *change.*" (64–66)

Williams also lists five common patterns of abstract nominalization and how to revise them:

1. When the nominalization is the subject of an empty verb, change the nominalization to a verb and find a new subject: "Our *intention* is" becomes "We *intend.*"

2. When the nominalization follows an empty verb, change the nominalization to a verb that can replace the empty verb: "The committee has no *expectation*" becomes "The committee does not *expect.*"

3. When the nominalization follows a *there is* or *there are,* change the nominalization to a verb that replaces the *is* or *are* and find a subject: "There is a *need* for further *study*" becomes "The staff *must study.*"

4. When a nominalization in a subject is linked to another nominalization in the predicate by a verb or a phrase that expresses some kind of logical connection such as cause and effect, condition and consequence, revise as follows: (a) Change both abstractions to verbs, (b) find the subject of those verbs, and (c) link the new clauses with a word that expresses the logical connection: "the group's failure was the result of its chairman's resignation" becomes "the group failed because its chairman resigned."

5. When you have two nominalizations in a row, turn at least the first into a verb. Then either leave the second as it is or turn it into a verb in a clause beginning with *how* or *why:* "There was first a *review* of the evolution of the medial dorsal fin" becomes "First, she *reviewed* the *evolution* of the medial dorsal fin." (55–57)

On Choosing between Active and Passive Voice (47b)

Both active and passive voices are natural to English speakers. When people are asked to recall a passage or sentence, they will regularly remember the verb as active even when it was passive in the original. Yet, occasions do occur when the passive is more natural and memorable. For instance, when relating something that happened to ourselves, we use the passive voice as often as the active:

> I was bruised by the fall.
>
> The fall bruised me.

Otto Jespersen notes in *Essentials of English Grammar,* "As a rule the person or thing that is the centre of interest at the moment is made the subject of the sentence, and therefore the verb is in some cases put in the active, in others in the passive." (120)

As a rule of thumb, Joseph Williams, in *Style: Ten Lessons in Clarity and Grace,* suggests avoiding all "unnecessary" passive construction (81). That is, when an active construction says exactly what the passive construction says and works as effectively (often more so), then the student ought to use the active voice. In choosing between active and passive, Williams says we ought to ask ourselves three questions. "Must your readers know who is performing the action? Are you able to maintain a logical consistency in the subjects of your sentences? Would an active or passive better help readers move from one sentence to the next?" (82). If the writer finds she is shifting from one subject to another from sentence to sentence in a passage, then she ought to try revising these sentences in the active voice.

The writing instructor needs to be aware that there are contexts in which the passive voice is expected and may even be preferred. A reporter protecting his or her source will write, "It is reported that. . . ." In such cases, the reader must be the final judge. However, in some academic settings, passive voice is not just expected; it is commanded by the conventions of the discipline. In scientific writing, for example, the writer is expected to remain objective; the third person reflects that objectivity better than the first person. Williams calls the voice used in such situations "the objective passive" (88).

(47c)   On Creating Special Effects

Linguistic special effects are not unlike the special effects produced for films; they can be spectacular and obvious or quiet and subtle; they ought to be meaningful, not simply ornamental. Of course, the choice of special effects—which to use, when to use them, whether to use them at all—

depends on the overall rhetorical effects sought. The style of James Joyce probably is not appropriate for a business report. Students need to recognize that different rhetorical situations involve different reader expectations. Special effects — now including color, graphics, even sound — may make for livelier prose, but not always more appropriate prose.

FOR MULTILINGUAL WRITERS: CREATING SPECIAL EFFECTS WITH MULTIPLE NEGATIVES

(47c1)

Most speakers of English sometimes use more than one negative at a time — saying, for instance, "I can't hardly see you." Multiple negatives, in fact, have a long history in English (and can be found in the works of Chaucer and Shakespeare, for example). It was only in the eighteenth century, in an effort to make English more "logical," that double negatives came to be seen as incorrect. In fact, double negatives are used for emphasis in many areas of the South — to say, for example, "Can't nothing be done."

For all their use in regional and ethnic varieties of English (and in many other languages, including French and Russian), multiple negatives are not used in standard academic English. In college writing, students may well have reason to quote passages that include multiple negatives, whether they are quoting Shakespeare, Toni Morrison, or their grandmother, but they should be made aware that they should not otherwise use multiple negatives.

June Jordan describes a time in one of her classes when she wrote the opening lines of Alice Walker's *The Color Purple* on the board and then asked students to "translate" it into standard English, with the following result:

Walker: "You better not never tell nobody but God. It'd kill your mammy."

Standard English: Absolutely, one should never confide in anybody besides God. Your secrets could prove devastating to your mother.

On Inverted Word Order

(47c3)

Readers come to sentences with certain expectations, conditioned by familiarity to recognize typical patterns of language. For English speakers, one of these patterns is the subject-verb-object structure of the basic declarative sentence. Expectations change when we read a question or an imperative; we expect inversions then. But inversions in declarative sentences surprise us, and that surprise can be used to good effect.

As with any special effect, some inversions are less ornamental than others. Look at this sentence:

> Dolly she called Dollyheart, but Verena she called That One.
> – Truman Capote, *The Glass Harp*

This sentence is much clearer in emphasis in its inverted form than if structured conventionally:

> She called Dolly Dollyheart, but she called Verena That One.

Placement within a sentence alters the emphasis that a word gets. Look at this sentence:

> Gone are the potted plants, the Christmas cheeses, the toys for the children that were regularly issued by the old Francis Cleary.
> – Mary McCarthy, *Cast a Cold Eye*

Note the drastic change in emphasis when we restructure the sentence into its conventional form:

> The potted plants, the Christmas cheeses, the toys for the children that were regularly issued by the old Francis Cleary are gone.

FOR TEACHING: READING WITH AN EYE FOR PROSE STYLE

Students can produce remarkably effective and amusing imitations. Have them complete the "Three Little Pigs" story begun on *Handbook* p. 735, or create completely new imitations of their own, and ask them to bring in several representative pieces by the author being imitated. Then ask students to identify the *precise* characteristics that are being imitated. How, for instance, do we *know* that the passage here imitates Poe?

As an additional example, offer students the following opening of "Three Little Pigs" as told by Thomas Paine (first-year student Jill Stover is parodying, of course, Paine's *Common Sense*).

"Swine Sense"

> . . . In the preceding pages, the author has carefully excluded any thing that is personal among Oinkers. Only clear fact and common swine-sense are included within this pamphlet. The interests of Oink are also those of pigs

around the world. The senseless murdering of innocent pigs, the breaking of a long withstanding mutual trust, and the undermining of our brave new society, Oink, is the harming of all those to whom God hath given feeling and a curly tail.

■ **USEFUL READINGS**

Havelock, Eric A. "The Character and Content of the Code." *The Literate Revolution in Greece and Its Cultural Consequences.* Princeton: Princeton UP, 1982. 140 – 44. Havelock identifies the characteristics of memorable oral speech: parataxis, echoes, correspondences and symmetries, foreshadowing, and repetition.

Jespersen, Otto. *Essentials of English Grammar.* Tuscaloosa: U of Alabama P, 1965.

Lanham, Richard A. *Analyzing Prose.* New York: Macmillan, 1992. Lanham provides a full system for stylistic analyses.

Skorczewski, Dawn. "Everybody Has Their Own Ideas: Responding to Cliché in Student Writing." *CCC* 52.2 (Dec. 2000): 220–39. Skorczewski considers cliché as a form of memorable prose that allows teachers to learn about the discursive contexts of students.

Weathers, Winston. *An Alternate Style: Options in Composition.* Rochelle Park: Hayden P, 1980. This hard-to-find classic is well worth seeking out. In it, Weathers summarizes the characteristics of "school" essays — which he calls "Grammar A" — and contrasts these with the experimental features of "Grammar B," ending with ways to help students experiment with style as one means of creating memorable prose.

Williams, Joseph M. *Style: Ten Lessons in Clarity and Grace.* 6th ed. New York: Addison-Wesley, 2002. Williams deals with many aspects of memorable prose style.

PUNCTUATION CONVENTIONS

48 ⬇ Using Commas

The commas are the most useful and usable of all the stops. It is highly important to put them in place as you go along. If you try to come back after doing a paragraph and stick them in the various spots that tempt you you will discover that they tend to swarm like minnows into all sorts of crevices whose existence you hadn't realized and before you know it the whole long sentence becomes immobilized and lashed up squirming in commas. Better to use them sparingly, and with affection, precisely when the need for each one arises, nicely, by itself.

– Lewis Thomas

A world that has only periods is a world without inflections. It is a world without shade. It has a music without sharps and flats. It is a martial music. It has a jackboot rhythm. Words cannot bend and curve. A comma, by comparison, catches the gentle drift of the mind in thought, turning in on itself and back on itself, reversing, redoubling and returning along the course of its own sweet river music while the semicolon brings clauses and thoughts together with all the silent discretion of a hostess arranging guests around her dinner table.

– Pico Iyer

The first system of punctuation was introduced circa 260 B.C. by a librarian in Alexandria named Aristophanes. His system can be considered a forerunner of our own, but it was ignored in his own time, and Greek and Latin generally observed no punctuation at all until about the ninth century A.D. Aristophanes' system used three marks: the *periodos* (a dot set high on the line), the *kolon* (a dot set on the line), and the *komma* (a dot set halfway between the top and bottom of letters). Ancient Greece was, of course, preeminently an oral culture, and these marks signaled not grammatical units but places for the speaker to breathe. Punctuation took on grammatical functions, as opposed to performative ones, as a part of the emergence of a print culture. In "Historical Backgrounds of Elizabethan and Jacobean Punctuation Theory," Walter Ong notes that medieval grammarians

> *never* refer to the position of a punctuation mark in terms of grammatical structure. For the most part, they are content to indicate where a *distinctio* [period] may (not where it must or must not) occur, and if one wishes to breathe

oftener than would be usual, there is no objection, apparently, to inserting the marks 'ex abundanti.' (351)

The concept of punctuation as breathing marks continued through the sixteenth and seventeenth centuries. Today, most handbooks define the proper uses of commas in grammatical terms, although this chapter does note the stylistic uses of commas (for rhythm, emphasis, and clarity).

FOR TEACHING: COMMA CHOICES

The following paragraph from "Homeless" by Anna Quindlen is reproduced without any of the commas Quindlen used. Ask students to add commas where they think they're necessary or would be helpful. Then have them look through this chapter to see if their choices are appropriate. Have they used any unnecessary commas? Can they see places where they need to add any? Use their findings for class discussion.

> They were not pictures of family or friends or even a dog or cat its eyes brown-red in the flashbulb's light. They were pictures of a house. It was like a thousand houses in a hundred towns not suburb not city but somewhere in between with aluminum siding and a chain-link fence a narrow driveway running up to a one-car garage and a patch of backyard. The house was yellow. I looked on the back for a date or a name but neither was there. There was no need for discussion. I knew what she was trying to tell me for it was something I had often felt. She was not adrift alone anonymous although her bags and her raincoat with the grime shadowing its creases had made me believe she was. She had a house or at least once upon a time had had one. Inside were curtains a couch a stove potholders. You are where you live. She was somebody.

FOR TEACHING: USING COMMAS AFTER INTRODUCTORY ELEMENTS

Ask students to bring in examples of sentences with introductory elements. (Have them look for sentences where introductory elements are set off by commas as well as ones where they're *not* set off by commas.) Put several examples up for discussion of how the comma (or the lack of a comma) affects readers' understanding of an author's intended meaning. You might also try repunctuating the examples, adding or deleting commas, and then considering the difference a comma makes.

(48a)

The comma, the most ubiquitous and flexible, not to say slippery, of all stops, is the least susceptible to hard and fast rules.
– G. V. CAREY

FOR TEACHING: USING COMMAS TO SEPARATE ITEMS IN A SERIES

Consider using sentence-combining exercises like the following one to help students practice using commas.

> Erin gathered the blocks.
> She took careful aim.
> She flung handful after handful at her little brother.
> She finally relented.
>
> Erin gathered the blocks, took careful aim, and flung handful after handful at her little brother before finally relenting.

To further develop your students' skills with commas in a series, challenge them to construct long sentences with multiple modifiers. Francis Christensen's analysis of cumulative sentences in "A Generative Rhetoric of the Sentence" contains some good models for students to imitate, including this one by William Faulkner: "Calico-coated, small-bodied, with delicate legs and pink faces in which their mismatched eyes rolled wild and subdued, they huddled, gaudy motionless and alert, wild as deer, deadly as rattlesnakes, quiet as doves."

You might give your students a few simple sentences — for example, *They huddled* — and ask them to expand them, either individually or collaboratively, into sentences like Faulkner's, paying close attention to punctuation as they go.

FOR COLLABORATIVE WORK: COMMAS AND STYLE

Consider sharing the following passage with your students, asking them to work together in groups to identify the grammatical reasons for Mark Twain's commas. Then ask the groups to rewrite some or all of the passage, combining sentences or eliminating commas by shortening sentences. Finally, discuss Twain's stylistic reasons for punctuating this passage as he does. What effects have your students achieved by punctuating the passage differently?

> The bull started up, and got along well for about ten feet, then slipped and slid back. I breathed easier. He tried it again — got a little higher — slipped again. But he came at it once more, and this time he was careful. He got gradually higher and higher, and my spirits went down more and more. Up he came — an inch at a time — with his eyes hot, and his tongue hanging out. Higher and higher — hitched his foot over the stump of a limb, and looked up,

Popping in a comma can be like slipping on the necklace that gives an outfit quiet elegance, or like catching the sound of running water that complements, as it completes, the silence of a Japanese landscape.
— Pico Iyer

as much as to say, "You are my meat, friend." Up again—higher and higher, and getting more excited the higher he got. He was within ten feet of me! I took a long breath—and then said I, "It is now or never." I had the coil of the lariat all ready; I paid it out slowly, till it hung right over his head; all of a sudden I let go of the slack, and the slip noose fell fairly round his neck! Quicker than lightning I out with the allen and let him have it in the face. It was an awful roar, and must have scared the bull out of his senses. When the smoke cleared away, there he was, dangling in the air, twenty foot from the ground, and going out of one convulsion into another faster than you could count! I didn't stop to count, anyhow—I shinned down the tree and shot for home.

— MARK TWAIN, *Roughing It*

TEACHING WITH TECHNOLOGY: USING COMMAS TO FACILITATE UNDERSTANDING   (48i)

To show your students how significantly commas facilitate our understanding of texts, post the following sentence on your class listserv and ask students to supply the proper punctuation:

woman without her man is nothing

Many professors of English using this exercise find that, consistently and over time, the men write "Woman, without her man, is nothing," whereas the women write "Woman! Without her, man is nothing." Discuss these differences with your students.

FOR TEACHING: CHECKING FOR UNNECESSARY COMMAS   (48j)

Students often punctuate with commas in a way that reflects regular speaking patterns. For this reason, they may find it difficult to determine when commas are unnecessary. To help them learn how to check for unnecessary commas, use a little humor. Share with your students the following passage from Dave Barry's humor column:

We shall commence today's column right at the outset with a "punctuation" question:

Q. I, am never sure, when, to use, commas.

A. You should use a comma whenever you have a need to pause in a sentence.

EXAMPLE: "So me and Tiffany were at the mall and she ate like four of those big fudge squares which is why her butt is the size of a Volkswagen Jetta I don't know WHAT Jason sees in, wait a minute I'm getting another call."

To indicate a longer pause, use more commas:

EXAMPLE: "Then the earth,,,,,,,,,, cooled off."

– DAVE BARRY, "Grammar Tends to Slip after Drinking a Giraffe"

FOR TEACHING: REVISING COMMAS

Write the Frost poem on *Handbook* p. 753 on the board, and read it aloud. Then try changing its comma structure — perhaps by ending line 4 with a comma instead of a period, or by adding commas in line 7 after *that* and *destruction*. Read the poem aloud each way, and ask students to describe the different effects. Finally, ask them to decide which one they prefer, and why.

FOR TEACHING: USING COMMAS IN YOUR OWN WRITING

Ask your students to read the following passage aloud, listening for the use of commas. Then have them read it again, mentally deleting the commas and noting how their absence affects meaning and rhythm. Finally, have them choose two of the sentences to use as a model, and create a similar pair of sentences of their own.

> The most important fact about a comma is that there are places where it must not be used. That is, there are places where a comma alters the meaning of a statement. Max Beerbohm was being witty when he used a comma in writing about Frank Harris, and many good writers.
> – BERGEN EVANS AND CORNELIA EVANS

I ran across many words whose meanings I did not know, and I either looked them up in a dictionary or, before I had a chance to do that, encountered the word in a context that made its meaning clear. But what strange world was this? I concluded the book with the conviction that I had somehow overlooked something terribly important in life. I had once tried to write, had once reveled in feeling, had let my crude imagination roam, but the impulse to dream had been slowly beaten out of me by experience. Now it surged up again and I hungered for books, new ways of looking and seeing. It was not a matter of believing or disbelieving what I read, but of feeling something new, of being affected by something that made the look of the world different.

– RICHARD WRIGHT, "The Library Card"

■ **USEFUL READINGS**

Barry, Dave. "Grammar Tends to Slip after Drinking a Giraffe." *Miami Herald* 25 Feb. 2001.

Christensen, Francis. "A Generative Rhetoric of the Sentence." *Rhetoric and Composition.* Ed. Richard Graves. Upper Montclair: Boynton, 1984.

Dawkins, John. "Teaching Punctuation as a Rhetorical Tool." *CCC* 46 (1995): 533–48. Dawkins argues that punctuation choices are always *rhetorical* choices and proposes a method for teaching students to recognize subtle rhetorical effects and to make good choices by "analyz[ing] their semantic and rhetorical intentions and then matching those intentions to readers' needs."

Ong, Walter. "Historical Backgrounds of Elizabethan and Jacobean Punctuation Theory." *PMLA* 59 (1944): 349–60. Despite the title, both the history of punctuation and Renaissance attitudes are treated equally.

Period Styles: A History of Punctuation. New York: Herb Lubalin Study Center of Design and Typography, Cooper Union for the Advancement of Science and Art, 1988. See the first essay, "Period Styles: A Punctuated History."

Shaughnessy, Mina. *Errors and Expectations: A Guide for the Teacher of Basic Writing.* New York: Oxford UP, 1977. See "Handwriting and Punctuation," particularly pp. 18–24, for a discussion of how basic writers use commas and periods.

Thomas, Lewis. "Notes on Punctuation." *New England Journal of Medicine* 296 (1977): 1103–05. This witty personal essay is remarkable for its erudition—perhaps more so because it was written by a medical researcher (turned essayist) and published originally in a medical journal.

Williams, Joseph M. *Style: Ten Lessons in Style and Grace.* 6th ed. New York: Addison-Wesley, 2001. Williams groups nonrestrictive modifiers under the heading "loose or nonspecifying commentary."

49 ▼ Using Semicolons

Among punctuation marks, the semicolon is a relative latecomer, lagging behind the comma, colon and period, most linguists agree. Of course, punctuation itself did not become a standard part of written discourse until the late 18th century. Composition had been a haphazard enterprise at best, with writers employing punctuation marks when and how they chose. —JULIA KELLER, "Secrets of the Semicolon"

The distinction between the Greek semicolon [·], a raised point whose aim is to keep the voice from being lowered, and the German one, which accomplishes the lowering with its period and its hanging lower part and yet keeps the voice suspended by incorporating the comma — truly a dialectical image — seems to reproduce the distinction between classical antiquity and the Christian Era, finitude refracted through the infinite. . . . History has left its residue in punctuation marks, and it is history, far more than meaning or grammatical function, that looks out at us, rigidified and trembling slightly, from every mark of punctuation.

— ADORNO

In classical Greek, groups of words comparable to what we call sentences were set off and called *colons*. A semicolon, therefore, is literally half a colon, or half of a sentence divided by the punctuation mark we call a *semicolon*. Lewis Thomas demonstrates effective use of the semicolon as he defines it, noting:

> The semicolon tells you that there is still some question about the preceding full sentence; something needs to be added. . . . It is almost always a greater pleasure to come across a semicolon than a period. The period tells you that is that; if you didn't get all the meaning you wanted or expected, you got all the writer intended to parcel out and now you have to move along. But with a semicolon there you get a pleasant little feeling of expectancy; there is more to come; read on; it will get clearer. — LEWIS THOMAS, "Notes on Punctuation"

As Thomas suggests, semicolons have the effect of creating a pause stronger than that of a comma but not as strong as the full pause of a period. Their primary uses are to link coordinate independent clauses and to separate items in a series.

The semicolon as we know it today was introduced in the seventh century A.D. During the eighth century, an inverted semicolon was used to indicate a vocal pause halfway between the comma and the semicolon. By the fifteenth century, however, the inverted semicolon had fallen out of favor.

On Semicolons and Academic Discourse

Bergen and Cornelia Evans claim that the semicolon is most appropriate for formal writing. "If a writer wishes to use an informal narrative style he should avoid semicolons as much as possible" (440). However, George Summey Jr., in *American Punctuation,* argues against thinking of the semicolon as "a stiff and formal mark that ought to be seldom used": "It is actually used by good current writers today and might well be used oftener if our writers would take the trouble to drop some of their *and*'s and *but*'s and use patterns that take a semicolon and no conjunction." The problem is not with the semicolon, Summey says, but with the "awkward patterns" and "stiff wording" with which it has been associated (98).

William and Mary Morris suggest that one reason for the lack of use of the semicolon is "the trend toward short, trenchant sentences" in journalism (547). But, in fact, the absence of the semicolon in less formal writing is changing. Still, the tendency to use the semicolon remains a stylistic choice. Some writers like Annie Dillard, whose *Pilgrim at Tinker Creek* is definitely not a formal piece, seem fond of the semicolon, while other writers, like John McPhee, rarely use it. Donald Barthelme's short story "Sentence" consists of one long sentence (or actually of a part of one sentence). While it includes numerous instances of dashes, parentheses, quotation marks, question marks, exclamation points, and commas, it has only one semicolon. The reason might be that the semicolon seems too close to being end punctuation, and the story is meant to give us the feeling of continuousness and endlessness. The period, incidentally, doesn't appear at all.

Theodor Haeker was rightfully alarmed by the fact that the semicolon is dying out; this told him that no one can write a period, a sentence containing several balanced clauses, any more. Part of this incapacity is the fear of page-long paragraphs, a fear created by the marketplace — by the consumer who does not want to tax himself and to whom first editors and then writers accommodated for the sake of their incomes. . . . It starts with the loss of the semicolon; it ends with the ratification of imbecility by a reasonableness purged of all admixtures.
    – ADORNO

FOR TEACHING: USING SEMICOLONS TO LINK INDEPENDENT CLAUSES   **(49a)**

The writer of the following paragraph chose not to use any semicolons, although there are several places where she might have. Ask students to read the paragraph carefully to find at least two such places and then decide whether they would have used a semicolon.

It is appropriate, I think, that Bob's Surplus has a communal dressing room. I used to shop only in places where I could count on a private dressing room with a mirror inside. My impulse then was to hide my weaknesses. Now I believe in sharing them. There are other women in the dressing room at Bob's Surplus trying on blue jeans who look as bad as I do. We take comfort from one another. Sometimes a woman will ask me which of two items looks better. I always give a definite answer. It's the least I can do. I figure we are all in this together, and I emerge from the dressing room not only with a new pair of jeans but with a renewed sense of belonging to a human community. — PHYLLIS ROSE, "Shopping and Other Spiritual Adventures"

(49c)

... only a person who can perceive the different weights of strong and weak phrasings in musical form can really feel the distinction between the comma and the semicolon.
— ADORNO

On Checking for Overused Semicolons

Mina Shaughnessy notes that semicolons are rarely used by beginning writers, who typically read little and so are unfamiliar with the form. They sometimes "strain the resources of the comma" to cover situations requiring other marks, including semicolons. Thus, comma splices may result (23, 33–34).

The opposite problem can occur once students have been introduced to semicolons; they may begin to overuse them. Part of the problem is the power of the semicolon itself. Shaughnessy notes that "as its form suggests, it has the linking power of a comma and the terminating authority of a period. Given the difficulties of the unpracticed writer with both linking and sustaining sentences, the semicolon must appear as something of a bargain" (34). Punctuation marks produce different psychological effects — on the writer as well as the reader. If the writer resists putting an end to a sentence because he or she fears having to start another, the instructor may see an overuse of semicolons.

Sometimes a semicolon marks the frontier between a thought and a triviality.
— ERICH HELLER, Commenting on the thought of Wittgenstein

Ultimately, the writer must get a feel for when to use semicolons to link ideas. Shaughnessy goes on to note that use of the semicolon, unlike the period and the comma, depends on the situation, on the relationships of ideas as much as on conventional formal requirements. George Summey Jr. states that the semicolon is "the most clearly specialized balancing and coordinating mark" and is "not a general-purpose mark like the comma" (97).

(49d)

On Checking for Misused Semicolons

One can imagine writers getting away with never using semicolons, except perhaps the rare use with a series of items. From this perspective, the semicolon becomes more a stylistic device than a grammatical one, which is not something you can say about the period, for instance. Clearly, then, the choice of a semicolon over another punctuation mark is often a rhetorical choice.

George Summey Jr. offers these flexible guidelines for when to choose the semicolon:

> What mark should be used in a given case — comma or semicolon, semicolon or period — will depend only in part on the length of the groups. Circumstances that may make the semicolon preferable to the comma are length and complexity of the groups, the absence of a connective, or a shift of grammatical subject. And any of these same circumstances may make the period better than the semicolon. Each case must be settled by the writer according to the immediate situation. The more important a group is in its context, the more reason for preferring semicolon to comma or period to semicolon. (99)

FOR COLLABORATIVE WORK: CHECKING FOR MISUSED SEMICOLONS

In "Secrets of the Semicolon" Julia Keller gives a brief history and user's guide to the semicolon. Read the following passage to your students:

> Once dismissed as a fussy, somewhat effete affectation, the white-gloved cousin to the calloused, workaholic comma or brutally abrupt period, the semicolon may be coming into its own. Most people, truth to tell, still seem somewhat intimidated by the semicolon; it smacks of deep thoughts and book-lined studies, of long pauses accompanied by rhythmic strokes of the chin. Semicolons function several ways in sentences. They can divide coordinate clauses that are complete in themselves; they can replace commas, indicating a longer pause; they can separate items in a list. But semicolons historically were deftly avoided. They were the fine china of the punctuation world, when plastic forks would do.

When you are done, ask your students to keep these guidelines in mind and look over the passage in groups, checking for overused and misused semicolons. Finally, have them work in peer-review groups to assess each other's writing.

FOR TEACHING: SEMICOLONS AND PARALLELISM

Semicolons often work well in creating a strong sense of parallelism:

> Last season, I liked *Frasier;* this season, I love it. But it's not my opinion that has changed. It's the show. Last year, *Frasier* was good; this year, it's getting great.
> – JEFF JARVIS

Ask students to take a piece of writing they are working on and look for a passage that could be emphasized by using semicolons to create paral-

(49d) ....

Semicolons function several ways in sentences. They can divide coordinate clauses that are complete in themselves; they can replace commas, indicating a longer pause; they can separate items in a list.
– JULIA KELLER

392   Chapter 49 Using Semicolons

lelism. Then ask them to bring their experiments to class for discussion about the rhetorical effects semicolons can create.

■ USEFUL READINGS

Baker, Nicholson. "The History of Punctuation." *The Size of Thoughts*. New York: Vantage, 1997.

Barthelme, Donald. "Sentence." *City Life*. New York: Farrar, 1970.

Evans, Cornelia, and Bergen Evans. *A Dictionary of Contemporary English Usage*. New York: Random, 1957.

Keller, Julia. "Secrets of the Semicolon." *Chicago Tribune* 12 May 1999: 1.

Morris, William, and Mary Morris. *Harper Dictionary of Contemporary Usage*. New York: Harper, 1975.

Shaughnessy, Mina. *Errors and Expectations*. New York: Oxford UP, 1977.

Summey, George, Jr. *American Punctuation*. New York: Ronald, 1949.

Thomas, Lewis. "Notes on Punctuation." *The Medusa and the Snail*. New York: Penguin, 1995.

⚡ Using End Punctuation

50

> *Punctuation has long been considered the stronghold of inflexible and prescriptive rules. This tradition is unfortunate. To a great degree, punctuation is variable, flexible, and even imaginative.*
>
> – WILLIAM D. DRAKE

End punctuation — a period, question mark, or exclamation point — tells readers they have reached the end of one unit of thought and can pause and take a mental breath before moving on to the next one. Student writers need to be guided by meaning in their choice of end punctuation, understanding, however, that they can sometimes use it for special effect. Ask them to look, for instance, at the way end punctuation guides readers in the following three sentences:

Am I tired.

Am I tired?

Am I tired!

The end punctuation tells how to read each sentence: the first as a dry, matter-of-fact statement; the second as a puzzled or perhaps ironic query; the last as a note of exasperation.

In order to use end punctuation of any kind, of course, the student must first have a sense of what a traditionally punctuated sentence is. As Mina Shaughnessy points out in *Errors and Expectations,* end punctuation requires "a familiarity with the sentence as a grammatical unit and with the process whereby simple sentences are enlarged so as to include various types of subordinate structures" (27). Beginning writers will have been producing sentences orally for a long time before they come to produce them in writing, but writing is an abstract operation, not a natural operation like speaking. We speak, producing whole thoughts in subjects and predicates, without reflection; writing requires a great deal of reflecting

For many beginning writers, the need to mark off sentences inhibits the progress of their thoughts. In speech, they can produce sentences as easily and unconsciously as they can walk; in writing, they must stop to deliberate over what is and what is not a sentence.

– MINA SHAUGHNESSY

on what we are doing. Thus you may want to review the *Handbook* chapter on sentence production (Chapter 31).

You may also encounter "a psychological resistance to the period" (Shaughnessy 18). The period imposes an end to the thought that the student may have had difficulty in beginning. The period tells the writer that he or she must begin again, a task that the inexperienced writer may find fearful.

Also, students sometimes become overly concerned with end punctuation. Shaughnessy believes that such concern suggests a perception of the sentence as a whole unit that ought not to be divided or modified in any way.

(50a–c)

FOR COLLABORATIVE WORK: UNDERSTANDING END PUNCTUATION

Ask students to work in small groups to imagine they work for a company that is preparing to launch a new product. First, they should decide what the product is — some sort of food or drink, an automobile, the latest laptop computer, or something else — and what its name should be. Then they should write a headline and some copy for the product's first advertisement. Finally, ask that they note the way they have used end punctuation — where they have placed periods, question marks, and exclamation points, and compare their advertisement with those of several other groups. Use their findings to begin a class discussion on the rhetorical effects of end punctuation.

FOR MULTILINGUAL WRITERS: USING END PUNCTUATION

The exclamation point has been variously called the note of admiration, the shriek of surprise, the astonisher or paralyzer, the period that blew its top.
— George Summey, Jr.

Because the European system of punctuation marks can differ markedly from those in other cultures, multilingual writers need to memorize which punctuation marks can *begin* a line — and which cannot.

End punctuation, including [’!:”).?;] cannot begin a line, but some punctuation can [(“]. As a result multilingual writers will want to look carefully at the ways English texts are punctuated on the page.

(50b)

On Using Question Marks

The question mark appeared in the eighth century. Lewis Thomas, in his "Notes on Punctuation," claims the question mark is not, "strictly speaking," a stop, but rather an "indicator of tone." Yet question marks also indicate grammatical meaning. A sentence like *Joseph danced the boogaloo* may be either declarative or interrogative, depending on the context.

> Joseph danced the boogaloo.
>
> Joseph danced the boogaloo?

John Wilson, in *The Elements of Punctuation,* describes the dual function of the question mark, along with the exclamation point, parenthesis, and dash:

> They are rhetorical, so far as they help to exhibit the force and intensity of a style which is rhetorical in its structure; but they are also grammatical, because they often serve to indicate, in connection with other marks, the nature, construction, and sense of the passages in which they occur. (92)

On Using Exclamation Points   (50c)

The exclamation point was rarely used before the Renaissance. It differs fundamentally from the other two end punctuation marks. While the period and the question mark function grammatically (as well as "rhetorically"—that is, phonologically—in the case of the question mark), the exclamation point functions almost entirely to indicate a change in voice. While it does mark the end of a sentence, it does not do so always, and when it does, it could be replaced with a period or question mark.

Attitudes toward the exclamation point have ranged from disgust to simple tolerance. Rarely has anyone exclaimed the praises of the exclamation point. At best, commentators describe it neutrally, as did the author of *A Treatise of Stops, Points, or Pauses* in 1680, calling it "a Note of Admiration, wondering, or crying out." Typically, we encounter descriptions like that of George Summey Jr. who notes that, at the time he was writing *American Punctuation* (1949), typewriters did not possess exclamation-point keys. Instead, the mark was made by striking a period, backspacing, and then striking an apostrophe. Summey calls this procedure "more trouble than the mark is likely to be worth" (90).

■ **USEFUL READINGS**

Shaughnessy, Mina. *Errors and Expectations: A Guide for the Teacher of Basic Writing.* New York: Oxford UP, 1977. Chapter 2, "Handwriting and Punctuation," focuses on end punctuation.

Summey, George, Jr. *American Punctuation*. New York: Ronald, 1949.

Thomas, Lewis. "Notes on Punctuation." *New England Journal of Medicine* 296 (1977): 1103 – 05. This witty personal essay is remarkable for its erudition — perhaps more so because it was written by a medical researcher (turned essayist) and published originally in a medical journal.

Wilson, John. Jr. *The Elements of Punctuation*. Boston, 1856.

▼ Using Apostrophes

51

As a mark of the possessive case, the apostrophe has an unusual history. In Old English, the endings of nouns changed according to the noun's grammatical function — a noun used as a subject, for example, had a different ending from one used as a direct object. By the fourteenth century, Middle English had dropped most of this complicated system, yet possessive and plural endings remained: *Haroldes sword* was still used to mean "the sword of Harold." Then in the sixteenth century, scholars concluded that the ending *-es* and its variants were actually contractions of *his*. Believing that *Haroldes sword* meant "Harold his sword," they began using an apostrophe instead of the *e: Harold's sword*.

Even though this theory was later discredited, the possessive ending retained the apostrophe because it was a useful way to distinguish between possessive and plural forms in writing. Today we use the apostrophe primarily to signal possessive case, contractions and other omissions of words and letters, and certain plural forms.

One of the special difficulties in teaching today's students to use apostrophes is tied to the differences between speaking and writing. Our students will often omit apostrophes in writing because they do not hear them in oral discourse. Though it can be argued that indeed we *do* hear some punctuation (through intonation, rhythm, pauses, and breathing), the apostrophe is decidedly "silent"; based on sound alone, there is no way to distinguish *cant* from *can't, isnt* from *isn't, Joes* from *Joe's*. A student may be very adept at spoken discourse (as most are), but less practiced with the conventions of written English and, hence, have difficulty remembering to insert apostrophes. Indeed, some linguists suggest that English, with its tendency to rely on word order and to drop inflections, may someday be *without* apostrophes.

(51a) On Using Apostrophes to Signal Possessive Case

Although there is some disagreement over adding just an apostrophe rather than an apostrophe and *-s* to singular nouns ending in *-s*, the most authoritative sources on usage recommend using an apostrophe and an -s with all singular nouns, including those words ending with *-s*. Here are some additional examples:

> *Nogales's* hot and dry summers
> *Cass's* research into the squash melon
> the *princess's* last visit

Exceptions, however, are proper names that end in an "eez" sound — often Greek or hellenized names.

> *Aristophanes'* comedies
> *B. F. Yerkes'* research

(51b) On Using Apostrophes to Signal Contractions

Typically, contractions have a less formal tone than the combined words written out in full. As a general rule, writers are probably wise to limit the use of contractions in formal settings, including letters of application, business letters, legal documents, and papers for college courses. Yet even in formal contexts, contractions may sometimes be appropriate where the alternative would sound overly contrived. The rhetorical considerations of purpose, content, context, and audience should guide the writer's use of contractions. Fred Astaire would have sounded somewhat stiff singing "Is it not romantic?" while Abraham Lincoln would have struck an incongruously chatty tone had he said, "With firmness in the right, as God gives us to see the right, let's strive on to finish the work we're in."

FOR COLLABORATIVE WORK: APOSTROPHES AND THE RHYTHMS OF SPEECH

Ask students to practice reading aloud the rhyme on *Handbook* p. 770, first with all the contractions written out and omitted letters restored and then as Hurston wrote it. Ask them then to work together to describe the difference, considering, for example, which version sounds more like speech and which version sounds more formal.

■ **USEFUL READINGS**

Flesch, Rudolf. *The ABC of Style: A Guide to Plain English.* New York: Harper, 1964. See pp. 29–30 on the use of contractions in writing.

Hashimoto, Irwin. "Pain and Suffering: Apostrophes and Academic Life." *Journal of Basic Writing* 7.2 (1988): 91–98. Hashimoto humorously discusses students' frequent problems with apostrophes. He places "a large chunk of the blame" on a handbook tradition that leads us to look for simple, clear rules and overlook "the ugly truth" that the rules for apostrophes are really quite messy.

52

▼ Using Quotation Marks

By necessity, by proclivity, — and by delight, we all quote.

– RALPH WALDO EMERSON

Before the seventeenth century, there was no regulated punctuation mark to indicate quotations. In ancient Greek texts, the *paragraphos* (a short horizontal line used to divide texts into units) was used to indicate changes in dialogue. Quotations and direct speech were simply introduced with phrases like *he said,* without any punctuation. During Shakespeare's time, however, commas and inverted commas were generally placed at the start of a passage. Shakespeare scholar Margreta de Grazia tells us that these commas were used interchangeably with the pointing index finger (☞) directing the reader's eye to passages of special note. According to Grazia, both signals — commas and ☞ — appeared in the margin, the place where aids to the reader were supplied. Such signals never appeared within the text itself. And these signals primarily indicated to the reader that a passage was important — not that it originated elsewhere.

Although quotation marks now are exclusionary, marking off private property, during Shakespeare's time, they signaled communal ground or commonplaces. They marked material to be copied by each reader in his copybook or commonplace book, thereby assuring that the commonplaces would become more common still. By simply perusing the margins of a text, readers might lift material for their own personalized storehouse of wise and therefore widely applicable sayings.

By the mid-seventeenth century, the double comma was placed within the text, before a sentence to indicate its importance: „ *The time to act is now.* The double comma was later used to enclose quotations, and printers began to edge both margins of quoted materials with double commas.

Inverted commas is the British label for *quotation marks,* a label that indeed recalls the origin of the marks in the seventeenth century. However, Wilson Follett points out that, although either expression is acceptable, *inverted commas* is an inaccurate label:

> The opening signs (' ") consist of commas both inverted and reversed; the closing signs (' ") are neither inverted nor reversed, but merely superior — i.e., above the line. (186)

Today, theorists are questioning the ideologies surrounding practices of quotation. An early critique of such practices appears in the work of Bakhtin and Volosinov, who question the ways in which quotation perpetuates a view of language as the property of a radically unique individual rather than as a set of socially constructed systems.

On Punctuation before Quotations (52a)

As a general rule, a writer can decide whether or not to use a comma or colon before a quotation by reading aloud the sentence or passage containing the quotation. If the quotation follows smoothly from the text that precedes it, no comma or colon is necessary. For instance, the quotation in the following sentence needs no comma or colon:

> Mannes argues that television commercials "contribute to the diminution of human worth and the fragmenting of our psyches."

However, if the quoted words do not fit syntactically into the larger sentence, then they should be preceded by a comma or colon, as in the following sentence:

> When Ralph Waldo Emerson was asked to take part in directly promoting abolition, he said: "I have my own spirits in prison — spirits in deeper prisons — whom no man visits if I do not."

FOR COLLABORATIVE WORK: USING QUOTATION MARKS IN INTERVIEWS (52a)

Ask students to bring the interviews assigned in Thinking about Your Own Use of Quotation Marks (on p. 778) to class. Then ask them to work in pairs, trading interviews and reading them with special attention to use of quotation marks. Are they used accurately throughout? Are any uses of quotation marks confusing or unclear? What suggestions could they give each other for revision?

(52a3)

FOR COLLABORATIVE WORK: USING QUOTATION MARKS TO SIGNAL DIALOGUE

Divide the class into groups of three. Using one of the following sentences as an opener, have two members of each group take on the roles involved and produce a dialogue. The third person of the group records the dialogue, and together afterwards, the group members decide on how it should be punctuated.

1. One roommate asks the other, "What should we do tonight?"
2. One sibling says to the other, "Oh no you don't."
3. As I turned the corner, I heard someone say "Stop right there."

(52a–c)

FOR COLLABORATIVE WORK: USING QUOTATION MARKS

Divide the class into groups of three, and ask each group to compose a one- or two-page passage that includes as many of the following as possible: direct quotations, quotations within quotations, dialogue, titles, definitions, and special-emphasis words or phrases.

(52d)

On Checking for Misused Quotations Marks

Lewis Thomas offers the following advice for using quotation marks: (1) quote exact words; (2) do not string together thoughts that the author did not intend to be connected; (3) do not use quotation marks to qualify ideas that you would like to disown; (4) do not put them around clichés to avoid your responsibility in using them.

(52d–e)

FOR TEACHING: REVISING QUOTATION MARKS

Ask students to read each of the following sentences, deleting quotation marks used inappropriately, moving those placed incorrectly, and using more formal language in place of slang expressions in quotation marks.

In "Bartleby the Scrivener" Bartleby states time and again, "I would prefer not to."

1. The grandmother in O'Connor's story shows she is still misguided when she says, "You've got good blood! I know you wouldn't shoot a lady"!

2. What is Hawthorne telling the readers in "Rappaccini's Daughter?"

3. Very quietly, Chun Lee said, "I know the answer".

4. This "typical American" is Ruby Turpin, who in the course of the story receives a "message" that brings about a "change" in her life.

5. Being "overweight" is a problem because "excess pounds" are hard to lose and can be "dangerous" to a person's health.

6. One of Joyce Carol Oates's most shocking stories is "The Bingo Master;" the triumph of brutality is devastating.

7. Macbeth "bumps off" Duncan to gain the throne for himself.

8. In his article "The Death of Broadway", Thomas M. Disch writes that "chore-ographers are, literally, a dying breed[1]".

9. "Know thyself — " this is the quest of the main characters in both Ibsen's *Peer Gynt* and Lewis's *Till We Have Faces*.

10. One thought flashed through my mind as I finished *"In Search of Our Mothers' Gardens:"* I want to read more of this writer's books.

Quotation marks should be used only when something is quoted and if need be when the text wants to distance itself from a word it is referring to. They are to be rejected as an ironic device. For they exempt the writer from the spirit whose claim is inherent in irony, and they violate the very concept of irony by separating it from the matter at hand and presenting a prede-termined judgment on the subject.

– ADORNO

Answers

1. The grandmother in O'Connor's story shows she is still misguided when she says, "You've got good blood! I know you wouldn't shoot a lady!"

2. What is Hawthorne telling the readers in "Rappaccini's Daughter"?

3. Very quietly, Chun Lee said, "I know the answer."

4. This "typical American" is Ruby Turpin, who in the course of the story receives a message that brings about a change in her life.

5. Being overweight is a problem because excess pounds are hard to lose and can be dangerous to a person's health.

6. One of Joyce Carol Oates's most shocking stories is "The Bingo Master"; the triumph of brutality is devastating.

7. Macbeth murders Duncan to gain the throne for himself.

8. In his article "The Death of Broadway," Thomas M. Disch writes that "chore-ographers are, literally, a dying breed."[1]

9. "Know thyself" — this is the quest of the main characters in both Ibsen's *Peer Gynt* and Lewis's *Till We Have Faces*.

10. One thought flashed through my mind as I finished *In Search of Our Mothers' Gardens:* "I want to read more of this writer's books."

■ **USEFUL READINGS**

Follet, Wilson. *Modern American Usage*. New York: Hill, 1966.

Shaughnessy, Mina. *Errors and Expectations: A Guide for the Teacher of Basic Writing.* New York: Oxford UP, 1977. See chapter 2, an insightful discussion of punctuation. In particular, Shaughnessy claims that basic writers rarely use quotation marks.

Thomas, Lewis. "Notes on Punctuation." *New England Journal of Medicine* 296 (1977): 1103–05.

Volosinov, Valentin N. "Exposition of the Problem of Reported Speech." *Marxism and the Philosophy of Language.* Cambridge: Harvard UP, 1973. Here Volosinov mounts a powerful critique of quotation practices, revealing the ways they are inevitably embedded in ideology.

Using Other Punctuation Marks

Parentheses, brackets, dashes, and slashes developed well after the technology of the written word first appeared, but the colon was one of the first punctuation marks used. Since most discourse was oral rather than written, punctuation evolved to mark places where speakers paused or breathed rather than grammatical units. The first system of punctuation, created by Aristophanes in the second century B.C., used only three marks: the period, colon, and comma. Six centuries later, St. Jerome (A.D. 400) punctuated his translation of the Vulgate Bible using a rhetorical system of colons and commas to mark breathing points. The elocutionary nature of punctuation developed further during the tenth to thirteenth centuries with the addition of marks to denote places where the speakers should raise their voices (the *punctus elevatus, punctus interrogativus,* and *punctus circumflexus*) and confirmed the use of the colon as a breathing stop, particularly between verses of the Psalms. However, over time, written discourse became less connected to oral discourse, especially after the invention of printing, and punctuation began to take on more rhetorical or grammatical functions. Parentheses, brackets, dashes, and slashes functioned primarily to indicate grammatical divisions. Parentheses began to appear around 1500, and dashes by 1700, but the slash (also called a virgule or solidus) has been with us a little longer. Virgules first appeared in the thirteenth and fourteenth centuries as a form of light stop; after about 1450 the virgule, which was originally placed high, began to appear on the base line and developed a curve. Today we know this mark as a comma.

On Using Parentheses

The term *parentheses* derives from the classical Greek figure of speech *parenthesis*, which denotes the act of inserting a verbal unit (a word, phrase, or sentence) into a position that interrupts the sentence flow. Such material can be punctuated with dashes or commas as well as with parentheses.

for life's not a paragraph and death i think is no parenthesis.
– E. E. CUMMINGS

On Using Dashes

You may want to share Adorno's thoughts on dashes with students. Ask them to write up a brief explanation of what *they* think the dash is used for.

A parenthesis is a convenient device, but a writer indulges his own convenience at the expense of his readers' if his parenthesis is so long that a reader, when he comes to the end of it, has little chance of remembering where he was when it began.
– H. W. FOWLER

> In the dash, thought becomes aware of its fragmentary character. It is no accident that in the era of the progressive degeneration of language, this mark of punctuation is neglected precisely insofar as it fulfills its function: when it separates things that feign a connection. All the dash claims to do now is to prepare us in a foolish way for surprises that by that very token are no longer surprising.
> – ADORNO

> The test of a writer's sensitivity in punctuating is the way he handles parenthetical material. The cautious writer will tend to place that material between dashes and not in round brackets [i.e., what is commonly called parentheses, ( )], for brackets take the parenthesis completely out of the sentence, creating enclaves, as it were, whereas nothing in good prose should be unnecessary to the overall structure. By admitting such superfluousness, brackets implicitly renounce the claim to the integrity of the linguistic form. . . . Dashes, in contrast, which block off the parenthetical material from the flow of the sentence without shutting it up in a prison, capture both connection and detachment.
> – ADORNO

FOR TEACHING: USING DASHES

Emily Dickinson published very few poems during her lifetime. But privately, she bound her manuscripts into packets or "fascicles," folded sheets of paper sewn together by hand, which give the impression of being little "books," meant to be read by others. Her capitalization and punctuation were very unconventional. Especially curious is her use of dashes as an almost universal punctuation mark, sometimes occurring in places that break up sentences into ungrammatical units.

The first editor of Dickinson's work systematically eliminated the dashes, and in fact, until the middle of the twentieth century, editors always normalized her mechanics. In 1950, Edith Perry Stamm proposed a theory to explain Dickinson's dashes. She claims that Dickinson's system of dashes indicated various spoken intonations. Most experts discount Stamm's theory, because it seems likely that if Dickinson had wanted to indicate intonation, she would have made her marks clearer to distinguish.

Ask students to read the following brief Dickinson poem—with her original dashes restored—at least twice, first ignoring the dashes and then using them to guide their reading. Then ask students to work in small groups to decide what effect the final dash has. Finally, ask them to try composing a four-line poem that uses dashes to guide reading and meaning.

> Much Madness is divinest Sense—
> To a discerning Eye—
> Much Sense—the starkest Madness—
> 'Tis the Majority
> In this, as All, prevail—
> Assent—and you are sane—
> Demur—you're straightway dangerous—
> And handled with a Chain—
> — EMILY DICKINSON

For additional practice, ask students to read some other poems with dashes and study the effects they bring to the poem. They might even try to repunctuate the poem, replacing dashes with colons or parentheses, for instance, to appreciate the difference. Other poems with dashes you might suggest include:

"Birches" and "Mending Wall," Robert Frost

"The Love Song of J. Alfred Prufrock," T. S. Eliot

"The Ruined Maid," Thomas Hardy

"Daddy," Sylvia Plath

On Using Colons   (53d)

In Greek, the word *colon* denoted a unit of prose with certain rhythmical qualities, linking it to oral delivery. But today, colons function primarily

---

The stately colon, the confiding parenthesis and the gently pausing comma demand to know: what's behind today's big dash to the dash? Why has this lingua interruptus—expressing uncertainty, jerking the reader around, setting up startling conclusions, imitating patterns of speech—come to dominate our prose?
— WILLIAM SAFIRE

The dash is a handy device, informal and essentially playful, telling you that you're about to take off on a different tack but still in some way connected to the present course—only you have to remember that the dash is there, and either put in a second dash at the end of the notion to let the reader know that he's back on course, or else end the sentence, as here, with a period.
— LEWIS THOMAS

to indicate a kind of grammatical equality or identification between the material located on one side and that on the other side. One of the benefits of the colon is the leisure it allows the writer to explain without having to write full sentences.

.... **(53f)**

On Using Ellipses

Ellipses are purely rhetorical or grammatical in function. They derive from the classical Greek scheme *ellipsis,* which refers to the omission of a word or words from a text. Classical rhetoricians had in mind a conscious omission that would be implied by the context:

> And he to England shall along with you.   – HAMLET

> So let the class invent its own assignments. If it wants more sophistication, fine.   – PETER ELBOW

Undiluted dashiness has become the mark of the slapdash writer who fails to take the trouble to differentiate among the pauses of punctuation.
– WILLIAM SAFIRE

Have students quote parts of the preceeding excerpts in sentences indicating omissions, as explained on the *Handbook* p. 787. Teach your students how to recognize the use of ellipses by sharing with them a variety of examples and pointing out instances in their own writing.

.... **(53g)**

FOR TEACHING: ONLINE PUNCTUATION

More and more, we see new forms of punctuation being used by online writers. Ask your students what kinds of marks they use most often in emails and instant-message communications. Review the list on *Handbook* p. 788. Then ask students to write up a brief "introduction" for their favorite punctuation mark, giving examples of where and when to use the mark online. Share with them the following humorous piece by Mark Harmon:

> I write in praise of the interrobang, a punctuation mark that looks something like a question mark with an exclamation point superimposed on it. It is the perfect punctuation mark for parents, as in: "You got home when?!" or "You left your brother where?!" or "You did/ate/pierced what?!" Unfortunately, the interrobang is not available on any keyboard that I know of, so we still are obliged to use both question mark and exclamation point as punctuation for such expressions of shock, disbelief, incredulity, outrage, anger, or puzzlement. . . . One might think that Internet users—who have done so much for / and @ — might have a soft spot for the interrobang. Instead, they seem content

to use colons, semicolons, hyphens, and parentheses to create sideways faces at the close of sentences.

■ **USEFUL READINGS**

Baker, Nicholson. "The History of Punctuation." *The Size of Thoughts.* New York: Vantage, 1997. 70–88. Baker remarks on "newer forms of emotional punctuation called 'smileys' or 'emoticons'—a sideways facial expression at the close of an email paragraph—e.g., :-) and >%-(. The semicolon collaborates in the 'wink' or 'smirk,' thus —;-)."

The Chicago Manual of Style. 14th ed. Chicago: U of Chicago P, 1993. See chapter 5, "Punctuation," which discusses colons, dashes, parentheses, brackets, and hyphens.

Hale, Constance, ed. *Wired Style: Principles of English Usage in the Digital Age.* New York: Broadway, 1999. Online at <http://hotwired.lycos.com/hardwired/wiredstyle>.

Harmon, Mark D. "Crossing a Question Mark with an Exclamation Point." *Chronicle of Higher Education* 28 July 2000: B7.

Palacas, Arthur L. "Parentheticals and Personal Voice." *Written Communication* 6 (1989): 506–27. Based on a sample of professional writing, Palacas argues that one clear source of "voice" is appositive and parenthetical structures.

Safire, William. "On Language." *New York Times Magazine* 28 May 2000: 19.

PART 10

UNDERSTANDING MECHANICAL CONVENTIONS

54 ⬇ Using Capitals

Originally, a large letter usually marked the beginning of a sentence, and that letter could be either upper- or lowercase. The *Codex Alexandrinus* (a fifth-century copy of the Bible) is one of the first documents that uses large letters to mark off each sentence. A full lowercase set of characters existed as early as A.D. 510, and the mixing of lowercase and uppercase characters developed from this date. By the time printing became established (in the mid-1500s), capital letters always signaled the start of a sentence (as in the Gutenberg Bible), but they were also liberally scattered throughout manuscripts at the printer's discretion. By the seventeenth century, the use of capital letters had become more or less standardized; they were used at the beginning of sentences and for proper names and titles. The *Encyclopaedia Britannica* (1975) notes that standardizing the usage of uppercase and lowercase letters was a crucial development:

> Three of the most important components [of a system of punctuation] are the space left blank between words; the identification of the first line of a new paragraph; and the uppercase, or capital, letter written at the beginning of a sentence and at the beginning of a proper name or a title.

Today, we take blank space and paragraph indentation for granted. However, our elaborate conventions for the use of capital letters — especially in online discourse — take more time and effort for students to recognize and adhere to.

On the Rhetorical Function of Capitalization

The use of capitals may seem simply conventional, but the conventions involved have rhetorical functions. In *Modern Punctuation*, George Summey Jr. lists three general functions of capitalization:

1. "As an aid to clearness." (Capitalizing proper nouns to distinguish them from common nouns and capitalizing the first letter of a sentence aid the logos of the writer's work.)
2. "For courtesy or reverence." (Capitalizing names and titles aid the writer's ethos.)
3. "For emphasis." (Although generally out of fashion nowadays, capitalizing words such as *nature* can possibly aid a writer's logos or pathos.) (165)

FOR MULTILINGUAL WRITERS: DIFFERENCES IN CAPITALIZATION STYLES

The Chicago Manual of Style advises writers that "Articles . . . , coordinating conjunctions . . . , and prepositions, regardless of length, are lowercased unless they are the first or last word of the title or subtitle" (282–83). The *Handbook* follows this advice. We recognize and discuss with our students that rules for capitalization (as well as punctuation and mechanics in general) are conventions, agreements between readers and writers. These rules may differ from publisher to publisher, between English and psychology, and from instructor to instructor. Students need to know the conventions they are asked to write in. To work from a position of strength, students should become familiar with the basic rules that have achieved the consensus in standard academic English (the rules summarized in the *Handbook*), and then find out how those rules differ in other disciplines or from one instructor to another.

FOR TEACHING: CAPITALIZATION AND POETRY   **(54a)** ....

Ask your students to read the poem by e. e. cummings on p. 615 of the *Handbook,* paying particular attention to capitalization. Discuss how cummings's placement of capitals helps readers understand the poem. Compare the capitalization in this poem to the choices made by Emily Dickinson on p. 800.

On Capitalizing Proper Nouns   **(54b)** ....

The eighteenth century saw a movement to begin proper nouns with lowercase letters. In a letter to his son, dated April 13, 1752, Lord Chesterfield denounced the fashion:

It offends my eyes to see *rome, france, caesar, henry the fourth,* etc. begin with small letters; and I do not conceive that there can be any reason for doing it half so strong as the reason of long usage to the contrary. This is an affectation of Voltaire.

However, in the first draft of the Declaration of Independence, Thomas Jefferson did not capitalize words that usually received capitalization in the eighteenth century, including *nature, creator,* and even *god.*

(54c) FOR TEACHING: CAPITALIZING TITLES OF WORKS

Consider encouraging your students to act as researchers by asking them to bring to class examples of how capitalization rules are used for titles. Direct them to student newspapers, print advertisements, labels on bottles and cans, and billboards for examples, and ask them to determine what they feel are appropriate and inappropriate uses (when capitals *should* be used), and effective and ineffective uses (when capitals help focus attention). Try to direct attention to the context of language use; what may be appropriate in an advertisement may be inappropriate in a formal paper for your class.

FOR TEACHING: CAPITALIZATION AND SPECIAL EFFECTS

Writers often capitalize words or even whole passages to add a special emphasis (WOW! ZAP!). The writer Dave Barry uses this technique in his humorous newspaper columns: "Today, I saw a chicken driving a car. (I AM NOT MAKING THIS UP.)" Ask students to look through the local newspaper, noting examples of capital letters used for emphasis and to bring some examples to class for comparison with those found by classmates.

For examples of how a writer of serious intentions may use capitalization for different kinds of emphasis, refer your students to the excerpt from Cynthia Ozick's "We Are the Crazy Lady" on *Handbook* p. 814.

(54f) TEACHING WITH TECHNOLOGY: CAPITALIZATION IN EMAIL

Ask students to spend a few minutes writing an email message to someone they haven't seen for some time, giving the person they've chosen an update on their activities. Then ask students to discuss with one another all the words they capitalized — and why.

■ USEFUL READINGS

The Chicago Manual of Style. 14th ed. Chicago: U of Chicago P, 1993. See chapter 7, "Names and Terms," for a discussion of when to use capital letters; section 7.127 comments on articles in titles.

Period Styles: A History of Punctuation. New York: Herb Lubalin Study Center of Design and Typography in the Cooper Union for the Advancement of Science and Art, 1988. See the first essay, "Period Styles: A Punctuated History."

Summey, George, Jr. *Modern Punctuation.* New York: Oxford UP, 1919.

55

▼ Using Abbreviations and Numbers

As the opening to Chapter 55 in the *Handbook* suggests, students may be most familiar with the numbers and abbreviations they find in the phone book (or on the Internet or in the *TV Guide* listings). Point out to them the way both abbreviations and numbers function in the following excerpt, and then ask them to jot down the major places in which they ordinarily encounter abbreviations and numbers.

> *AAA — CHICAGO MOTOR CLUB*
> *Emergency 24 Hr. Road Service*
>   *Toll Free* *800-262-6327*
> *Membership Services and Insurance*
>   *68 E. Wacker Pl.* *372-1818*

On Abbreviations

The controversy over whether to abbreviate or spell out a word can become heated. On the one hand, commentators William and Mary Morris take the conservative approach: "Generally speaking, *abbreviations* are to be avoided in formal writing" (2). On the other hand, commentators like Rudolf Flesch take a different view: "It's a superstition that abbreviations shouldn't be used in serious writing and that it's good style to spell everything out. Nonsense: use abbreviations whenever they are customary and won't attract the attention of the reader" (3).

Flesch's statement points to an important aspect of abbreviation usage: choosing whether to use abbreviations or spell out the words is a rhetorical decision. As the authors of *Words into Type* note, "An abbreviation that can be used in certain branches of writing might be poor form in others" (100). For instance, *vs.* for *versus* is acceptable in legal writing, but not, to conservative taste, in some other formal writing. The writer must once again recognize and evaluate her or his audience. One rule of thumb, however, does apply across disciplines: when in doubt, spell it out. Today, writers find abbreviations in many World Wide Web addresses and sites, and the conventions surrounding these uses of abbreviations are still very much in flux.

On the History of Abbreviations

Writers have always used abbreviations, whether on stone, paper, or computer screens. *SPQR, Senatus Populusque Romanus,* the insignia of Rome, was the most famous abbreviation of Western antiquity. For the several centuries preceding our own, the use of abbreviations declined, but since World War II, we have experienced a veritable flood of abbreviated words, especially in the United States. Just looking at the way some companies and products are spelled will indicate the extent to which people in the United States abbreviate:

EZ for *easy* as in EZ Sleep Motel.

X for *ex-* as in X-cel Optical Co.

Hi for *high* as in Hi-Lo Oil Co.

Also, our abbreviations, taking the general meaning of that word, involve much more than this chapter suggests. *Laser, radar, scuba, snafu,* and *sonar* are among the acronyms that are now integral parts of the English lexicon. Abbreviations as well as acronyms can become pronounceable words themselves. Abbreviating has become an important way of coining new words: *ad* for *advertisement; auto* for *automobile; bra* for *brassiere; exam* for *examination; lab* for *laboratory; phone* for *telephone; photo* for *photograph.*

Ask your students to compile a list of all the new computer-related abbreviations they can think of.

On Differences in Abbreviation Styles

In presenting the form of common abbreviations, the *Handbook* conforms with *The Chicago Manual of Style.* However, you may want to take note that in some instances *The MLA Handbook* prescribes different usages. For example, the MLA editors use no periods with *AD, BC,* or *NB.*

(55b)

On Using Abbreviations with years: B.C., B.C.E. and A.D.

Most of us don't always remember that while B.C.E. and B.C. follow a date, A.D. precedes it. Even columnist and conservative grammarian William Safire admits an infamous mistake regarding the use of A.D. As a speech-writer at the White House, he approved the wording of the plaque left on the moon by the first American astronauts to land there. It reads "July 1969, A.D." Safire expresses the wish that "some descendant of mine will take a sharp stylus on some weekend rocket to the moon and, while await-ing a transfer rocket to Mars, will draw a little arrow placing it in front of the word *July*. This will show that human beings in the early days of space were grammatically fallible; that mankind . . . is forever editing, and that a little precision is a dangerous thing."

(55d)

On Using Other Kinds of Abbreviations: *i.e.* and *e.g.*

Two Latin abbreviations, *e.g.* and *i.e.*, can easily be confused, although their meanings are rarely interchangeable. *E.g.* means "for example" (from the Latin *exempli gratia*). It introduces an instance or examples of that to which it refers. *I.e.* means "that is" (from the Latin *id est*). It introduces a repetition in different words, a restatement or amplification of ideas just preceding it.

(55e)

FOR TEACHING: SPELLING OUT NUMBERS

You might be asked to specify relatedness as a factor in deciding whether to use a numeral or spell out the number. *The Chicago Manual of Style* states:

> Numbers applicable to the same category should be treated alike within the same context, whether a paragraph or a series of paragraphs; do not use nu-merals for some and spell out others. (296)

Here is an example:

> The English Department has 75 graduate students in six major areas: 29 in lit-erature; 25 in rhetoric and composition; 8 in literary theory; 6 in linguistics; 4 in folklore; and 3 in film.

In this sentence, all the numerals relate to student population. However, the spelled-out number (*six*) relates to *major areas*. Therefore, the writer is permitted to spell out numbers and use numerals in the same sentence. The key factor in deciding whether to spell it out or not is rhetorical: which way would cause less confusion? Spelling out the one number that is unrelated to the seven other numbers distinguishes it so that the reader will not confuse it with the others.

■ **USEFUL READINGS**

The Chicago Manual of Style. 14th ed. Chicago: U of Chicago P, 1993. The *Manual* provides complete information on the standard form and punctuation of abbreviations.

Flesch, Rudolf. *The ABC of Style.* New York: Harper, 1964.

Mencken, H. L. *The American Language.* 5th ed. New York: Knopf, 1999. The author provides a readable discussion of abbreviations.

Morris, William, and Mary Morris. *Harper Dictionary of Contemporary Usage.* New York: Harper, 1975. This usage guide differs somewhat from others by relying on a panel of writers to discuss problems of usage.

Skillin, Marjorie E., and Robert Malcolm Gay. *Words into Type.* 3rd ed. Englewood Cliffs: Prentice, 1974.

56 ⬇ Using Italics

Italic is one of the three families of type that have dominated Western ty-pography since the invention of printing. The other two are roman (the type used here) and 𝔟𝔩𝔞𝔠𝔨 𝔩𝔢𝔱𝔱𝔢𝔯 (also referred to as Old English or Gothic but not to be confused with newer Gothic typefaces). Black letter type is used today almost exclusively for decoration. Roman is the name for the kind of type that is used predominantly in printing in the West today. Italic falls in between, having both technical uses (to indicate titles, etc.) and rhetorical uses (to indicate emphasis). Each of the three major types has its origins in calligraphy.

Black letter type developed out of decorative handwriting usually as-sociated with Germany and England. Roman letters developed first as capitals — in Rome, of course. Italic letters were based on the cursive writ-ing used by chancery scribes in Italy to speed up their work.

The preferred type of the earliest printers was black letter. However, the first printers in Italy, Konrad Sweynheim and Arnold Pannartz, found it inappropriate for the Humanist movement that was sweeping fifteenth-century Italy. They searched calligraphic history for a more "Humanistic" type and developed what they called "Antiqua." In time, Antiqua became what we know of as "roman." For many years, black letter continued to be used for non-Humanist texts, ecclesiastical writings, and legal works.

The first printer to use italic type was Aldus Manutius, who worked in Venice in the late fifteenth century. His type designer, Francesco Griffo of Bologna, modeled his italic design on the cursive letters used in the papal chanceries of the time. Italic type first appeared in a series of Latin pocketbook-size texts, aimed at the new audience of Renaissance readers who had the Humanist love for Latin writers. The series succeeded im-mediately. The first volume, the "Aldine Virgil," appeared in 1501.

Today, word processors and some email programs allow for italics. If your students *don't* have access to such programs, they can still indicate italics by <u>underlining</u>.

On the History of Print Types

Printing was introduced into England in 1474 by William Caxton, who used a rather striking black letter type. His assistant and eventual successor, Wynkyn de Worde, introduced italic type to England in 1524.

The French, however, were to be the most influential printers in England, establishing the dominance of roman type. As early as 1518, Richard Pinson, a Norman, introduced roman type into England and established a forty-year printing career that issued more than four hundred printed works. In 1540, Claude Garamond, the first commercial typefounder, designed and cut a roman type, referred to as the "Garamond type." It quickly displaced most of the other types used in Europe. However, in 1672, when King Louis XIV ordered the creation of a new type based on "scientific principles," typecutter Philippe Grandjean designed *Roman du Roi,* which immediately overtook Garamond as the preferred type.

In 1734, William Caslon introduced a refined version of the Garamond type, which became what we think of as the traditional roman type. The Caslon type won wide acceptance and was introduced into the American colonies by Benjamin Franklin. The official copies of the Declaration of Independence were printed in Caslon's roman type.

On Using Italics for Titles   (56a)

Newspapers provide an inexpensive, always available source of writing on which students can model much of their own use of conventions. However, in some cases, a newspaper may not be a good resource for models of italics usage. Traditionally, they have used quotation marks in place of italics. Today, many major newspapers, including the *New York Times, Washington Post, Chicago Tribune,* and *Los Angeles Times,* italicize their headlines. They use a number of different typefaces in order to produce variety, especially on front pages, which are full of different news stories. However, they continue to use quotation marks to indicate any titles, including those of books, plays, and magazines, despite style manuals that say these titles ought to be italicized.

·····································(56e) **On Using Italics for Special Emphasis**

Writers may want to use italics to emphasize parts of a work for a variety of different reasons. Fowler suggests several:

1. To emphasize the main point of the phrase or clause or sentence.
2. To stress a contrast with reader expectations (and, of course, reveal the writer's awareness of the contrast).
3. To stress a contrast with another word, phrase, etc., within proximity (with both words, phrases, etc., usually italicized).
4. To suggest a stress upon a word or phrase, if it were spoken aloud.
5. To suggest that that which is being emphasized deserves more consideration or "thinking over" than the reader would normally give it: "They [italics] pull up the reader and tell him not to read on, or he will miss some peculiarity in the italicized word. The particular point he is to notice is left to his own discernment . . ." (313).

Whether or not to use italics for emphasis is still being debated and probably will continue to be debated as long as some writers feel the need for that special emphasis. Fowler calls it "a primitive way of soliciting attention" (313). Yet, as *The Chicago Manual of Style* states, "Writers have probably always felt the need for devices to give special expression . . ." (209).

·····································(56e) **FOR TEACHING: USING ITALICS FOR SPECIAL EMPHASIS**

A visitors' guide of Chicago provides the following listing:

> *Gold Coast Dogs* (418 North State). Chicago is serious about hot dogs. A good Chicago hot dog is an all-beef critter with natural casing, in a steamed bun and topped with your choice of the following (aka *everything*): yellow mustard, relish, raw chopped onion, tomato wedges, a dill pickle sliced lengthwise, maybe jalapeño peppers if you're perverse, and celery salt. A good Chicago hot dog *never* touches catsup, brown mustard, cooked onions, cheese, or sauerkraut.

Ask students to identify the purposes for which italics are used in the passage. Then ask them to find examples of italics in other sources and to bring in two or three interesting examples to compare with those discovered by classmates.

■ **USEFUL READINGS**

The Chicago Manual of Style. 14th ed. Chicago: U of Chicago P, 1993. The *Manual* provides full guidance in the use of italics.

Fowler, Henry. *A Dictionary of Modern English Usage.* 2nd ed. New York: Oxford UP, 1965.

"Printing, Typography, and Photoengraving." *The New Encyclopaedia Britannica: Macropaedia.* 1987. This article provides a brief history and discussion of the nature of typography.

57 ⬇ Using Hyphens

the lady whose odd smile is the merest hyphen
— KARL SHAPIRO

The "merest" hyphen is used to divide words at the end of a line and to link words or word parts (such as *hand-me-down* or *bye-bye*). As such, it serves purposes both mechanical and rhetorical. Its mechanical uses are fairly straightforward, with simple rules that tell us when and where we can divide a word at the end of a line. The rhetorical ones, however, are somewhat more complicated, for though they are governed in some cases by rules, they are defined in other cases by the needs of readers. You can use the following anecdote to point out the rhetorical usefulness of a hyphen:

> I came across a word I thought was a series of typos for *collaborators*. Reading it again, I realized the word was *colaborers*. But a hyphen would have [prevented] all the confusion. — STEWART BEACH

Indeed, had the word included a hyphen — *co-laborers* — its meaning would have been instantly clear.

On the History of Hyphens

Early Greek grammarians placed a short line *under* a compound to indicate that it was not to be read as two words. This sign did not appear *within* the line because paper was so scarce, the same reason that most Greek and early Latin manuscripts appear with no spaces between words. But even after spacing had been introduced, it was haphazard at best. Greek manuscripts never perfectly divided text into words, and it was only in the eleventh century that hyphens began appearing in Latin manuscripts. As A. C. Partridge reminds us, though, the use of the hyphen did

Hooray for the hyphen! Or, rather, Hoo-ray!
— GEORGE PLIMPTON

424

not become systematic until the twelfth century, and even then, the hyphen was sometimes repeated at the beginning of the next line (58). By the sixteenth century, hyphens were commonplace and used for the same purposes that we use them today, although they appeared in manuscripts doubled, like an equal sign (=), and slanted.

FOR TEACHING: USING HYPHENS TO DIVIDE WORDS AT THE END OF A LINE   **(57a)**

After reviewing the rules on p. 815 of the *Handbook*, share with your students the following amusing anecdote by Dave Barry about using hyphens to divide words at the end of a line:

> According to a *Washington Post* news item concerning an internal memo distributed by IRS deputy chief counsel, Marlene Gross, Gross "does not want to receive any memorandums, letters, etc. with hyphenated words." A second memo stated that Gross "does not want hyphenated words in letters, memos, unless it is at the end of the sentence." The *Post* does not say why Gross feels so strongly about hyphens. But it's quite common for people to develop hostility toward punctuation. I myself fly into a homicidal rage when I see business names featuring apostrophes on either side of the letter 'n,' such as "The Chew 'n' Swallow Café."

FOR COLLABORATIVE WORK: USING HYPHENS WITH COMPOUND WORDS   **(57b)**

Consider the following excerpt from a modern translation of *Beowulf.* Read it aloud to the class, and then ask students to suggest synonyms for the compounded terms. Finally, read both the excerpt and the version with their synonyms, and attempt to describe the difference in tone that results.

> There was stone paving on the path that brought
> the war-band on its way. The war-coats shone
> and the links of hard hand-locked iron
> sang in their harness as they stepped along
> in their gear of grim aspect, going to the hall.
> Sea-wearied, they then set against the wall
> their broad shields of special temper,
> and bowed to bench, battle-shirts clinking,
> the war-dress of warriors. The weapons of the
> seamen stood in the spear-rack, stacked together,
> an ash-wood grey-tipped. These iron-shirted
> men were handsomely armed.

FOR TEACHING: USING HYPHENS WITH COMPOUND WORDS

Consider reading Paul Fussell's "Notes on Class" with your class, focusing on the way he uses hyphenated compounds to name social classes. Because the topic of his essay — class divisions in society — is "a dirty little secret," no names exist to designate the distinctions Fussell wishes to make:

Top Out-of-Sight	Mid-Proletarian
Upper Class	Low-Proletarian
Upper-Middle-Class	Destitute
Middle Class	Bottom Out-of-Sight
High-Proletarian	

Fussell also uses hyphens to create compound words to express his ideas: *pseudo-genteel, shape-change, quasi-official,* and *dark-suited first-generation aspirants* ("Notes on Class," from *The Boy Scout Handbook and Other Observations* [New York: Oxford UP, 1982]).

More recently, English has been absorbing large numbers of compounds derived from the computer industry. *Wired Style* offers good advice on how to deal with hyphenating (or *not* hyphenating) these new terms.

■ **USEFUL READINGS**

Hare, Constance, ed. *Wired Style: Principles of English Usage in the Digital Age.* San Francisco: Hardwired, 1996.

Partridge, A. C. *Orthography in Shakespeare and Elizabethan Drama.* Lincoln: U of Nebraska P, 1964. For a concise and informative discussion of how the major punctuation marks evolved, see appendix VIII, "The Historical Development of Punctuation Marks."

Teall, Edward N. *Meet Mr. Hyphen and Put Him in His Place.* New York: Funk, 1937. See chapter 1 for a short history of hyphens.

Webb, Robert A. *The Washington Post Deskbook on Style.* 2nd ed. New York: McGraw, 1989. See the entry under "hyphens" for rules and illustrative examples.

PART 11

FOR MULTILINGUAL WRITERS

58 ▼ Learning U.S. Academic Conventions

> *America is woven of many strands. I would recognize them and let it so remain. Our fate is to become one, and yet many. This is not prophecy, but description.*
> — RALPH ELLISON

Within the many strands of U.S. culture are countless multilingual students who encounter American academic conventions as confusing restrictions on the ways of reading, writing, and thinking that they have known for so long. Whether we consider these U.S. conventions in terms of "contrastive rhetorics" or "second-language issues," we need to be sensitive to the fact that U.S. academic conventions comprise a culture with a discourse and philosophy that can intimidate many multilingual students.

If the assumption "we all know good writing when we see it" governs our approach to teaching composition, how will we incorporate a concern for multilingual writers whose ways of engaging texts, assuming expectations for readers and writers, and personal or academic voices may not conform to such models? The notes provided here and the readings listed at the end of this chapter can begin to suggest alternative ways of approaching the teaching of writing to multilingual students. In particular, recent work by Diane Belcher, Ilona Leki, and Vivian Zamel—to name a few—offer us suggestions on how to teach students U.S. academic conventions in a way that takes Ralph Ellison's tribute to America to heart.

America's future walks through the doors of our schools each day.
— MARY JEAN LETENDRE

(58a) FOR TEACHING: WRITING U.S.A. STYLE

While the "process movement" has been all the rage in composition studies, Ilona Leki tells us that ESL teaching has only recently shifted from structure-based language instruction to process-based instruction. In order to achieve the task of teaching your students how to produce effective academic writing, you will need to engage your multilingual students using a process model, not a transmission model of writing pedagogy.

Share with your students Min-Zhan Lu's moving personal essay, "From Silence to Words: Writing as Struggle" (available in Sondra Perl's collection, *Landmark Essays on Writing Process*), and have them discuss Lu's writing process. What academic styles did she encounter on her journey? What academic conventions have your students encountered? What counts as "standard" in their home countries? When did they make their second (or third) language acquisition?

You might also share with students stories about famous novelists who chose to write in second languages, such as Joseph Conrad and Samuel Beckett. How did these writers master the particular style of a given audience and make their living by it? What can your students learn from such tales? How have cultures and expectations for assimilation changed since Conrad and Beckett? How are they different in the United States versus England or France?

America's future will be determined by the home and the school. The child becomes largely what he is taught; hence we must watch what we teach, and how we live.
–Jane Addams

FOR COLLABORATIVE WORK: UNDERSTANDING EXPECTATIONS FOR READERS

(58b)

Ilona Leki advocates immersion in language, especially reading, as vital for developing writing skills. In her book, *Understanding ESL Writers*, Leki recommends classroom practices, analyzes student writing, and surveys findings of contrastive rhetoric for several cultures. Similarly, Vivian Zamel, in "Writing One's Way into Reading," argues that reading and writing are interactive, mutually beneficial tasks.

Building off this research, have students in your classes share the inventories they created for section 58b of the *Handbook*. How do native speakers approach a text in contrast to multilingual speakers? What expectations do readers of various discourse communities hold?

America is a land of wonders, in which everything is in constant motion and every change seems an improvement. . . . No natural boundary seems to be set to the efforts of man; and in his eyes, what is not yet done is only what he has not yet attempted to do.
– Alexis de Tocqueville

FOR MULTILINGUAL WRITERS: UNDERSTANDING EXPECTATIONS FOR WRITERS

(58c)

Sandra Cisneros tells her readers to "write about what makes you different." Indeed, for multilingual writers, their own experience is a veritable treasure trove of material for academic, professional, and personal essays.

Candace Spigelman sees strategic versions of "the personal" as a legitimate form of academic writing. Using her case for conceptualizing personal writing through principles of rhetorical argument, encourage your students to make claims, warrants, appeals to authority, and other persuasive arguments using their own experiences in their writing.

TEACHING WITH TECHNOLOGY: UNDERSTANDING EXPECTATIONS FOR TEXTS

In her 1997 address to the Conference on College Composition and Communication, Cynthia Selfe discussed contemporary expectations for texts in a technological age:

> Technological literacy—meaning computer skills and the ability to use computers and other technology to improve learning, productivity and performance—has become as fundamental to a person's ability to navigate through society as traditional skills like reading, writing and arithmetic. (par. 1)

In *Literacy and Computers*, Cynthia Selfe and Susan Hilligoss expand further on the significance of technologically mediated texts for U.S. academic conventions:

America is the only country left where we teach languages so that no pupil can speak them.
– JOHN ERSKINE

> Technology, along with the issues that surround its use in reading- and writing-intensive classrooms, both physically and intellectually disrupts the ways in which we make meaning—the ways in which we communicate. Computers change the ways in which we read, construct, and interpret texts. In doing so, technology forces us to rethink what it means to be human. We need more problems like this. (1)

Share the preceding passages with your students. Do they agree that technology has transformed U.S. academic conventions? How does America's access to computers change what it means to write across the globe? How do students from other countries and cultures respond to new technological environments? What expectations for texts do they need to learn? How can we assess digital literacy and teach writing in a newly mediated environment?

FOR COLLABORATIVE WORK: UNDERSTANDING EXPECTATIONS FOR TEXTS

Give students the following quotation on an electronic discussion board:

> The last time somebody said, "I find I can write much better with a word processor," I replied, "They used to say the same thing about drugs."
> – ROY BLOUNT JR.

Then ask them to write a brief essay—to be posted to the discussion board—about the textual and cultural allusions inherent in the passage, and to create a thesis concerning whether they agree with it. To further the dialogue, ask each student to respond to one other student's post. Choose a few postings from the class to generate discussion on how expectations for texts are changing today with the increasing use of computers.

■ **USEFUL READINGS**

Bartholomae, David. "Inventing the University." *When a Writer Can't Write: Studies in Writer's Block and Other Composing Process Problems*. Ed. Mike Rose. New York: Guilford, 1985. 135–65. Bartholomae argues that to succeed in college, students must learn to speak the language of the university, to "try on the peculiar ways of knowing, selecting, evaluating, reporting, concluding, and arguing" that are already valued by various academic discourse communities.

Belcher, Diane, and George Braine, eds. *Academic Writing in a Second Language: Essays on Research and Pedagogy*. Norwood, NJ: Ablex, 1995.

Bizzaro, Resa Crane. "Places as Teacher-Scholars in Composition Studies: Comparing Transition Narratives." *CCC* 53.3 (Feb. 2002): 487–506. Through personal narrative, professional interviews, and a synthesis of theoretical claims, Bizzaro discusses the experiences of Native Americans and other minorities in order to offer those marginalized by ethnicity, race, class, and gender a model for entering the profession of rhetoric and composition.

Carson, Joan G., and Ilona Leki, eds. *Reading in the Composition Classroom: Second Language Perspectives*. Boston: Heinle, 1993. The authors examine how reading and writing are increasingly being taught together in ESL courses—not as technical skills but as processes imbued in cultural contexts.

Connor, Ulla. *Contrastive Rhetoric: Cross-cultural Aspects of Second-Language Writing*. New York: Cambridge UP, 1996.

Cope, Bill, and Mary Kalantzis, eds. *Multiliteracies: Literacy Learning and the Design of Social Futures*. London: Routledge, 2000. This collection of essays from the New London Group (NLG), which includes the famous 1996 *Harvard Educational Review* manifesto, "Pedagogy of Multiliteracies: Designing Social Futures," analyzes and responds to the globalized, "fast-capitalism" economy that both fragments cultures and produces new forms of writing in terms of multimedia and information technology. With consequences for theories of public and private spheres as well as for curricula, this volume offers new perspectives on negotiating changes in literacy and writing.

Cummins, Jim. "The Sanitized Curriculum: Educational Disempowerment in a Nation at Risk." *Richness in Writing: Empowering ESL Students*. Ed. Donna M.

Johnson and Duane H. Roen. White Plains: Longman, 1989. The authors discuss how, in 1983, university curricula across the country shifted policies from "equity" to "excellence" with the consequence that increased standards and tough pedagogical strategies threatened to disempower multilingual and minority students in particular.

Ferdman, Bernardo M., Rose-Marie Weber, and Arnulfo G. Ramirez, eds. *Literacy across Languages and Cultures.* Albany: State U of New York P, 1994. The essays in this collection reveal that meeting the English literacy needs of members of linguistic and cultural minorities in the United States requires rethinking many assumptions about literacy itself, especially because most research concentrates on first-language literacy.

Henry, Jim. "Writing Workplace Cultures." *CCC* 53.2 (Dec. 2001). Online at <http://www.ncte.org/ccc/2/53.2/henry/article.html>. Henry examines the dramatic changes wrought by globalization (or "fast capitalism") on both the workplace and the writing produced in it.

Huckin, Thomas, Margot Haynes, and James Coady. *Second Language Reading and Vocabulary Learning.* Norwood: Ablex, 1993. A presentation on research into the ways that ESL students learn vocabulary, including analyses of L1 vocabulary learning and the efficacy of contextual guessing, investigation of the assumption that reading improves vocabulary acquisition, and evaluation of pedagogical practices for improving vocabulary.

Kutz, Eleanor, Suzy Q. Groden, and Vivian Zamel. *The Discovery of Competence: Teaching and Learning with Diverse Student Writers.* Portsmouth: Boynton/Cook, 1993. A call to approach students in terms of competence, not error. The authors argue that teachers need to understand the complexities of language acquisition and help students acquire new competencies in academic discourse by building bridges between old and new languages.

Leki, Ilona. *Understanding ESL Writers: A Guide for Teachers.* Portsmouth: Boynton/Cook, 1992.

Lu, Min-Zhan. "From Silence to Words: Writing as Struggle." *CE* 49 (Apr. 1987): In this personal essay, Lu takes us on a journey between discourse communities and offers compelling points for writing teachers to ponder.

Okawa, Gail Y. "Diving for Pearls: Mentoring as Cultural and Activist Practice among Academics of Color." *CCC* 53.3 (Feb. 2002): 507–32. Okawa discusses the mentorship views of two senior scholars, Geneva Smitherman and Victor Villanueva, and offers insight into the complexities and costs of building a multiethnic/multiracial professoriate in our discipline.

Pennycook, Alastair. "Borrowing Others' Words: Text, Ownership, Memory, and Plagiarism." *TESOL Quarterly* 30 (Summer 1996): 201–30. In an interesting perspective on plagiarism, Pennycook argues that memorizing the words of others and other acts of language learning differ significantly across cultures, and that understanding the complex issues related to textual borrowing makes Western notions of plagiarism confusing and hypocritical.

Perl, Sondra. *Landmark Essays on Writing Process*. Davis: Hermagoras P, 1994.

Selfe, Cynthia. "Technology and Literacy: A Story about the Perils of Not Paying Attention." *CCC* 50.3 (Feb. 1999): 411–36.

Selfe, Cynthia L., and Susan Hilligoss. *Literacy and Computers: The Complications of Teaching and Learning with Technology*. New York: MLA, 1994. This crucial collection of essays on using computers in literacy education addresses how computer technology changes literacy instruction and how to use collaborative computer networks and hypertext; it also includes suggestions for further research on literacy and technology.

Spigelman, Candace. "Argument and Evidence in the Case of the Personal." *CE* 64.1 (Sept. 2001): 63–87. Spigelman examines the strategic versions of "the personal" as rhetorical tropes in academic essays and as sources of evidence that might replace more empirically based models in the form of "narrative probability." She builds on Aristotelian rhetorical theory to argue that "narrative too offers claims, reasons and evidence for serious analysis and critique" (83). Her works-cited list provides particularly rich material for interested readers.

Tucker, Amy. *Decoding ESL: International Students in the American College Classroom*. Portsmouth: Boynton/Cook, 1995.

Valdes, Guadalupe. "Bilingual Minorities and Language Issues in Writing." *Written Communication* 9 (Jan. 1992): 85–136. Examining the complexity of bilingualism in the United States, Valdes charges that our profession must do more research on the kinds of writing that bilingual minorities are exposed to, on how mainstream teachers respond to these students' writing, and on the linguistic and social factors that affect their writing.

Zamel, Vivian. "Strangers in Academia: The Experiences of Faculty and ESL Students across the Curriculum." *CCC* 46.4 (Dec. 1995): 506–21.

——. "Writing One's Way into Reading." *TESOL Quarterly* 26 (1992): 463–85. Zamel argues that even though reading and writing are both acts of meaning-making, reading continues to be taught by a transmission or information-retrieval model. Reading is a transaction between the text and the reader's knowledge and experience, and writing can reveal and enhance this transaction by enabling students to engage the text through their responses; students thus become better readers by becoming better writers.

Zamel, Vivian, and Ruth Spack, eds. *Negotiating Academic Literacies: Teaching and Learning across Languages and Cultures*. Mahwah: Lawrence Erlbaum, 1998.

59 ▼ Understanding Nouns and Noun Phrases

Assessment of student writing is already a complex field of study, and the assessment of ESL student writing can be even trickier, especially when the teacher doesn't feel prepared to teach or evaluate ESL students. But in "Assessment of ESL Students in Mainstream College Composition," Lisa Hillenbrand addresses the major concerns of writing instructors by speaking to issues of "Unraveling the Rhetoric," "Moving Away from the Error Obsession," and "Methods of Marking and Evaluating." She offers several substantive practices for classroom instructors.

FOR COLLABORATIVE WORK: NOUNS IN SPECIFIC LANGUAGES

Break the class into groups and make a list of the distinguishing characteristics among *nouns* in each group member's native language. Have students work together to prepare a lesson about these characteristics to present to the other groups. When they take the time to see and hear their native languages through the eyes and ears of a "foreigner," students will be better able to teach their own languages as well as to become more adept at learning the nuances of other languages, in this case, standard academic English.

(59a) ## FOR TEACHING: DISTINGUISHING COUNT AND NONCOUNT NOUNS

As you talk with your class about count and noncount nouns, you will have to talk about the ways the English language is redundant. At the beginning of Chapter 34 in this book, you will find a discussion of this important issue. Ask your students to bring in an essay they're working on and to write out the first paragraph, giving themselves plenty of space to mark out the redundancies of their English prose, particularly as redundancy does or does not apply to instances involving count and noncount nouns.

FOR TEACHING: CHOOSING ARTICLES APPROPRIATELY

(59d) ⋯⋯⋯⋯⋯⋯⋯⋯⋯⋯⋯⋯

Ask students to copy out a passage from an in-progress essay and label as definite or indefinite the articles they used. They should be able to explain their choice of article. When students use nouns *without articles,* they should also be able to explain their syntactical decision.

■ USEFUL READINGS

Acton, William. "Some Pragmatic Dimensions of ESL Writing Tutorials." Educational Resources Information Center, 1981. ED 267 581. Acton describes an "editor" model that ESL students may use with one another, especially if they ask for assistance with particular problems of mechanics, syntax, usage, idiomatic expressions, coherence, and style. If students know what their problem areas are and can ask for help with those problems, they will progress more quickly toward near-native fluency in English.

Hillenbrand, Lisa. "Assessment of ESL Students in Mainstream College Composition." *TETYC* 21 (May 1994): 125–29.

Robinson, William S. "ESL and Dialect Features in the Writing of Asian American Students." *TETYC* 22 (Dec. 1995): 303–10.

Zamel, Vivian. "Strangers in Academia: The Experiences of Faculty and ESL Students across the Curriculum." *CCC* 46.4 (Dec. 1995): 506–21.

60

▼ Understanding Verbs and Verb Phrases

In "The Poetry of ESL Error," Melissa Allen discusses her evolution from an error-oriented, frustrated ESL instructor to a relaxed, fascinated instructor of ESL students. She writes that she began enjoying her teaching and her students when she realized that they were telling her things she didn't know; they were provoking her to think. "[T]hey were using the English language in interesting ways, with nuance and subtlety, with fascinating sounds and rhythms and silences. Even the errors sometimes had a certain something—poetry?" (120).

Her realization changed her attitude about the goal of ESL teaching, and she argues that to concentrate on making ESL students write like native speakers is to "deprive them, ourselves, and our language of much that is enriching about the way ESL students use English" (121). Hers is a compelling argument, which is most convincing in the list of "error-free" ESL sentences she includes. She describes these sentences as having "a nonnative flavor":

1. I went outside and smoked down my anger.
2. I cheered him on his success.
3. [I looked through the list of names] but my name didn't come out for me.
4. When I feel oppressed in the chest, I like to listen to rock music.
5. I imagined she was a ferocious person who had timid ideas.
6. Your brain wants to eat more air than you are giving it.
7. Our music filled the room with warm heart.
8. It is useless to continue this barren argument.

FOR TEACHING: POETIC USES OF NONNATIVE ENGLISH

Ask for volunteers to share their "poetic" and other nonnative uses of English. If your students are working in groups, a native speaker of English might be able to locate such impressive examples of English usage.

■ **USEFUL READINGS**

Allen, Melissa. "The Poetry of ESL Error." *TETYC* 22 (May 1994): 120–24.

Goldstein, Lynn M., and Susan M. Conrad. "Student Input and Negotiation of Meaning in ESL Writing Conferences." *TESOL Quarterly* 24 (1990): 443–60. Conferencing in and of itself does not necessarily lead to student input or successful revision. Only when students negotiate meaning with the teacher is there a high percentage of successful revisions. The authors encourage teachers to discuss conference goals and examine their own conference behavior, especially in terms of trying to control the students' discourse.

Hafernick, Johnnie Johnson. "The How and Why of Peer Editing in the ESL Writing Class." Educational Resources Information Center (ERIC), 1983. ED 253 064. Hafernick discusses the advantages of peer editing and includes specific guidelines for ensuring efficient and successful editing days.

Hvitfeldt, Christina. "Guided Peer Critique in ESL at the College Level." ERIC, 1986. ED 282 438. If writing students follow specific guidelines, they will better analyze and critique student papers. Hvitfeldt includes sample peer-critique forms.

Keh, Claudia L. "Feedback in the Writing Process: A Model and Methods for Implementation." *English Language Teaching Journal* 44 (1990): 294–304. Feedback is a fundamental element of the process approach to writing: peer feedback, often focused on sentence-level concerns, raises audience awareness and allows peer learning/teaching; instructor feedback should also stay with higher-order concerns and follow established guidelines.

61

 Understanding
Prepositions and
Prepositional Phrases

Sandra Savignon, pioneer in communicative competence, is credited with influencing second-language teaching worldwide. Her work focuses on theoretical and research bases for language teaching, curriculum design, and testing procedures that encourage the learner to combine rule-based knowledge of several areas in order to negotiate meaning in a second language. In *Communicative Competence: Theory and Classroom Practice,* the phrase "communicative competence" includes "knowledge of sociolinguistic rules, or the appropriateness of an utterance in addition to knowledge of grammar rules." As she notes, "the development of the learners' communicative abilities is seen to depend not so much on the time they spend rehearsing grammatical patterns as on the opportunities they are given to interpret, to express, and to negotiate meaning in real-life situations."

(61a)

FOR COLLABORATIVE WORK: USING PREPOSITIONS IDIOMATICALLY

Ask your students to break into groups and discuss their language backgrounds. First, consider an American attitude that all people should either know or learn English. What is their response? Second, they may want to consider the idea that everyone — including those smug Americans — should learn at least one foreign language. What are the advantages of knowing another language? another culture? Finally, ask students to focus on any prepositions and prepositional phrases they have used in this discussion, noting those that seemed problematic. Use these examples for class discussion.

■ **USEFUL READINGS**

Chenoweth, N. Ann. "The Need to Teach Rewriting." *English Language Teaching Journal* 41 (1987): 25–29. Teachers who correct only sentence-level errors reinforce students' attention to only the sentence. Therefore, Chenoweth argues for assigning revisions rather than new essays.

Robb, Thomas, Steven Ross, and Ian Shortreed. "Salience of Feedback on Error and Its Effects on EFL Writing Quality." *TESOL Quarterly* 20 (1986): 83–93. Although research in ESL concludes that instructors should concentrate on higher-level concerns, most instructors continue to respond more frequently to issues of mechanics, syntax, and spelling. Instructors need to remember that the direct correction of surface errors is not a significant way to improve student writing ability.

Savignon, Sandra J. *Communicative Competence: Theory and Classroom Practice.* Reading: Addison, 1983.

——. "Communicative Language Learning." *Theory into Practice* 26 (1987): 235–42.

62 ⬇️ Forming Clauses and Sentences

In "Dictation as a Measure of Communicative Competence," Sandra Savignon argues that a student's success in taking dictation is a strong indicator of that student's language proficiency, for that student is *hearing* the language correctly. You might use the following passage for such an exercise:

> In prerevolutionary Cambodian society, whether a family belonged to the upper class or the peasantry, and whether they were ethnic Cambodian, or of Chinese or Vietnamese origin, the mother dealt with all household matters, child rearing in particular, and the prosperity, well-being, and reputation of the household depended mostly on her. The father dealt with the outside world and provided major family support. Because social norms based on Buddhist teachings promoted male-female equality, many women engaged in business ventures. When necessary, children helped their mothers to earn extra income, and there was usually a strong empathy between mothers and children. Even after children married and set up their own nuclear households, they continued to interact closely with their parents and siblings for mutual physical, emotional, and financial needs.
>
> The legal and cultural norm of duty to family members based on Buddhist precepts covered such things as parental authority, arrangement of proper marriages for children, provision of support in the event of divorce and in old age, inheritance, adoption, guardianship, and provision of proper funeral arrangements.
>
> Children generally received a great deal of affection in the first years of life not only from parents, but also from other adults and adolescents. But as they grew, older children were expected to conform to norms of politeness and obedience. Although some competition was present in games, the stress was on playing rather than winning. . . .
>
> By age 10 or so, both sexes had been taught basic skills necessary to be useful members of society. Boys, particularly in villages, learned agricultural techniques, while girls learned household duties. In adolescent years, the

two sexes were segregated in school, which was strictly a place for education, and not for entertainment or romance. Premarital sex was deplored and sexual knowledge not considered suitable for children because it was considered to lead to desire and trouble. Adults also did not display physical love publicly even after marriage. Ideally, marriages were arranged by parents.

– Usha Welaratna, "A Khmer Perspective"

You may also ask your students to read aloud their dictations, taking care to notice whether, as they read aloud, they correct any of the mistakes they've made in their transcriptions.

FOR TEACHING: FORMING CLAUSES AND SENTENCES

Read aloud to the class the following passage from Amy Tan's "The Language of Discretion," and then ask students to list her allegations. After you have written their lists of allegations on the board, ask students to respond to Tan's argument, providing examples from their own language when possible.

Having listened to both Chinese and English, I . . . tend to be suspicious of any comparisons between the two languages. Typically, one language — that of the person doing the comparing — is often used as the standard, the benchmark for a logical form of expression. And so the language being compared is always in danger of being judged deficient or superfluous, simplistic or unnecessarily complex, melodious or cacophonous. English speakers point out that Chinese is extremely difficult because it relies on variations in tone barely discernible to the human ear. By the same token, Chinese speakers tell me English is extremely difficult because it is inconsistent, a language of too many broken rules, of Mickey Mice and Donald Ducks.

Even more dangerous to my mind is the temptation to compare both language and behavior *in translation.* To listen to my mother speak English, one might think she has no concept of past or future tense, that she doesn't see the difference between singular and plural, that she is gender blind because she calls my husband "she." If one were not careful, one might also generalize that, based on the way my mother talks, all Chinese people take a circumlocutory route to get to the point. It is, in fact, my mother's idiosyncratic behavior to ramble a bit.   – Amy Tan, "The Language of Discretion"

■ **USEFUL READINGS**

Belcher, Diane, and George Braine, eds. *Academic Writing in a Second Language: Essays on Research and Pedagogy.* Norwood, NJ: Ablex, 1995. A "must-read" for teachers of writing.

Charles, Maggie. "Responding to Problems in Written English Using a Student Self-Monitoring Technique." *English Language Teaching Journal* 44 (1990): 286–93. Charles describes the ideal revision situation as editor-writer conferences between students and instructors. She outlines a procedure for student self-monitoring in which students engage in a written dialogue with instructors from their first draft through their final revision; such an approach gives students control, motivates them to read and incorporate comments, and encourages them to analyze their writing by placing themselves in the position of the reader.

Savignon, Sandra. "Dictation as a Measure of Communicative Competence." *Language Learning* 32 (1982): 33–51.

Spack, Ruth, and Catherine Sadow. "Student-Teacher Working Journals in ESL Freshman Composition." *TESOL Quarterly* 17 (1983): 575–93. Students and instructors exchange dialogic journals that focus on classroom issues. All students participate in the class and in the construction of their essay topics; instructors receive feedback on their techniques and topics. Journal writing has a positive impact on ESL students' writing attitudes and habits.

PART 12

ACADEMIC AND PROFESSIONAL WRITING

63

▼ Understanding Disciplinary Discourse

A college education should equip one to entertain three things: a friend, an idea and oneself.

— THOMAS EHRLICH

The belief that writing should be the concern of the entire school community underlies this chapter on understanding disciplinary discourse. According to Art Young and Toby Fulwiler, composition researchers and theorists such as James Britton, Janet Emig, James Kinneavy, James Moffett, Mina Shaughnessy, and Lillian Bridwell-Bowles have all variously suggested that student writing will not improve until students see writing at the center of their academic experience. They will learn to value it and practice it when it is incorporated usefully into the daily process of learning in all disciplines. Writing-across-the-curriculum programs work toward these goals. Over the last two decades, dozens of these programs have emerged in U.S. colleges and universities. Individual programs may differ in scope and practice, but all of them aim to improve student writing by encouraging faculty from across the disciplines to use writing regularly and thoughtfully in their classrooms.

On Writing in Specific Disciplines

Writing in the disciplines — sometimes called writing across the curriculum, writing in the content areas, language for learning, writing to learn — has two histories that Anne Herrington and Charles Moran refer to as "extraordinarily different yet intimately related" (3). In *Writing, Teaching, and Learning in the Disciplines,* they begin with two historical perspectives, the British one given by Nancy Martin and the American one discussed by David Russell. In these essays, we see how theorists and educators such as Douglas Barnes, James Britton, and Harold Rosen from the United Kingdom, and Wayne Booth, James Moffett, and Albert Kitzhaber from the

United States came together to provide an impetus for what came to be known as the writing-in-the-disciplines movement, a movement that has persisted for over twenty years. Today, many universities consider writing in the disciplines to be a central concern and use general education requirements to ensure that students are writing in their classes in a number of disciplines. This chapter aims to assist students in using skills and techniques from their writing courses to situate their writing in other disciplines successfully.

**FOR COLLABORATIVE WORK: ANALYZING
ACADEMIC ASSIGNMENTS AND EXPECTATIONS**

(63a)

If your students can provide assignments from various disciplines, have them carry out an analysis using the questions in the "Analyzing an Assignment in Any Discipline" checklist in 63a. Let them work in groups to analyze the assignments and their expectations.

**FOR MULTILINGUAL WRITERS: ANALYZING
ACADEMIC ASSIGNMENTS AND EXPECTATIONS**

(63a)

Writers from diverse national backgrounds have to consider cultural expectations as well as disciplinary specifications when approaching an assignment. They might need additional clarification on the various standards for disciplinary work. Encourage your multilingual students to visit their teachers during office hours or to make an appointment to review the assignment expectations before commencing a task. This communication will often prevent misunderstandings and will help expedite the learning process.

A teacher affects eternity; he can never tell where his influence stops.
—Henry Brooks Adams

FOR COLLABORATIVE WORK: UNDERSTANDING DISCIPLINARY VOCABULARIES

(63b)

Ask students to work in groups of three. Each student should bring to class two copies of a short passage of approximately one hundred words taken from an article, an essay, or a textbook in a field with which he or she is familiar. Have students give a copy to each of their partners and ask them (1) to list terms, phrases, or concepts that seem to involve specialized or highly technical language and (2) to define and explain these terms. Have students retrieve their articles and their partners' lists, check their efforts, and then, in discussion, clarify the terms for them. Discuss their confusion or lack of it.

This exercise gives students familiar with a particular field practice explaining basic terms to an audience unfamiliar with that field. For example, the term *blastema* is basic knowledge to students in molecular genetics, as is *Cyrillic alphabet* to Slavic language majors. *Morpheme* is a basic concept to linguistics students, as is *hypotenuse* to geometry students. Thus, this exercise serves two purposes:

1. It helps students develop an awareness of how to adapt their language and explanations to audiences with different degrees of expertise or familiarity with a field's vocabulary.

2. It also allows students to test their own understanding of terms and concepts. One way we determine how well we ourselves understand these is to explain them to someone else.

For additional practice at recognizing and using particular disciplinary language, divide the class into groups of no more than three students who are working in the same major field or some fairly closely related field. Ask each group to compile a glossary of twenty key terms that are essential to a field or that overlap related fields. Have students alphabetize the terms and give a definition and explanation of each.

(63c)   TEACHING WITH TECHNOLOGY: IDENTIFYING THE STYLE OF A DISCIPLINE

June Jordan might well have added to the quotation cited here, "And there is a language of science, of law, of medicine." To get students thinking about the style of disciplines, ask them to write a journal entry about their experiences with writing in different disciplines. Some will have found writing difficult or easy regardless of discipline, but others will have noted differences in the experiences, assignments, and teachers' expectations associated with different subjects. These journal entries can be shared or simply written as preparation for an initial class discussion of disciplinary writing conventions.

There are many languages. There is the language of guns. There is the language of money. There is the language of human rights. There is the language of love.
— June Jordan

(63d)   FOR TEACHING: UNDERSTANDING THE USE OF EVIDENCE

In an intriguing letter to the editor, published in the *PMLA*, David Linton examines the way in which scholarly contributors to a *PMLA* roundtable on "The Status of Evidence" use evidence themselves to make their claims. Ask your students to write similar letters to editors of journals that they read across various disciplines. In their letters, they should analyze and comment on the use of evidence in three of the journal's articles.

Any place that anyone young can learn something useful from someone with experience is an educational institution.
–AL CAPP

ATTENTING TO DISABILITIES: USING CONVENTIONAL DISCIPLINARY PATTERNS AND FORMATS

(63e) ··················

Students with various disabilities may wish to offer alternative means of complying with disciplinary patterns and formats in order to accommodate their particular learning styles. A vision-impaired student, for example, might provide a verbal copy of an assignment by using voice-recording technology at your campus disability center. Take time to discuss possible variations in disciplinary formats with advisors from across the college campus. You might bring up the importance of attending to disabilities at the next faculty meeting to get the discussion started.

■ USEFUL READINGS

Bazerman, Charles. "Codifying the Social Scientific Style: The APA Publication Manual as a Behaviorist Rhetoric." *The Rhetoric of the Human Sciences: Language and Argument in Scholarship and Public Affairs.* Ed. John Nelson, Allan Megill, and Donald McClosky. Madison: Wisconsin UP, 1987. Bazerman argues that the disciplines are socially negotiated territories and conventions of disciplines are representations of actions produced through that discipline's process of inquiry—a process that is shaped and transformed by the contributions of those who work with and within the discipline.

Herrington, Anne, and Charles Moran, eds. *Writing, Teaching, and Learning in the Disciplines.* New York: MLA, 1992. This collection contains fourteen essays covering historical and theoretical perspectives on writing across the curriculum as well as a number of treatments of classroom practice.

Kasper, Loretta Francis. "Discipline-oriented ESC Reading Instruction." *TETYC* (Feb. 1995): 45–53. Kasper describes three different kinds of reading courses that use discipline-specific materials.

Kirsch, Gesa. *Women Writing the Academy.* Carbondale: Southern Illinois UP, 1993. Kirsch studies women's experiences in trying to inhabit various disciplinary languages and styles.

Langer, Judith A. "Speaking of Knowing: Conceptions of Understanding in Academic Disciplines." *Writing, Teaching, and Learning in the Disciplines.* Ed. Anne Herrington and Charles Moran. New York: MLA, 1992. 69–85.

LeFevre, K. B., and M. J. Dickerson. *Until I See What I Say: Teaching Writing in All Disciplines.* Burlington: IDC Publications, 1981. This book, written by English instructors, gives several ideas for teaching writing in other disciplines. This source might prove especially useful for ideas on revision, generating content, and teaching techniques.

Linton, David. "The Framing of Evidence." *PMLA* 112 (1997): 428–29.

MacDonald, Susan Peck. *Professional Academic Writing in the Humanities and Social Sciences.* Carbondale: Southern Illinois UP, 1994. The author examines the ways disciplinary genres and forms shape knowledge-making.

Malinowitz, Harriet. "A Feminist Critique of Writing in the Disciplines." *Feminism and Composition Studies.* Ed. Susan C. Jaratt and Lynn Wosham. New York: MLA, 1998. 291–312.

Marsella, Joy, Thomas L. Hilgers, and Clemence McLaress. "How Students Handle Writing Assignments in Six Disciplines." *Writing, Teaching, and Learning in the Disciplines.* Ed. Anne Herrington and Charles Moran. New York: MLA, 1992. 174–91.

Walvoord, Barbara E., and Lucille P. McCarthy. *Thinking and Writing in College: A Naturalistic Study of Students in Four Disciplines.* Urbana: NCTE, 1990. Useful reading for teachers of first-year writing whose students will go on to enter a variety of disciplines.

Young, Art, and Toby Fulwiler. *Writing across the Disciplines: Research into Practice.* Upper Montclair: Boynton, 1986. This is an informative collection of research on writing-across-the-discipline programs from four perspectives: purpose, evaluation, writing and learning connections, and politics and the effectiveness of these programs.

64 Writing for the Humanities

Books are the carriers of civilization. Without books, history is silent, literature dumb, science crippled, thought and speculation at a standstill.
— BARBARA TUCHMAN

FOR MULTILINGUAL WRITERS: BECOMING A STRONG READER OF TEXTS IN THE HUMANITIES

(64a)

After students have read through Jon Dorbolo's "The Debt of Justice," ask them to identify the elements that are culturally or contextually specific. What kinds of knowledge does the reader need to bring to a text to appreciate fully each allusion and historical reference? What familiarity with other texts of Western civilization are required of the reader of this text? How might multilingual writers make such unfamiliar materials familiar to the class and thus accentuate the importance of engaging actively with a text? Ask students to bring in a piece of regional writing and to present to the class the cultural allusions in the text that one must understand in order to be a strong reader of the text.

Every man's work, whether it be literature or music or pictures or architecture or anything else, is always a portrait of himself.
— SAMUEL BUTLER

FOR TEACHING: BECOMING A STRONG READER BY EXAMINING TEXTUAL EVIDENCE

(64a)

Ask students to go through Melissa Schraeder's essay on pp. 879–88 of the *Handbook,* noting every instance in which she uses material from the literary text — examples, quotations, and so on — to support her thesis. Point out the critical role such use of textual "evidence" plays in any essay whose writer adopts a text-based stance.

·································· (64b)

Great literature should do some good to the reader: must quicken his perception though dull, and sharpen his discrimination though blunt, and mellow the rawness of his personal opinions.
—A. E. Housman

FOR COLLABORATIVE WORK: BECOMING A STRONG WRITER OF TEXTS IN THE HUMANITIES

After students read the introduction to Chapter 64 of the *Handbook* ask them to choose a literary work, film, or painting that moves them. Then have them write a short essay about it, explaining to their peers how it moves them. Ask each student to respond to one other student's essay, engaging both the content of the essay and how learning about this person's relationship to the humanities has revealed the power of strong writing to move and persuade.

·································· (64b)

ATTENDING TO DISABILITIES: BECOMING A STRONG WRITER OF TEXTS IN THE HUMANITIES

As Mark Mossman reminds us, when you ask students to write autobiographical texts, be sure to include mention of disabilities. Make a space for discussion of disabilities when teaching how to write about the humanities. Have them research figures such as Lord Byron for the myths of creativity and writing that continue to affect people with disabilities in present-day Western civilization.

·································· (64b)

FOR TEACHING: BECOMING A STRONG WRITER THROUGH USE OF QUOTATIONS AND EXAMPLES

Call students' attention to the way quotations and examples from the novel are used as evidence in Melissa Schraeder's essay, and ask them to compare this kind of evidence with the evidence presented in the previous student essays.

·································· (64c)

FOR COLLABORATIVE WORK: BECOMING A STRONG WRITER BY ANALYZING INTRODUCTIONS

Put students into small groups and, by using the first paragraph of Melissa Schrader's essay (p. 879) as their text, ask students to identify the features of an introduction to a literary interpretation essay. Can they suggest ways to make the opening sentence more dramatic—perhaps by posing it as a question?

TEACHING WITH TECHNOLOGY: WEAVING IN SOURCES   **(64c)** ....

One of the difficulties students often have in writing essays about literature is weaving quotations smoothly into the text of their own. Refer students back to the discussion of quotations in Chapter 17 and ask them to evaluate the use of quotations in Melissa Schraeder's essay. Are quotations introduced clearly? Do they "fit in" to the preceding sentence? Does the student writer comment sufficiently on their significance?

TEACHING WITH TECHNOLOGY: USING NEW MEDIA TO EXPLORE TOPICS   **(64d)** ....

Your composition classroom is a wonderful place for students to begin exploring ways to write through new media. Have them transform their analysis of a literary text or film into a multimedia project that expands their learning by forcing them to bring in alternative perspectives. For a model of such a project, consult — as a class — the Web site on *Beloved* produced by Professor Gerald Lucas's class, <http://www.cas.usf.edu/~lucas /students/morrison/toni.htm>.

Then ask students to construct their own projects using new media. They might construct a Web site, for example, on which they post images corresponding to historical allusions in *Beloved,* or photographs from slave plantations. As they integrate texts — such as archival records from plantation owners, newspaper ads for runaway slaves, maps of the South, and photographs of hangings — they will get a much more concrete sense of the profound historical density of the novel and the way in which writing about literature through new media opens avenues to understanding topics in the humanities.

After the projects are completed, ask students to write a brief reflection on what they have learned about the different disciplines, how each discipline organizes knowledge, and how they can apply their writing and presentation strategies across various fields. How will strong reading and strong writing serve them well in history, literature, classics, modern languages, and film?

■ **USEFUL READINGS**

Commeyras, Michelle. "Using Literature to Teach Critical Thinking." *Journal of Reading* 32 (1989): 703–07.

Crowley, Sharon. *Composition in the University: Historical and Polemical Essays.* Pittsburgh: U of Pittsburgh P, 1998. Tracing the history of competing composition and literature programs, Crowley views composition as a "policing mechanism" resulting from composition specialists' middle-class affiliations and claims that while English departments have colonized composition, writing in the university need not depend on first-year college English.

Elbow, Peter. "The Cultures of Literature and Composition: What Could Each Learn from the Other?" *CE* 64.5 (May 2002): 533–46.

———. "The War between Reading and Writing—and How to End It." *Critical Theory and the Teaching of Literature: Politics, Curriculum, Pedagogy.* Urbana: NCTE, 1995. Elbow examines the war between writing and literature in university English departments. His analysis covers sites of conflict, the privilege of reading over writing, the benefits of ceasing the battle, and strategies for conflict resolution.

Gere, Anne Ruggles. "Composition and Literature: The Continuing Conversation." *CE* 51 (Oct. 1989): 617–22.

Glenn, Cheryl. "The Reading-Writing Connection: What's Process Got to Do with It?" *When Writing Teachers Teach Literature.* Ed. Toby Fulwiler and Art Young. Portsmouth: Boynton, 1995. Glenn charts in detail the ways she uses writing to teach a survey-of-English-literature course.

Harmon, William. *A Handbook to Literature.* 9th ed. Upper Saddle River: Prentice, 2003. A useful and convenient reference guide to literary terminology.

Lindemann, Erika. "Freshman English: No Place for Literature." *CE* 55 (1993): 311–16.

Lynn, Stephen. "A Passage into Critical Theory." *CE* 52 (1990): 258–71. This is a brief guide for teachers to some schools of critical theory including new criticism, structuralism, deconstruction, psychological criticism, and feminist criticism. Lynn offers concrete examples of these critical approaches by applying each of them to the same passage.

MacDonald, Susan Peck, and Charles R. Cooper. "Contributions of Academic and Dialogue Journals to Writing about Literature." *Writing, Teaching, and Learning in the Disciplines.* Ed. Anne Herrington and Charles Moran. New York: MLA, 1992. 137–55.

Mossman, Mark. "Visible Disability in the College Classroom." *CE* 64.6 (July 2002): 645–59. Mossman argues for the importance of visible narratives of disability to transform the culture of the classroom; he contends that we need to include disability when we ask students to write autobiographical texts.

Schilb, John. *Between the Lines: Relating Composition Theory and Literary Theory.* Portsmouth: Boynton/Cook, 1996. Assessing differing definitions of rhetoric (irony to literary theory; persuasion to composition theory), Schilb traces the divergences in the fields at conferences and university departments since the

1960s. Looking alternatively to postmodernism, personal writing, and collaboration, Schilb identifies potential new trends and argues for theories tested by pedagogy.

Tate, Gary. "A Place for Literature in Freshman Composition." *CE* 55 (1993): 317–21.

■ **USEFUL WEB SITE**

The Voice of the Shuttle

http://vos.ucsb.edu/

By Alan Liu, this is one of the richest humanities sites. The literature resources include cross links to world literature and minority literatures and offer searches by subject and period. In addition, this site has an extensive literary theory page that is very useful for undergraduates.

65

▼ Writing for the Social Sciences

Nothing has such power to broaden the mind as the ability to investigate systematically and truly all that comes under thy observation in life.
– MARCUS AURELIUS

In a recent article for *College English,* Peter Elbow compares his experiences as both a composition teacher and a teacher of literature. What characterizes composition for him is its focus on useful instruction:

> When I finally came to see myself as a composition person, I felt an enormous relief at finally feeling *useful* — as though I could make an actual difference for people. I'd never felt solidly useful trying to teach and write about literature. I'm proud that composition is the only discipline I know, outside of schools of education, where members feel their field has a built-in relationship to teaching and to students. (536)

The idea of writing instruction as inherently useful — related to purpose and student goals — is nowhere more appropriate than in composition classes, where we may need to teach students to write for the social sciences. Indeed, many students in our first-year classes go on to major in such fields as psychology, economics, anthropology, political science, and sociology. We can help prepare them for their future majors and careers through a focus on writing as a process of discovering knowledge in a particular field, for a particular audience. The same rhetorical foundations that they need to write a compelling public-policy analysis will help them craft a careful psychological study. At the same time, we can serve our students best if we help foster their spirit of inquiry, show them how to seek out the resources they need to pursue their own research interests, and lead them toward viewing writing as a critical means of communicating across all disciplines.

A sense of curiosity is nature's original school of education.
    –NORMAN VINCENT
        PEALE

454

TEACHING WITH TECHNOLOGY: BECOMING A
STRONG READER OF TEXTS IN THE SOCIAL SCIENCES

(65a) ....

If you are teaching a composition class in which you use social science readings, you may find it difficult to tell how comprehensively students have processed the material. One solution, suggested by Joe Law in *Writing across the Curriculum*, is to design weekly quizzes for students to complete on a computer during class or through a course Web site. Law also has students log their reading, research, and field-observation notes through technological means so that his responses can be quickly returned to each student.

Anthropology is the most humanistic of the sciences and the most scientific of the humanities.
–Alfred L. Kroeber

FOR TEACHING: BECOMING A STRONG
WRITER OF TEXTS IN THE SOCIAL SCIENCES

(65b) ....

One way for students to master the material of the social sciences is through writing assignments that engage their critical and imaginative skills. In "Writing to Learn History," Donald Holsinger advocates using a variety of writing projects to engage students in the subject matter: course journals, simple writing exercises as preparation for in-class discussions, and detailed response papers that challenge students to write about specific statements and questions rather than vague topics. In addition, Holsinger suggests that an excellent way for students to become strong writers of texts in the social sciences is to have them write frequently and freely. Perhaps assign larger projects in developmental steps such that students have to work through stages of writing. Have students revise and resubmit their work as if it were being submitted to a journal in the field. Finally, have your students write to different audiences and from different perspectives.

FOR COLLABORATIVE WORK: BECOMING A
STRONG WRITER OF TEXTS IN THE SOCIAL SCIENCES

(65b) ....

You might get students started on creative and engaging writing projects by asking them to look at various models of scholarly writing in the social sciences. Divide the class into groups of three, and send them to the library to find several journal articles from different publications for a particular field (psychology, anthropology, political science, sociology,

Anthropology provides a scientific basis for dealing with the crucial dilemma of the world today: how can peoples of different appearance . . . and dissimilar ways of life get along peaceably together?
  –CLYDE KLUCKHOHN

economics, education, and so on). Ask each group to perform a rhetorical analysis on the writing in the articles, assessing it for disciplinary-specific terminology, construction of knowledge (quantitative or qualitative), use of evidence, and formal properties (organization, voice, and subsections). Then ask each group to compose a "mock" article to be published in one of the journals. Have them model their text on one of the examples and then write a brief reflection about what they have learned from this "pedagogy of models."

(65c)

ATTENDING TO DISABILITIES: ADDRESSING ISSUES OF STYLE IN THE SOCIAL SCIENCES

While many of your students can consult the wealth of resources available online for tips on organizing and formatting their social science texts, others may not have access to all the resources they need. Consider your students with disabilities and how they might need the assistance of your campus disability resource center for help converting voice to text, text to audiotape, or images to Braille.

(65c)

FOR TEACHING: ADDRESSING ISSUES OF STYLE IN THE SOCIAL SCIENCES

Your students may feel hesitant to express their own individuality in their writing for social science purposes. You might wish to initiate a class discussion on what it means to write with an objective voice versus writing with the strategic use of ethos. Analyze Merlla McLaughlin's essay on pp. 906–15 of the *Handbook* for its uniqueness of style, format, and visual strategies. Ask students to write a short response on the appropriateness of her choices for her particular academic audience.

(65d)

FOR MULTILINGUAL WRITERS: RESEARCH SOURCES AND INFORMATION FOR THE SOCIAL SCIENCES

There are a number of Web sites that host a range of papers, resources, potential research questions, and collections of historical data. While you might discuss some of these with your students, you should also arrange to meet with a librarian in order to learn about your institution's database subscription services. You might choose to make an additional consultation with your librarian for multilingual writers.

Finally, don't forget the resources you have in your students. They will often share sources and potential leads with one another. When it comes to your multilingual students, you have an invaluable resource. What ideas and information can they share with the rest of the class from their perspective of knowing multiple languages and cultures? How might they serve as a potential interview pool for projects in sociology, political science, ethnography, and history? What preferences do they voice for their writing projects in terms of content, purpose, and perspective? Have your students write a short response to Merlla McLaughlin's essay on pp. 906–15 of the *Handbook* and identify different responses to conflict in their own cultures. How does one's experience shape one's response to Wilmot and Hocker's theory?

> *Education in our times must try to find whatever there is in students that might yearn for completion, and to reconstruct the learning that would enable them autonomously to seek that completion.*
> —ALLAN BLOOM

■ USEFUL READINGS

Abdalla, Adil E. A. "A Country Report Project for an International Economics Class." *Journal of Economic Education* 24.3 (Summer 1993): 231–36. In this semester-long, multipart writing project for an international economics class, each student wrote a report on a specific country, received instructor feedback and peer review, revised the report, and wrote a lengthy term paper, thereby using writing to comprehend economic theory, real-world phenomena, problems with data, and the research process.

Bazerman, Charles. "Codifying the Social Scientific Style: The APA Publication Manual as a Behaviorist Rhetoric." *The Rhetoric of the Human Sciences: Language and Argument in Scholarship and Public Affairs.* Ed. John Nelson, Allan Megill, and Donald McClosky. Madison: Wisconsin UP, 1987. Bazerman works within the discipline of psychology to give an interesting view of language and writing. He argues that the disciplines are socially negotiated territories and conventions of disciplines are representations of actions produced through that discipline's process of inquiry — a process that is shaped and transformed by the contributions of those who work with and within the discipline.

Carlisle, Marcia. "Talking History." *OAH Magazine of History* 9 (Winter 1995): 57–59. Arguing that students put more effort into writing essays than into class participation, Carlisle advocates establishing a computer discussion about history in order to generate critical discussion about the readings.

CCC 36 (1985). This entire issue is devoted to the role of writing in the academic and professional disciplines. Of special interest is "Learning to Write in the Social Sciences" (140–49).

Davidson, Lawrence S., and Elisabeth C. Gumnior. "Writing to Learn in a Business Economics Class." *Journal of Economic Education* 24.3 (Summer 1993): 237–43. The authors describe a course at the Indiana University Business School in which each student is assigned a country and has to research and write on a topic from the perspective of that country. The authors argue that recursive writing assignments (in which students receive feedback and revise their drafts) make students more interactive, force them to spend more time on task, and give them a more accurate sense of economics as a discipline.

Elbow, Peter. "The Cultures of Literature and Composition: What Could Each Learn from the Other?" *College English* 64.5 (May 2002): 533–46. Describing his career as both a literature and a composition professional, Elbow contrasts the fields, identifies his relief at teaching something *"useful"* in composition, and points out how both fields might learn from one another.

Hemmeter, Thomas, and David Connors. "Research Papers in Economics: A Collaborative Approach." *Journal of Advanced Composition* 7 (1987): 81–91. Hemmeter and Connors describe their collaboratively taught course combining writing instruction with an advanced-level economics course. The essay focuses especially on the writing of the "end-of-the-term research paper."

Herrington, Anne, and Charles Moran, eds. *Writing, Teaching, and Learning in the Disciplines.* New York: MLA, 1992. This collection contains fourteen essays covering historical and theoretical perspectives on writing across the curriculum as well as a number of treatments of classroom practice.

Holsinger, Donald C. "Writing to Learn History." *Social Studies Review* (Fall 1991): 59–64. Holsinger suggests a number of ways that professors can use writing to engage students in the subject of history, from in-class writing exercises and responses to course journals, process writing, and multiple-perspectives projects.

Johnson, William A., Jr., Richard P. Rettig, Gregory M. Scott, and Stephen M. Garrison. *The Sociology Student Writer's Manual.* 3rd ed. Upper Saddle River: Prentice, 2002.

Law, Joe. "Critical Thinking and Computer-aided Instruction in Sociology 200." *Writing across the Curriculum* 8 (March, 1998): 1+. Law suggests using computers to test student comprehension of readings in large, lecture-size class settings.

MacDonald, Susan Peck. *Professional Academic Writing in the Humanities and Social Sciences.* Carbondale: Southern Illinois UP, 1994. The author examines the ways disciplinary genres and forms shape knowledge-making.

Odell, Lee, Dixie Goswami, and Doris Quick. "Writing Outside the English Composition Class: Implications for Teaching and for Learning." *Literacy for Life: The Demand for Reading and Writing.* Ed. Richard W. Bailey and Robin Melanie Fosheim. New York: MLA, 1983. 175–94. The authors assess the writing of both political science and economics majors as well as of legislative analysts; their conclusion that analysts more effectively address audience and context suggests that a pedagogy informed by such practical purposes will strengthen student writing.

Shamoon, Linda K., and Robert A. Schwegler. "Sociologists Reading Student Texts: Expectations and Perceptions." *Writing Instructor 7* (Winter 1988): 71–81. This article examines the expectations and perceptions that instructors have of their students' writing. A group of sociology instructors are asked two questions: (1) To what extent are instructors' expectations and perceptions discipline specific? (2) What features of good expository writing do college instructors look for — thesis statements? topic sentences? paragraph coherence?

Sociology Writing Group. *A Guide to Writing Sociology Papers.* 5th ed. New York: Worth, 2001.

■ **USEFUL WEB SITES**

Exercising the Sociological Imagination

http://www.trinity.edu/mkearl/index.html#in

A dynamic Web site hosting links to exciting research topics, questions, and steps toward reading and writing in the social sciences.

Social Sciences: General Advice for Non-Majors

http://www.dartmouth.edu/~compose/student/soc_sciences/write.html

Dartmouth College's Composition Center Web site includes this step-by-step guide for undergraduates to writing social science papers.

66 Writing for the Natural and Applied Sciences

By looking at writing ecologically we understand better how important writing is — and just how hard it is to teach. —Marilyn Cooper

The best scientist is open to experience and begins with romance — the idea that anything is possible.
—RAY BRADBURY

"What is a scientist after all? It is a curious man looking through a keyhole, the keyhole of nature, trying to know what's going on." Thus wrote Jacques Cousteau. Many of the students in your writing classes will go on to pursue scientific majors and careers. But remember that curiosity — the spirit of inquiry that drives research — is crucial to successful writing for any purpose. Teaching students to recognize and cultivate their own spirit of inquiry will help make them more effective writers in your composition classes and in their future professions.

.... **(66a)**

TEACHING WITH TECHNOLOGY: BECOMING A STRONG READER OF TEXTS IN THE SCIENCES

The famous physicist Robert Millikan wrote that being a strong reader — having what he called the "habit of attention" — was crucial to academic success: "Cultivate the habit of attention and try to gain opportunities to hear wise men and women talk. Indifference and inattention are the two most dangerous monsters that you'll ever meet. Interest and attention will insure to you an education." You can teach your students to become strong readers of texts in the sciences by asking them to peruse online journals available through your library's database and conduct a detailed analysis of the differences between them. Have them make a list of key figures cited often on a particular topic, ways in which different fields organize information, and the audience addressed by each article. Ask them to work through the questions at the end of 66a in the *Handbook* and write up a brief report to post to the class as a whole.

**FOR COLLABORATIVE WORK: BECOMING A
STRONG WRITER IN THE NATURAL AND APPLIED SCIENCES**

(66b) ....

Have students work in peer-review groups on their literature reviews, research reports, and lab reports. You can get them started by modeling a peer review of Tara Gupta's application in the *Handbook* (p. 926). Ask students to suggest revisions, alternatives in format and presentation, and an alternate introduction. As a class, make the changes collaboratively, using the board or an overhead projector. Be sure to emphasize to students the point made in 66c — that most scientific writing is collaborative.

**FOR COLLABORATIVE WORK: CONSIDERING
THE SPECIAL CHALLENGES OF SCIENTIFIC WRITING**

(66c) ....

Ask students to share their responses to the question on p. 937 of the *Handbook* concerning the functions of textual elements in scientific writing. Then have them interview their science professor to obtain his or her response. Begin a dialogue in class about the rhetorical purpose of composition elements across the natural and applied sciences. If students understand the reasons for following particular writing guidelines, they will be more prone to follow them and write well.

*Facts are the air of
scientists. Without them
you can never fly.*
–LINUS PAULING

■ **USEFUL READINGS**

CCC 36 (1985). This entire issue is devoted to the role of writing in the academic and professional disciplines. Of special interest is "A Freshman Writing Course in Parallel with a Science Course" (160–65).

Dobrin, Sidney I., and Christian R. Weisser. "Breaking Ground in Ecocomposition: Exploring Relationships between Discourse and Environment." *CE* 64.5 (May 2002): 566–89. In a foundational article on the mutual relationship between ecology and composition, the authors argue for place and environment as critical categories in academic inquiry and for the importance of ecological approaches to composition.

Haas, Christina. "Learning to Read Biology." *Written Communication* 11 (1994): 43–84. This case study follows the development of one student's changing perceptions of literacy, focusing on her own reading and writing as well as her views about those activities, her representations of the nature of texts, and her understanding of the relationship between knowledge and written discourse within her disciplinary field of biology.

Manual for Design Report Writing in Engineering. Sponsored by Michigan Technological University, National Science Foundation, and Whirlpool Foundation,
1991. This manual, written in collaboration with several senior engineering
students and tested in engineering design courses for ten years, gives concise
and useful guidelines for advanced engineering students, from conceptualizing an audience to ethics and politics in writing design reports.

McMillan, Victoria E. *Writing Papers in the Biological Sciences.* 3rd ed. Boston: Bedford,
2001.

Michaelson, Herbert B. *How to Write and Publish Engineering Papers and Reports.* 3rd
ed. Phoenix: Oryx, 1990. In clear language, this book outlines several proven
methods and techniques for preparing, writing, and submitting technical papers for school, business, or publication.

Powell, Alfred. "A Chemist's View of Writing, Reading, and Thinking across the
Curriculum." *CCC* 36 (1985): 414–18. Powell, a chemistry professor, outlines
numerous discipline-based writing and reading projects that he assigns in a
two-semester course sequence in organic chemistry.

Ross, Carolyn. *Writing Nature: An Ecological Reader for Writers.* Boston: Bedford,
1995.

Weisser, Christian R. "Ecocomposition and the Greening of Identity." *Ecocomposition: Theoretical and Pedagogical Approaches.* Ed. Christian R. Weisser and Sidney
I. Dobrin. Albany: SUNY P, 2001. 81–95. An examination of how social con-
structionist approaches to composition have changed our conception of identity by emphasizing the wide range of external influences and social conventions that shape human experience.

Weisser, Christian R., and Sidney I. Dobrin, eds. *Ecocomposition: Theoretical and
Pedagogical Approaches.* Albany: SUNY P, 2001. A groundbreaking collection of
essays bringing together scientific approaches to ecology and composition
theorists.

Winsor, Dorothy A. "Engineering Writing/Writing Engineering." *CCC* 41 (1990):
58–69. A useful general article on how engineers think and write differently
about engineering, this article employs a case study to suggest similarities and
differences in how engineers construct knowledge through language.

67 ▼ Writing for Business

Learning is about more than simply acquiring new knowledge and insights; it is also crucial to unlearn old knowledge that has outlived its relevance. Thus, forgetting is probably at least as important as learning.

– GARY RYAN BLAIR

All professional activities require strong and persuasive writing as well as adherence to the formal conventions of a particular audience. Companies and business organizations look for solid, well-written, and carefully constructed cover letters and résumés that attend to the rhetorical situation. Grants and business proposals can be highly successful if attention is given to the writing process for each of these important genres. As writing teachers, we often find that our students need advice and instruction in writing for business situations. You can help them develop their business-writing strategies by leading them through the sections in the *Handbook* on becoming strong readers and writers of texts in business.

On Becoming a Strong Writer of Texts in Business

(67b)

In a study of strong business writing, Lee Odell and Dixie Goswami examined writing done by administrators and caseworkers. By interviewing the study participants and analyzing the writing samples they collected, the authors found that while workers in different positions write differently and justify their writing choices differently, all writers are sensitive to rhetorical context. Their writing varied according to its type, audience, and subject. Nevertheless, what the study participants termed "acceptable writing" remained constant across different positions.

**FOR COLLABORATIVE WORK: BECOMING
A STRONG WRITER OF TEXTS IN BUSINESS**

*Success or failure in
business is caused more
by the mental attitude
even than by mental
capacities.*
–Sir Walter Scott

Keeping Odell and Goswami's findings in mind, ask your students to
form peer-review groups to analyze a series of business documents and
evaluate the documents comparatively. Then have them write a brief
memo detailing the qualities of "acceptable writing" in one of the documents. Make sure that they use the "Guidelines for Writing Effective
Memos" on p. 940 in order to write the most effective and succinct memo.

·····························(67c)

FOR COLLABORATIVE WORK: WRITING BUSINESS MEMOS

In groups of three or four, ask students to write a memo to students who
will be enrolled in your course next term. Suggest that students focus on
course activities, teacher expectations, and so forth. Then, to invite consideration of audience, have them write different versions to friends,
teachers, and so on. This will provide practice in a genre that is unfamiliar to many students.

·····························(67c)

FOR PEER RESPONSE: WRITING RÉSUMÉS

Because employers spend so little time reading an individual résumé, format, design, and just plain good writing are especially critical. For this exercise, ask students to bring in drafts of their résumés and, working in
groups of two or three, offer suggestions based on the guidelines in 67c.
You may want students to review the principles of document design in
Chapter 8.

·····························(67c)

**FOR MULTILINGUAL WRITERS: WRITING
BUSINESS MEMOS, EMAILS, LETTERS, AND RÉSUMÉS**

Cultural norms often determine the kinds of emails, memos, and reports
that are most appropriate for a given audience. Ask your students to share
a copy of an email from someone in their home country conducting a
business transaction.

■ **USEFUL READINGS**

Barbour, Dennis. "Collaborative Writing in the Business Writing Classroom: An Ethical Dilemma for the Teacher." *Bulletin of the Association for Business Communication* (Sept. 1990): 33–35. An examination of the difficulties inherent in grading collaborative writing in business communications courses.

Caudron, Shari. "Virtual Manners." *Workforce* 79.2 (Feb. 2000): 31–34. A discussion of email etiquette for business situations.

Davis, Ken. "Managing Your Writing." *College Accounting*. Ed. James Heintz and Robert W. Parry Jr. Mason: South-Western, 1993. 10–11. Discusses the writing process in terms of management strategies, with twelve steps meant to optimize the writer's time.

Laufer, Doug, and Rick Crosser. "The 'Writing-across-the-Curriculum' Concept in Accounting and Tax Courses." *Journal of Education for Business* (Nov./Dec. 1990): 83–87. Sample writing assignments and instruction for an accounting course.

Law, Joe. "Learning to Write with E-mail in Money and Banking." *Writing across the Curriculum* 7 (Jan. 1998): 1+. Practical advice for using electronic discussion lists in courses on money and banking.

Locker, Kitty O. *Business and Administration Communication*. 6th ed. Boston: Irwin/McGraw, 2003. Locker writes knowledgeably about oral and written communication, technology in the workplace, workplace ethics, organizational culture, and international and intercultural business communication.

Nelson, Sandra J., and Douglas C. Smith. "Maximizing Cohesion and Minimizing Conflict in Collaborative Writing Groups." *Bulletin of the Association for Business Communication* (June 1990): 59–62. Peer-review and collaborative writing strategies for business communication classes.

Odell, Lee, and Dixie Goswami. "Writing in a Non-Academic Setting." *Research in the Teaching of English* 16.3 (Oct. 1982): 201–23. An examination of writing standards across diverse business conditions.

Peek, Lucia E., and George S. Peek. "Using Practitioner Articles to Develop Computer, Writing, and Critical Thinking Skills: Examples from the Accounting Curriculum." *Bulletin of the Association for Business Communication* 53.4 (Dec. 1990): 17–19. The authors call for writing assignments in accounting classes that focus on the analysis and production of computer spreadsheets.

Tebeaux, Elizabeth. "Redesigning Professional Writing Courses to Meet the Needs of Writers in Business and Industry." *CCC* 36 (Dec. 1985): 419–28. Tebeaux describes the distinctions among technical, business, and science writing; she recommends changes in business writing courses to make a better match between the writing taught and the actual writing used on the job.

■ USEFUL WEB SITES

Purdue University's Online Writing Lab (OWL)

http://owl.english.purdue.edu

Purdue hosts a range of model documents for writing emails, résumés, and job-application letters.

Stanford University's Professional Writing Resources Page

http://www.stanford.edu/group/pwr/students/wr_resources/studrcl.html

Visit the many links provided with annotations for students in composition classes.

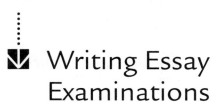

Writing Essay Examinations

Although widely used, standardized tests measure only editorial skills —
choosing the best sentence, recognizing correct usage, punctuation, and
capitalization. At least for this reason, they are not valid measures of
writing performance. — CHARLES R. COOPER AND LEE ODELL

Instructors have always wanted to assess the progress of their students, but writing tests are a rather new phenomenon in the history of education. Not until the mid-nineteenth century did writing tests become widespread. In 1874, Harvard led the way by introducing the first written entrance examination. Before that date, candidates were "promoted" on the basis of oral examinations. In the new test, students were required in an hour to produce a carefully thought out, carefully revised, unified, error-free essay on subjects such as a Shakespearean play, a novel like Scott's *Ivanhoe,* or dueling in the age of Queen Anne. Needless to say, many failed.

Ironically. before the institution of this exam, composition was not primarily considered a lower-level college or secondary school subject. Previously it had been an upper-division course that the student took for three years. James Berlin suggests that the new entrance exam was one of several related events caused by the shift in educational priorities from rhetoric to poetics (*Rhetoric and Reality* 23). After 1874, essay exams proliferated in the schools and colleges.

On How to Use Essay Exams

In their book, *Facts, Artifacts, and Counterfacts,* David Bartholomae and Anthony Petrosky suggest that asking students to write essay examinations is antithetical to the teaching of a drafting process of writing. Yet they hesitate to reject essay writing entirely. Exam writing "requires students to consolidate much of what they have learned in the course and to use their knowledge efficiently." But the emphasis can shift from ideas and organization to error control (101).

Given this hesitation, you may well wonder whether you should require essay exams. In many cases, however, exams are institutionally required and may even be institutionally composed, with the individual instructor having little choice in what goes into the test or how it is given — or sometimes how it is even graded. If the exams are institutionally imposed, you should find out as much as you can as early as you can in order to schedule preparation time, if needed.

If you are allowed the decision of whether or not to test a class, you need to clarify for yourself exactly what you expect your students to get out of it.

There are two reasons for giving such an exam. First, you may want to test your students' knowledge and abilities. In such a case, you will want to make sure that you either limit the topic or extend the time given so that students can complete the process — discover, narrow, and organize the topic; write, revise, and proofread the essay. Second, you may simply want to give your students experience writing under such conditions as practice for future exams in other college courses. In that case, you will want to actually spend class time on how to write under such conditions and then to simulate those conditions in an exam. In fact, essay writing is being used more frequently and in more and more disciplines. Instructors view essay examinations as better indicators of knowledge than multiple-choice tests and short-answer definitions.

FOR TEACHING: PLANNING ESSAY EXAMS

How you give an essay exam depends on how you view the function of exams. Before scheduling an exam, clarify in your own mind why you want to examine your students in this way. If you are interested in testing your students' writing abilities, consider these alternatives:

- Schedule the exam over two class periods. Students come to class on the first exam day with nothing but a pen; you provide test booklets. The assignment includes several topic choices. The student spends the first day deciding on a topic and a thesis, discovering support for that thesis, and writing a first draft. Take up all the exam booklets at the end of the first period. On the second day, return the booklets to the students, and they rewrite and proofread and correct their essays. At the end of the second day, they turn in the exams.

- Hand out topics several days ahead of time, assigning your students the task of deciding on a topic, finding a thesis, and discovering support for that thesis before the time of the exam. On the day before the exam, take up all of their preliminary work in order to ensure that a student does not arrive with a fully written essay. On the day of the exam, students should arrive with nothing but a pen. You return their preliminary work to them with an exam booklet, and they write their essay during class.

FOR TEACHING: EASING TEST ANXIETY

Students react in a variety of ways to exams. Naturally, most become anxious at the thought of being tested, but in some, the pressure can cause such an emotional distress that a person may become physically ill and intellectually paralyzed. Such a condition is often referred to as "test anxiety," and it is much more common among students than instructors sometimes realize. Allen J. Ottens, a psychological counselor and author of numerous papers and a book on test anxiety, writes that such anxiety "is a significant problem affecting a substantial number of students" (1).

Of course, instructors cannot read their students' minds, and often those who suffer from such anxiety are not readily apparent. However, you should become aware of the following symptoms of test anxiety:

1. Frequent panicky talk by a student about the exam and its terrible consequences.

2. Frequent self-belittling by the student and comparisons of himself or herself with other students.

3. Reminiscences of previous tests in which the student performed badly.

4. Performing irrelevant tasks that appear to be avoidance of performing tasks relevant to the test.

5. Attendance to what other students are doing during the test rather than attending to the student's own writing.

6. Too much clock-watching during an exam.

7. Physiological indicators, like trembling hands, unexplainable sweating, complaints of illness (which may be very real, by the way) on days when exams are scheduled.

8. Expressions or indications of embarrassment at asking questions.

9. A rushing through the exam so that the student misinterprets directions and/or does significantly worse than you expected.

10. Any other unusual behavior related to the exam.

11. And, of course, the student's explicit expression of fear of the exam.

Instructors themselves should not attempt to cure test anxiety in their students. It is a psychological problem best dealt with by the student and a psychologist or psychoanalyst. However, instructors can help the student.

Your reassurance that the student can perform up to his or her abilities can go a long way in building self-confidence in the face of the exam. Of course, you must also be honest as well as supporting; you should not tell the student he or she can perform better than you really think he or she can.

If you believe a student has test anxiety, set up a private conference. You will want to talk to students about any problems they have without others around. In the conference, you can approach the subject directly, presenting the reasons you are concerned, and asking the student if he or she is aware of any cause for concern. A student might already be aware of and dealing with test anxiety. If not, you will want to suggest that the student see a school counselor. You should make it clear that while test anxiety is serious, it is also a common problem, and one that can be resolved. You might also suggest that the student check the library or local bookstores for books on test anxiety, such as Allen J. Ottens's *Coping with Academic Anxiety.* Finally, be reassuring, but honest. You cannot dismiss any student from work required of all other students in the class, but you might be able to compromise. Would the student cope with the exam better if he or she took it alone? In that case, you should be able to arrange a time and room in the same way you would a makeup exam. Perhaps, further conferences to discuss improvements in his or her writing generally and strategies for dealing with exams would help. Perhaps, the tests count little in the overall grade the student will receive; you could reassure the student of that. In addition, preparing for an exam in a peer group can help reassure the student that he or she is able to contribute and do the work.

If a liberal education should teach students "how to think," not only in their own fields but in fields outside their own — that is, to understand "how the other fellow orders knowledge," then bulling, even in its purest form, expresses an important part of what a pluralist university holds dear, surely a more important part than the collecting of "facts that are facts" which schoolboys learn to do. Here, then, good bull appears not as ignorance at all but as an aspect of knowledge. It is both relevant and "true." In a university setting good bull is therefore of more value than "facts," which, without a frame of reference, are not even "true" at all.
–WILLIAM G. PERRY JR.

.... **(68d)**

ATTENDING TO DISABILITIES: DRAFTING YOUR ANSWER

Since writing is an expressive human activity, we believe the best response to it is a receptive, sympathetic human response.
– CHARLES R. COOPER
AND LEE ODELL

If you are giving essay exams to your writing class, make sure that you are familiar with the needs of all your students. Do any of them require untimed tests or particular testing facilities? Are there any disabilities that you need to accommodate? Do any students suffer from severe test anxiety? You can become attuned to these needs by handing out a brief information sheet on the first day of class. Ask students to write down any special concerns they have or any disabilities that they want you to know about. Guarantee confidentiality, and make sure you explain that you are asking for this information in order to better accommodate each student. In addition, you can hold a "test-run" essay exam during one class session and see if any of the students' drafts indicate a need for your attention or accommodation.

FOR COLLABORATIVE WORK: REVISING AND EDITING YOUR ANSWER   **(68c)**

Ask your students to generate, as a class, one or two questions that they might be likely to encounter on an essay exam for your course. Then hold a "dry run" essay examination in class. When the students are finished writing, have them work in peer-review groups to analyze each other's answers, making suggestions for both revision and editing. Ask them to implement the revision strategies discussed in Chapter 4 of the *Handbook*. You might also have them answer the questions in section 68e of the *Handbook*.

When students are done making comments for each other, have them discuss their suggested revisions. What strategies can they use from this exercise on the day of the actual test? What aspects of their answers should they be careful to revise or edit for the test itself?

FOR MULTILINGUAL WRITERS: CONSIDERING A SAMPLE ESSAY ANSWER   **(68f)**

Take time to meet with your multilingual students—in individual conferences or in small groups—to discuss the difficult or unfamiliar aspects of the student essay in section 68f of the *Handbook*. How does analyzing a sample essay bring to light the additional strategies that multilingual writers need to include in preparing for essay exams? Should they keep an evolving list of new vocabulary words throughout the term? practice their exam answers in peer-review groups and then check whether their essays fulfill the question prompt adequately? review areas of cultural knowledge with a tutor prior to the exam?

TEACHING WITH TECHNOLOGY: ANALYZING AND EVALUATING YOUR ANSWER   **(68g)**

Conduct the collaboration exercise in section 68g of the *Handbook* in a computer-equipped classroom. Ask students to bring in excerpted essay prompts from their classes. Then, with students working on computers, have them collaborate to compose a list of features: What similarities and differences exist between the questions? What common strategies can they develop to tackle essay exams? Finally, ask each group to create a brief PowerPoint presentation on both the features of and the strategies for success in answering essay examinations.

Organization and neatness have merit in essay exams.
     –JOE LANDSBERGER

■ USEFUL READINGS

Bartholomae, David, and Anthony Petrosky. *Facts, Artifacts, and Counterfacts: Theory and Method for a Reading and Writing Course.* Upper Montclair: Boynton, 1986.

Berlin, James A. *Rhetoric and Reality: Writing Instruction in American Colleges, 1900–1985.* Carbondale: Southern Illinois UP, 1987.

———. *Writing Instruction in Nineteenth-Century American Colleges.* Carbondale: Southern Illinois UP, 1984.

Chesla, Elizabeth. *Write Better Essays in Just 20 Minutes a Day: Your Guide to Great Grades and Top Test Scores.* New York: LearningExpress, 2000. This student's guide features college essay questions, strategies for tackling test anxiety, and advice on approaching the essay—from analysis and drafting to polishing critical writing assignments.

Greenberg, Karen, Harvey S. Weiner, and Richard A. Donovan. *Writing Assessment: Issues and Strategies.* New York: Longman, 1986. This collection includes twelve essays as well as an annotated bibliography of current research in assessment.

Jones, Bill, and Roy Johnson. *Making the Grade: A Study Programme.* Manchester, Engl.: Manchester UP, 1990. This two-volume book offers ideas on understanding assignments, planning and drafting essay exams, and using student learning strategies for success.

Ottens, Allen J. *Coping with Academic Anxiety.* New York: Rosen, 1984. This book is one of several that describe what is usually referred to as "test anxiety," and offers suggestions for coping with it.

Peters, Pamela. *Strategies for Student Writers: Guide to Writing Essays, Tutorial Papers, Exam Papers and Reports.* Hoboken: Wiley, 1987. A comprehensive writing guide that takes students from various disciplines through the steps for writing, editing, and evaluating essay exams.

■ **USEFUL WEB SITES**

The Essay-type Exam

> http://www.iss.stthomas.edu/studyguides/tsttak4.htm
>
> *Part of Joe Landsberger's Web site on study guides and strategies, this page offers excellent concrete advice, links, and strategies for students.*

Managing Your Test Anxiety

> http://www.sdc.uwo.ca/learning/mcanx.html
>
> *A helpful resource page from the University of Western Ontario, Canada.*

Writing Essay Exams

> http://departments.colgate.edu/diw/essayexam.html
>
> *Guidelines from Colgate University's writing center.*

69 ▼ Assembling a Writing Portfolio

One salutary result of the "process" movement in composition studies has been the increased understanding of how and when particular student writers move back and forth among the acts of inventing, revising, drafting, editing, rethinking, drafting, and so on, most often in non-linear and highly recursive ways. In turn, these new understandings have highlighted the importance of critical thinking to writing, not only in terms of invention and expression of ideas but also in more global ways. Often referred to as "metadiscourse," this high-order kind of critical thinking calls on writers to step back and survey their own work, analyzing its strengths and weaknesses, and articulating its inner workings—its diction, syntax, and rhetoric. Research in composition indicates that the ability to exercise this kind of critical thinking is an important part of what enables growth in writing.

One of the best ways to capture the kinds of changes that take place over time with the writing process is by assembling a writing portfolio. Increasingly, writing teachers are turning to portfolios for final grade assessments. At the same time, the benefits to the student of assembling a writing portfolio are immeasurable. By tracking, compiling, and reflecting on their work, the way their writing has changed, and how they have developed strategies of invention, composition, and delivery, students produce a metadiscourse about the recursive nature of their writing lives. Moreover, once introduced to the value of assembling and maintaining a writing portfolio, students often continue the practice throughout their academic and professional careers. In this way, they continue to learn about themselves as writers and as critical thinkers.

Write about what makes you different.
– SANDRA CISNEROS

Exploratory writing can have a range of postures, from the personal to the objective.
– WILLIAM J. MCCLEARY

On Portfolios

The growing use of portfolios in writing classes seems clearly related to the need for more open and inclusive ways of testing and measuring student performances. In the face of more and more national and state initiatives to test and certify and decertify students from kindergarten through graduate school, many scholars and teachers of writing have argued that such initiatives will inevitably fail if they are tied only to reductive quantified measures (such as multiple-choice tests or fill-in-the-blanks) to indicate skill in writing, or even if they are tied to one-shot timed writing examinations. One solution to this dilemma is to look at more than one piece of student writing as a means of assessment, and to look at that student's writings across time as well as across genres and modes of discourse. In short, one powerful alternative to traditional forms of measurement in writing is portfolio assessment.

Advocates of portfolios argue that they give a better picture of students' writing abilities, that they allow for some attention to process as well as product in the assessment, that in spite of difficulties with reliability, they are more accurate in their assessment of students and more satisfying for teachers to use and respond to, and that they promote a much more sophisticated understanding of the complexities involved in writing. As Pat Belanoff and Marcia Dickson point out in *Portfolios: Process and Product,* portfolios *reward* rather than punish "the essential things we try to place at the heart of our writing courses: exploratory writing, in which the writer questions deeply . . . ; discussion with peers and with teacher; feedback on drafts from peer and teacher; and extensive, substantive revision."

It would do us all good to remember that the focus of portfolio assessment is the student, not the instructor.
– MARCIA DICKSON

On the Meaning of *Portfolio*

As Richard Larson argues in "Using Portfolios in the Assessment of Writing" (in Belanoff and Dickson, 1991), *portfolio* should designate "an ordered compilation of writings. A casual gathering up of papers one has written over a year or two probably does not deserve to be called a 'portfolio.' A portfolio ideally should be a deliberate compilation, gathered according to some plan, for use by an identified reader or readers for specific needs or purposes." Teachers who wish to use portfolios in their classrooms or programs might well begin by following Larson's lead here: determine the principles by which the portfolio will be compiled, decide how it will be organized, identify the intended audience(s) for the portfolio, and enumerate the purposes the portfolio will serve. Today, many teachers and students are moving portfolios online, creating "Web folios" that offer exciting opportunities for writers to represent themselves and their work.

(69a) On Considering the Purpose and Audience for a Portfolio

The overlapping terms *portfolio, journal, log, diary,* and *daybook* refer to a wide range of writing practices whose origins may be as old as writing itself. Until the Renaissance, most journals were essentially public or semi-public documents, such as daily accounting or business records, chronicles of public bodies or historical events, and travel journals. With the intellectual and social changes of the Renaissance and Reformation, however, come the beginnings of what we now think of as the journal, or "the book of the self." Thus, while we may think of the journal as a relatively new pedagogical instrument, introduced in the 1960s as an aid to prewriting, it actually has a much longer affiliation with education. Schoolchildren from the Tudor era right up through the early twentieth century have kept commonplace books filled with observations, facts, and quotations from their reading as a source of ideas. Journals or portfolios have also been kept to monitor or track the development of a specific skill or the whole intellect, as the locus of prewriting or drafting, as a place to develop fluency and to experiment with language, and as a place to connect and explore the public and private selves.

(69b) FOR COLLABORATIVE WORK: SELECTING WORK FOR A PORTFOLIO

If possible, engage your students in developing the criteria by which their portfolios will be evaluated. Ask them to work in groups to come up with at least half a dozen (more if possible) items they think are characteristic of first-rate portfolios. Use these lists as the basis for class discussion on how you can recognize these characteristics in the pieces of writing in the portfolio and how credit should be apportioned for them. Then if the portfolio is to be a major part of your course, you might wish to have students form groups of three to work together as an editorial board responding to one another's portfolios throughout the term.

(69b) FOR MULTILINGUAL WRITERS: SELECTING WORK FOR A PORTFOLIO

Yu Ren Dong advocates asking multilingual students to write autobiographies about their native literacy experiences in order to facilitate more responsive and effective instruction. Such literacy autobiographies can work particularly well when students develop them into comprehensive writing portfolios. Do they have samples of their writing from earlier years and in multiple languages? Can they compose short, self-reflective introductions to each sample in order to lead the reader through the portfolio? Their narrative of literacy education will trace developmental turns in their writing process across years and languages. Ask them to conclude with a critical reflection on the goals they seek to achieve next in their writing process.

FOR TEACHING: COMPLETING A PORTFOLIO

(69c)

When giving students guidance on what elements to include in their portfolios, be sure to spend time discussing the importance of organization and format. Susan Hilligoss and Tharon Howard delineate some of the key concerns students should keep in mind when designing portfolios:

> A portfolio is a unique genre, with much opportunity for visual creativity, yet it calls for many of the navigational features of more conventional long documents. Because it projects your ethos and because readers may be rushed or unfamiliar with portfolio layouts, the portfolio should have a unified look, visual impact that supports your ethos and the communicative purpose, and clear organization. (87)

TEACHING WITH TECHNOLOGY: DEVELOPING AN ELECTRONIC PORTFOLIO

(69d)

Leading the field forward, Carl Young and Margo Figgins use an electronic portfolio, called the Q-folio, in research and writing classrooms at the University of Virginia. They designed and implemented the tool in the classroom in order to "reawaken the imagination to critical inquiry and reinvent traditional notions of research and composition portfolios." (par. 1)

More and more students keep track of all their writing on their computers. You can transform this careful habit into a productive and dynamic electronic portfolio. Walk students through the questions in section 69d of the *Handbook*. Then help them brainstorm ways of compiling these digital portraits of themselves through imaginative and informative electronic portfolios. Remember to attend to disabilities; review the guidelines provided throughout this manual to make sure that all interested readers can access the electronic materials.

■ **USEFUL READINGS**

Belanoff, Pat, and Marcia Dickson, eds. *Portfolios: Process and Product.* Portsmouth: Boynton/Cook, 1991. A classic in the field, this anthology is vital to any teacher or program using portfolios as classroom-based or programmatic assessment tools. The anthology provides case-study examples from liberal arts and land-grant secondary institutions; advice for how to structure portfolios in the composition, basic writing, and biology classrooms; theoretical pieces on the connections between portfolios and learning; and the political questions and consequences of instituting portfolio-based assessment programs.

Bishop, Wendy. "Designing a Writing Portfolio Evaluation System." *English Record* 40.2 (1990): 21–25.

Dong, Yu Ren. "The Need to Understand ESL Students' Native Language Writing Experiences." *TETYC* 26.3 (Mar. 1999): 277–85.

Elbow, Peter, and Pat Belanoff. "Portfolios as a Substitute for Proficiency Examinations." *CCC* 37 (1986): 336–39.

——. "Using Portfolios to Increase Collaboration and Community in a Writing Program." *WPA: Journal of the Council of Writing Program Administrators* 9 (Spring 1986): 27–40.

Hilligoss, Susan, and Tharon Howard. *Visual Communication: A Writer's Guide.* 2nd ed. New York: Longman, 2002. This book provides brief but specific guidelines on the visual design of portfolios and other texts.

Larson, Richard L. "Portfolios in the Assessment of Writing: A Political Perspective." *Assessment of Writing: Politics, Policies, Practices.* Ed. Edward White. New York: MLA, 1996. 271–83. Larson examines the issues of power relations in portfolio assessment, particularly consent, as instructors may be forced to use this method, and privacy, as student writing may be assessed by outside parties. He advocates an approach in which administration works with instructors to gain their acceptance of the portfolio method, and that makes clear the uses to which such assessment will be put.

Murphy, Sandra, and Barbara Grant. "Portfolio Approaches to Assessment: Breakthrough or More of the Same?" *Assessment of Writing: Politics, Policies, Practices.* Ed. Edward White. New York: MLA, 1996. 284–300. The authors examine various theoretical models of how the portfolio method aids in the assessment of student writing, and further discuss the problems and practicalities of implementing such models, in particular decisions regarding standardization versus contextualization and top-down versus collaborative assessment.

Nelson, Alexis. "Views from the Underside: Proficiency Portfolios in First-Year Composition." *TETYC* 26.3 (Mar. 1999): 243–53. Students' stories about portfolio assessment shed light on how they work and why they sometimes don't.

"Portfolio Assessment: An Annotated Bibliography." *Quarterly of the National Writing Project and the Center for the Study of Writing* 10 (Oct. 1988): 23–24.

Yancey, Kathleen Blake, and Irwin Weiser, eds. *Situating Portfolios: Four Perspectives.* Logan: Utah State UP, 1997. One of the most recent anthologies on portfolios in English, this collection explores four contexts for writing portfolios: the theory behind portfolios in the field and their power as assessment tools for secondary educational institutions; portfolio pedagogy, especially in terms of student literacy and the classroom community; portfolios as reflective and professional instruments for teachers themselves; and the interstices of technology and portfolios, in particular hypertext portfolios, email, and the electronic classroom. All four contexts address how portfolios transform student writing and the teaching of composition.

Young, Carl. A., and Margo A. Figgins. "The Q-folio in Action: Using a Web-based Electronic Portfolio to Reinvent Traditional Notions of Inquiry, Research, and Portfolios." *Contemporary Issues in Technology and Teacher Education* 2.2 (2002). Online at <http://www.citejournal.org/vol2/iss2/english/article1.cfm>. A discussion of the design and implementation of the Q-folio at the University of Virginia as an electronic tool for transforming the imagination and traditional composition.

■ **USEFUL WEB SITE**

Portfolio Resources

> http://www.cstw.ohio-state.edu
>
> *The Ohio State University Center for the Study and Teaching of Writing's site includes many portfolio resources as well as examples of student writing portfolios.*

Answers to Selected Exercises

Here are answers to all exercises that have specific answers. Exercises for which answers will vary are not covered here.

EXERCISE 5.4: Suggested Answers

Repeated key words include: *Information Superhighway; vast; computer.*

EXERCISE 5.5: Suggested Answers

I must make, I must confess, I have been, I have almost; first; confessions/confess; white moderate, White Citizen's Counciler, white moderate; who is more devoted, who prefers, who constantly says, who paternalistically believes, who lives, who constantly advises; to "order" than to justice, a negative peace which is the absence of tension to a positive peace which is the presence of justice; I agree with you, but I cannot agree with; timetable, mythical concept of time, "more convenient season"; Shallow understanding from people of good will, absolute understanding from people of ill will; Lukewarm acceptance, outright rejection.

EXERCISE 13.1: Suggested Answers

1. Arguable
2. Arguable, depending on the acceptance of scientific data
3. Arguable
4. Not arguable
5. Arguable
6. Not arguable, unless students want to discuss boiling temperatures at different air pressures
7. Arguable
8. Arguable, depending on the acceptance of statistical reports
9. Arguable
10. Arguable, although some studies continue to show correlations between reduced speed and lower accident rates. More readily verifiable is the correlation between speed limit and mortality rate.

EXERCISE 13.3: Suggested Answers

1. The Palestinian-Israeli conflict can be managed but not solved. Thesis: The U.S. government should not attempt to solve the Palestinian-Israeli conflict because (1) it is essentially religious, not political; (2) neither side has a tradition of compromise; and (3) both sides will accept nothing less than possession of the same territories.
2. Prison inmates retain basic human rights, including the right not to be tested for HIV. Thesis: Mandatory testing of prisoners for HIV is wrong because it would infringe on their basic right to privacy.
3. Free access to computers is an unrealistic goal. Thesis: Students should not have free access to computers because (1) the cost would

481

be prohibitive; and (2) they don't have equal access to other facilities such as study carrells, musical instruments, practice fields, and sports equipment.

4. The new federal student-loan program is a step in the right direction. Thesis: The new federal student-loan program should be supported because (1) it ensures access to higher education for many more people; (2) it does not add substantially to the budget deficit because the funds will be repaid; and (3) its success may encourage the government to develop other useful programs.

5. Cloning of humans would be a disaster for humanity. Thesis: Cloning of human beings should be banned by law because (1) it would reduce the beneficial genetic diversity created by sexual reproduction; (2) it would create severe psychological problems for individuals created in this way; and (3) it would encourage unscrupulous people to try to create their own "master race," "slave race," or some other category of clones.

EXERCISE 13.4: Answers

The copywriters work to establish credibility by:

1. Demonstrating knowledge (we invest your money in companies that are successful, stable, and have a positive history of caring for people and the planet).

2. Establishing common ground (we all want to invest our money wisely and responsibly; we want financial as well as social benefits).

3. Demonstrating fairness (by investing only in socially responsible funds and by investing minimums of $250, which makes the company accessible to lower-income investors).

4. Appealing to logical judgment (we have seven mutual fund portfolios to meet a range of investment objectives).

In addition, by "hearting" North, Central, and South Americas, this ad excludes the controversial African investments that "socially responsible" investors find so offensive.

EXERCISE 13.6: Suggested Answers

1. Whatever promotes the best interests of all concerned and violates no one's rights is morally acceptable.

2. Women should not be exposed to a higher risk of death.

3. Only those who can talk can feel pain.

EXERCISE 13.7: Suggested Answers

Examples/precedents/narratives: All the examples are vague and without specific support; they are "claims" rather than examples or precedents. "We have a positive history of caring for people and the planet."

Authority and testimony: The ad uses terms such as "IRAs," "403B7 Plans," and "Automatic Investment programs," which give the ad authority. Subtle testimonies to the accessibility and decency of the investment program are the mention of "minimum" investments of $250 as well as the name of the company itself, "Working Assets, Common Holdings." The ad works to give responsibility to the reader by asking the reader to read the prospectus carefully before investing or sending money—a kindly warning to the reader about any kind of investment with any company.

Causes and effects: By investing your money in a financially and *socially* responsible company, you invest in the welfare of the planet and the people. Big jump—but somewhat convincing.

Induction and deduction: Deduction. "Working Assets puts your money where your heart is" is the initial pronouncement that is somewhat supported by the information that follows. That initial sentence tries to serve as a kind of initial thesis sentence.

Logical fallacies: The ad is begging the question by saying that Working Assets is responsible because it has a history of being responsible. This ad also oversimplifies issues related to investing policies, the stability and success of investment companies, and the consequences of investment policies.

EXERCISE 13.9: Suggested Answers

1. Concern over basic human rights if banned; concern over harm to the environment and to smokers and nonsmokers as well.
2. Fear of terrorist hijackings; concern over possible invasion of privacy; anger over failure of past security measures.
3. Fear of radiation leakage; anger at the government for putting innocent citizens in danger; pride in technological achievement; distress at increased electricity bills to pay for a new power plant.
4. Joy over the rebirth of overt religious conviction; distaste for the perceived abuse of emotional appeals and misuse of money; amusement by others' gullibility.
5. Concern for the health of student-athletes; disbelief that coaches and administrators would want to win at all costs; anger that their insistence on perfection would cause athletes to turn to drugs to stimulate performance, to relieve stress, and to relax.

EXERCISE 25.1: Suggested Answers

Feeling their oats. One year old is an exciting age. Babies are changing in lots of ways—in their eating, in how they get around, in what they want to do, and in how they feel about themselves and other people. When they were little and helpless, you could put them where you wanted them, give them the playthings you thought suitable, feed them the foods you knew were best. Most of the time they were willing to let you be the boss, and took it all in good spirit. It's more complicated now that they are around a year old. They seem to realize that they're not meant to be baby dolls the rest of their lives, that they're human beings with ideas and wills of their own.

By 15 to 18 months, many children's behavior makes it clear that they're heading for what is often called "the terrible twos." When you suggest something that doesn't appeal to them, they feel they must assert themselves. Their nature tells them to. They just say "No" in words or actions, even about

things that they like to do. The psychologists call it "negativism"; many parents call it "that terrible *no* stage." But stop and think what would happen to children who never felt like saying "No." They'd become robots. You wouldn't be able to resist the temptation to boss them all the time, and they'd stop learning and developing. When they were old enough to go out into the world, to school and later to work, everybody else would take advantage of them, too. They'd never be good for anything.

– BENJAMIN SPOCK, *Baby and Child Care* (1985)

THINKING CRITICALLY ABOUT HOW LANGUAGE CAN BUILD COMMON GROUND: Suggested Answers

The poet asserts his own individuality in lines 6, 7–15, 21–24. He forges common ground with the reader in lines 16–20 perhaps; lines 25–40 definitely. The poet addresses racism in lines 34–40.

EXERCISE 27.2: Suggested Answers

1. Desdemona's attitude is that of a submissive victim; she simply lies down and dies, accepting her death as inevitable.
2. All candidates strive for the same results: to discredit their opponents and to persuade the majority of voters that they are qualified for the position.
3. Often, instead of dismissing an incompetent teacher, school officials will transfer the person to another school in order to avoid the problems involved in a dismissal.
4. The angrier she became over his actions, the more he rebelled and continued doing what he pleased.
5. My family lived in Trinidad for the first ten years of my life, and we experienced many hardships, but when we came to America, we thought our prospects were good.

EXERCISE 27.3: Answers

1. attentively
2. rapturous
3. dramatically
4. frugal

484   Answers to Selected Exercises

EXERCISE 27.4: Suggested Answers

1. *racing:* charging, tearing, marching. These alternatives each connote a different context and set of circumstances, giving the reader a different impression of the Burmans' action. *Charging* suggests an attack, whereas *racing* gives the impression of the Burmans competing against one another and the author *me* to arrive at a destination. *Marching* suggests regimented, ordered, or determined movement, and *tearing* a frenzied, excited, wild, or uncontrolled pace. *Rise:* stand; *rattling:* heaving, pulsing; *mound:* mountain, hump

2. *tragic:* distressing, alarming, disturbing; *consumes:* defeats, feeds on, erodes; *displays:* champions, thrives on, builds up, promotes; *drama:* excitement, tension, vitality

3. *hauling:* drawing; *briskly:* quickly; *businesslike:* efficient, matter-of-fact; *blow:* club, smack

4. *girl:* young lady, miss

5. *abide:* tolerate; *turns:* changes; *vital:* alive; *hold still:* contain their energy

EXERCISE 27.5: Suggested Answers

1. The entryway of the building looked like a garbage dump; paper was littered about, all kinds of bottles lay shattered, and rotting cantaloupe and chicken parts gave off an unbearable odor.

2. Cooing, singing, twittering — the early morning beckoning of birds outside my window makes it a treat to get up.

3. The feast at Mom's on Sunday was delicious as usual: roast chicken, garlic and sage stuffing, sweet garden peas, gallons of gravy, and half a fresh-baked apple pie each.

4. The valet stepped cautiously yet excitedly toward my Porsche.

5. Erin raced up, then retreated, then charged again, finally wetting her chubby toes in the surf.

FOR COLLABORATION: Suggested Answers

1. *like a magnolia corsage* (simile): this simile makes vivid and concrete Mom Willie's Southern heritage and suggests how positively she values it — and how proudly she "displays" it.

2. *deep and soft like water moving in a cavern* (simile): this simile compares the sound of her voice to water in a cavern.

3. *lounging* (metaphor): compares the horse in pasture to people relaxing; *cuddling up* (metaphor): emphasizes the pleasure the writer has reading mysteries; *top priority* (metaphor): reading is an activity of official importance.

EXERCISE 28.2: Answers

1. rhetoric: from ME *rethorike* < L *rhetorica* < Gr *rhetor,* orator < *eirein,* to speak

2. student: from ME < L *studere,* to study

3. curry: from Tamil *kari,* sauce

4. whine: from ME *whinen* < Indo-European *kwein,* to whiz, hiss, whistle

5. apple: from ME *appel* < OE *aeppel,* fruit, apple, eyeball, anything round

6. sex: from ME < L *sexus* < *secare,* to cut

7. okra: a word of West African origin

8. tortilla: from Sp, diminutive of *torta,* cake

9. cinema: from Fr *cinématographe* < Gr *kinema,* motion + *graphein,* to write

10. video: from L, I see < *videre,* to see

EXERCISE 28.3: Suggested Answers

1. *coerce:* (syn.) make, force, compel, constrain, oblige, drive

2. *prevaricate:* (syn.) equivocate, lie, palter, fib

3. *parameter:* (syn.) characteristic, element, factor

4. *odious:* (syn.) disgusting, ghastly, hideous, unpleasant

5. *awesome:* (syn.) impressive, overwhelming

6. *obfuscate:* (syn.) darken, confuse

EXERCISE 28.4: Suggested Answers

1. The *OED* lists a sixteenth-century definition of *dogmatism* as the preaching of new doctrine, the positive assertion of opinion, and a way of thinking based on principles that have not been tested by reflection.

   Webster's New World Dictionary gives both the idea of asserting opinion as well as the notion that this opinion usually occurs without reference to evidence.

2. The *OED* defines *alienate* as to make strange or turn away from, to transfer ownership, and to change or alter something.

   Webster's New World Dictionary adds two slightly different meanings: to cause to be withdrawn from society, and to transfer affection.

3. The *OED* defines *discriminate* as to make or constitute a difference, to distinguish with the mind or intellect, and to make a distinction.

   Webster's New World Dictionary also includes the notion of discernment or observing distinctions and adds the idea of showing partiality or prejudice.

4. The *OED* defines *hopefully* as an adverb: "In a hopeful manner, with a feeling of hope; with ground for hope, promisingly."

   Webster's New World Dictionary also lists adverb uses.

5. The *OED* defines *humanism* as belief in the mere humanity of Christ, the quality of being human, a system of thought concerned with merely human interests, and the Renaissance study of Greek and Roman culture.

   Webster's New World Dictionary describes the philosophical basis of modern *humanism* in detail: "a modern, nontheistic, rationalist movement that holds that man is capable of self-fulfillment, ethical conduct, etc. without the recourse of supernaturalism."

6. Both the *OED* and *Webster's New World Dictionary* define *culture* as the cultivation of the soil, the production of a particular commodity, the growth of microorganisms in a prepared substance, the development of the intellect, and the ideas or customs of a group.

   The *OED* includes two obsolete definitions: worship, and the training of the human body.

EXERCISE 29.1: Suggested Answers

1. *terrestrial:* worldly, earthy, mundane; consisting of, living on, or growing on land
2. *scriptorium:* a writing room; a room in a monastery for copying manuscripts; writing and studying
3. *geothermal:* having to do with the heat of the earth's interior
4. *lucent:* giving off light; shining; translucent or clear
5. *beneficent:* doing good; resulting in benefit
6. *audiology:* the science of hearing; the evaluation of hearing defects
7. *vacuous:* empty of matter; showing lack of intelligence, interest, or thought; characterized by lack of purpose
8. *pathogenic:* producing disease
9. *juridical:* of judicial proceedings, jurisprudence, or law
10. *graphology:* the study of handwriting

FOR COLLABORATION: Suggested Answers

1. *remit:* send again or send back; release from the guilt or penalty of, refrain from, desist from an activity
2. *subterranean:* beneath earth; of or relating to the area under the surface of the earth
3. *translucent:* across or over light; permitting the passage of light, clear or transparent
4. *monograph:* write a single writing; a learned treatise on a small area of learning
5. *distend:* stretch apart or away; extend, enlarge from internal pressure
6. *superscript:* write over or above; a distinguishing symbol written immediately above

or above and to the right of another character

7. *deport:* carry from; carry away, send out of the country by legal deportation, behave or comport oneself

8. *neologism:* a recent word or thought; a word, usage, or expression that is often disapproved of because of its newness or barbarousness

9. *inaudible:* hear not; not capable of being heard

10. *apathetic:* without feeling or not suffering; having or showing little or no feeling or emotion; having or showing little or no interest or concern

EXERCISE 29.2: Suggested Answers

1. *contemplative:* of or inclined to contemplation; thoughtful, meditative

2. *fanciful:* full of fancy; indulging in fancies; imaginative in a playful way; whimsical

3. *impairment:* reduction, injury

4. *liquefy:* to change into a liquid

5. *barrenness:* not being able to produce offspring; emptiness

6. *defiance:* the act of defying; bold resistance to authority or opposition

7. *merciless:* having no mercy; pitiless, cruel

8. *redden:* to make red; to become red

9. *standardize:* to make standard or uniform

10. *satirist:* a writer of satires

THINKING CRITICALLY ABOUT VOCABULARY: Suggested Answers

1. *eradicated:* tore out by the roots, got rid of, wiped out, destroyed
   propensities: natural inclinations or tendencies

2. *synchrony:* the fact or state of simultaneous occurrence

EXERCISE 30.1: Answers

1. They're; their; there

2. to; too

3. beginning; a lot
4. noticeable; until
5. occurred; before
6. believe; lose
7. you're; definitely; your
8. affects; success; than; its
9. received; through
10. develop; truly; successful
11. cannot; separate
12. where; and
13. arguments; against; environment
14. businesses; dependent
15. Heroes; necessary
16. experience; exercise
17. professor; accept
18. categories; final
19. roommates; without
20. occasion; whether; weather
21. may be; therefore; immediately
22. woman's
23. occurrences; every day
24. It's; all right; sense
25. Apparently

EXERCISE 30.2: Answers

If *you're* looking for summer fun, *accept* the friendly *advice* of thousands of happy adventurers: spend three *weeks* kayaking *through* the inside passage *to* Alaska. For ten years, Outings, Inc., has *led* groups of novice kayakers *past* some of the most breathtaking scenery in North America. *Their* goal is simple: to give participants the time of *their* lives. As one of last year's adventurers said, *"It's* a trip I will remember vividly, one that *affected* me powerfully."

EXERCISE 30.3: Answers

1. sleigh	6. caffeine
2. conscience	7. chief
3. ancient	8. receive
4. leisure	9. achieve
5. pierce	10. heiress

EXERCISE 30.4: Answers

1. futurism
2. wholly
3. argument
4. lonely
5. malicious
6. dyeing
7. hopeful
8. continuous
9. exercising
10. outrageous

EXERCISE 30.5: Answers

1. lonelier
2. carrying
3. defiance
4. studious
5. supplied
6. dutiful
7. likelihood
8. obeyed
9. rainiest
10. coyly

EXERCISE 30.6: Answers

1. occurred
2. fastest
3. skipper
4. reference
5. commitment
6. regrettable
7. submitted
8. frantically
9. benefited
10. weeping

EXERCISE 30.7: Answers

1. tomatoes
2. hooves
3. volunteers
4. babies
5. dishes
6. spoofs
7. beaches
8. yourselves
9. golf clubs
10. roses
11. stepchildren
12. turkeys
13. heirs apparent
14. radios
15. phenomena

EXERCISE 30.8: Answers

For me, the *ideal occupation* is an *arrangement* in which I would play with a band for six months and tour the other six months of the year. I wouldn't want to teach music because I would *probably* have to teach in a school where many students are forced by *their parents* to take music. When children are forced to do something, *it's likely* that they won't enjoy it. If I were able to both tour *and* teach, however, I would be happy.

I'm *really* glad that I've gotten involved in music; it looks as if I'm destined to be a *professional* musician. *Surely* I don't know what else I could do; I *doubt* I'd be a good *administrator* or business executive or lawyer. And the idea of being a doctor or *dentist* and probing around people's *bodies* or looking at teeth that have huge, *rotting* cavities isn't appealing to me. The more I think about it, the *happier* I am with my music. I *definitely* plan to pursue that career.

The misspellings in this passage can be attributed to three causes:

1. The writer's reliance on pronunciation as a guide for spelling, thus leading to leaving out unpronounced consonants and vowels and to additions and substitutions of wrong letters as in *ideel, ocupation, arangement, probly, parrents, likly, an, realy, profesional, surly, dout, administrater, bussiness, denist,* and *definately.*
2. The writer's difficulty distinguishing homonyms as in *there* and *its.*
3. The writer's unfamiliarity with rules governing addition of suffixes to words ending in *y* as in *bodys* and *happyer.*

EXERCISE 31.1: Answers

1. My foot got tangled in the computer cord.
2. Her first afternoon as a kindergarten teacher had left her exhausted.
3. Dr. Burns is almost certainly going to recommend surgery.
4. Our office manager, a stern taskmaster with a fondness for Chanel suits, has been terrifying interns since 1976.
5. Hearing his petulant voice on the radio always forces me to change the station.

EXERCISE 31.2: Answers

1. we will
2. had been leaking
3. agree; do need

4. can collect; might run; should finish
5. would be

EXERCISE 31.3: Answers

Nouns are set in italics; articles are set in boldface.
  1. *Halloween;* **the;** *children; candy*
  2. *plagiarism*
  3. *Thanksgiving;* **a;** *season; turkeys*
  4. **The;** *crocuses' buds;* **a;** *frost;* **the;** *ground;* **a;** *field; ice*
  5. **the;** *row; people;* **a;** *man; hair;* **a;** *woman; jeans*

EXERCISE 31.4: Answers

Pronouns are set in italics; antecedents are set in boldface.
  1. *She; everyone*
  2. **Jane;** *one; she*
  3. *Who;* **jeans;** *them;* **designer;** *himself; them*
  4. **They;** *themselves*
  5. **People;** *who;* **those;** *who*

EXERCISE 31.5: Answers

Adjectives are set in italics; adverbs are set in boldface.
  1. **Because; perilously;** *short;* **quickly;** *the; final*
  2. **Nevertheless;** *her; teenaged;* **eventually;** *his; poor*
  3. *The;* **somewhat;** *shy;* **reluctantly;** *six; exuberant*
  4. *The; huge; red; lovely; the;* **disappointingly**
  5. *the; youngest; the; a; brilliant*

EXERCISE 31.6: Suggested Answers

  1. A corporation can fire undependable employees.
  2. The thin, dirty abandoned dog limped sadly along the hot asphalt road.
  3. In the pastoral painting, a dirt road curves between the rolling hills.
  4. The tall, white candles gleamed brightly on the well-scrubbed tablecloth.
  5. Contract workers quickly installed a new telephone cable.

EXERCISE 31.7: Answers

  1. of; from; until
  2. through; across; into
  3. according to; at
  4. During; down; between
  5. about; from; in

EXERCISE 31.8: Answers

  1. after; and; both . . . and; so
  2. but
  3. not only . . . but also
  4. Although; and; as if
  5. because; but; still

EXERCISE 31.9: Answers

Complete subjects are set in italics; simple subjects are set in boldface.
  1. *A* **shortage** *of affordable housing near the university*
  2. *the new* **elevator**
  3. *some representative* **photographs**
  4. *Japanese* **animation,** *with its cutting-edge graphics and futuristic plots*
  5. *Some* **women** *worried about osteoporosis*

EXERCISE 31.10: Answers

Predicates are set in italics.
  1. *is new to this route:* LV — is; SC — new
  2. *made us a nation:* TV — made; DO — us; OC — nation
  3. *seems likely in this case:* IV — seems; SC — likely
  4. *will never die:* IV — will . . . die
  5. *promise consumers the world:* TV — promise; IO — consumers; DO — world

EXERCISE 31.11: Answers

  1. VERBAL (PART) — Approaching the rope; PREP — into the icy pond
  2. APP — the motel clerk; VERBAL (INF) — to be certified as a river guide; PREP — as a river guide
  3. VERBAL (PART) — outlined against the sky; PREP — against the sky

4. VERBAL (PART) — Floating on my back; PREP — on my back
5. ABSO — her fingers clutching the fence; VERBAL (PART) — clutching the fence
6. VERBAL (GER) — Learning to drive a car with a manual transmission; VERBAL (INF) — to drive a car with a manual transmission; PREP — with a manual transmission
7. VERBAL (PART) — Shocked into silence; PREP — into silence; VERBAL (PART) — fixed on the odd creature; PREP — on the odd creature
8. VERBAL (PART) — Dancing with abandon; PREP — with abandon; VERBAL (INF) — to play their instruments
9. APP — a quiet man as a rule; PREP — as a rule; PREP — in the shower; VERBAL (PART) — singing at the top of his lungs; PREP — at the top of his lungs; PREP — of his lungs
10. PREP — of recreation; VERBAL (GER) — taking a nap

EXERCISE 31.12: Answers

1. IND — I don't know what happened to my grade school friends; REL — what; DEP — because I moved away during junior high school
2. IND — She immediately recognized the officer; DEP — who walked into the coffee shop; REL — who
3. DEP — When she was deemed old enough to understand; SUB CONJ — when; IND — she was told the truth; IND — she finally knew why her father had left home; REL — why
4. IND — The trip was longer; DEP — than I had remembered; REL — than
5. IND — I could see that he was very tired; REL — that; IND — I had to ask him a few questions

EXERCISE 31.13: Suggested Answers

1. The last guests, who had stayed much later than we expected, finally left.
2. After working on his paper until five in the morning, Primo desperately wanted a cup of coffee before he went to class.

3. The new computer, which had been programmed by an employee who had long since left the company, made a strange noise.
4. Rob, who was a collector of jazz records, always borrowed money from his friends.
5. When the police shut down the outdoor concert, the crowd grew louder and more disorderly.

EXERCISE 31.14: Answers

1. complex, declarative
2. compound, interrogative
3. simple, declarative
4. simple, imperative
5. compound-complex, declarative

EXERCISE 32.1: Answers

1. Who (subjective)
2. Whomever (direct object of *recommends*)
3. Whom (direct object of *trust*)
4. Whom (object of preposition, *with*)
5. Whom (direct object of *benefit*)

EXERCISE 32.2: Answers

1. she
2. whom
3. them
4. me
5. he
6. their
7. he
8. whoever
9. we
10. whom

FOR COLLABORATION: Answers

1. her and him → she and I
2. I → me
3. who → whom
4. (correct)
5. him → his
6. him → he
7. me → I
8. (correct)
9. (correct)
10. whomever → whoever

EXERCISE 33.1: Answers

1. let, came, torn
2. made, found
3. began
4. wound, forgotten (OR forgot)
5. made, knew
6. woke, flown
7. sprang, swam
8. thrown, been
9. broken, lost
10. went, seen

EXERCISE 33.2: Answers

1. lies
2. laid
3. sat
4. Sitting
5. rise

EXERCISE 33.3: Answers

1. *predict/are predicting* — present action that may be seen as ongoing
2. *have feared/have been fearing* — action begun in past continues
3. *emigrated* — completed action
4. *sent/has sent* — started in past, may be seen as ongoing to the present
5. *will meet/will be meeting* — future (continuing) action
6. *ate/were eating* — past action, completed
7. *will have finished* — future action completed by a certain time
8. *will have watched* — future action completed by a certain time
9. *expresses* — literary work
10. *rises* — general truth

EXERCISE 33.4: Answers

1. When he *was* twenty-one, he *wanted to become* a millionaire by the age of thirty.
2. *Having left* England in December, the settlers *arrived* in Virginia in May.

3. They *had hoped* to plant their garden by now.
4. *Having worked* with great dedication as an un-paid summer intern at the magazine, Roberto called his former supervisor in the fall to ask about a paid position.
5. When we walked home from school, we often *stopped* for ice cream.

EXERCISE 33.5: Answers

1. The storm *uprooted* huge pine trees.
2. A superhero with amazing crime-fighting powers *was drawn* by the comic-book artist.
3. For months, the mother kangaroo *protects, feeds,* and *teaches* her baby to survive.
4. The first snow of winter *covered* the lawns and rooftops.
5. A sleek new building to house a modern art collection *was designed* by a team of architects.

EXERCISE 33.6: Answers

1. was → were
2. was → were
3. (correct)
4. was → were
5. knows → know

EXERCISE 34.1: Answers

1. know
2. races
3. rewards
4. supplies
5. stops
6. was
7. cares
8. holds
9. frighten
10. leaves

EXERCISE 34.2: Answers

1. is → are
2. (correct; *talking and getting up* is considered a single unit)

3. (correct)
4. (correct)
5. were → was; a word referred to as a word is singular
6. convince → convinces; "neither/nor"
7. sits → sit
8. (correct; *most* refers to voters)
9. are → is
10. intimidates → intimidate; "neither/nor"
11. make → makes
12. (correct; *who* refers to *one*)
13. were → was; *Our Tapes* is singular, a title
14. was (second verb) → were; *that* refers to *countries*
15. reveal → reveals

THINKING CRITICALLY ABOUT SUBJECT-VERB AGREEMENT: Suggested Answers

none of these assumptions about marriage *add up*; plural, *none* refers to *assumptions*

Between the public statistic and the private reality *lies* a sea of contradictions; singular subject is *sea*

Marriage *seems* to me; *Marriage* is singular

the divorce rate — with or without new babies in the house — *remains* constant; *divorce rate* is singular

The fabric of men-and-women-as-they-once-were *is* so thick; *fabric* is singular

no amount of patching *can weave* that cloth together; *amount* is singular

but even stronger *is* the growing perception; singular, subject is *perception*

that only people who *are* real to themselves; plural, *who* refers to *people*

that only people who are real to themselves *can connect*; *people* is plural

Two shall be as one *is* over; singular, *Two shall be as one* is an expression that forms a singular subject

no matter how lonely we get; *we* is plural

EXERCISE 35.1: Suggested Answers

1. With tuition on the rise, students have to save money wherever they can.

2. Roommates do not always get along, but they can usually manage to tolerate each other temporarily.
3. Congress usually resists presidential attempts to encroach on what it considers congressional authority.
4. We voted on whether Franklin or Lucille would have a chance to join the club.
5. If there is a doctor in the house, he or she should step forward now and offer to help.
6. Every dog and cat has its own personality that could never be cloned.
7. Neither the scouts nor their leaders knew the way out of the forest.
8. (correct)
9. Celebrities can sometimes convince themselves that they really are special and talented.
10. I often turn on the fan and the light and neglect to turn them off.

THINKING CRITICALLY ABOUT PRONOUN AGREEMENT: Suggested Answers

After the birth of human beings, their early years are obscurely spent in the toils or pleasures of childhood. As they grow up, the world receives them, when their adulthood begins, and they enter into contact with their fellows. They are then studied for the first time, and it is imagined that the germ of the vices and the virtues of the maturer years is then formed. This, if I am not mistaken, is a great error. We must begin higher up; we must watch infants in their mothers' arms; we must see the first images which the external world casts upon the dark mirror of their minds, the first occurrences which they witness; we must hear the first words which awaken the sleeping powers of thought, and stand by their earliest efforts — if we would understand the prejudices, the habits, and the passions which will rule their lives. The entire human being is, so to speak, to be seen in the cradle of the child.

EXERCISE 36.1: Answers

1. completely → obsessed
2. ridiculously → behaved
3. bad → they
4. really → hot and humid; frequently → below zero
5. loudly → talked
6. badly → hurt
7. well → performed
8. terrific → Aneil
9. good → stew
10. strictly → brought up

EXERCISE 36.2: Answers

1. Aidan reads both science fiction and true crime books, but he likes science fiction best.
2. According to the article, walking is healthier [not healthy] than jogging.
3. The crown is set with some of the most precious gemstones in the world.
4. Women tend to live longer than men; hence, more of the elderly are women.
5. Minneapolis is the larger of the Twin Cities.
6. She came up with a perfect plan for revenge.
7. My graduation day will be the happiest day of my life.
8. The student cafeteria is operated by a college food service, part of a chain.
9. Commuting by train or bus is more energy efficient than commuting by car.
10. Seeing grizzly bears in Glacier National Park was a more exciting experience for the children than going to Disneyland.

EXERCISE 37.1: Suggested Answers

1. Before Sasha flew to Brazil, she hurried to call her sister. Before her sister flew to Brazil, Sasha hurried to call her.
2. Lear divides his kingdom between the two older daughters, Goneril and Regan, whose extravagant professions of love are more flattering than the simple affection of the youngest daughter, Cordelia. The consequences of this error in judgment soon become apparent, as the older daughters prove neither grateful nor kind to him.
3. New England helped shape many aspects of American culture, including education, religion, and government. As New Englanders moved west, they carried their institutions with them.
4. When drug therapy is combined with psychotherapy, the patients relate better and are more responsive to their therapists, and they are less vulnerable to what disturbs them.
5. Before opening for business next to the cleaners, the restaurant burned down.
6. Texans often hear about the influence of big oil corporations.
7. Jonathan had an interview with a person who convinced him to keep looking for a job in advertising.
8. She dropped off a friend who had gone to the party with her.
9. Many employees resented smoking, so the company policy prohibited it.
10. In his poems, Derek Walcott often describes the landscape of St. Lucia.

EXERCISE 38.1: Suggested Answers

1. The greed of the 1980s gave way to the occupational insecurity of the 1990s, which in turn gave way to reinforced family ties in the early 2000s.
2. The dean asked that we close the door and then sit down.
3. The editor thought she had eliminated all the errors when she spotted yet another misplaced modifier.
4. She studied the package, wondered what it could be, and tore off the wrapping.
5. Suddenly, we heard an explosion of wings off to our right, and we could see a hundred or more ducks lifting off from the water.

6. After the suspect was searched, he was fed at taxpayers' expense.
7. The upstairs noise irritated him until he figured out its source — a kitten.
8. A cloud of snow powder rose as skis and poles flew in every direction.
9. The instructor told us to read the next two stories before the next class and that she might give us a quiz on them.
10. Workers with computer skills were in great demand, and a programmer could almost name his or her salary.
11. I think it better that Grandfather die painlessly and with dignity than that he continue to live in terrible pain.
12. I liked the sense of individualism, the crowd yelling for me, and the feeling that I was in command.
13. Oscar Wilde wrote that books are not moral or immoral but "either well written or poorly written."
14. Put the ground beans in the filter cone, pour in the water, turn on the machine, and then sit back and enjoy the smell of the coffee.
15. The aroma, which wafts through the house, lures the adults from their beds.

THINKING CRITICALLY ABOUT SHIFTS: Suggested Answers

third-person singular (*It has been* . . .) → first-person plural (*our time* . . .) → third-person singular (*There is no delusion.* . . .) → second-person singular (*your head* . . .) → third-person singular (*The human mind* . . .) → first-person plural (*and we are obliged* . . .) → third-person singular (*It is all very well.* . . .) → second-person singular (*your awareness* . . .)

(Note the shift in mood from the indicative to the imperative in the next-to-last sentence.)

EXERCISE 39.1: Suggested Answers

1. Listeners prefer talk shows to classical music, so the radio station is changing its programming.

2. Clothing designers recycle looks — nothing is original anymore.
3. Some students read more online than in print; some do the opposite.
4. Mexicans observe Day of the Dead, but it is not a mournful holiday.
5. After a Hollywood actor played a dog in three movies, he became typecast.
6. He found life lessons in the canine world; for example, he learned the value of persistence.
7. You adopted the rabbit — now you feed him.
8. Even though the West Indian woman has lived in New England for years, she always feels betrayed by winter.
9. The colorful restaurant on the roof of the Pompidou Center indeed looks like a set for the Jetsons.
10. A popular restauranteur opened a barbecue joint in a jazz club. Critics applauded the joint venture.

EXERCISE 40.1: Suggested Answers

1. Small, long-veined, fuzzy green leaves add to the appeal of this newly developed variety of carrot.
2. Many Americans yearn to live with gusto.
3. The region has dry, sandy soil, blown into strange formations by the ever-present wind.
4. Exploring sculpture and video, Paul McCartney has gone beyond music.
5. Hong Kong offers numerous museums and celebrates all the performing arts.
6. Diners in Creole restaurants might try shrimp gumbo or order turtle soup.
7. Tupperware parties go back to the late 1940s. At Tupperware parties, hosts are salespersons.
8. He was making his friend feel better by joking that time heals all haircuts.
9. Joan Didion has investigated politics and explored human emotions.
10. Mary Wollstonecraft believed in universal public education and in education that forms the heart and strengthens the body.

EXERCISE 40.2: Suggested Answers

1. *dependent-clause fragment:* As soon as the seventy-five-year-old cellist walked onstage, the audience burst into applause.
2. *verbal-phrase fragment:* The patient has only one goal, to smoke behind the doctor's back.
3. *noun-phrase fragment:* Lust is an emotion that someone famously said he had felt in his heart.
4. *dependent-clause fragment:* The director lowered his fee, which had started out in the stratosphere.
5. *prepositional-phrase fragment:* In the United States of all places, genealogy is the most popular hobby today.
6. *appositive-phrase fragment.* Forster stopped writing novels after *A Passage to India,* one of the greatest novels of the twentieth century.
7. *subordinate-clause fragment.* Sylvia Plath achieved new status because of *Ariel,* her final book of poems.
8. *compound-predicate fragment.* I loved *Beloved* and knew Toni Morrison deserved the Nobel Prize.
9. *relative-clause fragment.* The president appointed five members who drew up a set of bylaws.
10. *subordinate-clause fragment.* Because the younger generation often rejects the ways of its elders, one might say that rebellion is normal.

EXERCISE 41.1: Suggested Answers

1. Relating his amusing stories, the comedian had the audience in stitches.
2. The tanks toppled almost all the government buildings on the square.
3. The victim died from friendly fire, apparently.
4. While helping my father clean his attic, I found and offered to frame the citation that the mayor had given him for outstanding service.
5. All-night public transportation, which connects the university and downtown, is a new service.

6. Doctors recommend a new, painless test for cancer.
7. In my mind, I went through the process of taxiing and taking off.
8. Before I decided to buy the stock, I knew the investment would pay off dramatically.
9. The bank offered flood insurance underwritten by the federal government to the homeowners.
10. The maintenance worker shut down the turbine that was revolving out of control.

EXERCISE 41.2: Suggested Answers

1. The candidate quickly promised to reduce class size. The candidate promised to reduce class size quickly.
2. She suggested that she would take the summer after graduation off. After graduation, she suggested that she would take the summer off.
3. The collector who originally owned the painting planned to leave it to a museum. The collector who owned the painting planned originally to leave it to a museum.
4. Doctors can now restore limbs that have been partially severed to functioning condition. Doctors can now restore limbs that have been severed to partially functioning condition.
5. The speaker said he would answer questions when he finished his talk. When he finished his talk, the speaker said he would answer questions.

EXERCISE 41.3: Suggested Answers

1. Statistics irrefutably tell us that strong economic times have led to increases in the college dropout rate.
2. Due to its shock value in negotiations, sometimes a radical proposal stimulates creative thinking by parties to a conflict.
3. The architect wanted to design public buildings eventually.

4. Bookstores sold fifty thousand copies in the first week after publication.

5. Because of the sudden trading, the stock exchange became a chaotic circus.

EXERCISE 41.4: Suggested Answers

1. Determined to increase its audience share, producers of news shows may make them entertainment.

2. Craving instant updates, young adults are responsible for the gain in popularity of all-news stations.

3. To provide comic relief, newscasters attribute heat waves and blizzards to the weather forecaster.

4. Chosen for their looks, newscasters may have weak journalistic credentials.

5. As a visual medium, the televised format is not suited for presenting complex issues.

EXERCISE 41.5: Suggested Answers

1. However unhappy I am with my part-time job, it helps me pay the rent.

2. While one drinks eight glasses of water a day, one's weight often drops.

3. When waiters are faced with a busy restaurant full of hungry people, their jobs can become very stressful.

4. Although Americans are careful of their pronunciation, Parisians cannot understand their French.

5. Even though it is costly, my family travels for two weeks every summer.

EXERCISE 42.1: Suggested Answers

1. A political career would satisfy my desire for public service. My desire for public service makes me interested in a political career.

2. Many people would suffer if air pollution standards were relaxed. The reason air-pollution standards should not be relaxed is that many people would suffer.

3. By not prosecuting white-collar crime as vigorously as we prosecute violent crime, we encourage white-collar criminals to ignore the law. We must prosecute white-collar crime as vigorously as violent crime unless we want to encourage white-collar criminals to ignore the law.

4. Irony occurs when you expect one thing and get something else. The experience of expecting one thing and getting something else is irony.

5. One common side effect of the medication is growth of hair on women's faces. Women grow hair on their faces as a common side effect of the medication.

EXERCISE 42.2: Suggested Answers

1. My new stepmother makes my father happier than the last one did.

2. Argentina and Peru were colonized by Spain, and Brazil was colonized by Portugal.

3. She argued that children are even more important for men than they are for women.

4. Were the traffic jams in Texas any worse than those in many other states in the South and West?

5. The personalities of first-born offspring are different from those of middle children.

EXERCISE 43.1: Suggested Answers

1. The producers were pleased with their film, at the festivals, in the reviews, and at the box office.

2. If we are to judge by reports in newspapers the next morning, more important than who wins Best Actress is what she wears to accept the award.

3. From the sightseeing boat, we saw a whale dive toward the photographer, lift itself out of the water, and crash its tail on the waves.

4. The presence of the Indian in these movies always conjures up destructive stereotypes of

drunkenness, horse thieves, and bloodthirsty war parties.

5. Victorian women were warned that smoking would cause them to grow a moustache, contract tuberculosis, become sterile, or die young.

EXERCISE 43.2: Suggested Answers

1. Many forms of hazing occur, such as physical and mental abuse.
2. Many people tend to expand their sentences by adding unnecessary words.
3. World hunger is a major problem.
4. The first-time tourist to New York was really proud of finishing Monday's *Times* crossword puzzle but had no idea that the puzzle is easiest on Monday so that everyone who tries it feels a sense of accomplishment.
5. The stock market seems a source of anxiety to investors who don't understand the important principle of cycles.

EXERCISE 44.1: Suggested Answers

The bull-riding arena was fairly crowded, but this made no impression on me, for I had made a decision. It was now time to prove myself, and I was scared. I walked to the entry window and laid my money on the counter. The clerk held up a Stetson hat filled with slips of paper. I reached in and picked one. The slip held the number of the bull I was to ride, so I headed toward the stock corral.

EXERCISE 44.2: Suggested Answers

1. The *Hindenburg,* a gigantic airship, was destroyed in an explosion.
2. In South Africa, you can explore a savanna, where magnificent wildlife roam, or world-class cities.
3. When Stephen King stole traffic cones in 1970, he was arrested and fined one hundred dollars.
4. The mayor, still a man of paradoxes, tells about selling Christmas wreaths at the same

time that he was studying for his bar mitzvah.

5. In the mid-seventies, skateboarding originated in Venice, California, where, because of a drought, the swimming pools were empty.

EXERCISE 45.1: Suggested Answers

1. Before we depart, we must pack, notify the post office, and board the dog.
2. My favorite pastimes include reading, exercising, and talking with friends.
3. We must either walk quickly or drive slowly.
4. I want not only hot fudge but also whipped cream.
5. Graduates find that the job market shrinks, narrows, and tightens.

EXERCISE 45.2: Suggested Answers

1. I remember watching it the first time, realizing I'd never seen anything like it, and immediately vowing never to miss an episode of *Saturday Night Live.*
2. Just as my parents grew up devoted to *I Love Lucy,* so I grew up committed to *Cheers.*
3. *Lucy* often concerned telling white lies, fooling a husband, and getting into and out of jams.
4. It was impossible to watch *Cheers* and not to see a little of yourself in one of the characters.
5. TV networks now face the question of either coming up with new situations or acknowledging the death of the sitcom.

EXERCISE 45.3: Suggested Answers

Growing up in a large city provides a very different experience from growing up in a suburb. Suburban children undoubtedly enjoy many advantages over city children, including lawns, trees, and better schools. However, in recent years many people who were raised in the suburbs but who moved to large cities as young adults are deciding to bring up their own children in an urban setting. Their reasons for doing so include being able to enjoy the cultural advantages of the city, being able to spend more time with their children if they do not have to commute far to work, and being able to expose their children to a greater diversity of social and economic groups. Just as their own parents left the city for the space and calm of suburbia, so today's parents are returning to it for the crowds and excitement. Wherever they bring up their children, though, parents have never found nor ever will find utopia.

THINKING CRITICALLY ABOUT PARALLELISM: Suggested Answers

The richness of the scene was in *its plainness, its natural condition — of horse, of ring, of girl,* even to the girl's bare feet that gripped the bare back of her proud and ridiculous mount. The enchantment grew not *out of anything that happened or was performed* but *out of something that seemed to go round and around and around with the girl,* attending her, a steady gleam in the shape of a circle — a ring *of ambition, of happiness, of youth.* (And the positive pleasures of equilibrium under difficulties.) In a week or two, *all would be changed, all (or almost all) lost; the girl would wear makeup, the horse would wear gold, the ring would be painted, the bark would be clean for the feet of the horse, the girl's feet would be clean for the slippers that she'd wear.* All, all would be lost.

EXERCISE 46.1: Suggested Answers

To play bridge, you need to have the proper materials — a full deck of playing cards minus the jokers, a score pad, and a pen or pencil — and four players with a knowledge of suit and card ranking. The players are divided into two partnerships, which are usually decided by drawing cards from a shuffled deck; the two players who draw the highest cards and the two who draw the lowest cards are partners and sit across from each other. The person who draws the highest card during partnership is the first dealer. The dealer, starting clockwise with the person on the left, deals each player one facedown card at a time until all four players have thirteen cards apiece. After the deal, the players sort their cards by suit, usually alternating black and red suits, and then arrange the cards in ranking order, from the highest, the ace, to the lowest, the deuce. The five highest cards, the ace, king, queen, jack, and ten, are referred to as honors, and the one suit that outranks every other one, which is designated at the start of the game, is called the trump suit.

EXERCISE 46.2: Suggested Answers

1. *Periodic:* Not knowing their names, not answering their questions, and not reading their stories, the politician clearly did not understand reporters. *Cumulative:* The politician clearly did not understand reporters, whose names he did not know, whose questions he did not answer, and whose stories he did not read.
2. *Periodic:* When a premature summer on Thursday gives way to more winter on Monday and a human easily grabs a jacket again, an apple tree may founder. *Cumulative:* An apple tree may founder when a premature summer on Thursday gives way to more winter on Monday, although a human easily grabs a jacket again.

EXERCISE 47.1: Suggested Answers

1. Someone made mistakes. (The passive is probably better in this case because *someone* sounds limp. Furthermore, it may turn out that the maker of mistakes was a group, not an individual.)
2. A Dallas design team helped the first lady in her decor. (The active is preferable only if the writer wants to put the emphasis on the team rather than on the first lady.)
3. When murdering civilians was denied by the soldiers, that denial was questioned by journalists. (In this case, the active voice is much easier to follow.)

4. A longtime enemy assassinated the leader of the rebels. (Probably if the murderer is known, the active voice is preferable. When we don't know who the assassin is, we usually go with a passive construction.)
5. In a patient with celiac disease, the body's immunological response to gluten damages the intestine. (Perhaps because both versions are long and technical, neither seems significantly better.)

EXERCISE 47.2: Suggested Answers

Those responsible for evaluating education have long resisted measuring the effectiveness of methods and teachers in terms of the results secured. They have emphasized teachers' procedures and have seldom examined their products, that is, what their pupils are able to do. However, we are beginning to see an increasing number of bold proposals that assume the American public expects the schools to show improved results. As public support of education increases, the taxpayers will increasingly insist on judging a teacher on his or her ability to enhance pupils' learning.

EXERCISE 48.1: Answers

1. At the worst possible moment, a computer crash made me lose my document.
2. Unfortunately, the door to the kennel had been left open.
3. Certain of her ability to earn a high score on the test, Katrina got a good night's sleep.
4. Whenever someone unexpectedly rings the doorbell, his dog goes berserk.
5. Therefore, answering the seemingly simple question is very difficult.
6. (no comma needed)
7. A tray of cheese puffs in one hand and a pile of napkins in the other, the waiter moved slowly around the room.
8. To find a good day-care provider, parents usually need plenty of time and money.

9. After the hurricane moved on, the citizens of the town assessed the damage.
10. Startled by the explosion, the workers dropped to the ground.

EXERCISE 48.2: Suggested Answers

1. The chef did not want to serve a heavy dessert, *for* she was planning to have a rich stew for the main course.
2. The children are usually well behaved, *but* they forgot their manners at their grandmother's house.
3. I studied ten of Verdi's operas, *yet* I have only begun to appreciate the wealth of his creativity.
4. The playwright disliked arguing with the directors, *so* she avoided rehearsals.
5. Tropical fish do not bark, *nor* are they cuddly pets.

EXERCISE 48.3: Answers

1. (no commas needed)
2. (no commas needed)
3. I would feel right at home in the city dump, which bears a striking resemblance to my bedroom.
4. The rescue workers, exhausted and discouraged, stared ahead without speaking.
5. (no commas needed)
6. The Zunis, an ancient tribe, live in New Mexico.
7. (no commas needed)
8. Genevieve de Gaulle-Anthonioz, a niece of the former president of France, spent time in a Nazi concentration camp during World War II.
9. Birds' hearts have four chambers, whereas reptiles' have three.
10. (no commas needed)

EXERCISE 48.4: Answers

1. They found employment in truck driving, farming, and mining.
2. We bought zucchini, peppers, and tomatoes at the market.

3. A high center of gravity, a narrow wheel base, and the fact that a typical owner drives the vehicle at highway speeds all contribute to SUV rollovers.

4. Anouk enrolled in courses in history, statistics, and geometry.

5. The tiny, brown-eyed Lafayette twins were the only children in the kindergarten class who could already read.

6. Supermarket cashiers need to know several skills: how to bag groceries properly, how to make correct change, and how to identify dozens of different fruits and vegetables.

7. The ball sailed over the fence, across the road, and through the Wilsons' living room window.

8. I timidly offered to help a loud, overbearing, lavishly dressed customer.

9. (no commas needed)

10. These Dick Vitale clones insist on calling every play, judging every move, and telling everyone within earshot exactly what is wrong with the team.

EXERCISE 48.5: Answers

1. One must consider the society as a whole, not just its parts.

2. Many of the parents and students did, in fact, support the position of the teacher who resigned.

3. Her friends did not know about her illness, did they?

4. The drought this year will, it appears, prevent him from watering his flower garden.

5. Ladies and gentlemen, I bid you farewell.

EXERCISE 48.6: Answers

1. (no commas needed)

2. More than 350,000 people gathered for the protest on the Washington Mall.

3. The *Titanic* hit an iceberg on April 14, 1912, and sank in about two hours, drowning 1,503 people.

4. MLA headquarters are at 10 Astor Place, New York, New York 10003.

5. The nameplate read *Donald Good, R.N.,* and looked quite impressive.

EXERCISE 48.7: Answers

1. (no comma needed)

2. My professor insisted, "The cutting edge gets dull very quickly."

3. (no comma needed)

4. "Neat people are lazier and meaner than sloppy people," according to Suzanne Britt.

5. (no comma needed)

FOR COLLABORATION: Answers

1. Awards are given for best actor, best actress, best supporting actor, and best supporting actress every year.

2. Observers watch facial expressions and gestures and interpret them.

3. We could see nothing except jagged peaks for miles around.

4. Everyone in the high school auditorium that night felt strongly about the proposed zoning changes.

5. Clothes that had to be ironed were too much trouble.

6. Before we got into the sun-baked car, we opened the doors and waited for a few minutes.

7. Students with high scores on standardized tests do not necessarily get high grades in college.

8. The photographer Edward Curtis is known for his depiction of the West.

9. We all took panicked, hasty looks at our notebooks.

10. An invitation to buy prescription drugs online and an offer for golf balls were two of the junk email messages waiting in my computer's mailbox.

THINKING CRITICALLY ABOUT YOUR USE OF COMMAS

McCarthy's version:

And here was another strange thing about Myers. He not only did nothing for a living but he appeared to have no history. He came from Elkhart, Indiana, but beyond this fact nobody seemed to know anything about him — not even how he had met my aunt Margaret. Reconstructed from his conversation, a picture of Elkhart emerged for us that showed it as a flat place consisting chiefly of ball parks, poolrooms, and hardware stores. Aunt Margaret came from Chicago, which consisted of the Loop, Marshall Field's, assorted priests and monsignors, and the black-and-white problem. How had these two worlds impinged? Where our family spoke freely of its relations, real and imaginary, Myers spoke of no one, not even a parent. At the very beginning, when my father's old touring car, which had been shipped on, still remained in our garage, Myers had certain seedy cronies whom he took riding in it or who simply sat in it in our driveway, as if anchored in a houseboat; but when the car went, they went or were banished. Uncle Myers and Aunt Margaret had no friends, no couples with whom they exchanged visits — only a middle-aged, black-haired, small, emaciated woman with a German name and a yellowed skin whom we were taken to see one afternoon because she was dying of cancer. . . .

EXERCISE 49.1: Answers

1. Joining the chorus was a great experience for Will; it helped him express his musical talent and gave him a social life.
2. City life offers many advantages; in many ways, however, life in a small town is much more pleasant.
3. Florida's mild winter climate is ideal for bicycling; in addition, the terrain is very flat.
4. The voting machines in poorer counties were most likely to reject correctly punched ballots; therefore, the voting system favors people in wealthier areas.
5. The debate over political correctness affects more than the curriculum; it also affects students' social relationships.

EXERCISE 50.1: Answers

1. Please attend the meeting on Tuesday at 10:00 A.M. in Room 401.
2. Cleopatra committed suicide in 30 B.C.E. when she was about thirty-nine years old.
3. "Have you lost something, Charles?" I inquired.
4. Trish asked the receptionist if Dr. Margolies had office hours that afternoon.
5. A voluntary effort by the AMA could help contain hospital costs.

EXERCISE 50.2: Answers

1. Social scientists face difficult questions: should they use their knowledge to shape society? merely describe human behavior? try to do both?
2. Did the employees realize that the company was in danger of bankruptcy?
3. "Can I play this?" asked Manuel.
4. (correct; indirect question)
5. The judge asked, "What is your verdict?"

EXERCISE 50.3: Suggested Answers

1. The court denied a New Jersey woman's petition to continue raising tigers in her backyard!
2. I screamed at Jamie, "You rat! You tricked me!"
3. "This time we're starting early!" she shouted.
4. Help! I can't swim!
5. Oh no! We've lost the house!

EXERCISE 51.2: Answers

1. Grammar is *everybody's* favorite subject.
2. *Britney Spears's* musical career may not last as long as *Madonna's* has.

3. She insists that her personal life is *nobody's* business.
4. *Carol and Jim's* income dropped drastically after Jim lost his job.
5. Parents often question their *children's* choice of friends.
6. Many smokers disregard the *surgeon general's* warnings.
7. *A.J.'s* older *brother's* name is Griffin.
8. The *trees'* leaves were turning brown all over the county during the long drought.
9. This dog has a *beagle's* ears and a *St. Bernard's* nose and feet.
10. *Michelle Kwan's* and *Sarah Hughes's* performances in the long program brought Hughes a gold medal and Kwan a bronze.

EXERCISE 51.3: Answers

1. There was a big revival at my Auntie *Reed's* church.
2. I heard the songs and the minister saying: "Why *don't* you come?"
3. Finally Westley said to me in a whisper: . . . "*I'm* tired *o'* sitting here. *Let's* get up and be saved."
4. So I decided that maybe to save further trouble, *I'd* better lie. . . .
5. That night . . . I cried, in bed alone, and *couldn't* stop.

FOR COLLABORATION: Answers

1. His great-uncle Ray's contribution helped him finish the film.
2. Zillah couldn't finish painting the garage before dark.
3. Each of the dogs in the shelter has its own charm, but there's no way to find a home for every one.
4. If you went to Hollywood, you'd have to forget about how difficult it'd be to get a job in the film industry.
5. It's late; let's go out for pizza instead of making supper.

EXERCISE 52.2: Answers

1. Kowinski uses the term *mallaise* to mean physical and pyschological disturbances caused by mall contact.
2. My favorite article in *People* magazine every year is "The Sexiest Man Alive."
3. "The little that is known about gorillas certainly makes you want to know more," writes Alan Moorehead in his essay, "A Most Forgiving Ape."
4. The "fun" of surgery begins before the operation ever takes place.
5. Should "America the Beautiful" replace "The Star-Spangled Banner" as the national anthem?
6. Sylvia Nasar describes the brilliant mathematician's youth and early career in the book's first section, which is called "A Beautiful Mind."
7. Many viewers were stunned when Jackie Jr. was killed in "The Army of One," the last episode of *The Sopranos'* third season.
8. The Beatles song "Love Me Do" catapulted the band to international stardom.
9. My dictionary defines *isolation* as "the quality or state of being alone."
10. When my teacher assigned Chaucer's *Canterbury Tales,* I never expected to read a poem as hilarious and bawdy as "The Miller's Tale."

FOR COLLABORATION: Suggested Answers

An article called "Their Game, Their Gold" appeared in the *New York Times* the morning after Canada won the gold medal in men's hockey at the 2002 Olympics in Park City, Utah. Sportswriter George Vecsey described the final match as "so fast, so furious, so full of skill that it will live in the memories of all who witnessed it" and noted, "The game itself deserved a gold metal." The Canadian men's hockey team had not won a gold medal at the Olympics since 1952, fifty years to the day before their winning match in Utah. Wayne Gretzky, one of the sport's most admired players and the executive director of the winning team, said that his country desperately needed to win the tournament.

EXERCISE 53.1: Answers

1. While doing online research on the Federal Communications Commission, Mario found the links at <www.google.com> very helpful.
2. During my research, I found that a flat-rate income tax (a single-rate tax with no deductions) has its problems.
3. The health care expert informed readers that "as we progress through middle age, we experiences intimations of our own morality [*sic*]."
4. The speaker pointed out that some hospitals train nurses in this pseudoscientific technique (he was referring to therapeutic touch [TT]), which had been discredited by many rigorous studies.
5. Albert made the following suggestions: (1) clean the dishes as soon as they are used; (2) put items away when they are no longer needed; and (3) make a schedule for vacuuming, dusting, doing laundry, and other household chores.

EXERCISE 53.2: Answers

1. Many people would have ignored the children's taunts — but not Ace.
2. Even if marijuana is dangerous — an assertion disputed by many studies — it is certainly no more harmful to human health than alcohol and cigarettes, which remain legal.
3. If you want to do well on a test — and why wouldn't you? — remember that a little anxiety can improve your performance.
4. Union Carbide's plant in Bhopal, India, sprang a leak — a leak that killed more than 2,000 people and injured an additional 200,000.
5. Fair-skinned people — and especially those with red hair — should use a strong sunscreen.

EXERCISE 53.3: Answers

1. The article made one point forcefully and repeatedly: the United States must end its dependence on foreign oil.
2. Another example is taken from Psalm 139:16.
3. (correct)
4. The president declared: "Not over my dead body will they raise your taxes."
5. Watching television in the wee hours of the morning had given me just two things: lines under my eyes and an irrational desire to purchase hair-care and cleaning products.
6. Ghandi urged four rules: tell the truth even in business, adopt more sanitary habits, abolish caste and religious divisions, and learn English.
7. (correct)
8. According to *The Birds of Heaven: Travels with Cranes,* eleven of the fifteen crane species on earth are endangered.
9. Even more important was what money represented: success, prestige, and power.
10. Two buses go to Denver: one at 9:38 A.M. and one at 2:55 P.M.

EXERCISE 54.1: Answers

1. The town in the South where I was raised had a statue of a Civil War soldier in the center of Main Street.
2. We had a choice of fast-food, Chinese, or Italian restaurants.
3. Reporters speculated about the secret location where Vice President Cheney had remained for several weeks.
4. The Council of Trent was convened to draw up the Catholic response to the Protestant Reformation.
5. We drove east over the Hudson River on the Tappan Zee Bridge.
6. Every artist on a major label seems to want a Lexus or a Lincoln Navigator and a chauffeur to drive it.

7. Accepting an award for his score for the film *The High and Mighty,* Dmitri Tiomkin thanked Beethoven, Brahms, Wagner, and Strauss.
8. My French teacher in high school showed us films by François Truffaut, including *Small Change* and *The 400 Blows,* but I could hardly understand a word.
9. American soldiers went to Afghanistan in the fall of 2001, after the attacks on the World Trade Center and the Pentagon.
10. In the backseat, the children sang "The Itsy Bitsy Spider" over and over until their mother thought she would scream.

EXERCISE 55.1: Answers

1. The Thursday night NBC show set in an emergency room remains popular even though cast members have changed over the years.
2. An MX missile, which is 71 feet long and 92 inches around, weighs 190,000 pounds.
3. Almost every evening [or afternoon], my neighbor stops by and borrows things she never returns—for example, milk, coffee, or a couple of onions.
4. Enron officials met with the vice president of the United States to discuss the administration's energy policy, but soon afterward the Texas company declared bankruptcy.
5. A large corporation like AT&T may help finance an employee's M.B.A.
6. Unfortunately, the five-cent candy bar is a relic of the past.
7. The Grammy Awards are sometimes held in New York City, but the Oscars always take place in Los Angeles.
8. The local National Public Radio station has a broadcast range of seventy-five miles.
9. After less than a year at the University of Virginia, Poe left and joined the U.S. Army.
10. In spite of its old-fashioned name, the National Association for the Advancement of

Colored People is a thoroughly modern organization.

EXERCISE 55.2: Answers

1. Three hundred seven miles long and eighty-two miles wide, the island offered little of interest.
2. In the seventies, teenagers watched television shows about the fifties, and in the late nineties, a show about the seventies was popular.
3. You could travel around the city for only sixty-five cents. (An amount of money is spelled out if it can be stated in three or fewer words, such as *sixty-five cents,* and if it appears in a discussion involving infrequent use of numbers. In a discussion involving many numbers, 65¢ might be more acceptable.)
4. As far as she knew, nothing of interest had happened on June 8, 1972, except her birth.
5. The senator who voted against the measure received 6,817 angry emails and only 12 in support of her decision.
6. He was pleased that he had scored in the seventy-ninth percentile in math.
7. (correct)
8. In that age group, the risk is estimated to be about 1 in 2,500.
9. (correct)
10. The amulet measured $1\frac{1}{8}$ by $2\frac{2}{3}$ inches.

THINKING CRITICALLY ABOUT ABBREVIATIONS AND NUMBERS: Answers

All semi-pro leagues, it should be understood, are self-sustaining, and have no farm affiliation or other connection with the *26* major-league clubs, or with the *17* leagues and *152* teams . . . that make up the National Association—the minors, that is. There is no central body of semi-pro teams, and semi-pro players are not included among the *650* major-leaguers, the *2,500*-odd minor-leaguers, plus all the managers, coaches, presidents, commissioners, front-office people, and scouts, who, taken together, constitute the great tent called organized ball. (A much diminished tent, at that; back in 1949, the minors included *59* leagues, about *448* teams, and perhaps *10,000* players.) Also outside the tent, but perhaps within its shade, are *5* college leagues, ranging across the country from Cape Cod to Alaska, where the most promising freshman, sophomore, and junior-college ballplayers . . . compete against each other . . .

– Roger Angell, "In the Country"

EXERCISE 56.1: Answers

1. Guests often stayed in the bathroom for long periods reading *Spamku,* a book of haiku about luncheon meat.
2. While shopping at Poverty Records, a second-hand store, Joan found a copy of *The Velvet Underground and Nico* with its banana sticker still intact.
3. Georgetown offers a potpourri of cultures and styles.
4. The word *veterinary* comes from the Latin *veterinarius.*
5. Niko Tinbergen's essay "The Bee-Hunters of Hulshorst" is a diary of experiments on *Philanthus triangulum Fabr,* the bee-killer wasp.
6. Flying the *Glamorous Glennis,* named for his wife, Chuck Yeager was the first pilot to fly faster than the speed of sound.
7. The *Washington Post* provides extensive coverage of Congress.
8. The monster in the Old English epic *Beowulf* got to tell his own side of the story in John Gardner's novel *Grendel.*
9. W. H. Auden wrote a poem describing Brueghel's painting *Landscape with the Fall of Icarus.*
10. While listening to *Prairie Home Companion* on my local public radio station, I heard the singers who perform "I Am a Man of Constant Sorrow" in the movie *O Brother, Where Art Thou?*

EXERCISE 57.1: Answers

1. pass*able; pass-able
2. ech*o; do not hyphenate leaving just one letter on either line
3. stripped; do not break one-syllable words
4. ne*ces*si*ty; ne-ces-si-ty
5. an*te*cham*ber; ante-chamber
6. well*liked; well-liked
7. have*n't; do not break contractions
8. hop*ing; hop-ing
9. a*non*y*mous; anon-y-mous
10. breathe; do not hyphenate one-syllable words

FOR COLLABORATION: Answers

1. anti-inflammatory
2. pre-Industrial Revolution
3. pro- and anti-handgun lobbyists
4. (correct)
5. a what-me-worry look
6. self-important
7. bride-to-be
8. seven hundred thirty-three
9. bumper-to-bumper traffic
10. a politician who is fast-talking (*Fast-talk* is commonly found in dictionaries; thus hyphenation is correct even though the compound adjective comes after the noun.)

EXERCISE 57.2: Answers

1. (correct)
2. The drumbeating and hand clapping signaled that the parade was near.
3. I bought a five-pound bag of sugar and two and three-quarter pounds of ground turkey.
4. After he spent four weeks in an alcohol rehabilitation program, he apologized to his wife for twenty-two years of heavy drinking.
5. We urged him to be open-minded and to temper his insensitive views.
6. Both pro- and anti-State Department groups registered complaints.

7. The employees found John difficult to work for because of his rudeness and huge ego.
8. In the early years of the western frontier, people had no one to turn to for help when lawlessness got out of hand.
9. The governor-elect joked about the preelection polls.
10. Her heavily rouged cheeks and blue eye shadow made her look like a circus clown.

EXERCISE 59.1: Answers

1. Before the middle of the nineteenth century, surgery was usually a terrifying, painful ordeal.
2. Because anesthesia did not exist yet, the only painkiller available for surgical patients was whiskey.
3. The pain of surgical procedures could be so severe that many people were willing to die rather than have surgery.
4. In 1846, one of the hospitals in Boston gave ether to a patient before he had surgery.
5. The patient, who had a large tumor on his neck, slept peacefully as doctors removed it.

EXERCISE 59.2: Answers

Hollywood is famous for hiring various experts to teach people technically what most of us learn informally. A case in point is the story about the children of one movie couple who noticed a new child in the neighborhood climbing a tree. The children immediately wanted to be given the name of his instructor in tree climbing.

EXERCISE 60.1: Answers

1. Over the last forty years, average temperatures in the Arctic have increased by several degrees.
2. A few years ago, a robin was observed in Inuit territory in northern Canada.
3. Inuit people in previous generations would never have seen a robin near their homes.

4. The Inuit language, which is called Inuktitut, has no word for *robin*.
5. Many Inuits are concerned that warmer temperatures may change their way of life.

EXERCISE 60.2: Answers

The notion that a chill <u>puts</u> you at risk of catching a cold is nearly universal. Yet science <u>has found</u> no evidence for it. One of the first studies on the matter <u>was led</u> by Sir Christopher Andrewes. He <u>took</u> a group of volunteers and <u>inoculated</u> them with a cold virus; previously, half of the group <u>had been kept</u> warm, and the other half <u>had been made</u> to take a bath and then to stand for half an hour without a towel while the wind <u>was blowing</u> on them. The chilled group <u>got</u> no more colds than the warm group.

EXERCISE 61.1: Answers

1. (correct) *lay off:* phrasal verb
2. (correct) *count on:* prepositional verb
3. (correct) *pick up:* phrasal verb
4. *look at:* prepositional verb
   As I looked at the newspaper, I was surprised to see that I was qualified for a job that paid much better than mine.
5. (correct) *give up:* phrasal verb

EXERCISE 62.1: Suggested Answers

1. The scholar who finally deciphered hieroglyphics was Jean François Champollion.
2. Champollion enjoyed studying the languages of the Middle East.
3. (correct)
4. It was of great importance that he knew Coptic, a later form of the Egyptian language.
5. In 1822 Champollion wrote a paper in which he presented his decipherment of hieroglyphics.
6. If the Rosetta Stone had not been discovered, it would have been much more difficult to decipher hieroglyphics.